CONSUMER DEMAND AND LABOR SUPPLY
Goods, Monetary Assets, and Time

STUDIES IN MATHEMATICAL AND MANAGERIAL ECONOMICS

Editors

HENRI THEIL

HERBERT GLEJSER

VOLUME 29

NORTH-HOLLAND PUBLISHING COMPANY
AMSTERDAM – NEW YORK – OXFORD

CONSUMER DEMAND AND LABOR SUPPLY

GOODS, MONETARY ASSETS, AND TIME

WILLIAM A. BARNETT
Board of Governors of the Federal Reserve System

NORTH-HOLLAND PUBLISHING COMPANY
AMSTERDAM – NEW YORK – OXFORD

© NORTH-HOLLAND PUBLISHING COMPANY – 1981

All rights reserved. No part of this publication may be reproduced, stored in a retrieval system, or transmitted, in any form or by any means, electronic, mechanical, photocopying, recording or otherwise, without the prior permission of the copyright owner.

ISBN 0 444 86097 5

Publishers:
NORTH-HOLLAND PUBLISHING COMPANY
AMSTERDAM – NEW YORK – OXFORD

Sole distributors for the U.S.A. and Canada:
ELSEVIER/NORTH-HOLLAND INC.
52 VANDERBILT AVENUE
NEW YORK, N.Y. 10017

Library of Congress Cataloging in Publication Data

Barnett, William A
    Consumer demand and labor supply.

    (Studies in mathematical and managerial economics ; v. 29)
    Bibliography: p.
    Includes indexes.
    1. Consumption (Economics)--Mathematical models.
    2. Demand (Economic theory)--Mathematical models.
    3. Labor supply--Mathematical models. I. Title.
    II. Series.
    HB820.B37   338.5'21'0724   80-25640
    ISBN 0-444-86097-5 (Elsevier North-Holland)

Printed in The Netherlands

INTRODUCTION TO THE SERIES

This is a series of books concerned with the quantitative approach to problems in the social and administrative sciences. The studies are in particular in the overlapping areas of mathematical economics, econometrics, operational research, and management science. Also, the mathematical and statistical techniques which belong to the apparatus of modern social and administrative sciences have their place in this series. A well-balanced mixture of pure theory and practical applications is envisaged, which ought to be useful for universities and for research workers in business and government.

The Editors hope that the volumes of this series, all of which relate to such a young and vigorous field of research activity, will contribute to the exchange of scientific information at a truly international level.

THE EDITORS

CONTENTS

Introduction to the series   v
Foreword   xi
Preface   xii
List of tables   xv
List of figures   xvii
Technical notes   xviii

PART I. UNIFICATION OF GOODS DEMAND AND LABOR SUPPLY

Chapter 1. Introduction   3
    1.1. Objective   3
    1.2. Overview   3
    1.3. Two-stage decisions   8
    1.4. Intertemporal allocation   13

Chapter 2. Consumption theory   17
    2.1. Introduction   17
    2.2. The household model   18
    2.3. Demand per household member   23
    2.4. The full-employment-equivalent price of leisure   31
    2.5. Application of the shadow price of leisure   36

Chapter 3. Specifications and aggregation theory   43
    3.1. Empirical demand systems   43
    3.2. The CSE model   44
    3.3. The Rotterdam model   49
    3.4. Theoretical foundations for the Rotterdam model   55
    3.5. Aggregation over consumers   58
    3.6. The components of the remainder term   66
    3.7. The Rotterdam model approximation   68
    3.8. Summary and conclusion   72

Chapter 4.	Statistical theory	75
	4.1. Introduction	76
	4.2. Weak convergence	80
	4.3. Lemmas and properties	83
	4.4. Convergence in distribution	88
	4.5. Asymptotic efficiency	91
	4.6. The asymptotic likelihood ratio test	92
	4.7. Asymptotic standard errors with nuisance parameters	96
Chapter 5.	Data and results	99
	5.1. Description of the data	99
	5.2. The price of leisure	101
	5.3. Further discussion of price of leisure results	108
	5.4. The specification	114
	5.5. Estimates (absolute price version)	120
	5.6. Separability in leisure	133
	5.7. The Rotterdam model in relative prices	135
	5.8. Residual analysis	144
	5.9. Model fit	149
	5.10. Conclusions	154

PART II. NEW MODELS AND APPROACHES

Introduction to Part II		158
Chapter 6.	Recursive subaggregation and a generalized hypocycloidal demand model	159
	6.1. Introduction	159
	6.2. The model	160
	6.3. Estimation	165
	6.4. Results	170
	6.5. Elasticities and duality	178
Chapter 7.	Aggregation of monetary assets	185
	7.1. Introduction	185
	7.2. Objectives	187
	7.3. The consumer's decision	193
	7.4. Conditional current period allocation	199
	7.5. Preference structure over financial assets	200

7.6.	Recursive estimation approach	203
7.7.	Data	204
7.8.	Estimation of passbook branch	207
7.9.	Transactions balances	212
7.10.	Empirical selection of blocking	217
7.11.	Statistical index numbers	219
7.12.	Information content of the index	227
7.13.	Conclusion	230

Chapter 8. **Decision structure** — 233
- 8.1. Introduction — 233
- 8.2. The household production function approach — 234
- 8.3. Identification of the structural form — 238
- 8.4. The Pollak and Wachter critique — 242
- 8.5. The preference independence transformation — 249
- 8.6. Application to Chapter 5 estimates — 254

Chapter 9. **Implicit utility models** — 259
- 9.1. Introduction — 259
- 9.2. Theoretical properties of the model — 262
- 9.3. Additive structural errors — 267
- 9.4. Alternative approaches — 271
- 9.5. Control theoretic approach — 274
- 9.6. Conclusion — 277

APPENDICES

Appendix A. **Appendix to Chapter 2** — 281
- A1. Section 2.2 proofs — 281
- A2. Relationship between problems (2.2) and (2.3) — 283
- A3. Relationship between problems (2.3) and (2.5) — 285
- A4. Properties of the shadow price of leisure — 286
- A5. Extension to the full-employment boundary — 299

Appendix B. **Appendix to Chapter 3** — 303
- B1. Integrability and aggregation theory — 303
- B2. The remainder terms — 307
- B3. The Rotterdam model specification — 313
- B4. Locally integrable models — 319

Appendix C.	Appendix to Chapter 4		323
	C1.	Eisenpress nonlinear FIML program	323
	C2.	Chapter 4 proofs	331
Appendix D.	Appendix to Chapter 5		347
	D1.	Data sources	347
Appendix E.	Appendix to Chapter 7		351
	E1.	Other monetary assets	351

Bibliography   355
Author index   365
Subject index   369

FOREWORD

William Barnett's book will be much appreciated by those who believe in a thorough and systematic approach to applied economic analysis. His starting point is the microeconomic theory of consumer demand and labor supply. Next he explicitly considers the problem of aggregation over consumers, using a random coefficients model. The third step is statistical inference, and the fourth is a hard look at the data and their limitations. Then, finally, the statistical methods are applied to the data in order to test and estimate the model derived from economic theory. It is this systematic step-by-step approach which makes this book the work of a complete econometrician.

In addition, the book shows considerable versatility in terms of the economic models used. They all have in common that they are inspired by the system-wide approach which handles several equations simultaneously rather than each separately, but they employ different parameterizations and include the modeling of the demand for monetary assets. The book should be welcomed as an important addition to the growing literature on the system-wide approach to economic analysis.

Chicago, May 1980 HENRI THEIL

PREFACE

The purpose of this book is to present a unified treatment of the author's research and of related research in the fields of consumer demand and labor supply modeling. This research spans the range of current demand analysis from applied empirical research to fundamental economic theory. We present new demand models, new economic theory, new statistical theory, and extensive empirical results. Although the book is basically a research monograph, it could be used as an introduction to current areas of intensive research in empirical commodity, leisure, and monetary-asset demand modeling.

The book is divided into two parts. Part I consists of Chapters 1–5, while Part II consists of Chapters 6–9. Part I contains a systematic treatment of a single empirical problem: the unification of labor supply and goods demand modeling. Part I uses existing modeling and statistical procedures and methodologies, but develops new theory supporting those procedures and methodologies. The fully developed theory is implemented empirically. We explore the implications of our results for the conventional dichotomy between consumption expenditure allocation modeling and labor supply modeling. Part II contains new models and methodologies. In particular, Part II contains two new demand models. In addition it also contains a new method based upon the household production function approach along with a related method using a preference independence transformation and a money market model generating theoretical price and quantity indices of monetary asset services. The index numbers are found to be substantially preferable to conventional monetary summation aggregates.

Contents of Part I

Chapter 1 presents an introductory discussion of Part I with particular emphasis upon the aggregation conditions necessary and sufficient for the conventional separation of labor economics from demand systems modeling. Chapter 2 contains the economic theory developed to support our joint modeling of goods demand and labor supply. That theory includes our household model and our results on the shadow price of leisure. Chapter 3 presents the specification and a new theoretical analysis supporting the foundations of the Rotterdam model. Chapter 4 presents the statistical theory needed to support our nonlinear maximum likelihood inferences. Chapter 5 contains our empirical results on the joint modeling of goods demand and labor supply.

Contents of Part II

Chapter 6 presents a new inverse demand model. Chapter 7 presents estimates of a fully nested money market model, generating exact monetary asset quantity and user-cost aggregates at multiple levels of aggregation. The exact aggregates can be approximated by parameter-free statistical index numbers. Chapter 8 contains a theoretical analysis of the controversial household production function approach to demand modeling and comparison of that approach with a related approach using a preference independence transformation. Chapter 9 presents estimates of a new implicit utility demand model.

Acknowledgements

I am indebted to Kenneth Kopecky, Alfred Norman, and Ryuzo Sato for their collaboration in the research which forms the basis for Chapter 9. Much of the work in Part I was initiated in my Ph.D. thesis research at Carnegie-Mellon University. My thesis adviser, whose assistance was extensive, was Paul Shaman. I am particularly indebted to Henri Theil for his valuable and extensive comments on each draft of this book and for his advice and encouragement throughout this effort. Partial financial support for this research was provided under National Science Foundation Grant no. SOC76-84459, while the author was a research associate at the University of Chicago.

Many of the results in this book were first written into a sequence of papers which have appeared in various journals. Useful comments on those papers were received from Richard Berner, William Brainard, David Cass, W. E. Diewert, Franklin Fisher, James Heckman, Donald Hester, David Humphrey, Nicholas Kiefer, Arthur Kruse, Lawrence Lau, E. Malinvaud, Eileen Mauskopf, John Paulus, P. C. B. Phillips, Robert Pollak, James Ramsey, Leonard Rapping, Robert Rasche, P. A. V. B.

Swamy, Peter Tinsley, and the participants at numerous university and NBER conferences and annual Econometric Society Meetings. Harry Eisenpress and John Davison provided extensive assistance in the design and implementation of the computer algorithm used in Chapters 6 and 7. Edwin Price assisted in the selection and aggregation of the data used in Chapter 6. My wife, Maxine, provided careful proofreading and editorial assistance. I am indebted to Debra Bellows and Judith Elofson for their expert technical typing. Finally, I wish to thank Tatsuo Hatta, Richard Miller, Carl Christ, and Ailsa Roëll, who read and commented on the manuscript of this book while I was visiting at the Johns Hopkins University.

Washington, D.C., May 1980   WILLIAM A. BARNETT

LIST OF TABLES

5.1.	Maximum likelihood estimates of the CSE model (no intercept, $\alpha = 2.3$, $\Gamma = 1$)	104
5.2.	Maximum likelihood estimates of the CSE model (no intercept, $\alpha = 3.1$)	105
5.3.	Two-step generalized least squares estimates of the absolute price version of the Rotterdam model	121
5.4.	Maximum likelihood estimates of the absolute price version of the Rotterdam model	121
5.5.	Average elasticities from maximum likelihood estimation of the absolute price version of the Rotterdam model	123
5.6.	t-Ratios from maximum likelihood estimation of the absolute price version of the Rotterdam model	130
5.7.	Maximum likelihood estimates of the absolute price version of the Rotterdam model with intercept	132
5.8.	Maximum likelihood estimates of the absolute price version of the Rotterdam model with weak separability in leisure imposed	134
5.9.	Maximum likelihood estimates of the absolute price version of the Rotterdam model without leisure	135
5.10.	Two-step generalized least squares estimates of the first blocking of the relative price version of the Rotterdam model	138
5.11.	Derivatives of the derived parameters in two-step generalized least squares estimation of the first blocking	139
5.12.	Estimated covariance matrix of two-step generalized least squares coefficient estimators of the Rotterdam model's first blocking	139
5.13.	Maximum likelihood estimates of the relative price version of the Rotterdam model	140
5.14.	Two-step generalized least squares estimates of the final blocking of the relative price version of the Rotterdam model	141
5.15.	Derivatives of the derived parameters in two-step generalized least squares estimation of the final blocking	141

5.16.	Estimated covariance matrix of two-step generalized least squares coefficient estimators of the Rotterdam model's final blocking	142
5.17.	Conditional maximum likelihood estimates of the fully additive relative price version of the Rotterdam model	143
5.18.	Information inaccuracies with leisure included	151
5.19.	Information inaccuracies with leisure deleted	153
6.1.	Parameter estimates of the protein block (group 1)	172
6.2.	Parameter estimates of the other foods block (group 2)	173
6.3.	Parameter estimates of the miscellaneous goods block (group 3)	173
6.4.	Parameter estimates of the aggregate model	177
6.5.	Estimated Hicks–Allen price elasticities	182
6.6.	Estimated expenditure elasticities	183
7.1.	Passbook branch parameter estimates	210
7.2.	Parameter estimates with transaction balances and aggregated savings	215
7.3.	GNP velocities of three monetary quantity index numbers	223
7.4.	Specifications of policy targets (Y_t)	229
7.5.	Components of monetary aggregates	229
7.6.	Sample estimates of percent information gain from summation to Divisia aggregation of monetary assets	229
7.7.	ARIMA estimates of percent information gain from summation to Divisia aggregation of monetary assets	230
8.1.	Matrix A	241
8.2.	Matrix Q	241
8.3.	Bordered composition matrices and conditional income elasticities for selected years, 1890–1955	256
D1.	Prices and quantities of perishables, semidurables, durables, services, and leisure, 1890–1955	348
E1.	Substitution elasticities between other monetary substitutes	352

LIST OF FIGURES

5.1.	Generalized variance of the fit as α is varied	104
5.2.	Comparison of the wage rate and the shadow price of leisure	106
5.3.	Stability over time of leisure's share in full income	107
5.4.	Stability of durables' share in full and in ordinary income	108
5.5.	Slutsky cross elasticity of each good with the price of leisure	110
5.6.	Each parameter's t-ratio in the perishables equation	125
5.7.	Each parameter's t-ratio in the semidurables equation	126
5.8.	Each parameter's t-ratio in the durables equation	127
5.9.	Each parameter's t-ratio in the services equation	128
5.10.	Each parameter's t-ratio in the leisure equation	129
5.11.	Empirical distribution function of the transformed residuals for the absolute price version model	146
5.12.	Empirical distribution function of the transformed residuals for the relative price version model	147
7.1.	Seasonally adjusted velocity (normalized)	224
7.2.	Ten-year government bond rate	225
8.1.	Conditional full-income elasticities of the three transformed goods, 1890–1955	257
A1.	Excess demand price of leisure	298
A2.	A shadow price interpretation of the equivalent price of leisure	299

TECHNICAL NOTES

This volume consists of two parts. Part I contains five chapters and Part II contains four chapters. Each chapter contains a number of sections. For example, section 3.2 is the second section of Chapter 3.

Formulae are indicated by two numbers, the first of which refers to the chapter and the second to the order of occurrence. Thus, eq. (3.2) is the second equation in Chapter 3. Similarly, tables, figures, assumptions, theorems, and corollaries are indicated by two numbers, the first of which refers to the chapter and the second to the order of occurrence: table 5.1 is the first table in Chapter 5, theorem 3.2 is the second theorem in Chapter 3, etc.

Matrices are indicated by boldface italic uppercase letters (like $\boldsymbol{A}$), column vectors by boldface italic lowercase letters ($\boldsymbol{a}$), and row vectors by boldface italic lowercase letters with a prime added ($\boldsymbol{a}'$) to indicate that they are transposes of the corresponding column vector.

The radical (square root symbol) $\sqrt{}$ is used as an operator. It operates on the expression in parentheses immediately following the operator. When not immediately followed by a left parenthesis, the radical operates on the variable immediately following the operator. Thus, $\sqrt{(bx+y)}a = (bx+y)^{1/2}a$ and $(1/\sqrt{T})Y = (1/\sqrt{(T)})Y = (1/T^{1/2})Y$.

PART I

UNIFICATION OF GOODS DEMAND AND LABOR SUPPLY

CHAPTER 1

INTRODUCTION

1.1. Objectives

Consideration of new demand models will be reserved for Part II. In Part I we consider the application of existing models and theory to the unification of two previously independent areas of economic research. Until relatively recently, labor economics and demand systems analysis were separate fields of research. But in recent years the importance of interactions between labor supply and goods demand has become increasingly evident and has become the subject of much research. In Chapters 1, 2, 3, and 5 we develop a unified approach to the joint modeling of goods expenditure allocation and labor supply. In the current chapter we consider the issues motivating this unification, and we briefly outline our approach and results.

1.2. Overview

Part I explores, both theoretically and empirically, the relationship between the demand for goods and the demand for leisure. Particular attention is paid to the acceptability of the aggregation conditions necessary and sufficient for the existence of separate labor supply and consumption allocation decisions; other central issues relate to the problems involved in modeling the effects of involuntary unemployment.

Empirical studies of the allocation of consumer expenditure and of the supply of labor conventionally have proceeded separately. Yet some theoretical research on labor supply has indicated that the demand for leisure may be, at least in part, a derived demand induced by the consumption of time-consuming goods. If this hypothesis were useful, even as an approximation, then interactions between goods and leisure consumption would be substantial. Such interactions also have been central to a recent literature on the efficiency and allocative effects of wage and commodity taxes. The relationship between that literature and demand interactions has been discussed by Abbott and Ashenfelter (1976).

At present we restrict attention to a single period model. In that case conventional empirical work would be based upon the assumption that households make their decisions in two stages. Each household would be given an endowed annual "full income" which includes the market value of its time. In the first stage the household would allocate full income over leisure and aggregate commodity expenditure. In the second stage the household would allocate aggregate commodity expenditure over individual goods. The aggregation conditions necessary and sufficient for the consistency of such a two-stage decision with the preferences of a household will be considered below. As we shall see, those conditions are not weak, and if they are not satisfied the usual functions and index numbers needed to formulate the two-stage decision process do not exist.[1]

Without the aggregation conditions, the usual commodity demand and labor supply functions do not exist. Those functions degenerate into functions incompatible with the theory from which they were derived. Equations seemingly reasonable relative to a given theoretical criterion become unreasonable when viewed as a system relative to the same theoretical criterion – a problem not uncommon in the construction of large econometric models. Our carefully modeled rational economic units are no longer rational. To avoid such a possibility we shall construct, jointly estimate, and explore a complete system of demand functions, including a leisure demand function, without the imposition of conditions sufficient for a two-stage decision. We shall then test for the acceptability of those aggregation conditions.

Owen (1964, 1970, 1971) has considered the interaction between the demand for leisure and the demand for recreational goods. He found that recreational goods and leisure are Cournot complements. This interaction is easily understood in terms of the time-using nature of recreational goods and of the resulting joint consumption of leisure time with the consumption of recreational goods. In Part I of this book the emphasis will be on the information available from the joint modeling and estimation of leisure demand with the demands for all goods. As Mincer has observed in his introduction to Owen's book (1970, p. vii): "It soon becomes clear, of course, that recreation is but one of many uses of consumption time...

---

[1] Examples of studies accepting those conditions include Betancourt (1971a, b), Christensen and Jorgensen (1968), and Christensen (1968).

Consequently, the demand for non-work time is a demand derived from the demand for consumption activities, such as recreation. And the study of labor supply becomes a special case of a generalized approach to the theory of consumption." In our applications of such a generalized approach, one interaction becomes conspicuously important: the time-saving interaction between the consumption of durables and the consumption of leisure.

If a consistent two-stage decision does not exist, then a stationary utility function in goods alone does not exist. The existing empirical studies which do accept the two-stage decision process have been plagued by unexplained time trends, as would be expected if the two-stage decision process did not apply. The nature of the difficulty is well summarized in the conclusion to Powell et al.'s study (1968, p. 120) of US consumption:

> The final puzzle...is the question of how one should interpret estimated trends.... Apparently, autonomous trends in consumption have been ... important. It is fair criticism to claim that an approach which "explains" observed consumer behavior in terms of unexplained autonomously occurring changes in consumer habits does not explain consumer behavior at all.... Any attempt to suppress trends makes interpretation of the data ... almost impossible ... the prescription seems to be "More research."

In a similar study on Australian consumption, Powell (1966, p. 674) concluded that "very large trends are evident and no explanation has been offered for their sign or their magnitude. Investigation of this puzzle certainly offers a challenge to further theoretical and empirical work, connected, in its way, with the problem of economic development."

A household model is constructed which extends the Prais–Houthakker homogeneity postulate to permit the modeling of the decisions of a representative household and to permit the construction of a theoretically meaningful definition of per capita leisure. When unemployment exists, it is sometimes argued that the "price of leisure" drops below the wage rate. An issue during our research was the question of how to model the relationship between unemployment and the consumption of goods and leisure. It was postulated by Owen (1970) that that relationship can be captured by permitting the "price of leisure" to drop below the wage rate when unemployment is positive. A similar formulation was used by Grossman (1973) and by Christensen (1968, p. 47). Unfortunately, the marginal concept on which such theorizing was based was not made clear. While

Owen's discussion of this subject provides intuitive support for his contentions, the meaning of the "price of leisure" in such a context was not isolated.[2]

In Chapter 2 a full-employment-equivalent concept of the price of leisure will be defined and explored. Existence and uniqueness will be proved and its properties investigated, and it will be shown that the full-employment-equivalent price of leisure can be related to a shadow price concept. It will be demonstrated both theoretically and empirically that the price of leisure does vary inversely with the unemployment rate, and it will be shown that if the price of leisure is defined to equal the wage rate independently of the unemployment rate, then the supply of labor function cannot be identified. The construction uses Kuhn–Tucker conditions to eliminate the corner solutions generated by involuntary unemployment. Our results are in agreement with those derived by Heckman (1974) in a different but similar context.

New theoretical foundations are derived for the Rotterdam model. Under weak assumptions and a new interpretation, the Rotterdam model is proved to be highly flexible at the aggregate level and to provide powerful tests of theory. Since we use aggregate data, we find the Rotterdam model, with our associated new theory, to be particularly well suited to the purposes of Part I. Other models are developed for other purposes in Part II.

A system of demand functions, including a leisure demand function, is estimated. The system is nonlinear in its parameters. The existing literature on sampling from a fixed distribution is not relevant to a model with exogenous variables, while the literature on nonlinear least squares and nonlinear generalized least squares is not directly applicable. The alternative generalized least squares approach does not provide convenient hypothesis tests and is not invariant to the deletion of arbitrary equations, although such deletion is required to impose demand homogeneity.

Proofs are provided in Chapter 4 to support large sample inference by nonlinear maximum likelihood methods in the class of models we use. Regularity conditions are derived sufficient to ensure consistency, asymptotic normality, and asymptotic efficiency of maximum likelihood estimators in nonlinear models. The limiting distribution of the asymptotic likelihood ratio criterion is derived, and a method of dealing with nuisance parameters is presented. The proofs extend the classical maximum likelihood estimation results on sampling from a fixed distribution to our class

---

[2] Mathematically, Owen's approach amounts to adding a term containing the shadow price of leisure to each side of the budget constraint. Hence that term and therefore the shadow price of leisure could be cancelled out again.

of nonidentically distributed observations. Our proofs build upon Malinvaud's work on nonlinear generalized least squares.

Our empirical work results in a precisely estimated price of leisure series covering 60 years of US history. Estimation and testing with an extended version of the Rotterdam model provides strong support for the joint treatment of labor supply and commodity demand. Although the labor supply function is found to be inelastic in all of its explanatory variables, highly significant specific and Hicks–Allen substitutability is found to exist between leisure and durables demand. This interaction is to be expected, since durables tend to be time-saving goods. Consider, for example, washing machines, dishwashers, outboard motors, electric typewriters, or electronic calculators. At constant full income levels the household can be expected to substitute such goods for leisure time as the price of leisure rises or as time becomes more scarce. Such substitutability is the obvious analog to the substitutability of capital goods for labor time in the theory of the firm. Capturing the time-saving properties of durables is seen to lead to uniform reductions in average information inaccuracy measures. The properties of the model and the precision of the estimators are shown to be excellent, and unexplained exogenous time trends in preferences are found not to exist.

It frequently is asserted that leisure consumption has experienced a long-run trend interrupted by a post-war structural change. It is commonly believed that the income elasticity of the supply of labor dropped severely shortly after the Second World War, resulting in an end to the long-run decline in the workweek. When labor market behavior is explored in terms of leisure's share in full income, we find no evidence of a change in preferences. In fact, the share of leisure is seen to be nearly constant throughout US economic history, and if it trended upward during any period of that history, it was the Second World War. In this study, all consumption quantities are measured as shares in full income. By that allocation, leisure's, durables', and semidurables' shares all have tended to remain unchanged over the long run. No unexplained structural shifts were observed.

All relevant economic theory, including the derived price of leisure theory, is accepted empirically. Alternative approaches are formulated, tested, and rejected. The likelihood function is explored to investigate the limiting cases characterizing conventional methods. In the neighborhood of such limits, the properties of the model deteriorate severely. Sign reversal is exhibited by leisure's own-price Slutsky elasticity, and the precision of all parameter estimators decays rapidly as the limits are approached.

It is interesting to consider the implications of these findings for the forecasting of durable goods consumption. During a recession, the representative household possesses an excess supply of free time available for menial household tasks, in the sense that the household has unemployed time that it willingly would sell in the labor market if it could. This excess time includes both time from involuntarily unemployed household members and from employed members working the depressed workweek typical of recession periods. Hence, there is little incentive to economize on the use of time through the purchase of consumer durables. Even with the current stock of durables, the household has excess time. But as the economy recovers from the recession, free household time becomes scarce, idle household members find work, and the workweek of employed members increases. As a means of economizing on the use of scarce time, the household buys durables. During expansions, consumers substitute time-saving durables for increasingly scarce leisure as involuntarily unemployed time decreases and as the workweek expands. Any model that does not permit this substitution between leisure and durables would tend to underestimate the demand for durables during economic expansions.

1.3. Two-stage decisions

Consider a household that is faced with the problem of allocating full income over leisure and goods. At present we shall explore this problem in a simple single period model. As a matter of style, let us use the term "full income" to refer to single period aggregate expenditure on goods and leisure, and let us treat it as given. In the next section we shall consider briefly the intertemporal issues involved in such a choice of explanatory variables.

The household must choose a vector of commodity consumption quantities, $x \geqslant 0$, and a quantity of leisure $\ell \in [0, k]$ to

$$\begin{aligned} \text{maximize} \quad & U(x, \ell) \\ \text{subject to} \quad & x'p + p_L \ell = m. \end{aligned} \quad (1.1)$$

Here p_L is the price of leisure, to be operationalized in Chapter 2, p is the vector of prices of consumer goods, k is the total amount of annual time available to the household for market employment, u is a strictly quasiconcave, monotonically increasing, twice continuously differentiable utility function, and m is the household's full income. Only values of (m, p, p_L)

will be considered that lead to positive consumption of all goods. We now seek to explore the possibility of separating the labor supply decision from the commodity consumption allocation decision.

In terms of statistical efficiency, the resulting demand functions, including the leisure demand function, are best estimated jointly, whether or not a consistent two-stage decision exists.[3] In fact, it is desirable to estimate the entire consumption sector jointly – if not a model of the complete economy. In a very simple model, labor supply would be a determining factor in income, which would then be an explanatory variable in a consumption function determining consumption. Aggregate consumption expenditure finally would serve as an explanatory variable in a system of commodity demand functions. Clearly, we have a system of simultaneous equations, most likely having correlated disturbances.

In the approach that we shall take, aggregate expenditure on goods and leisure ("full consumption" expenditure) could be viewed as determined by a consumption function of the sort estimated by Christensen and Jorgenson (1968). Full consumption then serves as an explanatory variable in each equation in a system of commodity and leisure demand functions. We examine only one aspect of that joint estimation problem: the allocation of full consumption over goods and leisure.

We thereby deal with systems of seemingly unrelated regression equations with cross equation parameter restrictions, and gains in joint estimation exist. In this chapter we seek the conditions required merely to ensure the *existence* of specifications providing separation of labor supply from commodity demand. This existence question is independent of the method of estimation considered.

In conventional empirical commodity demand and labor supply studies, the consumer is assumed to make his decision in two stages. In the first stage, which is the conventional domain of the labor economist, the consumer allocates full income over leisure and aggregate commodity expenditure. In the second stage, which is the conventional domain of the demand systems modeler, the consumer allocates aggregate commodity expenditure over goods.

Studies not using this two-stage decision are rare but do exist in recent research. A test for consistent two-stage maximization was attempted by Abbott and Ashenfelter (1976). However, their paper is flawed by modeling and methodological problems. We shall mention some of those prob-

---

[3] The gains in efficiency depend upon the properties of the error structure. See Theil (1976, chs. 7 and 8).

lems in later chapters. Our approach is based upon Barnett's (1979b), which was acquired concurrently with, but independently of, Abbott and Ashenfelter's. Other more distantly related papers (not testing for a two-stage consistent decision) include Diewert (1974a), Darrough (1977), Owen (1971), Christensen (1968), Kiefer (1975, 1977), and Betancourt (1971a, b).

In the first stage of the two-stage decision it is assumed that for some index of aggregate commodity consumption, $y=y(x)$, the household chooses $y \geq 0$ and leisure consumption, $\ell \in [0, k]$, to

maximize $v(y, \ell)$

subject to $p^*y + p_L\ell = m$,

where m is full income (full consumption), $p^* = p^*(p)$ is an index of commodity prices, p_L is the price of leisure, and v is a neoclassical utility function. In the second stage the household chooses a vector of commodity quantities, $x \geq 0$, to

maximize $y(x)$
subject to $x'p = p^*y$.

Our objective is to find necessary and sufficient conditions on u such that for every $(p, p_L, m) > 0$ the solution for (ℓ, x) to the two-stage decision will be the same as the solution to problem (1.1) for some price index $p^* = p^*(p)$, some quantity index $y = y(x)$, and some utility function v. In that case we shall say that the two-stage decision is consistent. Without the acceptance of those conditions, the usual dichotomized commodity demand and labor supply functions do not exist, and we must treat labor supply and consumption allocation jointly. From a well-known theorem in aggregation theory, we can determine that under usual neoclassical assumptions, the necessary and sufficient conditions we seek are the existence of a linearly homogeneous function $y(x)$ and a function v such that $u(x, \ell) = v(y(x), \ell)$. See Green (1964, p. 154), Green (1971, theorem 4), or Katzner (1970, p. 143).

The utility function u is defined to be weakly separable in leisure if the marginal rate of substitution between any two goods is independent of the quantity of leisure consumed. It can be shown that there exists v and y such that $u(x, \ell) = v(y(x), \ell)$ if and only if u is weakly separable in leisure. This result follows from Goldman and Uzawa (1964, theorem 2). Hence, we find that a consistent two-stage decision exists if two conditions are satisfied. The first condition is that u is weakly separable in leisure, so that $u(x, \ell) = v(y(x), \ell)$. This ensures the existence of a utility function, $y(x)$, solely in goods. The second condition is that the utility function in goods is linearly homogeneous.

The second stage of the conventional two-stage decision process permits the generation of a complete system of demand functions for goods alone. But the linear homogeneity of the quantity index (and utility function) $y(x)$ in goods is very restrictive. It results in the totally unacceptable property of unitary income elasticity of all demand functions. Empirical demand functions exhibiting that property are widely viewed as being of little practical value, since they violate Engel's law. Since the linear homogeneity assumption is unacceptably strong, it is interesting to consider whether the consistency conditions can be weakened. The only way to weaken the consistency conditions without losing consistency is to redefine the two-stage decision. A useful means of doing so is to convert it to a three-stage decision. In the first stage, subsistence quantities of each good and of leisure are purchased. The next two stages are identical to those of the previously defined two-stage decision, except that the household is now allocating the income remaining after the purchase of the subsistence quantities of goods and leisure.

This multistage decision can be used to support various useful empirical systems of demand functions, such as Stone's Linear Expenditure System. The three-stage decision need not require a linearly homogeneous utility function in goods. However, it should be observed that in terms of the supernumerary quantities (quantities in excess of subsistence levels) that actually are subject to choice, the three-stage decision is identical to the two-stage decision. Hence, the utility function in goods has the unappealing property of being linearly homogeneous in supernumerary quantities. Since the three-stage decision is equivalent to the two-stage decision under a redefinition of "goods," we shall consider the two-stage decision in much of the work to follow. Where useful, goods can be redefined to be measured in supernumerary quantities.

Alternatively, we could dispense with the homogeneity assumption entirely by altering the two-stage decision in a different manner. We could require that the two-stage decision provide the correct consumption quantities only for differential changes in prices and income, and we could define the resulting differential two-stage decision in a manner using two differential price indices (Divisia and Frisch), rather than only the one index used in the global two-stage decision defined above. This differential approach has been developed and used by Theil. See Theil (1979, section 9.1, footnote 1). The differential approach does not require homotheticity in supernumerary quantities (or any other form of marginal homotheticity). Nevertheless, the three-stage approach described above (with the single price index, p^*) corresponds to the decomposition underlying the usual separation of labor supply from consumer demand models. Since the weak separability assumption is necessary for either global or differential decomposition, we shall concentrate on exploring that assumption.

Weak separability is an extremely important separability condition: without weak separability a utility function in goods alone does not even exist. By its definition, weak separability defines a sort of orthogonality of preferences, with preferences in the space of goods being independent of the leisure dimension of the commodity space. To see the implications of this assumption, it is instructive to consider the implications of weak separability for the Slutsky terms. Goldman and Uzawa (1964, theorem 5) and Katzner (1970, theorem 5.2-5) have provided proofs that can be applied to demonstrate that u is weakly separable if and only if the Slutsky compensated derivative $K_i(m, p, p_L)$ between good i and the price of leisure is of the form

$$K_i(m, p, p_L) = c(m, p, p_L) \frac{\partial x_i(m, p, p_L)}{\partial m}, \quad \text{for } i=1,\ldots,n, \quad (1.2)$$

where $c(m, p, p_L)$ is a function of (m, p, p_L) and $x_i(m, p, p_L)$ is the household's demand function for good i.

Now, suppose all goods are normal goods, so that $\partial x_i / \partial m$ is positive for all i. Furthermore, suppose good j is an aggregate of recreational goods, which Owen's work would lead us to believe is Cournot complementary with leisure. If good j is also a Hicks-Allen complement for leisure, then its Slutsky term, K_j, is negative. Hence, $c(m, p, p_L)$ is negative. We then are led to the conclusion that every K_i, $i=1,\ldots,n$, is negative and therefore that all goods are Hicks-Allen complements for leisure. But our work below will demonstrate that durables and leisure are Hicks-Allen substitutes.

Many anecdotes of that sort can be generated from inspection of (1.2). For example, by observing the proportionality between $K_i(m, p, p_L)$ and $\partial x_i / \partial m$, we can easily generate numerous counterintuitive relationships between a good's degree of substitutability with leisure and a good's position on a luxury-necessity scale. As is well known, $c(m, p, p_L)$ serves as a group norm, and in a study in which one hopes to explore potentially complicated interactions between goods and leisure, the imposition of such a norm carries heavy costs. Nevertheless, it should be observed that the two-stage decision leads to major simplifications, and in many contexts it is undoubtedly a powerful tool. As will be seen below, weak separability assumptions alone can lead to large decreases in the numbers of parameters to be estimated.

It should be observed that nonweakly-separable utility interactions between leisure and goods can exist and can influence the demand for goods even if the labor market is not cleared. The conclusions of this section are not changed if leisure consumption is determined involuntarily, although the results then are most conveniently restated in terms of shadow prices and a shadow income level. These complications are considered in section 2.2.

1.4. Intertemporal allocation

In the previous sections we have dealt with single period allocation. The simplest interpretation is acquired by postulating a single period world, and our terminology frequently will be suggestive of such a world. Hence, we refer to the consumer's allocation of all current "income" or "full income" over current period consumption of goods and leisure. No mention is made of savings. Those terminological conventions are common in the demand systems literature, and they will be particularly useful when we introduce distributional issues involving income and expenditure shares over both goods and consumers. However, it should be understood that we actually are dealing with current period consumption expenditure allocation over goods and leisure, not current period actual income allocation over goods, leisure, and savings. In this section we discuss briefly the assumptions under which current period expenditure can be allocated over goods and leisure by simple single period constrained utility maximization within a multiperiod world. Acceptance of at least one of those assumptions will be implicit in the rest of the book.

A function $f(z_1, z_2, \ldots, z_N)$ is blockwise weakly separable in N blocks if there exist a function F and functions, $g_1, \ldots, g_N$, such that $f(z_1, z_2, \ldots, z_N) = F(g_1(z_1), g_2(z_2), \ldots, g_N(z_N))$. We assume that the consumer's intertemporal utility function, defined over all current and future goods and leisure consumption quantities, is blockwise weakly separable in two blocks. One block contains current consumption quantities of goods and leisure, and the other block contains future consumption quantities of goods and leisure. Under this assumption, a conditional utility function exists solely in current goods and leisure quantities. This result is analogous to that discussed in section 1.3.

We now see that our function u is that conditional current period utility function. Similarly, we see that m is the consumer's actual current period consumption of goods and leisure. The consumer selects m by first maximizing his complete intertemporal utility function subject to a full wealth constraint. He then sums his resulting current period expenditure on goods and leisure to acquire m. The decision problem we consider in Part I of this book is the maximization of current period conditional utility subject to the constraint that current period expenditure on goods and leisure not exceed m. Under appropriate stationary assumptions and assumptions on expectations, the solution to that conditional single period allocation problem at any period of time would be the same as the solution for those quantities to the full intertemporal allocation decision. In the intertemporal decision, replanning is assumed in each period. These issues have been considered in detail by Christensen and Jorgenson (1968) and by Christensen (1968). See also section 8.7 of Theil (1976).

In future chapters we take m as given to the consumer during each period. We do not explicitly consider the means by which m has been determined. As discussed above, m could have been determined by solution of the full intertemporal decision, as seen by the consumer during the current period. If so, then our blockwise weak separability assumption is sufficient to justify our single period allocation modeling procedure. However, in a sense, our single period allocation decision becomes redundant, since the prior solution to the full intertemporal allocation problem already has solved for everything. Hence, a consumer would have no reason to solve the single period decision after already having solved the full intertemporal allocation decision during the same period. Nevertheless, we can, in principle, say that the consumer acts *as if* he were solving the single period allocation decision alone during each successive period. We take that approach.

In some cases it is useful to be able to explain m in a manner that is independent of the single period allocation of m over current consumption of goods and leisure. Weak separability is not sufficient to provide that facility. Either a stronger assumption (homogeneous separability) is required on preferences, or further assumptions are required on the behavior of prices or price expectations (as in the Hicksian aggregation conditions). Christensen and Jorgenson (1968) have explained m under the homogeneous separability condition using a full consumption function. The result is an extension of the Modigliani–Brumberg–Ando consumption function to the explanation of current period full consumption of goods and leisure, rather than of ordinary goods consumption. Such a consumption function logically could be adjoined to our model to explain m; the use of Christensen and Jorgenson's consumption function would not necessarily imply acceptance of their assumptions if restrictions on the behavior of relative prices or of price expectations were permitted. Since we do not consider the explanation of m, we need not accept assumptions sufficient for its explanation, and hence we do not further pursue such assumption structures.

However, weak separability of the household's intertemporal utility function with respect to further consumption *is* implicit in our single period models to follow. Without weak separability between present and future consumption, a single period utility function does not exist. But weak separability with respect to the future may not be an unreasonable approximation. We need only assume that households, faced with an uncertain future, act *as if* their utility functions were weakly separable with respect to the future. The imposition of the resulting group norms implied by weak separability is not unappealing, and when faced with the formidable task of modeling expectations the simplifications made possible by intertemporal weak separability are most welcome.

CHAPTER 2

CONSUMPTION THEORY

2.1. Introduction

We take the household to be the decision unit. In this chapter we seek to convert the household's decision problem into an equivalent problem that can be used to derive a system of conventional demand functions. Those functions are to be in a form that can be modeled directly with existing empirical demand systems.

Two fundamental problems exist in establishing this transition: (1) the aggregation problem and (2) the problem of labor market corner solutions. The first problem arises when we seek to aggregate over household members. All household members consume goods. But not all household members are in the labor force, and not all members of the labor force need be employed. As a result of such complexities, demand aggregated over household members may depend upon such distributional variables as labor force participation rates. In sections 2.2 and 2.3 we explore these issues, and we establish assumptions sufficient to acquire per capita demand functions depending solely upon prices and per capita explanatory variables.

The second problem arises since labor markets need not be cleared. Hence per capita leisure consumption need not be on the per capita leisure demand function. To remove such corner solutions we introduce a shadow price of leisure in section 2.4. If the shadow price of leisure, rather than the market wage rate, is used as the price of leisure, and if a corresponding shadow value is used for full consumption expenditure (on goods and leisure), then the corner solutions are removed.

Solutions to the corresponding shadow problem then become regular interior solutions, and consumption of goods and leisure lies on the resulting demand functions. Hence, adjustment of wage rate and full expenditure data to shadow values is needed to permit identification of our system of goods and leisure demand functions. In section 2.5 we provide a method of accomplishing those adjustments.

2.2. The household model

2.2.1. Introduction

Time series studies of consumption allocation are generally formulated to model the per capita consumption of each good. When one is interested solely in the demand for commodities, this poses few conceptual problems if one postulates the existence of a "representative individual." Alternatively, the Rotterdam model permits a rigorous aggregation over individuals, without the existence of a representative consumer. But when leisure is introduced, complications arise for any demand model.

While everyone consumes goods and many spend labor income, less than half the population is employed. The relevant economic unit is the household rather than the individual. We shall consider household participation rates and unemployment in deriving a means of passing from a household decision problem to a per capita household model. This research is necessitated by the need to operationalize the concept of aggregate per capita leisure and to relate it to the decisions of households. Our approach results in the construction of a "representative individual" for an arbitrary household. Rigorous consideration of aggregation over households (or equivalently over representative individuals) will be reserved for Chapter 3. We shall define leisure to be nonmarket time rather than idle time or recreational time.

Recently, an extensive literature on household decisions has appeared in the "new home economics." The objective of that literature is to generalize neoclassical demand analysis to include household production and explicitly treated interactions between groups of household members. This current chapter seeks the maximum simplification rather than the maximum generality. We seek to accept assumptions sufficiently strong to permit the modeling of per capita leisure and goods consumption through the use of existing empirical demand systems and available data. The new home economics seeks disaggregation over household members, while the current chapter seeks simplifying aggregation to total labor supply. The difference in the approaches results from differences in the household aggregation level relevant to the objectives. We disaggregate over goods rather than over labor supply. In Chapter 8 we discuss the household production function approach.

The objective of this section is to formulate and explore a structure of assumptions sufficient to permit the inclusion of leisure demand in conventional empirical models of the allocation of consumption expenditure. In the literature on labor economics, the relevant decision unit is the household; but to use the resulting theory directly in construction of an empirical system of demand functions would lead to the introduction of household size as an explanatory variable. We explore a means of eliminating that explanatory variable and of dealing with the related questions of unemployment and labor force participation. The result will be a formulation conveniently stated in per capita terms and permitting an operationalization of the concept of leisure.

2.2.2. The household's decision problem

In this subsection we define the household's decision problem. Let N_h be the size of the arbitrarily selected household. Let ℓ_i be the number of annual hours of leisure demanded by household member i, and let x be the household's n-dimensional vector of annual total quantities demanded of the n available consumer goods. We assume that household preferences can be expressed as a single utility function of the form

$$u\left(x, \sum_{i=1}^{N_h} \ell_i, N_h\right).$$

The household utility function, u, is strictly monotonically increasing in goods and leisure and strictly quasiconcave. In addition, we assume that $\partial u/\partial N_h$ is negative, since an increase in N_h with household consumption held constant reduces consumption per household member. Discussions relevant to the existence of this household utility function can be found in Willis (1973) and Nerlove (1974). One set of conditions under which such a utility function can be derived rather than postulated can be found in what Nerlove (1974) has called the "Samuelsonian finesse". The selection of those quantities to be treated as given by the household will be explained after the budget constraint has been introduced and rearranged.

We define the following symbols. Let L_i be the number of annual hours of labor supplied by the ith member of the household. We also define the following symbols: w_i is the market wage for the ith member's labor, k_0 is the number of annual hours available for work per household member, I_K is annual household capital income, S is annual household savings, and p is the commodity price vector corresponding to the quantities, x. The scalar L_D^i is the number of annual hours of the ith member's labor demanded by firms. It is assumed that p is strictly positive and that $w_i > 0$ and $L_D^i < k_0$ for all i.

We now can define the household's current period decision problem to be to find $(x, \ell_1, \ldots, \ell_{N_h})$ to

$$\text{maximize} \quad u\left(x, \sum_{i=1}^{N_h} \ell_i, N_h\right)$$

$$\text{subject to} \quad x'p + S = I_K + \sum_{i=1}^{N_h} w_i L_i,$$

$$x \geq 0; \quad \ell_i = k_0 - L_i; \quad 0 \leq L_i \leq L_D^i; \quad i = 1, \ldots, N_h.$$

The value of L_D^i will not be assumed to be the same for all individuals, although typically for a given i we would expect L_D^i to approximate some standard workweek, or to equal zero. The relation of this model to the usual labor market theory is clear. The aggregate market demand for household member i's labor is perfectly elastic at the market wage w_i up to the value L_D^i, at which point the demand becomes perfectly inelastic. Observe that if $L_D^i = 0$, then household member i is either involuntarily unemployed or a nonmember of the work force, depending respectively upon whether the labor demand constraint $(L_i \leq L_D^i = 0)$ is or is not binding. A constraint will be said to be binding if its removal would result in a change in the household's decision.

In the household utility function, observe that aggregate household leisure is valued independently of its allocation over individuals. This is consistent with the inclusion of the aggregate household consumption vector x in the utility function, rather than the consumption vector of each household member. Since the model will be used solely to explain and forecast household aggregates, complications to the model needed to explain the allocation of such aggregates over individuals within a household will be avoided, with the adopted level of detail in modeling being that just sufficient to explain the relevant data in a statistically efficient manner.

In this model, household consumption will be affected by changes in the age–sex composition of the household only to the degree that such changes correlate with changes in household size, N_h, which does appear in the utility function. Time series consumption studies rarely explicitly consider the age–sex composition of the population or of the work force. Exceptions generally use adult equivalent scales, as in Muellbauer (1977).

2.2.3. Simplifications

In this subsection we acquire algebraic simplifications of the household's decision problem. Let N_0 be the number of able-bodied household members capable of work (conventionally defined to be those of not less than 16 years in age). By definition of the term "nonable-bodied", it follows that $L_D^i = 0$ for $i = N_0 + 1, \ldots, N_h$. So by imposing the labor demand constraint, we find that the budget constraint can be simplified to

$$x'p + S = I_K + \sum_{i=1}^{N_0} w_i L_i.$$

By defining household net capital income, I, by $I = I_K - S$, we can simplify the budget constraint further to obtain

$$x'p + \sum_{i=1}^{N_0} w_i \ell_i = I + k_0 \sum_{i=1}^{N_0} w_i.$$

Observe that

$$I_K + k_0 \sum_{i=1}^{N_0} w_i \quad \text{and} \quad I + k_0 \sum_{i=1}^{N_0} w_i$$

are versions of Becker's "full income". Note that the time valued in full income does not include the time of non-able-bodied household members, although their consumption of goods and leisure is included in the household's consumption vector. No market exists for their time. But since only aggregate leisure appears in the household's utility function, the household does not distinguish between the leisure of different household members regardless of whether or not the market does through different values of w_i and L_D^i for $i = 1, \ldots, N_h$.

The value of

$$I + k_0 \sum_{i=1}^{N_0} w_i$$

is taken as given to the household. We appeal to section 1.3 to justify our assumption here that

$$I + k_0 \sum_{i=1}^{N_0} w_i$$

is determined by the household in a prior decision allocating full wealth over present and future aggregates. Hence, the current chapter, as well as the rest of Part I, deals with the household's second stage decision problem, in which full income (or equivalently "full expenditure") is allocated over current goods and leisure. Contrary to common practice, we do not hold I constant, since that would not be consistent with any plausible second stage current period allocation decision.

Observing that $\ell_i = k_0$ for $i = N_0 + 1, \ldots, N_h$, we find that

$$\sum_{i=1}^{N_h} \ell_i = \sum_{i=1}^{N_0} \ell_i + (N_h - N_0)k_0.$$

We shall assume that all available able-bodied household labor, as valued by the market, is homogeneous in type and quality. Then we can define w such that $w_i = w$ for all $i = 1, \ldots, N$. To permit recognition of the existence of unemployment, we make no analogous assumptions regarding the L_D^i. The household's decision problem now can be stated as to choose $(x, \ell_1, \ldots, \ell_{N_0})$ to

$$\text{maximize} \quad u\left(x, \sum_{i=1}^{N_0} \ell_i + (N_h - N_0)k_0, N_h\right) \tag{2.1}$$

$$\text{subject to} \quad x'p + w \sum_{i=1}^{N_0} \ell_i = I + k_0 N_0 w,$$

$$x \geq 0; \quad k_0 \geq \ell_i \geq k_0 - L_D^i; \quad i = 1, \ldots, N_0.$$

Define $\ell = \sum_{i=1}^{N_0} \ell_i + (N_h - N_0)k_0$ and $\bar{\ell} = N_h k_0 - L_D$, where

$$L_D = \sum_{i=1}^{N_0} L_D^i.$$

Define household full income, m, by $m = I + N_h k_0 w$. Now define the alternative decision problem of choosing (x, ℓ) to

$$\text{maximize} \quad u(x, \ell, N_h)$$
$$\text{subject to} \quad x'p + w\ell = m, \quad x \geq 0, \tag{2.2}$$

$$N_h k_0 \geq \ell, \tag{2.2a}$$

$$\ell \geq \bar{\ell}. \tag{2.2b}$$

In section A1 of Appendix A we prove that if $(x, \ell_1, \ldots, \ell_{N_0})$ is the solution to problem (2.1), then

$$(x, \ell) = \left(x, \sum_{i=1}^{N_0} \ell_i + (N_h - N_0) k_0 \right)$$

is the unique solution to problem (2.2). In this research we are interested in explaining only aggregate data. Hence, we need only consider the aggregate values, (x, ℓ), which are the solution to problem (2.2).

In applications, one commonly would expect constraint (2.2a) not to be binding for all households, since if it were then unemployment would be universal throughout the economy. Also, observe that constraint (2.2b) does not exclude the possibility of the existence of an excess supply of the household's labor. The constraint merely asserts that if an excess supply of household labor exists, then supplied labor actually employed will be constrained not to exceed labor demand, and thereby will be chosen exactly to equal labor demand. An excess supply of household labor will exist whenever the solution for ℓ to problem (2.2) with constraint (2.2b) deleted is strictly less than $\bar{\ell}$. In such a case the household would wish to supply more labor than the economy will employ.

On the other hand, when an excess demand for the household's labor exists, constraint (2.2b) is not binding. Man-hours employed will then equal man-hours supplied, regardless of the quantity of man-hours demanded. In fact, our explicit link between $\bar{\ell}$ and labor demanded is merely an expositional device. In practice, we shall view $\bar{\ell}$ as "ex post" household leisure actually consumed, regardless of the form of rationing involved in its determination. We then say that leisure consumption is involuntary if (2.2b) is binding, without the need to explain the source of involuntariness, and we say that the household acts "as if" it were solving problem (2.2).

2.3. Demand per household member

2.3.1. Extended Prais–Houthakker homogeneity postulate

In this subsection we define an extended Prais–Houthakker homogeneity postulate which is sufficient to acquire demand per household member independently of household size. Letting $q = (x', \ell)'$, the solution to problem (2.2) becomes $q_i = D_i(m, p, w, \bar{\ell}, N_h)$, where the demand function D_i determines demand for good i by the household. To acquire demand per household member, the Prais–Houthakker homogeneity postulate will be applied in an extended form. The usual Prais–Houthakker postulate assumes that household demand functions are linearly homogeneous in household ordinary income and household size, N_h. See Prais and Houthakker (1971). We extend the postulate by assuming that D_i is linearly homogeneous in (m, ℓ, N_h), where m is household full income.

To see the rationale behind that extended postulate, let $\lambda = 2$ in its definition, $D_i(\lambda m, p, w, \lambda \ell, \lambda N_h) = \lambda D_i(m, p, w, \ell, N_h)$. The same result would follow if two identical households were to merge into one.

The ordinary Prais–Houthakker homogeneity postulate is used explicitly in many cross-section studies and implicitly in nearly all time series consumption studies. It is the postulate of no economies to scale in consumption, since it excludes the possibility of the use jointly by household members of purchased consumer goods. For example, the postulate excludes economies in the use of household space or in means of transportation through the joint household use of housing or of automobiles. The postulate similarly excludes diseconomies to scale in household consumption.

The postulate is implicit in all empirical demand function systems that specify per capita demand independent of household size. In the extended form defined above, the postulate assumes constant returns to scale in the consumption of leisure as well as goods, and thereby excludes economies in the joint consumption of leisure. The application of that extended postulate to the demand for leisure time appears to be at least as reasonable as the widely accepted applications of the ordinary postulate in the modeling of the demand for goods.

Observe that the extended postulate applies with equal force, regardless of whether constraint (2.2b) is or is not binding. Again, consider the case of the merger of two households. Suppose that constraint (2.2b) were binding before the merger. Then leisure demand per household would be equal to ℓ prior to the merger. After the merger, the demand for household labor would have doubled. Hence, if (2.2b) were binding before the merger, it would continue to be binding after the merger, since prices, wages, per capita income, and household composition are constant. Thus, leisure demand necessarily will equal 2ℓ after the merger, or twice the ℓ demand prior to the merger. Alternatively, if (2.2b) were not binding before the merger, it would not be binding after the merger, and the combined household would then choose to consume twice the leisure previously consumed per household, since again household composition, per capita income, prices, and wages would not have changed. Hence, it is clear that the assumption of linear homogeneity in $(m, \bar{\ell}, N_h)$ is an extension of the ordinary Prais–Houthakker homogeneity postulate.

For given household age–sex composition, exceptions to the postulate either in its usual or its extended form could be expected when consumption economies or diseconomies to scale exist. Historically the aggregate labor force participation rate has remained nearly constant over time, independent of average household size. In addition, average hours worked per employee commonly are believed to be explainable largely without reference to household size. Hence, the assumption of constant returns to scale in leisure consumption has been reasonable historically – considerably more so than the assumption of constant returns to scale in the consumption of many commodities. But perhaps more convincingly, it is difficult to conceive of how economies of joint leisure consumption could exist once the joint consumption of goods has been excluded through the ordinary Prais–Houthakker homogeneity postulate. Preferences for leisure now are widely believed to be related, at least partially, to the time required to consume goods, and one cannot consume one's own goods through the use of someone else's time.

It can be shown that the ordinary Prais–Houthakker postulate is implied by the extended postulate. In other words, if the extended postulate obtains, but we derive demand functions for goods with ordinary income as an explanatory variable, it follows that the usual Prais–Houthakker postulate will apply to the resulting commodity demand functions. The converse is not true.

2.3.2. Household per capita leisure

In this subsection we apply the extended Prais–Houthakker homogeneity postulate in order to acquire per capita consumption of goods and leisure. A primary objective is to provide a formula for computing per capita household leisure.

Let $x^* = x/N_h$, $q^* = (x^{*\prime}, \ell^*)'$, $I^* = I/N_h$, $m^* = m/N_h = I^* + k_0 w$, and

$$\bar{\ell}^* = \bar{\ell}/N_h = k_0 - (1/N_h) \sum_{i=1}^{N_0} L_D^i.$$

In Appendix A, section A2, we apply our extended Prais–Houthakker postulate to the solution to problem (2.2). We find that the solution also is the unique solution to the problem of finding $x^* \geq 0$, $\bar{\ell}^* \in [\ell^*, k_0]$ to

$$\text{maximize} \quad u^*(x^*, \ell^*)$$
$$\text{subject to} \quad x^{*\prime} p + \ell^* w = m^* \tag{2.3}$$

for some monotonically increasing, strictly quasiconcave function, u^*. We write the solution to (2.3) as $q_i^* = Q_i(m^*, p, w, \bar{\ell}^*)$.

In Appendix A, section A2, we also determine that

$$\ell^* = k_0 - \frac{r_0 \bar{L}}{N_h}, \tag{2.4}$$

where household members $r_0 + 1, \ldots, N_0$ are assumed to be unemployed and where

$$\bar{L} = (1/r_0) \sum_{i=1}^{r_0} L_i.$$

Hence, ℓ^* is household per capita leisure.

2.3.3. Aggregation over households

To assist in the interpretation of (2.4) and to simplify the remaining discussion in this chapter, we shall aggregate over households in this subsection by postulating the existence of a "representative household" (which should not be confused with the concept of "representative individual" used above). By definition, the representative household's consumption of every good and leisure always equals the economy's consumption per household, and the representative household's decision problem is the per capita analog of an actual household's decision. In Chapter 3 we shall drop the assumption of the existence of a representative household and acquire the same results under a more satisfactory theory of aggregation over representative individuals.

It has been argued that modeling aggregate data in terms of a representative decision unit leads to negligible aggregation errors. See Pearce (1964, pp. 124–126) and Dixon (1975). Although it will be convenient to apply this argument in the rest of this section, we will not adopt that position in our own aggregation theory in Chapter 3. We believe that representative decision units exist only under extremely strong assumptions which we accept in this chapter only to simplify the exposition. We shall use the same notation below in modeling the decision of the representative household as we previously did for an arbitrarily selected actual household. Hence, all of the above analysis in this section is now applicable with the decision unit redefined to be the representative household.

Letting z be the number of households in the economy, and recalling the definition of the representative household, we can see immediately that

$$\bar{L} = \frac{1}{zr_0}\left(z\sum_{i=1}^{r_0} L_i\right)$$

which is average hours worked per worker. Data on $\bar{L}$ is available. Similarly, we find that $r_0/N_h = zr_0/zN_h$, which is the employment rate out of total population. More directly, we can compute $r_0\bar{L}/N_h$ as man-hours employed per capita. Now observe that the first term of (2.4) is available man-hours per capita, while the second term is actual man-hours employed per capita. So ℓ^* is an aggregate per capita analog to $\ell_i = k_0 - L_i$, the leisure of an individual. Similarly, $x^* = zx/zN_h$, which is the per capita consumption vector of goods.

2.3.4. Rescaled available hours

Problem (2.3) with its associated solution $q_i^* = Q_i(m^*, p, w, \bar{\ell}^*)$, $i = 1,\ldots, n+1$, and the resulting definition of per capita leisure in (2.4) are the results that we sought above. They will be the basis for the theoretical and empirical work to follow. However, for some purposes it might be desirable to scale down the definition of per capita leisure, and we provide such a rescaling in this subsection. By the above definition, the market value of per capita leisure is large relative to total expenditure. In constructing an aggregate price index, for example, it might be desirable to prevent domination of that index by the price of leisure. Hence, we shall now derive a means of scaling down the quantity of leisure without affecting the theory already presented. Although our models will be based upon the results presented above, the scale factor derived below will be useful in exploring the robustness of our inferences to variations in the definition of leisure. That scaling would have the same effect on our model as variations in our constant k_0. But in our basic models we shall simply set k_0 at the value proposed by Kuznets (1952) in his study of the share of leisure in a generalized GNP index.

Let Γ be an arbitrary constant. Let $\tilde{\ell} = \Gamma k_0 - (r_0/N_h)\bar{L}$, and define the set $A(\tilde{\ell}^*) = [\tilde{\ell}^* - k_0(1-\Gamma), \Gamma k_0]$. Let $\tilde{m} = I^* + \Gamma k_0 w$, and let $\tilde{q} = (x^{*\prime}, \tilde{\ell})'$. In Appendix A, section A3, we prove that problem (2.3) can be restated as to choose $x^* \geq 0$ and $\tilde{\ell} \in A(\tilde{\ell}^*)$ to

maximize $u_\Gamma(x^*, \tilde{\ell})$

subject to $x^{*\prime} p + \tilde{\ell} w = \tilde{m}$, (2.5)

where u_Γ is a strictly quasiconcave, monotonically increasing function. Then, functions $\tilde{Q}_i$ exist such that the solution to problem (2.5) is $\tilde{q}_i = \tilde{Q}_i(\tilde{m}, p, w, \ell^*)$ for $i = 1, \ldots, n+1$.

Observe that the derivation above follows regardless of the value of Γ. But to provide an intuitive interpretation of Γ in terms of chosen leisure time, Γ could be selected to be an upper bound (preferably a least upper bound) to the labor force participation rate out of total population. When used in our work, Γ will be chosen to exceed the labor force participation rate for all past recorded US economic history and also to exceed the probable value of that rate over the forecasting range of the model. Since our model is not intended to explain allocation of aggregates over people, the labor force participation rate is not determined and not used by this model. Hence, it is not inconsistent now to view the least upper bound to that rate as being an exogenous constant.

It will now be shown that $nk_0\Gamma$ is a household analog to the per capita constant k_0. Specifically it will be shown that as k_0 is available labor hours per person, $(N_h k_0)\Gamma$ is available hours per household. First observe that

$$\tilde{\ell} = \Gamma k_0 - (r_0/N_h)\bar{L} \qquad (2.6)$$

by the definition of per capita leisure, $\tilde{\ell}$. Hence, the corresponding index of household leisure is $N_h \tilde{\ell} = \Gamma N_h k_0 - r_0 \bar{L}$, so that household leisure, $N_h \tilde{\ell}$, is $\Gamma N_h k_0$ minus household labor employed. Thus, $\Gamma N_h k_0$ is naturally interpreted as labor hours available to the household. Furthermore, with k_0 being labor hours available per household member, it then follows that ΓN_h must be the total number of household members who the household would consider providing to the labor market. Hence, the reason is clear for the interpretation of Γ as the least upper bound to the labor force participation rate. But recall that nothing would be changed in the theory if Γ were set at any other number. The constant Γ is in fact first a scaling factor that happens to have a particularly attractive interpretation if it is set by reference to the labor force participation rate.

With Γ selected as above, a close analogy exists between the means of selection of Γ and k_0. Both scale down leisure to exclude time which for sociological or survival reasons is certain to be consumed. The theory is independent of the choices of Γ and k_0, since each can be absorbed into the utility function, while in the budget constraint they result merely in the subtraction of a constant from both sides. Similarly, our method of choosing Γ as the maximum historic labor force participation rate out of total population is the analog to Kuznets' choice of k_0 as the historic least upper bound to the work week.

In the S-branch demand system (used in Chapter 7) and in the linear expenditure demand system (as well as in our g-hypo system in Chapter 6), consumption quantities enter the utility function in the form of "supernumerary" consumption in excess of subsistence levels. In an analogous manner, leisure, as defined above, could be viewed as supernumerary leisure. Also note that in the final formulation, Γ and k_0 appear only as the product Γk_0. Although the rationale behind Γk_0 depends upon separate choices of Γ and k_0, empirically we could view Γk_0 as a single constant. Nevertheless, to provide a determinate procedure for selecting Γk_0, we shall choose both Γ and k_0 as described above.

2.3.5. Change in notation

We have now completed the derivation of the household's decision problem and of the household's demand functions in a form that can be interpreted on a per capita basis. The notation will be simplified for future convenience. The change in notation is defined by

$$\left(x^*, \tilde{\ell}, u_\Gamma, \tilde{m}, I^*, \bar{\ell}^* - k_0(1-\Gamma), \Gamma k_0\right) \mapsto \left(x, \ell, u, m, I, \bar{\ell}, k_0\right). \tag{2.7}$$

We also change the notation for the demand functions as follows:

$$\tilde{Q}_{n+1} \mapsto \ell, \tilde{Q}_i \mapsto x_i^*, \quad \text{for } i=1,\ldots,n.$$

Then on a per capita basis, the representative household's decision problem becomes to find $x \geq 0$, $\ell \leq k_0$ to

maximize $u(x, \ell)$

subject to $x'p + \ell w = m$, $\ell \geq \bar{\ell}$, (2.8)

with solution $x_i^* = x_i^*(m, p, w, \bar{\ell})$, $i=1,\ldots,n$, and $\ell^* = \ell^*(m, p, w, \bar{\ell})$. Also observe that now $m = I + k_0 w$.

2.3.6. Conclusion

The implications and usefulness of the analysis presented in this section can be illustrated by considering the consequences of doing without it. Abbott and Ashenfelter (1976) attempted to model leisure and goods demand jointly, without explicit household homogeneity postulates. Their work appears to have been motivated by an earlier paper by Ashenfelter and Heckman (1974), who concluded that "we may eventually be able to integrate the consumer's demand for non-market time with his demand for goods and services to produce estimates of a truly complete system of consumer demand functions". In addition to the estimation of two highly restrictive models, Abbott and Ashenfelter (1976) estimated a version of the Rotterdam model, which is the basis for our inferences in Part I. Unlike our favorable results, their estimated model has very poor properties. In fact, even their own Slutsky coefficients were statistically insignificant. These difficulties can be traced to the lack of availability to them of our household model (and of our price of leisure theory presented in the next section, and to their use of an unconditional demand approach requiring a zero savings rate).

Without our theory, Abbott and Ashenfelter found that they could not model the consumption decisions of nonmembers of the labor force, who comprise over 50 percent of the population. Hence, Abbott and Ashenfelter chose solely to model the decisions of suppliers of market time. Since data on the time series consumption of employed workers is not available, Abbott and Ashenfelter were forced to impute total US consumption expenditure in all of its categories to employed workers; in effect, Abbott and Ashenfelter assumed that over 50 percent of the population consumes nothing. By simultaneously using hours of work data as labor supplied per person, Abbott and Ashenfelter's data overstates goods' share in full income by over 100 percent. The household model in our current section permits imputation of total consumption expenditure to the total population that actually consumed it. As a result of the theory in this chapter and the next, our empirical demand systems will be seen in Chapter 5 to achieve theoretically and empirically acceptable and plausible results.

2.3.7. Remaining issues

Since ℓ is constrained to lie within $[\bar{\ell}, k_0]$, corner solutions are possible, even if $x^* > 0$ is known to obtain. The right-hand boundary of $[\bar{\ell}, k_0]$ presents no difficulties, since it will never be binding. It would be binding only if universal unemployment existed, implying the total collapse of the economy. But the lower bound can and will be binding whenever involuntary unemployment exists. Hence, corner solutions are possible that are not considered in the formulations on which standard empirical demand models are based.

To use such a standard system of demand functions we must be able to adjust the data in such a manner as to eliminate corner solutions without changing consumers' decisions. In the next section it will be shown that (m, w) can be adjusted to shadow values $(\hat{m}, \hat{w})$ such that if $\hat{m}$ and $\hat{w}$ were the actual levels of full income and of the wage rate, then the same consumption choices of goods and leisure would be made, but without those choices leading to corner solutions.

2.4. The full-employment-equivalent price of leisure

2.4.1. Introduction

When as excess supply of labor exists, the representative household's labor supply is constrained not to exceed labor demanded per household. This fact was explicitly recognized in the formulation presented in the preceding section. But the usual leisure and commodity demand functions of economic theory are derived under the assumption that no such direct quantity constraints (other than non-negativity) exist; the consumer takes prices and income as given and then chooses quantities demanded. The objective of this section is to determine the conditions necessary and sufficient to identify and estimate the usual demand functions (without quantity constraints), when the available market data was generated by an optimization process that may have been labor demand constrained.

Our results provide a means of including leisure in any existing system of demand functions with only prices and total expenditure as explanatory variables. However, the price of leisure that will have to be used for this purpose will be shown to be a shadow price. The shadow price will equal the wage rate only when full employment exists. Otherwise the shadow price of leisure will be less than the wage rate. The shadow price of leisure results in equating all price ratios with corresponding marginal rates of substitution. Hence, the use of the shadow price of leisure permits us to pass to a shadow world in which the measured consumption quantities of goods and leisure are selected by households without quantity constraints (on employment or hours).

In the previous section we proved under certain assumptions that with per capita leisure defined as in (2.4) of that section, per capita data behaves as if it were generated by a single representative consumer. As a result, we now can formulate our aggregate model in terms of a representative consumer. The underlying assumptions will be weakened in Chapter 3.

2.4.2. Decision problems

The representative consumer's decision was presented as problem (2.8) in the previous section and is subject to the constraint

$$\ell \geqslant \bar{\ell}. \tag{2.9}$$

Throughout this subsection we assume that $(m, p, w) > 0$ and $\bar{\ell} \in (0, k_0)$.

For arbitrary scalars $\hat{m} > 0$ and $\hat{w} > 0$, we now define the separate problem of finding (x, ℓ) to

$$\begin{aligned} \text{maximize} \quad & u(x, \ell) \\ \text{subject to} \quad & x'p + \ell\hat{w} = \hat{m} \quad \text{and} \quad \ell \leqslant k_0, (x, \ell) \geqslant 0, \end{aligned} \tag{2.10}$$

with the solution $\hat{x} = \hat{x}(\hat{m}, p, \hat{w})$ and $\hat{\ell} = \hat{\ell}(\hat{m}, p, \hat{w})$, where $\hat{x}$ has components $\hat{x}_i$, $i = 1, \ldots, n$.

Problem (2.8) is the problem that the representative consumer actually solves. But the solution to problem (2.10) provides the demand functions of economic theory. So in order to use the data generated by the solution to problem (2.8) to estimate the functions defined by the solution to problem (2.10), we must establish some relationship between the two solutions. In this subsection we determine the values of $(\hat{w}, \hat{m})$ that equate the solutions of problems (2.3) and (2.10).

Observe that our objective is to estimate the functions $\hat{x}$ and $\hat{\ell}$. Points on these functions, no matter how acquired, are valuable. We shall demonstrate in this subsection that for any (m, p, w, ℓ) a shadow value of $(\hat{m}, \hat{w})$ can be determined such that the solutions of the two problems are the same. Then the actual measured values of (x^*, ℓ^*) can be used as data in fitting the functions $(\hat{x}, \hat{\ell})$, if each observed value of (m, w) is adjusted to the corresponding shadow value of $(\hat{m}, \hat{w})$. Then for given data, (x^*, ℓ^*), the value of $\hat{w}$ is the shadow price of leisure relating (x^*, ℓ^*) to its corresponding demand functions. Hence it is $\hat{w}$ rather than w that captures the concept of "the price of leisure" that we need. We shall call $\hat{w}$ the (full employment) equivalent price of leisure or the shadow price of leisure. In a different context, the concept also has been used by Heckman (1974). Similarly, we shall call $\hat{m}$ the equivalent or shadow full income level. Observe that $\hat{w}$ is not just the supply price, since m is adjusted to $\hat{m}$ in acquiring $\hat{w}$.

The demand functions $(\hat{x}, \hat{\ell})$ that we are identifying are essentially long-run or full-employment-equivalent concepts. In a conventional empirical demand model context, the concept of an instantaneous short-run demand function is not particularly useful. In the immediate short run, markets are out of equilibrium and rationing over consumers or producers is determined by bargaining power. That side of the market (supply or demand) which desires a solution at the lower quantity tends to be in control.

By estimating the standard neoclassical demand functions of problem (2.10) we are dealing with central tendencies rather than the current instant. The concept of a current rather than an equivalent (shadow) price of leisure is of little interest in our approach. The current price of leisure is the wage rate; if we were to regress man-hours on the wage rate with all else held constant, we would acquire, at best, an estimate of a labor demand function rather than an estimate of the labor supply function we seek.

When an excess supply of labor exists so that constraint (2.9) of problem (2.3) holds, current leisure is beyond the control of the representative consumer, but unless his utility function is weakly separable in leisure, leisure interacts with goods in his utility function thereby affecting his preferences for goods. Without weak separability in leisure, a utility function in goods alone does not exist, even when leisure is not subject to choice by the consumer. But when full employment exists, constraint (2.9) is not binding, and the solutions to problems (2.3) and (2.10) become identical to $\hat{w} = w$ and $\hat{m} = m$.

With $\hat{w}$ and $\hat{m}$ adjusted to equal the equivalent (shadow) price of leisure and the equivalent full-income level, all markets are cleared in the shadow world defined by problem (2.10), but they are not in equilibrium. Firms see a wage of w while consumers see a price of leisure of $\hat{w}$. The term "full-employment-equivalent price of leisure" was selected to reflect the market clearing property of the shadow world.

In a sense, all economic theory deals with equivalent problems. In reality, corner solutions are the rule rather than the exception. No consumer ever purchases a positive quantity of every good. But it is useful to pretend that consumers act as if average data had been generated by the choices of a representative consumer. What our empirical work will demonstrate is that while problem (2.4) may be a useful fiction in explaining actual data, the data adjustment required to pass to problem (4.2) is non-negligible.

2.4.3. Assumptions and definitions

Our results on the shadow price of leisure will be conditioned upon the assumptions and definitions provided in this subsection. We shall have repeated use for the following sets, which are collected together for convenient reference:

$$S_0 = \{(m, p, w, \bar{\ell}) > 0 : x^*(m, p, w, \bar{\ell}) > 0, \bar{\ell} \leq \ell^*(m, p, w, \bar{\ell}) < k_0\},$$

$$S_1 = \{(\hat{m}, p, \hat{w}) > 0 : \hat{x}(\hat{m}, p, \hat{w}) > 0, 0 < \hat{\ell}(\hat{m}, p, \hat{w}) < k_0\},$$

$$S = \{(m, p, w, \bar{\ell}) \in S_0 : \hat{\ell}(m, p, w) < \bar{\ell}\}.$$

On set S, constraint (2.9) of problem (2.3) clearly is binding.

We accept the usual assumption that leisure is a normal good. We can formalize that assumption as follows:

Assumption 2.1. $\partial \hat{\ell}(\hat{m}, p, \hat{w})/\partial m > 0$, for all $(\hat{m}, p, \hat{w}) \in S_1$.

Now define $\hat{I}$ such that $\hat{I} = \hat{m} - k_0 \hat{w}$. We call $\hat{I}$ the net capital income level corresponding to the equivalent income and wage levels $\hat{m}$ and $\hat{w}$. Then define the set S_2 by

$$S_2 = \{(\hat{I}, p, \hat{w}) > 0 : (\hat{m}, p, \hat{w}) \in S_1, \hat{m} = \hat{I} + k_0 \hat{w}\},$$

and define the function h on S_2 by

$$h(\hat{I}, p, \hat{w}) = \hat{\ell}(\hat{I} + k_0 \hat{w}, p, \hat{w}).$$

We make the following assumption about the function h.

Assumption 2.2. Let $\bar{\ell}$ be as given in problem (2.3). Then for all $(\hat{I}, p, \hat{w}) \in S_2$, the function h satisfies

$$\frac{\partial h(\hat{I}, p, \hat{w})}{\partial \hat{w}} < \frac{\partial \hat{\ell}(\hat{m}, p, \hat{w})}{\partial \hat{m}} (k_0 - \bar{\ell}).$$

In the literature on growth models and on labor economics, it is frequently assumed that the labor supply function is perfectly inelastic to changes in the price of leisure, when net capital income and other prices are held constant. In our notation that assumption states that $\partial h/\partial \hat{w}$ is always zero. Our assumption is weaker than the common one. Suppose that $\partial h/\partial \hat{w} = 0$ everywhere. Then assumption 2.2 would follow immediately from assumption 2.1, since $k_0 - \bar{\ell}$ is positive by the definition of $\bar{\ell}$. The inelasticity of labor supply is verified by our empirical results in Chapter 5.

Observe that usual views on $\partial h/\partial \hat{w}$ do *not* apply to $\partial \hat{\ell}/\partial \hat{w}$. The full-income-constant leisure demand function should be expected to be downward sloping, like any other demand function. To see this, let $(\hat{I}, p, \hat{w}) \in S_2$.

Then it follows that

$$\frac{\partial h}{\partial \hat{w}} = \frac{\partial}{\partial \hat{w}} \hat{\ell}(\hat{I} + k_0 \hat{w}, p, \hat{w}) = \frac{\partial \hat{\ell}}{\partial \hat{m}} \frac{\partial \hat{m}}{\partial \hat{w}} + \frac{\partial \hat{\ell}}{\partial \hat{w}} = \frac{\partial \hat{\ell}}{\partial \hat{m}} k_0 + \frac{\partial \hat{\ell}}{\partial \hat{w}}.$$

But if $\partial h / \partial \hat{w} = 0$, then

$$0 = \frac{\partial \hat{\ell}}{\partial \hat{m}} k_0 + \frac{\partial \hat{\ell}}{\partial \hat{w}} \quad \text{or} \quad \frac{\partial \hat{\ell}}{\partial \hat{w}} = -k_0 \frac{\partial \hat{\ell}}{\partial \hat{m}},$$

which is negative by assumption 2.1. Such considerations should lead us to expect that our full-income-constant leisure demand function is downward sloping.

We now formally define the concepts of that shadow (equivalent) price of leisure and the shadow (equivalent) full-income level.

Definition 2.1. Let $(m, p, w, \bar{\ell}) \in S_0$. Then $\hat{w} > 0$ is the equivalent price of leisure if there exists $\hat{m} > 0$ such that $\hat{x}(\hat{m}, p, \hat{w}) = x^*(m, p, w, \bar{\ell})$ and $\hat{\ell}(\hat{m}, p, \hat{w}) = \ell^*(m, p, w, \bar{\ell})$.

Definition 2.2. Let $(m, p, w, \bar{\ell}) \in S_0$. Then $\hat{m} > 0$ is the equivalent full-income level if there exists $\hat{w} > 0$ such that $\hat{x}(\hat{m}, p, \hat{w}) = x^*(m, p, w, \bar{\ell})$ and $\hat{\ell}(\hat{m}, p, \hat{w}) = \ell^*(m, p, w, \bar{\ell})$.

In short, if the income and leisure price levels in problem (2.10) are set equal to the shadow income and shadow leisure price levels, then the solution to problem (2.10) becomes identical to the solution to the labor-market-constrained problem (2.8). Hence, we can model and estimate the simpler problem (2.10) with its interior solutions, if the shadow price of leisure and the shadow income levels exist and are used.

2.4.4. Results

In Appendix A, section A4, we show that the shadow price of leisure and the shadow income level exist and are unique. We also show that the shadow price of leisure equals the wage rate if and only if the labor market is cleared. Furthermore, we show that the shadow price of leisure declines monotonically as the unemployment rate increases. We also provide an interpretation of the shadow price of leisure in terms of the Lagrange multipliers from the Kuhn–Tucker conditions for constrained maximization with corner solutions (quantity constraints on employed labor hours).

2.5. Applications of the shadow price of leisure

2.5.1. Theory

Having acquired the existence, uniqueness, and properties of the shadow price of leisure, we now seek to characterize the shadow price analytically. Our objective is to permit solving for or specifying the shadow price of leisure in applications. Define the function f such that $f(\hat{w}, m, \boldsymbol{p}, w, \bar{\ell}) = \bar{\ell}(m - \bar{\ell}(w - \hat{w}), \boldsymbol{p}, \hat{w})$. The following characterization is proved as theorem A3 in Appendix A.

Characterization. Let $(m, \boldsymbol{p}, w, \bar{\ell}) \in S$. If $\hat{w}$ is the equivalent price of leisure, then $\hat{m}$ is the equivalent full-income level if and only if $\hat{m} = m - \bar{\ell}(w - \hat{w})$. Furthermore, $\hat{w} > 0$ is the equivalent price of leisure if and only if it is the solution to

$$f(\hat{w}, m, \boldsymbol{p}, w, \bar{\ell}) = \bar{\ell}. \tag{2.11}$$

Furthermore, we prove in Appendix A, section A4, that the solution to (2.11) is unique for each $(m, \boldsymbol{p}, w, \bar{\ell}) \in S$. Hence, there exists a function, now to be defined as g, on S such that $\hat{w} = g(m, \boldsymbol{p}, w, \bar{\ell})$ is the solution for $\hat{w}$ to (2.9). The function g therefore *determines* the value of the shadow price of leisure for $(m, \boldsymbol{p}, w, \bar{\ell}) \in S$.

However, the set S excludes the possibility of full employment. In Appendix A, section A5, we extend the function g to a function, g^*, defined on the set S^* which contains S as well as the full-employment boundary of S. In applications, the specification of the function g^* can be important.

In some applications we are more interested in locating a fixed point of the function f in $\bar{\ell}$. That fixed point could be used to determine $\bar{L} = k_0 - \bar{\ell} =$ per capita man-hours employed. In Appendix A, section A5 we prove the existence and uniqueness of the fixed point and hence the existence of a function, ξ^*, such that $\bar{L} = \xi^*(\hat{w}, m, \boldsymbol{p}, w)$. In some cases, specification of ξ^* can be of value in applications. In general, g^* is of particular use with models derived from community utility functions, while ξ^* is of particular use in specifying models based upon approximations.

2.5.2. Approximate demand systems

If we use a community utility function, g^* determines the equivalent price of leisure. By our uniqueness result the adjustment of (w, m) to the equivalent price of leisure, $\hat{w}$, and its corresponding equivalent full-income level, $\hat{m} = m - (w - \hat{w})\ell$, is necessary and sufficient to the identification of the set of conventional demand functions, including the demand for leisure. But in generating a specification for the equivalent price of leisure for use in the Rotterdam model, a specification for ξ^* will be more useful. That specification will be used only as a means of determining the differences $w - \hat{w}$ (rather than the levels of $\hat{w}$) required to correct the wage rate data downwards when unemployment exists. Hence, a simple specification could be used. The simplest method would be to use a linear specification, as is common in such data correction procedures. But in this case a more sophisticated specification would appear to be desirable.

The function ξ^* will be approximated by a function having a constant elasticity in $\hat{w}$. The function's form in terms of the other variables will be constrained only by consistency with the function's elasticity in $\hat{w}$. Then $\partial \log \xi^*(\hat{w}, m, p, w)/\partial \log \hat{w} = \theta$, for some constant θ, or $(\hat{w}/\xi^*)(\partial \xi^*/\partial \hat{w}) = \theta$. Observe that $\theta > 0$, since $\partial \xi^*/\partial \hat{w} > 0$ (as shown in Appendix A, section A5), $\hat{w} > 0$, and $\xi^* > 0$. We solve the following differential equation for ξ^*:

$$\int \frac{d\xi^*}{\xi^*} = \theta \int \frac{d\hat{w}}{\hat{w}},$$

or $\log \xi^* = \theta \log \hat{w} + C(m, p, w)$, where $C(m, p, w)$ is an arbitrary function of (m, p, w). Finally, we get $\xi^* = K(m, p, w)\hat{w}^\theta$, where K is an arbitrary function of (m, p, w).

Now in general, $w = \hat{w}$ if and only if $\xi(\hat{w}, m, p, w) = k_0 - \bar{\ell}(m, p, w)$. So $k_0 - \bar{\ell} = K(m, p, w)w^\theta$. Thus,

$$K(m, p, w) = \frac{k_0 - \bar{\ell}}{w^\theta}. \tag{2.12}$$

Furthermore, by definition of ξ^*, $\xi^*(\hat{w}, m, p, w) = k_0 - \hat{\ell}$ if and only if $\hat{w}$ equals the equivalent price of leisure corresponding to the given data (m, p, w, ℓ). So let $\hat{w}$ be that equivalent price of leisure. Then $k_0 - \hat{\ell} = K(m, p, w)\hat{w}^\theta$. Substitute (2.12) into this result to eliminate the arbitrary function $K(m, p, w)$. We then obtain that

$$\frac{k_0 - \bar{\ell}}{k_0 - \hat{\ell}} = \left(\frac{\hat{w}}{w}\right)^\theta.$$

Let $\alpha_0 = 1/\theta > 0$. Then

$$\frac{\hat{w}}{w} = \left[\frac{k_0 - \bar{\ell}}{k_0 - \hat{\ell}}\right]^{\alpha_0}.$$

But $k_0 - \bar{\ell}$ is per capita man-hours employed, while $k_0 - \hat{\ell}$ is per capita labor supply. So $(k_0 - \bar{\ell})/(k_0 - \hat{\ell}) = E_0 =$ the man-hour employment rate. So,

$$\hat{w}/w = E_0^{\alpha_0}.$$

In practice we will not have data on the man-hours employment rate, E_0, although we will have data on the usual employment rate, E. Recall that E_0 is man-hours actually worked divided by man-hours supplied. To handle this problem, we assume for some constant κ that hours worked per full time equivalent employee divided by hours supplied per full time equivalent employee equals E^κ. Then $E_0 = E^\kappa E$, so $E_0^{\alpha_0} = E^{\alpha_0(\kappa+1)}$. Letting $\alpha = \alpha_0(\kappa+1)$, we obtain that

$$\hat{w}/w = E^\alpha. \tag{2.13}$$

This is the specification which will be used to approximate the desired data adjustment of w to $\hat{w}$.

Observe that no specific utility function or leisure demand function has been assumed. This specification should be viewed only as a local approximation to the specific function ξ^*, in a manner analogous to that in which our demand models themselves in Part I will be derived. The estimated value of θ could be interpreted as the average value (over the data) of the approximated elasticity, or more formally as an estimate of its value at a single point of approximation chosen internally to the convex closure of the data. But it should be observed carefully that *all* of the above analysis only provides a very elaborate data correction device. Our objective is to correct w in the direction of $\hat{w}$ through an empirical approximation. Both w and $\hat{w}$ are "prices of leisure" in some sense (with w nested within our specification for $\hat{w}$ at $\alpha = 0$), and we believe that our corrected values are preferable to the data on w, which commonly is used as the price of leisure.

We prefer our corrected values computed from wE^α on the grounds that they probably are closer to the true shadow price, $g(m, p, w, \bar{\ell})$, than is w. We do not claim to have computed the true shadow price in any sense. In order to do so in a convincing manner, we would have to deal with the very complicated problems of variations in wage rates and unemployment rates over households and the dependencies between the labor supplies of household members. Our assumptions are appropriate for the level of aggregation of our data, but our assumptions are not weak.

Since we shall be conditioning on a $\hat{w}_L$ series *as data*, our concern will be with the properties of our data correction from w to $\hat{w}$. Observe that our correction formula $\hat{w}=wE^\alpha$ is consistent with the theory of Appendix A, section A4, for all positive α. Also, observe that if $\alpha=0$, then $\hat{w}=w$ everywhere. Hence, in general our formula cannot be worse than the use of the wage rate as $\hat{w}$, since that possibility is a special case nested within our formula. The correction is linear in the employment rate when $\alpha=1$. The general properties of the correction are easily seen by plotting $\hat{w}_L/w$ versus E for various $\alpha \geqslant 0$. For a one-parameter correction, the formula is attractively flexible. While $\hat{w}$ will fluctuate below w cyclically, $\hat{w}$ will track w over the long run.

Greater functional flexibility in this data correction formula would result in serious aggregation problems. Although both E and w will vary across households, we seek to use aggregate data. Our aggregation over consumers in Chapter 3 uses an extension to Theil's (1971, pp. 570–572) stochastic convergence approach to aggregation. That approach acquires per capita aggregates as explanatory variables only for linear (or nearly linear) models. Since our version of the Rotterdam model depends upon $\log \hat{w}$, which equals the linear function $\log w + \alpha \log E$ for our formula, we can conveniently aggregate across households.

By comparison, Owen (1964, 1970, 1971) computed a current price of leisure series using a fundamentally different, heuristic argument in terms of human capital and on-the-job training costs. Nevertheless, his empirical results can be given meaning in terms of the above theory by viewing his current price of leisure specification, P_L, as the result of a linear approximation, but with his P_L interpreted as the equivalent price of leisure $\hat{w}$. Then it can be shown that his full-income measure corresponds to the equivalent full-income level, $\hat{m}$, since $\hat{m} = m - \bar{\ell}(w - \hat{w}) = I + w(k_0 - \bar{\ell}) + \bar{\ell}\hat{w}$, where $w(k_0 - \bar{\ell})$ is the value of labor supplied at the market wage, while $\bar{\ell}\hat{w}$ is the value of leisure consumption at the equivalent price of leisure. Hence, all of Owen's empirical results (although not his theory) can be related directly to the theory presented above and to the objectives of this analysis. Furthermore, Christensen's (1968) and Grossman's (1973) price of leisure data can be acquired by setting $\alpha=1$ in our specification.

2.5.3. Cobb–Douglas case

No community utility function is implied by the Rotterdam model, but to illustrate the above methodology in a more direct manner the relevant results for an integrable aggregate system will be derived. The most elementary system, the aggregate Cobb–Douglas system, will be used.

Although this choice simplifies the illustration, the Cobb–Douglas community utility function satisfies the homogeneity and separability conditions necessary and sufficient for the existence and consistency of the two-step decision process discussed in Chapter 1. Since we wish to test for, rather than to impose, those conditions, this example is of no practical empirical value to us. Nevertheless, some implications of the separability condition can be seen from this example. We also see that despite the possibility of the two-step decision, we still have $\hat{w}<w$ whenever unemployment exists.

The Cobb–Douglas demand function system is $q_i = c_i(\hat{m}/\hat{p}_i)$ for $i= 1,\ldots,n+1$ with $\sum_{i=1}^{n+1} c_i = 1$, where $q=(x', \hat{\ell})'$ and $\hat{p}=(p', \hat{w})'$. We first find $\hat{w}$ by solving $\hat{\ell}(m-(w-\hat{w})\bar{\ell}, p, \hat{w}) = \bar{\ell}$ for $\hat{w}$. This equality in the present case is $c\{[m-(w-\hat{w})\bar{\ell}]/\hat{w}\} = \bar{\ell}$, where we are letting $c=c_{n+1}$. Solving for $\hat{w}$, we find that

$$\hat{w} = \frac{c}{1-c} \frac{m-w\bar{\ell}}{\bar{\ell}}. \tag{2.14}$$

We could use this result to explore the properties of $\hat{w}$, but it is more informative to use unemployment rather than $\bar{\ell}$ as an explanatory variable, since limiting results are most easily examined in terms of unemployment levels.

Let $\hat{U}=$ unemployed man-hours $=[k_0 - \hat{\ell}(m, p, w)] - (k_0 - \bar{\ell}) = \bar{\ell} - \hat{\ell}$. But $\hat{\ell}(m, p, w) = c(m/w)$. So we see that $\hat{U} = \bar{\ell} - c(m/w)$. Observe that substitution for $\bar{\ell}$ has converted an identity into a specification-dependent equality. Thus,

$$\bar{\ell} = \hat{U} + c\frac{m}{w}. \tag{2.15}$$

Substituting this equality into (2.14) we conclude that

$$\frac{\hat{w}}{w} = \frac{c}{1-c} \frac{m - \hat{U}w - cm}{\hat{U}w + cm}. \tag{2.16}$$

This is the equivalent price of leisure ratio for the Cobb–Douglas system.

We now explore the properties of that ratio. First, let $\hat{U}=0$. Then we have that $\hat{w}/w = 1$ or $\hat{w} = w$, as required by our theory. Now let $\hat{U}$ increase from zero. Since $\hat{w}/w$ is decreasing in $\hat{U}$, we find that $\hat{w} < w$ for $\hat{U} > 0$, with $\hat{w}$ decreasing monotonically as $\hat{U}$ increases. These results are consistent with our theory.

We now find the equivalent full-income level, $\hat{m}$, by substituting (2.15) and (2.16) into $\hat{m} = m - (w - \hat{w})\ell$. We obtain that

$$\hat{m} = m - \frac{1}{1-k_0} \hat{U}w, \tag{2.17}$$

which is increasing in m. But $\hat{m}$ is decreasing both in w and $\hat{U}$. As a result, equivalent full income declines rapidly as the market value of unemployed time, $\hat{U}w$, increases.

We now explore the interaction between leisure and goods demand by substituting $(\hat{w}, \hat{m})$ into each commodity demand function. Consider the commodity demand functions

$$x_i = k_i \frac{\hat{m}}{p_i}, \quad \text{for } i = 1, \ldots, n. \tag{2.18}$$

We see that the consumption of each commodity is decreasing in the market value of unemployed man-hours (income lost to involuntary unemployment), $\hat{U}w$. The effect of the weak separability of the Cobb-Douglas function can now be seen. We shall show that the commodity demand functions above are identical to another system of Cobb-Douglas demand functions having different coefficients and a different index of income.

To acquire this result we need merely substitute (2.17) into (2.18) to obtain that $x_i = c_i(y/p_i)$, where $c_i = k_i/(1-k_0)$ and $y = (1-k_0)m - \hat{U}w$. Now

$$\sum_{i=1}^{n} c_i = \frac{1}{1-k_0} \sum_{i=1}^{n} k_i = 1,$$

so we have a complete system of demand functions for goods alone. To see the meaning of the new income index, y, we need only observe that $y = m - w(\hat{U} + k_0(m/w)) = m - \ell w$. But by the budget constraint to problem (2.3), $x^{*\prime}p = m - \ell w$. We find that $y = x^{*\prime}p$, which is expenditure on all goods other than leisure. Hence, if we know the value of y, we can explain the consumption of commodities using an ordinary Cobb-Douglas system of demand functions without regard to labor supply.

Since the Cobb-Douglas utility function satisfies the homogeneity as well as the separability condition for a two-step decision, we know that we could also formulate the index numbers and utility function required to model the consumer's selection of y in a prior decision. The system of commodity demand functions could not have been reduced to a complete system, as done above, if the weak separability condition had not been satisfied. Without weak separability in leisure, no utility function in goods alone exists.

All of the above results on the Cobb–Douglas system can be extended directly to Stone's Linear Expenditure system simply by changing all consumption quantities and the income level to the corresponding supernumerary values. But the linear expenditure system satisfies the homogeneous separability condition necessary and sufficient for a consistent two-stage decision. Hence, Stone's system also is not usable for our purposes, since leisure demand in that model can be separated from goods consumption allocation.

CHAPTER 3

SPECIFICATIONS AND AGGREGATION THEORY

3.1. Empirical demand systems

In this chapter we present the specifications we will be using in Part I. Two categories of empirical demand systems will be used in this book: approximate systems and exact systems. Exact systems are globally integrable in the sense that for any feasible value of the parameter vector, the system of demand functions can be shown to be derivable from a neoclassical utility function. Approximate systems are not integrable or are only locally integrable. With an exact system we can be certain that any parameter restrictions implied by the micro theory of demand have been imposed. With one exception, all such currently available exact systems implicitly impose strong restrictions on tastes. The exception will be considered in Chapter 6.

To provide greater flexibility, a literature has evolved on approximate systems. These systems impose theoretical restrictions through explicit side constraints on the parameters and thereby can permit the testing of theory. In addition some provide particularly informative parameterizations. Well-known examples include the widely used translog, generalized Leontief, generalized Cobb–Douglas, and Rotterdam models. Theil and Barten's Rotterdam model will be used extensively in this research. It is a very powerful empirical tool when its theoretical foundations are validly interpreted. We shall present rigorous foundations below.

The usefulness of a model's parameterization is of major concern in the generation of approximate models. Having chosen a parameterization, one seeks to improve the precision of one's estimators by imposing theoretically acceptable restrictions on the parameters. It should be observed that if the restrictions are correct, then they will tend approximately to be satisfied by a consistent estimator for a sufficiently large sample size. We do not impose theoretical restrictions as an end in themselves. We impose them to improve the efficiency of the estimators.

We should not be overly concerned about the lack of global integrability of approximate demand systems. It might appear that such systems are in some sense inadmissible, since they do not lie in the function space of demand functions. Having substituted an estimator for the parameters of such a model, we have a function valued estimator of an element of the demand function space. But if realizations of such a function valued estimator (stochastic process) do not lie in the space of the function we wish to estimate, it might appear that we have reason for concern. But we do not. To see this, we need only consider a simple example.

Suppose, for example, we wished to fit a function about which theory provides us with one and only one fact: we know that the function is not a polynomial. It is nevertheless clear that we can appeal to the Weierstrass Approximation Theorem to make a strong case for fitting a polynomial, although we would violate the only theory we have. Since the only constant known in nature is the speed of light, we can be certain that no demand function encountered in the "real world" can be parameterized. So in a more general sense, no parametric demand function is "exact." But of far greater importance is the fact that micro theory does not apply directly at the aggregate level, since community utility functions exist only under very strong assumptions. The concept of an exact model is of little theoretical significance at the aggregate level. Hence, we shall base our theoretical foundations for the Rotterdam model upon an explicit aggregation theory.

3.2. The CSE model

3.2.1. Introduction

In this section we present the model that will be used to generate data on the price of leisure. The model will be an approximate system of demand functions that does not impose any a priori restrictions on the nature of interactions between goods and leisure, although Slutsky price elasticities and income plasticities will be parameterized at the point of the model's local approximation. We shall call the model the Constant Slutsky Elasticity (CSE) model.

The CSE model is closely related to the absolute price version of the Rotterdam model (defined in section 3.3), since the CSE model can be acquired by dividing each equation of the Rotterdam model by the corresponding value share and reparameterizing in the obvious way. For our purposes this division by the value share is highly desirable. The parameter of our price of leisure equation is thereby removed from the left-hand side of the system of demand functions. Serious empirical problems would arise if we were to attempt to use the Rotterdam model for our present purpose.

For example, we would have to deal with a particularly troublesome singular error covariance matrix. The usual procedure of eliminating an arbitrary equation would not be usable as a means of circumventing the singularity problem. The reason is that the Jacobian of the transformation between the disturbance vector and the only logical choice for an endogenous vector would depend upon the parameter, α, of our price of leisure eq. (2.12). The resulting variable Jacobian would destroy the usual invariance of the maximum likelihood estimate to the choice of equation to be eliminated.

3.2.2. The differential form

Although our CSE model appears never to have been estimated with or without leisure, the complete differential form of the model can be found in an unpublished paper written by Goldberger (1967, pp. 23–24). Although Goldberger credits Stone (1953, p. 277) with the model, the relation between the CSE model and Stone's model is very distant. Let $p_{n+1} = \hat{w}$, where $\hat{w}$ is the shadow price of leisure, and let q_i be consumption of the ith "good", where we have defined the $n+1$th good to be leisure. Using the notation defined in mapping (2.6), we would have $q = (x', \ell)'$. The variables m and p_j are (equivalent) full income and the price of the jth good, respectively, while w_j is the share of the jth good in (equivalent) full income. Then the model in its differential form is

$$d\log q_i = \eta_{i0}\left[d\log m - \sum_{j=1}^{n+1} w_j d\log p_j\right] + \sum_{j=1}^{n+1} \eta_{ij} d\log p_j,$$

for $i = 1, \ldots, n+1$.

Since we will be using the shadow values $(\hat{m}, \hat{w})$ for (m, w) throughout the rest of Part I, we will always be in the shadow (equivalent) world, and hence $(\hat{x}, \hat{\ell}) = (x^*, \ell^*)$ by definitions 2.1 and 2.2. In the rest of Part I we use the symbols (m, ℓ, x) themselves to refer to $(\hat{m}, \hat{\ell}, \hat{x})$, although we shall retain the symbol $\hat{w}$.

The differential form is subject to the following restrictions:

Engel aggregation: $\quad \sum_{i=1}^{n+1} w_i \eta_{i0} = 1,$ (3.1)

Cournot aggregation: $\quad \sum_{i=1}^{n+1} w_i \eta_{ij} = 0, \quad j = 1, \ldots, n+1,$ (3.2)

Symmetry: $\quad w_i \eta_{ij} = w_j \eta_{ji}, \quad i, j = 1, \ldots, n+1,$ (3.3)

Homogeneity: $\quad \sum_{j=1}^{n+1} \eta_{ij} = 0, \quad i = 1, \ldots, n+1.$ (3.4)

The expression $\mathrm{d}\log m - \sum_{j=1}^{n+1} w_j \mathrm{d}\log p_j$ is an index of the differential log change in real income. Finally, η_{i0} is the income elasticity of the demand for the ith good, while η_{ij} is the Slutsky cross price elasticity of the ith good with respect to the jth price. The elasticities are not constants. These are all theoretical results that are true for any demand system.

3.2.3. Further analysis

At this point we might be tempted to ask whether the usual derivation of these relationships remains valid after leisure has been introduced. When income becomes full income, we should recognize that a functional dependency may exist between full income and the price of leisure. For example, current income can depend upon current labor income, or in terms of a full-consumption function we would expect m (current full consumption expenditure) to be a function of the value of wealth, where the value of human wealth depends upon the price of leisure. In Goldberger's derivation of the CSE model, no functional relationship was recognized between m and any price. Do we need to consider the fact that $\partial m / \partial \hat{w}$ is not zero?

The answer is that we need not. The functional relationship between full income and prices requires explicit treatment only in models in which full income is a function *solely* of prices. In that case it becomes impossible to vary full income and prices independently. Demand becomes a function solely of prices, and income is eliminated as an explanatory variable. Otherwise m can be held constant while $\hat{w}$ varies, if we permit compensating changes in other determinants of m (such as capital income). In general it is reasonable to believe that full income will be a function of at least one variable that is not a price. So throughout Goldberger's derivations we can interpret partial derivatives in such a manner that the functional relationship between m and $\hat{w}$ can be ignored. However, we should observe that when we hold full income constant while varying the price of leisure, compensating changes are taking place in other variables, such as in net capital income, I. With that understanding, leisure becomes just another good in conventional demand analysis and the inclusion of leisure becomes a special case rather than an extension.

We now simplify Goldberger's results. First we prove that Cournot aggregation is redundant. By symmetry, we know that $\eta_{ij} = (w_j/w_i)\eta_{ji}$. Substituting into the homogeneity restriction, we find that

$$\sum_{j=1}^{n+1} \frac{w_j}{w_i} \eta_{ji} = 0.$$

If we multiply through by w_i, we get that

$$\sum_{j=1}^{n+1} w_j \eta_{ji} = 0,$$

which is the Cournot aggregation restriction. Hence, we shall not impose restrictions (3.2).

We now demonstrate that the homogeneity restrictions can be eliminated by substitution. Let $S = \{1, \ldots, n+1\} - \{k\}$. Then by homogeneity, $\eta_{ik} = -\sum_{j \in S} \eta_{ij}$, so that

$$\sum_{j=1}^{n+1} \eta_{ij} d\log p_j = \sum_{j \in S} \eta_{ij} d\log p_j - \sum_{j \in S} \eta_{ij} d\log p_k$$

$$= \sum_{j \in S} \eta_{ij} (d\log p_j - d\log p_k).$$

Then the differential form becomes

$$d\log q_i = \eta_{i0} \left[d\log m - \sum_{j=1}^{n+1} w_j d\log p_j \right]$$

$$+ \sum_{j \in S} \eta_{ij} (d\log p_j - d\log p_k).$$

Thus we find that restrictions (3.4) can be eliminated by deflating the differential of the logarithm of each price by the differential of the logarithm of an arbitrarily selected price.

3.2.4. Empirical specification

We now treat the elasticities as locally constant parameters, add a stochastic error term to the differential form, and convert the differentials to finite changes using the single period finite log change operator, D. We get that

$$Dq_i = \eta_{i0}\left[Dm - \sum_{j=1}^{n+1} w_j Dp_j\right] + \sum_{j \in S} \eta_{ij}(Dp_j - Dp_k) + \varepsilon_i,$$

$i = 1, \ldots, n+1$.

Recall that the term in brackets is an index of the log change in real income. The same term appears in the Rotterdam model, and in both cases we shall measure it using the same approximate index. The log changes in prices and quantities will be measured directly, with the exception of the log change in the price of leisure. The price of leisure will be eliminated by the substitution of our eq. (2.12) ($\hat{w} = wE^\alpha$, where E is the employment rate, w is the wage rate, and α is a parameter). Our model has become nonlinear in its parameters. The nonlinearity appears in the income term as well as in the price of leisure term, as will be seen when we derive the real income index. Clearly (equivalent) real income must depend upon prices, including the (shadow) price of leisure.

Letting $\boldsymbol{\varepsilon} = (\varepsilon_1, \ldots, \varepsilon_{n+1})'$, we assume that the disturbances, $\boldsymbol{\varepsilon}$, are homoscedastic and uncorrelated over time. We further assume that $\boldsymbol{\varepsilon}$ is distributed as $N(\boldsymbol{O}, \boldsymbol{\Omega})$, where the contemporaneous covariance matrix, $\boldsymbol{\Omega}$, is unknown.

Observe that restrictions (3.1) and (3.3) still remain. But both restrictions depend upon the value shares, w_i, $i = 1, \ldots, n+1$, which vary over time. This is a common problem in such models (see, for example, Byron, 1970a, b), and we adopt the common solution. We impose the restrictions at the average values of the shares. However, we should observe that relative to the underlying economic theory, this procedure is not especially elegant. The best we can do is to accept the usual argument that if a restriction holds for all observed shares, it should hold approximately at the averages. In fact our most convincing arguments will be found in our results. All of our conclusions will be similar over all of our specifications, including the Rotterdam model, for which entirely rigorous theoretical foundations will be presented. Having faced the problem squarely, we shall blink and pass on.

3.2.5. Objectives

As we mentioned above, our price of leisure equation, $\hat{w} = wE^\alpha$, induces particularly troublesome singularity problems into the Rotterdam model's error structure. In demand systems, singularity problems tend to arise only if the budget constraint is satisfied. The budget constraint forces the demand functions to be linearly dependent and thereby forces the disturbance covariance matrix, Ω, to be singular. No such problems arise in the CSE model, since that model does not satisfy the budget constraint. Hence, we can estimate all equations jointly. The reader may (or may not) be comforted to learn that the double log model also violates the budget constraint, and the CSE model will serve *only* as a data adjustment device.

We now proceed to describe the Rotterdam model. While the CSE model is well suited to the estimation of our parameter α, the merits of the Rotterdam model are underscored by the difficulties we face with the CSE model. With the Rotterdam model, parameter restrictions will be easier to impose, the budget constraint will be satisfied, and no need will exist to impose restrictions at average shares. Our use of the CSE model will be restricted to the estimation of our price of leisure adjustment parameter, α. Hence, the CSE model is used solely as an elaborate data adjustment mechanism. Theoretical foundations for the Rotterdam model will be of far greater concern to us and will be developed in detail.

3.3. The Rotterdam model

3.3.1. Introduction

The CSE model not only permits us to estimate the parameter α, but also the income and Slutsky price elasticities. However, it would be desirable to acquire more direct information about preference interactions between goods and leisure. Specifically, it would be useful to be able to test for various utility separability conditions such as weak or strong separability. In addition, knowledge about specific (utility-based) interactions can provide information about preferences that cannot be deduced from Slutsky elasticities. To provide the ability to explore preferences in greater detail, we use the Rotterdam model. In Part I we treat the Rotterdam model as our basic system of demand functions. Elasticity estimates acquired from the CSE model will be used largely as a check on the corresponding elasticity estimates acquired from the generally preferable Rotterdam model.

From the CSE model we acquire an estimate of α, and we thereby can generate a price of leisure series from eq. (2.12). We condition on that series as data when we estimate the Rotterdam model. As will be seen below, the precision of our estimator of α will be very great, so the resulting price of leisure series is well defined. As discussed earlier, the Rotterdam model is inherently designed for use conditionally upon measurable price variables. Substitution of the equation $\hat{w} = wE^\alpha$ into the model with α unknown would seriously complicate the model's empirical properties. Furthermore, in practice the values of variables frequently are deduced rather than measured. For example, in the presentation of our data in the first section of Chapter 5 we use a splicing method based upon linear regression. Here we use an analogous device when we generate price of leisure data from a nonlinear regression.

It should be observed that in any model that treats the price of leisure as data, that data can be deduced from an empirical specification. For example, Christensen's (1968) and Grossman's (1973) price of leisure data can be shown to have been generated by our equation $\hat{w} = wE^\alpha$, with α set equal to one. Similarly, studies which use the wage rate as data implicitly set α to zero in our price of leisure equation. As we have seen from theorem A3 and corollaries A1 and A2 in Appendix A, an α of zero is theoretically unacceptable. Furthermore, the hypothesis of $\alpha = 0$ will be strongly rejected by our empirical work in Chapter 5. Since the precision of our estimator of α will be very great, we can be considerably more comfortable about our leisure price data than about any comparable series based upon an arbitrary choice of α. In contrast, it is interesting to observe that Owen's (1971) attempt to estimate a price of leisure specification led to such poor precision that the choice of his parameter value was essentially arbitrary.

In brief, we generate a price of leisure series through the estimation of the CSE model, and we then condition upon that series as data in our work with the Rotterdam model. Since the Rotterdam model is not usable when α is unknown, our use of an extraneous estimate of α is necessary. Since both E and w are exogenous, it follows that $\hat{w} = wE^\alpha$ is exogenous in the Rotterdam model. Our extraneous estimator of α from the CSE model is consistent and will be seen to have very high asymptotic precision. Since our sample is large, the price of leisure data that we are accepting in the Rotterdam model is good.

However, in interpreting the standard errors of our Rotterdam model estimators, we should recognize that the minor uncertainty about α tends to decrease the precision of our other estimators. So our standard errors should be interpreted conditionally upon α. We need not be overly concerned about such problems, since we shall find that our inferences are robust over a range of values of α that is very large relative to the precision of our α estimator. In addition, when estimates from the CSE model are compared with the corresponding estimates of the Rotterdam model, close agreement will be achieved in all areas, despite the fact that α is estimated jointly with all other parameters in the CSE model.

3.3.2. The absolute price version

Two versions of the Rotterdam model exist: the absolute price version and the relative price version. We shall be using both versions. The symbol w_{it}^* denotes $\frac{1}{2}(w_{i,t-1}+w_{it})$, which is the average value of the share of the ith good in full income during the time increment being considered. The log change operator is defined such that $\mathrm{D}p_{it}=\log p_{it}-\log p_{i,t-1}$. The absolute price version can be written in the following form:

$$w_{it}^*\mathrm{D}q_{it}=\bar{\mu}_i\left[\mathrm{D}m_t-\sum_{j=1}^{n+1}w_{jt}^*\mathrm{D}p_{jt}\right]$$
$$+\sum_{j\in S}\bar{\pi}_{ij}(\mathrm{D}p_{jt}-\mathrm{D}p_{kt})+\varepsilon_{it},\qquad i=1,\ldots,n+1,$$

where S is as defined earlier. Again we are deflating each $\mathrm{D}p_{jt}$ by $\mathrm{D}p_{kt}$ for some arbitrary good, k. Our assumptions on the error structure are the same as those for the CSE model. The parameters are the $\bar{\mu}_i$ and the $\bar{\pi}_{ij}$ values, which are subject to the following constraints:

$$\sum_{i=1}^{n+1}\bar{\mu}_i=1, \tag{3.5}$$

$$\bar{\pi}_{ij}=\bar{\pi}_{ji},\quad \text{for } i,j=1,\ldots,n+1, \tag{3.6}$$

the matrix $\left[\bar{\pi}_{ij}\right]$ is negative semidefinite and of rank n. \hfill (3.7)

The homogeneity restriction has already been eliminated by substitution. Observe that we have introduced a time subscript, t, to facilitate our discussion.

Recall from our discussion of the CSE model that $Dm_t - \sum_{j=1}^{n+1} w_{jt}^* Dp_{jt}$ is an index of the log change in real income. Theil (1971, pp. 331–332) has shown that that change can be approximated satisfactorily by $\sum_{i=1}^{n+1} w_{it}^* Dq_{it}$, which has desirable properties as an index number in the Rotterdam model. We shall use that approximation both in the Rotterdam model and in the CSE model.

Observe that the model is linear in the parameters. But since the model satisfies the budget constraint, we must consider possible singularity problems. Let $\varepsilon_t = (\varepsilon_{1t}, \ldots, \varepsilon_{n+1,t})'$. We are assuming that for some unknown covariance matrix Ω, ε_t is distributed as $N(O, \Omega)$ for all t. It can be shown that Ω must be singular. Barten (1969) has proved that with given price data, one equation is redundant, and the maximum likelihood estimates of the parameters are invariant to the equation deleted. In our applications, we always delete the equation for the kth good, where k is the same as that chosen arbitrarily in our price "deflator" Dp_k.

Having deleted the kth equation, we require a means of estimating the parameters of the kth equation. We can do so by the use of restrictions (3.5) and (3.6) after the other equations have been estimated. Observe that once we have deleted equation k, restriction (3.5) need not be imposed on the remaining equations, since it will be imposed in the estimation of μ_k. So in estimating the remaining equations the only equality restrictions we need impose are the symmetry conditions, (3.6). Restrictions (3.7) will not be imposed, although they will be verified.

The model commonly is derived from a theoretical differential form in which the $\bar{\pi}_{ij}$ and $\bar{\mu}_i$ values are functions of (m, p). In that differential form, the $\bar{\pi}_{ij}$ values are defined to equal functions

$$\pi_{ij}(m, p) = \frac{p_i p_j}{m} \frac{\partial q_i}{\partial p_j} = \eta_{ij} w_i,$$

where η_{ij} is the Slutsky elasticity of the ith good with respect to the jth price. The partial derivative $\partial q_i / \partial p_j$ is taken with real income held constant. Similarly, the $\bar{\mu}_i$ values are defined to equal functions $\mu_i(m, p) = p_i(\partial q_i / \partial m) = \eta_{i0} w_i$. From these observations we could impute meanings to the $\bar{\mu}_i$ and $\bar{\pi}_{ij}$ values. The $\bar{\mu}_i$ values are called the marginal budget shares and the $\bar{\pi}_{ij}$ values, the Slutsky coefficients. In sections 3.4–3.7 we shall derive the model in a new and highly rigorous manner. The resulting interpretation of the parameters will be somewhat different from the common interpretation.

3.3.3. The relative price version

The relative price version of the Rotterdam model is of the form

$$w_{it}^* Dq_{it} = \bar{\mu}_i D\bar{m}_t + \sum_{j=1}^{n+1} \bar{\nu}_{ij}\left(Dp_{jt} - \sum_{k=1}^{n+1} \bar{\mu}_k Dp_{kt}\right) + \varepsilon_{it},$$

for $i = 1, \ldots, n+1$. We define the symbol $D\bar{m}_t$ to be our real income log change index, $\sum_{i=1}^{n+1} w_{it}^* Dq_{it}$. The parameters $\bar{\mu}_i$ are again the marginal budget shares appearing in the absolute price version. The parameters of the specification are subject to the following parameter restrictions:

$$\sum_{i=1}^{n+1} \bar{\mu}_i = 1, \tag{3.8}$$

$$\bar{\nu}_{ij} = \bar{\nu}_{ji}, \quad \text{for } i, j = 1, \ldots, n+1, \tag{3.9}$$

the matrix $[\bar{\nu}_{ij}]$ is negative definite, $\tag{3.10}$

$$\sum_{j=1}^{n+1} \bar{\nu}_{ij} = \bar{\phi}\bar{\mu}_i, \quad i = 1, \ldots, n+1. \tag{3.11}$$

We accept the same assumptions on the error structure as for the absolute price version, and again we find that Ω is singular. The deletion of an arbitrary equation solves the singularity problem. The $\bar{\nu}_{ij}$ parameters acquire their interpretation from the underlying differential form in which $\bar{\nu}_{ij} = \lambda p_i p_j u^{ij}/m$, where λ is a Lagrange multiplier and u^{ij} is the (i,j)th element of the inverse of the Hessian matrix of $u(q)$ for our utility function, u. Since specific substitutes and specific complements are defined in terms of these cross partials, we see immediately that goods i and j are specific substitutes if $\bar{\nu}_{ij}$ is positive and specific complements if $\bar{\nu}_{ij}$ is negative.

In practice the model is never estimated in this form. In fact it can be shown that without a further restriction on the parameter matrix $[\bar{\nu}_{ij}]$, an identification problem exists. The preferred approach is to divide the goods subscripts into a collection $\{S_1, \ldots, S_G\}$ of mutually exclusive and exhaustive blocks such that the utility function takes the block additive form

$$u(q) = \sum_{g=1}^{G} u_g(q_g),$$

where q_g is the vector of q_i values such that $i \in S_g$. The Hessian matrix $[\partial u/\partial q_i \partial q_j]$ is then block diagonal with $\partial u/\partial q_i \partial q_j = 0$ for all i, j in different blocks. This blocking can be imposed by setting $\bar{\nu}_{ij}=0$ for all i, j in separate blocks. The parameter $\bar{\phi}$ is called the income flexibility, acquiring its meaning from the differential form in which

$$\bar{\phi} = \sum_{i=1}^{n+1} \sum_{j=1}^{n+1} \bar{\nu}_{ij} = \left(\frac{\partial \lambda}{\partial m} \frac{m}{\lambda}\right)^{-1}.$$

The parameter $\bar{\phi}$ carries little information of interest to us in this study, although all other parameters of both versions of the Rotterdam model will be useful.

By deleting an equation we find that we no longer need impose restriction (3.8). Restriction (3.10) will not be imposed but verified. However, it is known that the model can be simplified further. We can solve constraints (3.11) for $\bar{\nu}_{ii}$ for each $i=1,\ldots,n+1$ and eliminate the resulting restrictions by substitution into the specification. The result is

$$w_{it}^* \mathrm{D}q_{it} = \bar{\mu}_i \mathrm{D}\bar{m}_t + \bar{\phi} A_{it}(\bar{\mu}) + \sum_{j \neq i} \bar{\nu}_{ij}(\mathrm{D}p_{jt} - \mathrm{D}p_{it}) + \varepsilon_{it},$$

where $\bar{\mu} = (\bar{\mu}_1, \ldots, \bar{\mu}_{n+1})'$ and $A_{it}(\bar{\mu}) = \bar{\mu}_i[\mathrm{D}p_{it} - \mathrm{D}p_{kt} - \sum_{j \neq k} \bar{\mu}_j(\mathrm{D}p_{jt} - \mathrm{D}p_{kt})]$.

Observe that the model is nonlinear in its parameters. In addition to this nonlinearity, another statistical problem exists. We can acquire estimates of all parameters by using the parameter restrictions to acquire estimates of parameters that were eliminated by substitution or which appear only in the deleted equation, but the standard errors of those estimators are not immediately available. Theil (1971, pp. 598–602) has derived a means of acquiring those asymptotic standard errors using a derivation that is equally applicable to our estimation procedures. Suppose β is the vector of all parameters omitted from the model but estimated by the use of the restrictions, and let $\hat{\beta}$ be the resulting estimator. Theil has derived a consistent estimator of the covariance matrix of the limiting distribution of $\sqrt{(T)}(\hat{\beta}-\beta)$. The estimate is computed as follows.

First we solve the constraints for the vector β in terms of the parameters γ contained within the estimated model. Let us denote this functional relationship by $\beta = \beta(\gamma)$. Recall that we have estimated β using $\hat{\beta} = \beta(\hat{\gamma})$, where $\hat{\gamma}$ is our estimate of γ. We then compute the derivative $\partial \beta(\gamma)/\partial \gamma'$ (which is a matrix valued function of γ) that we shall call $D(\gamma)$. Furthermore, let V be the covariance matrix of the limiting distribution of $\sqrt{(T)}(\hat{\gamma}-\gamma)$. It then can be shown that $\sqrt{(T)}(\hat{\beta}-\beta) \xrightarrow{\mathscr{L}} N(\mathbf{0}, D(\gamma)VD(\gamma)')$ as $T \to \infty$. A consistent estimator of the limiting covariance matrix can be acquired from $D(\hat{\gamma})\hat{V}D(\hat{\gamma})'$, where $\hat{V}$ is a consistent estimator of V. So our estimate of the asymptotic covariance matrix of $\hat{\beta}$ is

$$\frac{1}{T}D(\hat{\gamma})\hat{V}D(\hat{\gamma})' = D(\hat{\gamma})\left[\frac{1}{T}\hat{V}\right]D(\hat{\gamma}),$$

where $(1/T)\hat{V}$ is our estimate of the asymptotic covariance matrix of $\hat{\gamma}$.[1]

3.4. Theoretical foundations for the Rotterdam model

3.4.1. The model's critique

In the previous section we presented both versions of the Rotterdam model with their usual interpretations. As in the latter sections of Chapter 2, we assumed the existence of a representative household. This is not satisfactory, since aggregation over households is a difficult and important issue and since the theoretical foundations of the Rotterdam model are controversial. In the current section we acquire our interpretation of the absolute price version of the Rotterdam model through rigorous aggregation over households. Our results are based upon those of Barnett (1979c).

We begin by accepting the generalized Prais–Houthakker homogeneity postulate presented in Chapter 2. Hence, a representative individual exists for each household. Throughout the rest of Part I we view those representative individuals as our basic consumers. We aggregate over those consumers in the remaining sections of this chapter.

A now widespread critique of the Rotterdam model correctly observes that the model's properties and theoretical implications are exactly known only in a highly restrictive and uninteresting special case.[2] Hence, the model currently can be related exactly to *available* theory only if that unacceptably restrictive special case is maintained. In this section we fill that gap in our knowledge which has been observed to exist by the model's critics. We derive the model's theoretical properties at the aggregate level over a much larger region of the macroparameter space than the tiny region within which the currently understood special case is defined.

---

[1] Theil's derivation of those results depends upon the assumption that the function $\beta(\gamma)$ has continuous second-order derivatives in a region containing the true value of γ as an interior point.

[2] The critique applies to the parameterized version of the model. The "differential approach" in theory uses the model's derivation prior to parameterization with variable coefficients. See Theil (1979).

As is well known, the aggregated (over consumers) Rotterdam model is integrable to a community utility function only if all consumers' preferences are Cobb-Douglas. If the model is not integrable in the aggregate, then its theoretical properties are not known. But Cobb-Douglas restrictions never have been imposed in the model's applications. Hence the model – as used – has no rigorous exact link with currently available theory. Furthermore, the model never convincingly has been shown to approximate any well-defined theoretical construct that need exist at the aggregate level without Cobb-Douglas preferences. Hence, no relationship has been established successfully between the model's existing applications and the currently available theory.

An unnecessarily pessimistic implication sometimes has been read into this valid critique. It has been asserted (without support) that in fact no theoretical foundations for the Rotterdam model could possibly exist without aggregate integrability and hence without Cobb-Douglas preferences. See, for example, Christensen, Jorgenson and Lau (1975), Phlips (1974), Jorgenson and Lau (1975), Christensen and Manser (1977), or Yoshihara (1969), who thereby directly impute to the Rotterdam model itself (as opposed to the investigated subset of its macroparameter space) the properties of a Cobb-Douglas system. We shall *provide* the missing theoretical foundations for the Rotterdam model's nonintegrable case.

Yet it is now widely recognized by theoreticians that integrability of *any* aggregate demand system is an unacceptably strong assumption. Hence, the region of the parameter space (the nonintegrable subset) over which the Rotterdam model's properties are not known is precisely that subset which is of theoretical interest. In section 3.5 we begin by deriving a general and highly informative theoretical construct which exists under assumptions substantially weaker than those necessary for aggregate integrability. We then derive strong theoretical restrictions implied by theory throughout the region on which our theoretical construct is defined. This provides a very general theoretical solution to the problem of demand aggregation, which increasingly has hindered demand studies and has been the subject of intensive research in the recent general equilibrium literature. In section 3.6 we show that the Rotterdam model provides a Taylor series local approximation to our new theoretical construct throughout the Rotterdam model's feasible parameter set.

3.4.2. Our approach

Our current knowledge of the Rotterdam model depends upon constancy of the model's coefficients. But we shall prove that the assumed constancy of the model's coefficients at the aggregate (macro) level does not imply constancy of the model's coefficients at the consumer (micro) level. Hence, the available results are applicable only at the aggregate level. At the macro level the model is integrable only on a negligible Lebesgue measure zero subspace of the parameter space, and it is *that* negligible subspace on which the model's critics have explored the model's properties. But integrability of *any* model at the aggregate level obtains only if a community utility function exists, and such aggregate utility functions exist only under extremely restrictive and implausible conditions. Hence, we currently only know that the model has highly restrictive properties on a negligible parameter subspace on which theory dictates that such properties *should* be restrictive. All applications of the model have been based upon its properties on the *rest* of the parameter space, and we shall prove, under weak assumptions, that useful and highly informative theoretical restrictions can be tested for or imposed *everywhere* on the model's parameter space, without necessarily depending upon or implying aggregate integrability. Paradoxically, the systems advocated by the Rotterdam model's critics *are* dependent upon aggregate integrability and thereby *are* subject to valid criticism for inherent theoretical restrictiveness. We shall expand upon this point in section 3.7.

As is now well known, few of the microeconomic properties of consumer demand systems carry over to aggregate commodity demand systems. By deriving a general *limiting stochastic transformation* of aggregate economic theory, we shall demonstrate, under clearly weak assumptions, that conditions necessary for integrability of *micro* demand systems imply specific theoretical restrictions on that limiting transformation. Far more will be proved about our aggregate stochastic transformation than is known about aggregate demand systems themselves under any comparably weak assumptions. Hence, a solution to the aggregation problem in demand theory lies in passing to a new space of limiting functions. Since these results are most easily acquired in terms of continuous time stochastic processes, we shall derive our model in terms of a continuous time consumption decision, rather than the usual discrete time finite period expenditure allocation decision.

As discussed in the previous section, two closely related versions of the Rotterdam model exist, the "relative price" version and the "absolute price" version. We shall derive the properties of the absolute price version, since its linearity in the parameters simplifies our proofs considerably. Our derivations and our results will differ from those currently available. We avoid approximations having unknown properties, and we minimize assumptions that are not necessary to the derivations.

3.5. Aggregation over consumers

3.5.1. The individual consumer's decision

Let N be the number of consumers, and n the number of goods, and define $\boldsymbol{m} = (m_1, \ldots, m_N)'$, where $m_c = m_c(t) > 0$ is consumer c's rate of total consumption expenditure at time t. Although we do not explicitly discuss leisure in this section, we could include leisure as a "good" by simply increasing n to $n+1$. Consumption is viewed as proceeding continuously over time. Let $\boldsymbol{q}_c(t) = (q_{1c}(t), \ldots, q_{nc}(t))' \in S_c$ be consumer c's consumption flow at time t, where $q_{ic}(t)$ is consumer c's instantaneous rate of consumption of good i and $S_c \subset R^n$ is consumer c's consumption set, which we assume to be a subset of the non-negative orthant. We do not restrict S_c to be just an affine transformation of the non-negative orthant, as is frequently done when the set of subsistence bundles is collapsed to a singleton. Let $\boldsymbol{p}(t) = (p_1(t), \ldots, p_n(t))' > \boldsymbol{0}$ be the vector of corresponding prices.

Let T be the time interval of interest (perhaps unbounded above). We assume that at each instant of time, $t \in T$, consumer c selects $\boldsymbol{q}_c \in S_c$ to maximize $u_c(\boldsymbol{q}_c)$ subject to $\boldsymbol{q}_c' \boldsymbol{p}(t) = m_c(t)$, where u_c is an instantaneous utility function reflecting unchanging consumer preferences over instantaneous consumption flows, $\boldsymbol{q}_c(t)$, at any $t \in T$. This is the continuous time instantaneous expenditure flow analog of the usual discrete time single period expenditure allocation decision. The continuous time version follows from intertemporal preference separability in a manner similar to that of the discrete time version. By intertemporal preference separability we mean that at time t the consumer's intertemporal utility function is of the form

$$\int_t^\infty \exp[-\delta_c(t,\tau)\tau] u_c[x_c(t,\tau)] \, \mathrm{d}\tau,$$

where $\langle x_c(t,\tau) : t < \tau \leq \infty \rangle$ is consumer c's future intertemporal consumption plan at time t. Note that $\boldsymbol{q}_c(t) = x_c(t,t)$. We assume that the consumer replans continuously in accordance with his latest price expectations and wealth. We could hold the rate of time preference, $\delta_c(t, \tau)$, constant if we sought intertemporally consistent planning in the Strotz sense. Our result on instantaneous current expenditure flow allocation is shown easily through a proof by contradiction. Also see Phlips (1974, ch. 10), and Lluch (1973).

In its finite change form, the Rotterdam model's conditional single period allocation specification is a block in a recursive intertemporal system, and thereby is empirically as well as theoretically separable. For this remarkably strong result, see Theil (1976, ch. 8). We assume that u_c has all of the usual neoclassical properties.[3] The solution to the consumer's current expenditure flow allocation decision can be written as $\boldsymbol{q}_c = \boldsymbol{q}_c(m_c(t), \boldsymbol{p}(t))$. Observe that we rather inelegantly have used $\boldsymbol{q}_c$ also to designate the composite function of time $\boldsymbol{q}_c(t)$, so that $\boldsymbol{q}_c(t) = \boldsymbol{q}_c(m_c(t), \boldsymbol{p}(t))$. We follow convention in referring to $m_c(t)$ as consumer c's instantaneous "income" at time t. Although this rather dubious convention is solely a matter of style, it does assist in distinguishing semantically between expenditure and income shares. We assume that for each consumer and for all $t \in T$,

$$\boldsymbol{q}_c(m_c(t), \boldsymbol{p}(t)) \text{ lies strictly within the interior of } S_c. \tag{3.12}$$

We now assume that each consumer's instantaneous utility function can be written as $u_c(\boldsymbol{q}_c) = u(\boldsymbol{q}_c, \boldsymbol{s}_c)$, where $\boldsymbol{s}_c$ is a finite dimensional vector of taste-determining factors (environmental, physiological, genetic, etc.) experienced by consumer c. The function u is fixed, and the vector $\boldsymbol{s}_c$ depends upon c but not upon t. We could view $\boldsymbol{s}_c$ (and thereby tastes) as fixed at birth. Observe that we now can introduce a function $\boldsymbol{q}$ such that

$$\boldsymbol{q}_c = \boldsymbol{q}(m_c(t), \boldsymbol{p}(t), \boldsymbol{s}_c). \tag{3.13}$$

Define consumer c's value (expenditure) share of the ith good by $w_{ic} = p_i q_{ic}/m_c$. Now differentiate the logarithm of (3.13) with respect to t and multiply through by w_{ic}. We then can determine that

$$w_{ic} \, \mathrm{d} \log q_{ic} / \mathrm{d} t = \mu_i(m_c, \boldsymbol{p}, \boldsymbol{s}_c) \, \mathrm{d} \log \overline{m}_c / \mathrm{d} t \\ + \sum_{j=1}^{n} \pi_{ij}(m_c, \boldsymbol{p}, \boldsymbol{s}_c) \, \mathrm{d} \log p_j / \mathrm{d} t, \tag{3.14}$$

where the consumer's marginal propensity to consume good i is $\mu_{ic} = \mu_i(m_c, \boldsymbol{p}, \boldsymbol{s}_c) = p_i \partial q_{ic} / \partial m_c$, and his Slutsky coefficients are defined for $i, j = 1, \dots, n$ by

$$\pi_{ijc} = \pi_{ij}(m_c, \boldsymbol{p}, \boldsymbol{s}_c) = \frac{p_i p_j}{m_c} \left. \frac{\partial q_{ic}}{\partial p_j} \right|_{\mu_c = \mathrm{constant}}.$$

---

[3]The implications of dropping the insatiability assumptions are considered in Barnett (1973).

The log rate of change in real income flow $d\log \bar{m}_c/dt$ is defined to equal

$$d\log m_c/dt - \sum_{k=1}^{n} w_{kc} d\log p_k/dt.$$

The motivation for this definition can be found in Theil (1975, pp. 27, 129). From Theil (1975, p. 49) we also can determine that for any $t \in T$

$$\sum_{i=1}^{n} \mu_i(m_c, p, s_c) = 1,$$

$$\sum_{j=1}^{n} \pi_{ij}(m_c, p, s_c) = 0,$$

and $[\pi_{ij}]$ is a symmetric negative semidefinite $n \times n$ matrix of rank $n-1$. (3.15)

Define the collections of variables $\boldsymbol{\mu}_c = (\mu_{1c}, \ldots, \mu_{nc})'$ and $\boldsymbol{\Pi}_c = [\pi_{ijc}]$ and the functions $\boldsymbol{\mu} = (\mu_1, \ldots, \mu_n)'$ and $\boldsymbol{\Pi} = [\pi_{ij}]$. Subject to assumption (3.12), results (3.14) and (3.15) are completely general implications of neoclassical demand theory.

3.5.2. The random microcoefficients

Taste-determining factors, s_c, are likely to vary over consumers, and we cannot reasonably expect to capture even the major components of s_c as explanatory variables in an estimable model. Hence, we shall view (3.14) as having random coefficients. We treat the existing finite population of consumers as a random sample of size N from an infinite population of "potential consumers" consistent with the current state (environmental, economic, etc.) of the world. Thus, s_c, $c = 1, \ldots, N$, are N independent and identically distributed random vectors. Observe that the randomness is across consumers. Once the N consumers have been drawn, they remain the same for all $t \in T$; the sample of consumers is not redrawn at each t. Hence, the random vectors s_c do not vary over time. We implicitly treat the N drawn consumers as having infinite lifetimes, although one could derive a finite lifetime analog depending upon demographic variables.

We assume that the income time path $\langle m_c(t): t \in T \rangle$ assigned to the cth drawn consumer is sampled randomly from an infinite population of potential income paths. The simplest case occurs when each consumer in the infinite population of potential consumers has a predetermined income time path. Then, when we select consumers at random from that population, both $m_c(t)$, $t \in T$, and s_c become random simultaneously through their joint dependency upon c. Alternatively, we could sample s_c in one stage and then randomly select $m_c(t)$, $t \in T$, in a second stage so that s_c and $m_c(t)$ become independently distributed for all $t \in T$. We do not restrict the properties of the joint distribution of $(s_c, m_c(t))$ for fixed $t \in T$ in any manner. They may be correlated.

We accept the following very weak assumption on the existence of our theoretical populations.

Assumption 3.1. For each $c = 1, \ldots, N$, $\langle m_c(t): t \in T \rangle$ is a continuous time, differentiable, positive stochastic process.[4] At any fixed $t \in T$, the N random vectors $(m_c(t), s_c')'$, $c = 1, \ldots, N$, are independently and identically distributed (i.i.d.) with distribution function H_t. The marginal distribution of s_c has distribution function G.

It follows from assumption 3.1 that at any $t \in T$, $m_c(t)$, $c = 1, \ldots, N$, are i.i.d. We denote the distribution function of the marginal distribution of $m_c(t)$ by F_t. The function F_t is the theoretical income distribution function at t, which can be approximated by the observable empirical income distribution function. Observe that income distribution, by either measure, is free to vary over time. We refer to the induced stochastic processes $\mu_c = \mu(m_c(t), p(t), s_c)$ and $\Pi_c = \Pi(m_c(t), p(t), s_c)$ as the model's microcoefficients. Since prices are assumed to be the same for all consumers, we treat them as nonstochastic. Our assumption can be weakened to proportionality of prices over consumers, as can be useful with the price of leisure. See Theil (1975, p. 150).

3.5.3. A general result on aggregation over consumers

We now aggregate over the random coefficient microequations (3.14) using Theil's (1971, pp. 570–573) convergence approach to aggregation. Theil's (1975) aggregation of the relative price version of the Rotterdam model implicitly accepts the model's parameterization of (3.14). We here seek a general theoretical result requiring no such assumption.

---

[4]Strictly speaking we should say that $m_c(t)$ is [a.s.] positive for all $t \in T \cap A^c$, where A has Lebesgue measure zero. We use the notation [a.s.] to designate "almost surely" in the conventional measure theoretic sense. We shall be rather casual in our treatment of such subtleties.

Define $\bar{\mu} = (\bar{\mu}_1, \ldots, \bar{\mu}_n)'$ and $\bar{\Pi} = [\bar{\pi}_{ij}]$ such that for $i, j = 1, \ldots, n$

$$\bar{\mu}_i = E(m_c \mu_{ic})/Em_c \tag{3.16}$$

and

$$\bar{\pi}_{ij} = E(m_c \pi_{ijc})/Em_c. \tag{3.17}$$

We call $(\bar{\mu}, \bar{\Pi})$ the macrocoefficients. They vary over time and are population versions of weighted average microcoefficients, with weights proportional to the corresponding incomes.

Theil (1975) has treated the macrocoefficients as the simple expectations of the microcoefficients. We would acquire that result as a special case if m_c were uncorrelated with the random microcoefficients. But such an assumption could be accepted only as an approximation, since the microcoefficients are themselves functions of m_c. We will not assume the lack of such a functional relationship, even when we introduce the Rotterdam model's parameterization of our general theoretical results. However, it should be observed that Theil's derivation relates to the model's relative price version, for which assumptions must be stronger to permit necessary simplifications and to ensure invariance of block independence to aggregation.

Let $v_c = d\log \overline{m}_c/dt$, and let $k_{ic} = m_c(\mu_{ic} - \bar{\mu}_i)$. Define the aggregated per capita variables:

$$Q_i = (1/N) \sum_{c=1}^{N} q_{ic}, \quad M = (1/N) \sum_{c=1}^{N} m_c \quad \text{and} \quad W_i = p_i Q_i / M.$$

We shall need the following weak assumptions on the finiteness of certain moments. In considering the plausibility of assumption 3.2, observe that the finiteness of the first two moments of v_c and k_{ic} is sufficient for the finiteness of $E(v_c k_{ic})$. Also observe that π_{ijc} and μ_{ic} typically will have an absolute value of less than one.

Assumption 3.2. For all $t \in T$ and $c = 1, \ldots, N$, the values of $\bar{\mu}, \bar{\Pi}, Em_c(t)$, Ev_c, and $E(v_c k_{ic})$, $i = 1, \ldots, n$ are finite.

Defining $d\log \overline{M}/dt$ to equal $d\log M/dt - \sum_{k=1}^{n} W_k d\log p_k/dt$, we now can prove the following theorem. We use the notation $o_p(1)$ to designate a random variable that converges in probability to 0 as $N \to \infty$. We use $\text{cov}(\cdot, \cdot)$ to designate a covariance.

Theorem 3.1. Except for a term of stochastic order $o_p(1)$, assumptions 3.1 and 3.2 imply that for $i=1,\ldots,n$

$$W_i \mathrm{d}\log Q_i/\mathrm{d}t = \bar{\mu}_i \mathrm{d}\log \overline{M}/\mathrm{d}t$$
$$+ \sum_{j=1}^{n} \bar{\pi}_{ij} \mathrm{d}\log p_j/\mathrm{d}t + \mathrm{cov}(k_{ic}, v_c)/Em_c. \quad (3.18)$$

Proof. Multiply (3.14) through by the cth drawn consumer's income share, m_c/NM, and sum over $c=1,\ldots,N$. Following Theil (1975), p. 150), we find that the left-hand side becomes $W_i \mathrm{d}\log Q_i/\mathrm{d}t$.

The right-hand side of the aggregated equation can be grouped into two terms. As shown by Theil (1975, p. 154), the first term on the right-hand side can be rearranged to equal

$$\bar{\mu}_i \mathrm{d}\log \overline{M}/\mathrm{d}t + z(t), \quad (3.19)$$

where

$$z(t) = \sum_{c=1}^{N} (m_c/NM)(\mu_{ic} - \bar{\mu}_i)\mathrm{d}\log \overline{m}_c/\mathrm{d}t.$$

We now seek the stochastic limit of $z(t)$ as N goes to infinity.

First observe that

$$z(t) = \left[\sum_{c=1}^{N} m_c/N\right]^{-1} (1/N) \sum_{c=1}^{N} m_c(\mu_{ic} - \bar{\mu}_i)\mathrm{d}\log \overline{m}_c/\mathrm{d}t. \quad (3.20)$$

Under assumption 3.1, $m_c(t)$, $c=1,\ldots,N$, are i.i.d. at time t. Then by assumption 3.2, we find from Khinchine's theorem that

$$(1/N) \sum_{c=1}^{N} m_c = Em_c + o_p(1).$$

From assumption 3.1 we know that $Em_c > 0$. Hence, by Slutsky's theorem it follows that

$$\left[\sum_{c=1}^{N} m_c/N\right]^{-1} = (1/Em_c) + o_p(1). \quad (3.21)$$

Now $k_{ic}v_c$, $c=1,\ldots,N$, are i.i.d. Hence, by assumption 3.2 and Khinchine's theorem, we see that

$$(1/N) \sum_{c=1}^{N} k_{ic}v_c = E(k_{ic}v_c) + o_p(1). \quad (3.22)$$

So by (3.20), (3.21), and (3.22), it follows that

$$z(t) = E(k_{ic}v_c)/Em_c + o_p(1). \tag{3.23}$$

Now $Ek_{ic} = E(m_c\mu_{ic}) - \bar{\mu}_i Em_c = 0$, by definition of $\bar{\mu}_i$. Hence, we find that $E(k_{ic}v_c) = \text{cov}(k_{ic}, v_c)$. Thus, by (3.23), it follows that $z(t) = \text{cov}(k_{ic}, v_c)/Em_c + o_p(1)$. So by (3.19), the first term on the right-hand side of the aggregate equation is $\bar{\mu}_i d\log \overline{M}/dt + \text{cov}(k_{ic}, v_c)/Em_c + o_p(1)$.

Similarly, the second term on the right-hand side of the aggregate equation can be written as $\sum_{j=1}^{n} a_{ijc}$, where

$$a_{ijc} = (d/dt)\log p_j \sum_{c=1}^{N}(m_c/NM)\pi_{ijc}$$

$$= (d/dt)\log p_j \left[\left(\sum_{c=1}^{N} m_c/N\right)^{-1}\left(\sum_{c=1}^{N} m_c\pi_{ijc}/N\right)\right].$$

Now by assumption 3.1 and Khinchine's theorem we know that

$$(1/N)\sum_{c=1}^{N} m_c\pi_{ijc} = E(m_c\pi_{ijc}) + o_p(1).$$

So by (3.21) and Slutsky's theorem, we have that $a_{ijc} = \bar{\pi}_{ij}d\log p_j/dt + o_p(1)$. Hence, the second term on the right-hand side of the aggregate equation is $\sum_{j=1}^{n}\bar{\pi}_{ij}d\log p_j/dt + o_p(1)$. Q.E.D.

We have deleted the $o_p(1)$ term in (3.18), since in applications N typically will be very large. With the exception of the last term, which we call the global (or globally small) remainder term, our aggregate system of eqs. (3.18) is the direct aggregate analog of our micro system (3.14). Observe that we still are considering a very general transformation of economic theory, since assumptions 3.1 and 3.2 are very weak. There is nothing local about the "approximation" we acquire by dropping the $o_p(1)$ term for large N. We have not expanded any function about some single point. The $o_p(1)$ term is arbitrarily small *everywhere* with arbitrarily high probability for sufficiently large N.

We now explore implications of economic theory as reflected in our limiting stochastic transformation of economic theory (3.18). Observe that the proofs of both theorems 3.1 and 3.2 lean heavily upon the particular functional structure of (3.14), especially upon its linearity in the microcoefficients.

Theorem 3.2. If assumptions 3.1 and 3.2 obtain, then for all $t \in T$: $\sum_{i=1}^{n} \bar{\mu}_i = 1$, $\overline{\Pi}$ is symmetric negative semidefinite of rank $n-1$, and $\sum_{j=1}^{n} \bar{\pi}_{ij} = 0$ for $i = 1, \ldots, n$.

Proof. By (3.15) we can find that $\sum_{i=1}^{n} m_c \mu_{ic}/Em_c = m_c/Em_c$. Taking the expectation of each side, we get that $\sum_{i=1}^{n} \bar{\mu}_i = 1$. The other results of theorem 3.2 are proved simply in an analogous manner. Q.E.D.

Observe that by theorem 3.2 and (3.15), we have that $\sum_i k_{ic} = 0$. We see that macrocoefficients $(\bar{\mu}, \overline{\Pi})$ have properties analogous to those of the microcoefficients (μ_c, Π_c). Theorem 3.2 is a general result in aggregation theory, since it has been derived under clearly weak assumptions.

By contrast, let us see what has happened in the space of aggregate demand functions as we have let N go to infinity. For finite N we have that

$$\bar{q} = (1/N) \sum_{c=1}^{N} q(m_c(t), p(t), s_c),$$

where $\bar{q} = (Q_1, \ldots, Q_n)'$. Now under our assumption 3.1, we find from Khinchine's theorem that $\bar{q} = Eq_c + o_p(1)$. Hence, for large N we can treat Eq_c as our per capita aggregate demand functions. But observe that we know very little about those functions other than a version of the budget constraint, which obtains for even finite N. In fact, micro theory is only distantly related to the properties of Eq_c, which does not even lie in the same function space as $q_c(m_c, p)$. Observe, for example, that Eq_c is not a function of income m_c, but rather is a *functional* depending upon the distribution function H_t. In a somewhat different context, Mossin (1968) has found conditions under which his "mean demand function" depends upon p and Em_c. But in general, passing to the limit as N goes to infinity provides no new information in the space of demand functions.

Observe that assumption 3.2 has not been used, and assumption 3.1 was accepted largely as a convenience. Our proofs have used Khinchine's Weak Law of Large Numbers. If we had used Chebychev's Weak Law of Large Numbers (see Rao, 1973, p. 112), the random variables assumed to be stochastically independent in assumption 3.1 could have been assumed to be only uncorrelated. The macroparameters then would have been limiting averages of expectations rather than just expectations.

We maintain that (3.18) is itself a more powerful *fundamental* theoretical construct than an aggregate demand system, since far more is known about (3.18) than about aggregate demand systems. The acquisition of comparably strong results on aggregate demand functions requires substantially stronger assumptions than our assumptions 3.1 and 3.2. Observe that theorem 3.2 was *not* acquired from any implicit or explicit assumption of integrability of (3.18). We have not aggregated over utility functions, and our results are not dependent upon or implicitly induced by any community utility function. The properties of the macrocoefficients provided by theorem 3.2 are necessary conditions for integrability of each *individual's* demand functions. Although those properties are defined in terms of the macrocoefficients, the properties are neither necessary nor sufficient for integrability of the aggregated system (3.18) itself. The relative price version of the Rotterdam model, not considered in this section, does aggregate over certain stochastic properties of preferences, but not over complete utility functions. In Appendix B, section B1, we consider the integrability properties of (3.18) in detail.

3.6. The components of the remainder term

By definition of v_c, we know that the global remainder term of (3.18) is

$$\frac{1}{Em_c}\text{cov}(v_c, k_{ic}) = \alpha_i(t) - \beta_i(t), \tag{3.24}$$

where

$$\alpha_i(t) = \frac{1}{Em_c}\text{cov}(k_{ic}, \text{d}\log m_c/\text{d}t) \tag{3.25}$$

and

$$\beta_i(t) = \frac{1}{Em_c}\text{cov}\left(k_{ic}, \sum_{k=1}^{n} w_{kc}\text{d}\log p_k/\text{d}t\right). \tag{3.26}$$

As we shall see in this section, the potential exists for confounding the term $\beta_i(t)$ with other terms in (3.18). However, this problem does not exist with the term $\alpha_i(t)$, which is an independent function of time.

The theoretical issues that we are considering in this section relate to the properties of the macrocoefficients, which appear only in the other terms of (3.18); hence, the properties of $\alpha_i(t)$ are not related to our objectives. However, the empirical implementation of our results would require some consideration of $\alpha_i(t)$. Hence, in Appendix B, section B2, we consider the properties of $\alpha_i(t)$, which we argue typically are negligibly small (except perhaps during periods of revolutionary shifts in income distribution).

This result actually is stronger than necessary. Since an intercept commonly is used with the Rotterdam model, we need only argue that $\alpha_i(t)$ can be approximated by a constant over all $t \in T$. That constant need not be zero. In fact we even could acquire our results if $\alpha_i(t)$ could be approximated by

$$a_{0i} + a_{1i} \mathrm{d}\log \overline{M}/\mathrm{d}t + \sum_{j=1}^{n} a_{2ij} \mathrm{d}\log p_j /\mathrm{d}t + u_{it},$$

where u_{it} is random and where the a values are constants adding up over i to zero and satisfying $a_{2ij} = a_{2ji}$ for all $i, j = 1, \ldots, n$.

One should recognize that the theoretical arguments in this section are not dependent upon acceptance of the assumptions to be considered in the next section. Our practice of dropping the $\alpha_i(t)$ terms in the analysis below is a simplification of little theoretical consequence. Even the *empirical* implementation of our results is not, in principle, dependent upon our ability to drop the $\alpha_i(t)$ terms. Since our interest is in inferences solely about the model's other terms, the $\alpha_i(t)$ nuisance terms could be approximated (somewhat inelegantly) uniformly and arbitrarily well by the polynomial time trend dictated by the Weierstrass Approximation Theorem. But the empirical evidence presented in Chapter 5 suggests that when leisure is admitted as one of the n goods, not even the zeroth order (intercept) term of that trend is statistically significant; intercepts appear in the model solely as proxies for apparent taste change over goods, and only when non-weakly-separable leisure consumption is ignored. In addition, we shall see that absorption of the statistically insignificant term $\alpha_i(t)$ into the error structure does not contaminate the error structure. Using a Kolmogorov–Smirnov test applied to orthogonally transformed residuals, we shall accept normality. All other hypotheses on the error structure have been accepted by Theil (1976) and Paulus (1972) using differing data, and will be accepted in our empirical tests in Chapter 5.

We now investigate the more important and potentially troublesome term $\beta_i(t)$. Let ρ_{ij} be the correlation coefficient between $m_c(\mu_{ic} - \bar{\mu}_i)/Em_c$ and w_{jc} in the consumer population. Then it follows that

$$\beta_i(t) = \sum_{j=1}^{n} \gamma_{ij}(t) \frac{\mathrm{d}\log p_j}{\mathrm{d}t},$$

where

$$\gamma_{ij}(t) = \rho_{ij} \theta_i (\mathrm{var}\, w_{jc})^{1/2}, \tag{3.27}$$

and where θ is as defined (and interpreted) in Appendix B, section B2.

Substituting this expression for $\beta_i(t)$ into (3.18) with the $\alpha_i(t)$ component of the global remainder dropped, we get that

$$W_i\frac{\mathrm{d}\log Q_i}{\mathrm{d}t} = \bar{\mu}_i\frac{\mathrm{d}\log \overline{M}}{\mathrm{d}t} + \sum_{j=1}^{n}\left[\bar{\pi}_{ij} - \gamma_{ij}(t)\right]\frac{\mathrm{d}\log p_j}{\mathrm{d}t}. \qquad (3.28)$$

Hence, we see that $\gamma_{ij}(t)$ can be viewed as the *asymptotic aggregation bias* of the (i,j)th Slutsky macrocoefficient $\bar{\pi}_{ij}$.[5] In Appendix B, section B2, we argue that the asymptotic aggregation biases are small.

Equation (3.28) and theorem 3.2 contain our results on aggregation in the differential approach (see footnote 1 above) to demand analysis. The next section parameterizes our theoretical results.

3.7. The Rotterdam model approximation

3.7.1. The finite change version

We now proceed to operationalize our results. We begin by dropping the Slutsky aggregation biases $[\gamma_{ij}]$ in (3.28). Observe that we argue in Appendix B, section B2, that both $\gamma_{ij}(t)$ and $\alpha_i(t)$ are small *uniformly* on $t\in T$. Hence, we are basing our model on a *global* approximation rather than on a local property applicable only at a single point. We therefore have referred to the remainder (last) term of (3.18) as the global (or globally small) remainder term. The empirical problems (correlation with other terms, specification error, etc.) resemble those associated with dropping the remainder terms of the translog or generalized Leontief–Taylor series approximations. Also observe that $\gamma_{ij}(t)$ and $\alpha_i(t)$ could average zero over $t\in T$ without being precisely zero everywhere on T, although we shall not explicitly pursue that possibility.

We now convert (3.28) into a finite change form having a stochastic error term. We assume that our observations are evenly spaced over time at time intervals of size Δt. Define $\bar{t}=t+\Delta t$, and define the finite log change operator D such that $\mathrm{D}x_t = \log x(\bar{t})-\log x(t)$. Then define $W_{it}^* = 1/2(W_i(\bar{t})+W_i(t))$ and $\mathrm{D}\overline{M}_t = \mathrm{D}M_t - \sum_{k=1}^{n}W_{kt}^*\mathrm{D}p_{kt}$, and let ε_{it} be a stochastic error term assumed to be uncorrelated with $\mathrm{D}\overline{M}_t$ and $\mathrm{D}p_{jt}$ for all $t\in T, j=1,\ldots,n$. Theoretical support for this assumption of uncorrelated errors and explanatory variables can be found in Theil's (1976, chs. 7 and 8) block recursiveness result. Then by adding the stochastic error term

---

[5] I am indebted to Henri Theil for pointing out this interpretation to me.

onto an approximate finite change analog to (3.28), we find in Appendix B, section B3, that

$$W_{it}^* \mathrm{D}Q_{it} = \bar{\mu}_i \mathrm{D}\overline{M}_t + \sum_{j=1}^{n} \bar{\pi}_{ij} \mathrm{D}p_{jt} + \varepsilon_{it}, \qquad i = 1, \ldots, n. \tag{3.29}$$

Passing to the finite change approximation introduces an approximation error, but the error will be *uniformly* small over all $t \in T$, if the finite changes are small. When we convert to finite changes, we usually approximate instantaneous flows by annual totals or annual averages. This tends to lead to the interpretation of t as a time in the interior of its year. Observe that this approximation is not local, since we do not restrict the variation in the levels of $(m(t), p(t))$ over $t \in T$. Using Swamy's (1971, pp. 15–16) approach or Theil's (1975, pp. 158–164) second moment model, we could have introduced the stochastic error at the micro level and aggregated over the stochastic errors as well as over the other terms in acquiring (3.29).

When the macroparameters are held constant (as discussed in the next subsection), the equation system (3.29) subject to the coefficient constraints of theorem 3.2 is the absolute price version of the Rotterdam model.

3.7.2. Constancy of the parameters

Theil (1967, pp. 203–204), Theil (1975, p. 105), and Barten (1974, pp. 13–14) have argued (under assumptions differing from ours) that variations in the macrocoefficients capture higher-order effects than those otherwise inherent in the corresponding terms. Empirical tests of the constancy of the macrocoefficients are available in Barten (1974), Theil and Brooks (1970), Paulus (1972), and Theil (1976, ch. 15). None of these studies detected explainable parameter variability, and none could reject the hypothesis of constant macroparameters. Further evidence on this subject is available in Deaton (1974a). In fact the usual empirical problem is to restrict further the already large number of free parameters, rather than to increase them. See Paulus (1975).

In this subsection we parameterize our theoretical system of equations (3.18). A fundamental objective of the parameterization considered below is simplicity of estimation. Alternative parameterizations are easily constructed, although they necessarily become nonlinear in the parameters.

We could, for example, derive the macrocoefficients for a world of identical translog consumers (although identical preferences over consumers need not and will not be assumed with the parameterization presented below).

We begin by considering plausible restrictions on the following stochastic processes:

$$m_c \mu_c / E(m_c) \tag{3.30}$$

and

$$m_c \pi_c / E(m_c). \tag{3.31}$$

The mean function of a stochastic process $x(t)$, $t \in T$, is the function of time $f(t) = Ex(t)$, $t \in T$. Consider the mean functions of the processes (3.30) and (3.31). We would expect that the (stochastic) numerator of those expressions would be subject to trends biased upwards as the result of long-run trends in nominal income, m_c. However, division by $E(m_c)$ tends, on the average, to deflate that trend; no reason remains to expect a bias necessarily towards positive (or negative) trends in the sample paths of (3.30) and (3.31) for a randomly selected abstract good. In other words, we have no general theory to guide us in the specification of the macroparameter paths.

We do not say that the macroparameters will not trend in one direction or another. We merely state that we are unable to anticipate the direction of such possible trends in advance. If we were considering a particular good, rather than a randomly selected abstract good, we might have prior subjective information, but we consider only theory at present. Hence, the following simplifying assumption merits some consideration, although we will not maintain that assumption.

Assumption 3.3. The stochastic processes (3.30) and (3.31) have constant mean functions.

We consider assumption 3.3 in detail in Appendix B, section B3, and we determine that the class of stochastic processes consistent with the assumption is large. The following result is immediate.

Tautology 3.1. The macrocoefficients (3.16) and (3.17) are constant if and only if assumption 3.3 obtains.

As observed in Appendix B, section B3, we have no prior reason to believe (for an arbitrarily selected unknown abstract good) that the mean function of any arbitrary *one* of the stochastic processes (3.30) and (3.31) will trend in some predictable predetermined direction. But to assume that *all* of these or any other macroparameters will be *jointly* constant over time is intuitively very difficult to accept. Such an assumption (like assumption 3.3) would be necessarily strong, since it would purport to define a large number of true constants in nature. Even more importantly, lack of knowledge of the form of a trend does not imply nonexistence of a trend. Although we have no theory suggesting the form or direction of those possible trends, we may well speculate on the merits of further (theoretically unguided and unrestricted) flexibility in the specification of the macroparameter paths. Hence, we shall not accept assumption 3.3. In fact in general, rich parameterizations reasonably can be accepted only through local approximations by which functions become constants tautologically through evaluation at a fixed single point of approximation. Precisely the same procedure was used to acquire tautologically constant parameters for such models (the class of "flexible functional forms") as the translog, generalized Leontief, and generalized Cobb–Douglas. We now use a Taylor series approximation to expand the macroparameters about such a point.

To simplify our discussion let us assume that H_t (the joint distribution of $m_c(t)$ and s_c at t) has finite moments, and let us stack those moments into the vector ξ_t. Now let $\phi_t = (\xi_t', p(t)')'$, and let ϕ_0 (perhaps corresponding to a midpoint year or to a centroid of $\{\phi_t: t \in T\}$) be the value of ϕ_t about which we shall expand the macroparameters. Expand each of the macroparameters in a complete infinite order Taylor series approximation about ϕ_0, and substitute these expansions for the macroparameters in (3.29). Finally let $\psi_t = (D\overline{M}_t, Dp_{1t}, \ldots, Dp_{nt}, \phi_t' - \phi_0')'$, which is a vector of changes. Dropping terms of the second or higher order in ψ_t, we get back (3.29) with parameters held constant through evaluation at ϕ_0. The class of "flexible functional forms" similarly drops a second-order remainder term from its demand system. We shall call our second-order remainder term the local remainder term to distinguish it from the global remainder term introduced earlier.

We now treat our model as a local approximation of the first order in ψ_t. Macroparameter constancy would obtain with a uniformly zero remainder term only if assumption 3.3 applied. Since we shall not maintain assumption 3.3, constancy of the macroparameters should be understood to imply the existence of a second-order remainder term. As with any such Taylor series approximation, the size of the remainder term will be small when we remain within a local neighborhood of the point of the approximation. In our case the merits of the approximation would be greatest when ψ_t remains small for all $t \in T$.

Our unwillingness to maintain assumption 3.3 should be no surprise. It is not our intention to argue that the model provides a perfect approximation (uniformly zero remainder term) under weak assumptions. The model does not. It *is* our intention to argue that the model approximates a theoretical construct (3.18), which *exists* under weak assumptions. The issue that we raise is not the merits of the approximator, but rather the existence of that which is being approximated. Engel curves do not become parallel by looking at them locally. Hence, by Gorman's necessary and sufficient conditions for the existence of a community utility function, the available competing models need not approximate anything that exists at the aggregate level—even locally.

The merits of the approximator depend upon whether the explanatory variables or the macroparameters vary more rapidly. The use of Taylor series approximations does raise statistical questions about the correlation between the remainder and the disturbance terms. But such problems with higher-order terms are inevitable with any model, and if the remainder is small with high probability, then correlation problems are minimized by the Schwartz inequality. The integrability properties of the parameterized Rotterdam model, (3.2), are considered in Appendix B, section B3. The Rotterdam model's theoretical foundations are compared with those of the class of "flexible functional forms" in Appendix B, section B4.

3.8. Summary and conclusion

We have shown that far more is known about our general stochastically limited differential equation (3.18) than is known about conventional aggregate demand systems. We then explored the properties (3.18) subject to the particular Rotterdam model parameterization. Prior results on the Rotterdam model's theoretical foundations related solely to a Lebesgue measure zero subset of the space of admissible (consistent with assumptions 3.1 and 3.2) macrocoefficients. We have extended the existing results to apply throughout the much larger feasible set used in the model's empirical applications, and we have found the model's generality to be expanded considerably on the complement of the previously investigated Lebesgue measure zero subset. In addition, theory tells us that aggregate demand properties on the negligible subset *should* be restrictive.

Continued analysis of the Rotterdam model's specific parameterization of (3.18) could profitably consider its potentially (although perhaps not typically) troublesome nonsymmetric asymptotic Slutsky aggregation bias. Acquisition of a more rigorously controllable Slutsky aggregation bias might be a fruitful objective in considering extensions of or alternatives to the Rotterdam model's particular parameterization of our fundamental theoretical construct (3.18). One potential generalization of the parameterization of the relative price version of the Rotterdam model has been proposed by Theil (1975, pp. 108–112). Its usefulness is not yet known, although negative results have been reported in Theil (1976, sec. 15.4). An alternative generalization is proposed in Theil (1976, sec. 7.3) and is considered further in sections 15.6–15.8 of the same source. A generalization based upon Nasse's (1970) model is discussed in Theil (1979) and used in Meisner (1979b) and Meisner and Clements (1979). An extension merging the Rotterdam model with Working's (1943) and Leser's (1963) model of Engel curves is contained in Clements and Theil (1979).

An empirical rejection of Slutsky symmetry with the current parameterization would reflect the existence of non-negligible nonsymmetric aggregation biases rather than any violations of theory. However, available empirical evidence tends to support our conjecture that the Rotterdam model's Slutsky aggregation bias is small. See, for example, Theil (1971, pp. 340–344) for a successful test of Slutsky symmetry. But such results cannot be viewed as conclusive for other potential data or goods.

The class of "flexible" functional forms (translog, etc.) are similar to the Rotterdam model in providing first-order Taylor series approximations to a theoretical system of equations. The Rotterdam model has the theoretical advantage of approximating a more general theoretical construct (our system (3.18)) than that which is approximated by the "flexible" forms. That which is approximated by the Rotterdam model exists under far weaker assumptions than that (the demand system of a representative consumer) which is approximated by the "flexible" forms. However, the "flexible" forms have the advantage of providing a better understood approximation to that which is being approximated (when it exists). The "flexible" forms acquire their approximation exclusively through dropping the remainder term of a first-order local Taylor expansion. The Rotterdam model acquires its approximation by dropping the remainder term of a first-order local Taylor expansion (our "locally small remainder term") *and* dropping an additional remainder term (our "globally small remainder term").

CHAPTER 4

STATISTICAL THEORY

In this chapter we present results in statistical theory. In particular, we derive those results on maximum likelihood estimation needed in our inferences. For nonlinear equation systems the properties of the maximum likelihood estimator (MLE) commonly have been deduced from related but inapplicable results in the statistical and econometric literature. In this section, under specific regularity conditions, we build upon the nonlinear generalized least squares (GLS) results of Malinvaud to derive the large sample properties of the maximum likelihood estimator and the limiting distribution of the asymptotic likelihood ratio statistic. We discuss iterative convergence conditions under which the iterated Aitken estimator locates a consistent local maximum of the likelihood function, and we derive results permitting convenient estimation of the asymptotic covariance matrix of any subset of our parameter estimators.

Our results are based upon those of Barnett (1976), whose regularity conditions are easily verified for the models we shall use in Chapters 5–7 of this book. Amemiya (1977) has derived related results for nonlinear structural (implicit) models, rather than for the systems of seemingly unrelated regression equations considered by Barnett (1976). But Amemiya's regularity conditions are considerably more difficult to verify than Barnett's for the explicit demand systems estimated in Chapters 5–7. We consider verification of those regularity conditions in this section, and we develop Barnett's results in detail for the class of models considered in Chapters 5–7. In Chapter 9 we have to appeal to Amemiya's results to support our full information maximum likelihood estimation of an implicit demand system, but we shall not attempt the formidable task of verifying his regularity conditions for that system.

4.1. Introduction

4.1.1. Earlier results

A special case in which the large sample properties of the maximum likelihood estimator are known is the case of models nonlinear in the parameters but linear in the variables (see Hausman, 1975). In that case we can reparameterize to linearize the model in the parameters. We can then apply the invariance property of maximum likelihood estimates to permit acquisition of the large sample properties of the maximum likelihood estimator of the original parameters. We need only use the results on linear models known from Koopmans, Rubin, and Leipnik (1950). However, this simplifying conclusion applies only if two conditions are satisfied: (1) the transformation between the original and the new parameters must be one-to-one, and (2) the transformed parameters must not be subject to nonlinear constraints. The relative price version of the Rotterdam model, although linear in the variables, does not satisfy those two conditions.

The properties of the full information maximum likelihood estimator for simultaneous equations nonlinear in the variables but linear in the parameters have been studied in depth by Hatanaka (1979). In the standard single equation case, the MLE is the same as the least squares estimator which has been studied by Gallant (1975a), Jennrich (1969), and Malinvaud (1970a, 1970b).

In the applied work on nonlinear systems of equations, the properties of maximum likelihood estimators frequently are inferred from the existing classical statistical literature on maximum likelihood estimation. For an overview of much of that literature, see Goldfeld and Quandt (1972). Relevant statistical theory can be found in their section 2.4. That statistical literature was developed for sampling from a fixed distribution. But the observations in a regression model are not identically distributed. From the well-known linear model case we should expect that at least a stationarity assumption will be required on the exogenous variables. Hence, the classical literature on sampling from a fixed distribution does not provide the regularity conditions we seek, and as Malinvaud (1970a, pp. 956–957) has observed: "one may be surprised to realize how little developed is the statistical theory of nonlinear regression. Research has been concentrated on problems raised by the computation of the estimates.... But little effort has been spent in exploring the conditions under which nonlinear regressions perform well." Malinvaud (1970b, p. 338) has further observed that "contrary to general belief, the asymptotic theory of maximum likelihood estimation is not sufficiently general in its present state, to cover the model in which we are interested", which is the model in which we are interested.

Recently, a literature has appeared on the estimation of nonlinear equation systems by generalized least squares. See, for example, Gallant (1975b) and Malinvaud (1970a, 1970b). Since many of the existing computer programs provide maximum likelihood estimates or the equivalent (for reduced forms) converged iterated Aitken (generalized least squares) estimates, the finite-step (unconverged iteration on the covariance matrix) generalized least squares estimator is not widely used, and a new algorithm for computing the MLE has recently appeared (see Berndt, Hall, Hall, and Hausman, 1974). A list of some available programs is contained in Bard (1973, pp. 323–324). Other programs are available from Harvard's TSP package and the National Bureau of Economic Research's program package. More recently completed programs include Wymer's RESIMUL (currently available from Clifford Wymer at the International Monetary Fund) and the extended Eisenpress program discussed in Appendix C, Section C1.

Moreover, when the generalized least squares estimation is used, verification of the regularity conditions needed to permit the construction of hypothesis tests requires burdensome individual consideration of the theoretical relationship between the existing model and an "asymptotically linear quasi-model." See, for example, Malinvaud (1970b, p. 359, footnote), and Jennrich (1969, p. 662). Furthermore, the finite-step generalized least squares estimator is not invariant to the equation deleted. Our nonlinear systems are empirical systems of demand functions in which an arbitrary equation is deleted to avoid matrix singularity problems. An estimator that is not invariant to that arbitrary choice cannot be used. In addition, in our class of models the maximum likelihood estimator has all of the desirable asymptotic properties of the finite-step generalized least squares estimator along with the additional properties of minimizing the generalized variance of the fit and reproducing the covariance matrix estimator from the residuals. Finally, for structural form equation systems, Jorgenson and Laffont (1974) have proved that the minimum distance (GLS) estimator is asymptotically inefficient. However, the literature on nonlinear generalized least squares theory provides valuable theoretical results that will be used extensively in our proofs.

Our starting point in the derivations to follow will be Malinvaud (1970b ch. 9, sec. 3). Contrary to some popular opinion (e.g. Jorgenson and Laffont, 1974, pp. 615 and 623), that section provides no immediate results on the asymptotic properties of the maximum likelihood estimator, although Malinvaud's section does prove the asymptotic efficiency of the finite-step GLS estimator. Iteration on the finite-step generalized least squares estimator until convergence of its covariance matrix estimator does produce a maximum likelihood estimate (at least locally), but Malinvaud's asymptotic results on the finite-step generalized least squares estimator need not carry over to the converged estimator unless the covariance matrix estimator retains its consistency upon convergence of the iteration. As we shall demonstrate, Malinvaud's iterative convergence assumption alone is not sufficient to ensure consistency as the number of iterations goes to infinity. A uniformity condition will be required.

Furthermore, the asymptotic properties relevant to the finite-step GLS estimator, whether or not applicable to the maximum likelihood estimator, are not those needed to support use of the maximum likelihood estimator. For example, to determine the limiting distribution of the asymptotic likelihood ratio statistic, we shall need the asymptotic distribution of all of our parameter estimators. But Malinvaud's results provide no information regarding the asymptotic distribution of the covariance matrix estimator. In addition, the most widely used and conveniently computed standard errors for maximum likelihood estimators are not found from Malinvaud's approach. With few exceptions, Malinvaud's results are directly applicable solely to this finite-step generalized least squares estimator. Those exceptions are his general lemmas on consistency and his algebraic results on the properties of the likelihood function itself. We shall use those lemmas and properties extensively.

4.1.2. The problem

The models we consider are of the form $y_t = g(x_t, \gamma_0) + \varepsilon_t$ with the random vectors ε_t, $t = 1, \ldots, T$, distributed identically and independently as $N(0, \Omega_0)$. The q-dimensional vector γ_0 and the matrix Ω_0 are the true values of the parameters γ and Ω. We shall delete the subscript 0 when no ambiguity results. The vector y_t contains the observations on the endogenous variables at time t, while x_t contains the exogenous variables. This class of models includes systems of seemingly unrelated regression equations and systems of simultaneous equations with additive errors in reduced form. Our results can be extended immediately to the "maximum likelihood" estimation of identified simultaneous equation systems in structural form by applying the invariance property of MLE's. The difference between "maximum likelihood" and full information maximum likelihood (FIML) estimation of a structural form is defined in Malinvaud (1970b).

We assume that any prior restrictions on γ have already been eliminated by substitution in arriving at the vector-valued function g. However, this is merely a notational convenience. We could have explicit analytic restrictions on γ, and all of our results would be unchanged. We would need only to eliminate those restrictions by substitution into the likelihood function in the proofs below. An alternative approach to the use and testing of parameter restrictions could be based upon generalization of the work of Silvey (1959).

Now let θ be a p-dimensional vector including γ and then the elements of Ω outside of its redundant lower left triangle. Let $f(y_t|\theta_0, x_t)$ be the density of the distribution of y_t. For notational convenience we define f_t such that $f_t(y_t|\theta_0) = f(y_t|\theta_0, x_t)$, and we assume that f_t is three times differentiable in θ.

We shall attempt to provide simplified proofs whenever possible by the use of results available from the literature on nonlinear generalized least squares. We begin by defining a generalized least squares estimator. Let S_T be a positive definite matrix [a.s.] for every positive integer T. The matrix S_T may be random. Then at any T and any realization of S_T, a generalized least squares estimate $\gamma(S_T)$ is a value of γ which minimizes $\Sigma_{t=1}^{T}[y_t - g_t(\gamma)]'S_T[y_t - g_t(\gamma)]$. We assume that $\gamma(S_T)$ exists and is single valued. Our proofs extend easily to the case in which an arbitrary value is chosen from a solution set. We accept assumptions 1, 2, and 3 presented and discussed in Malinvaud (1970b, pp. 331–332).

To permit access to existing results, the structure of assumptions to be accepted below will include many presented and discussed by Malinvaud in his work on generalized least squares. We shall refer to such assumptions as needed, without reproducing them. This practice will be followed whenever we use a lemma proved elsewhere. When we require such assumptions in our own proofs, the assumptions will be reproduced explicitly. All of our proofs are provided in Appendix C, Section C2. The results below will be related to a function N defined such that

$$N(\gamma) = (1/T) \sum_{t=1}^{T} [y_t - g_t(\gamma)][y_t - g_t(\gamma)]'. \qquad (4.1)$$

4.2. Weak convergence

4.2.1. Lemmas

We shall need the following lemma. This lemma can be proved by using the method applied by Malinvaud (1970b, p. 337) to his two-step procedure, but with his second stage residuals replaced by our less restrictively defined vector $\tilde{\varepsilon}_t = y_t - g_t(\tilde{\gamma})$.

Lemma 4.1. Let $\tilde{\gamma}$ be a weakly consistent estimator of γ_0. Then $N(\tilde{\gamma}) = \Omega_0 + o_p(1)$.

Since our later proofs will assume the existence of a consistent local maximum to the likelihood function, we now present a brief discussion of a means by which that consistency assumption can be shown to follow from existing results on nonlinear GLS. A more formal treatment of consistency is available in Phillips (1976). By accepting stronger regularity conditions (analogous to Jennrich's, 1969), Phillips proved strong consistency. We now state an initial consistency lemma which we show to be relevant to our class of models. Although it is a result which is usually difficult to obtain, we can exploit the desirable properties of our model to relate the lemma to a result proved by Malinvaud.

Lemma 4.2. Let $\tilde{\Omega}_T = A + o_p(1)$, where A is any positive definite matrix and where $\tilde{\Omega}_T$ is a sequence of [a.s] positive definite random matrices. Let $\gamma(\tilde{\Omega}_T)$ be the corresponding minimum distance estimator of γ_0. Then $\gamma(\tilde{\Omega}_T) = \gamma_0 + o_p(1)$ as $T \to \infty$.

First we indicate the general applicability of this lemma to a larger class of models than ours. Consider theorem 4.3 on p. 292 of the first edition of Malinvaud's book (1966). Our result follows immediately from that theorem if we accept assumption 4.3 on his p. 291. But that assumption is extremely awkward and very difficult to verify. We shall not attempt to verify that our models satisfy that condition. Nevertheless, Malinvaud's observations following that assumption indicate that it is very weak. Although this suggests that our lemma 4.2 is widely applicable to nonlinear models, it would be comforting to be able to check the relevant regularity conditions rather than merely to observe that they are "weak". We now show that our models satisfy regularity conditions sufficient to demonstrate this lemma.

Consider assumption 1 and conditions (i), (ii), (iii), and (iv) of Malinvaud (1970b, p. 331). As Malinvaud (1970a, p. 967) has proved in his theorem 3, our lemma 4.2 follows immediately from those regularity conditions. But they are the strongest regularity conditions Malinvaud has considered and undoubtedly are not widely applicable. Fortunately, when they do apply they are easily verified, and they do apply to our models. For a discussion of those regularity conditions, see sections 5 and 6 of Malinvaud (1970b). As is seen from Malinvaud's discussion on p. 966 of that paper and from a comparison of his assumptions with the properties of our models, all of the relevant conditions clearly are satisfied with one possible exception: his stationarity assumption on the process generating the "exogenous" variables is highly restrictive.

In all consistency proofs for regression models, some sort of stationarity assumption must be made about future values of the exogenous variables. But Malinvaud's assumptions here are particularly restrictive. Fortunately, stationarity assumptions regarding our exogenous variables are immediately acceptable. All of our exogenous variables (with one minor exception) in all of our models in Part I are either log changes in deflated variables or deflated log changes. Such deflated percentage changes tend to exhibit strong long-run stationarity properties. We can accept Malinvaud's stationarity assumption comfortably, and hence lemma 4.2 follows.

An obstacle remaining to our proof of the consistency of $\hat{\theta}$ is the verification of the assumption stated in lemma 4.2 above. A somewhat circuitous approach to its verification will be needed. In Appendix C, section C2, we prove the following simple lemma, which alternatively could be acquired from Bickel's (1967, p. 586) stronger result.

Lemma 4.3. Let X_{mt} be a double sequence of random variables for m, $t = 1, 2, \ldots$, and let X_t be a sequence of random variables. Let c be a constant scalar. Suppose $X_{mt} \xrightarrow{a.s.} X_t$ uniformly in t as $m \to \infty$. Also, let $X_{mt} = c + o_p(1)$ as $t \to \infty$ for any m. Then $X_t = c + o_p(1)$.

4.2.2. Consistency

To complete our consistency proof we must postulate an algorithm for locating a critical point of the likelihood function. Suppose we set $S_T = I$ for all $T = 1, 2, \ldots$, and compute the minimum distance estimator, $\gamma(S_T)$.

By lemma 4.2, $\gamma(S_T)$ is consistent. Then compute $\tilde{\Omega}_T$ such that

$$\tilde{\Omega}_T = \frac{1}{T} \sum_{t=1}^{T} \tilde{\varepsilon}_t \tilde{\varepsilon}_t',$$

where $\tilde{\varepsilon}_t = y_t - g_t(\gamma(S_T))$. By lemma 4.1, $\tilde{\Omega}_T = \Omega_0 + o_p(1)$. Hence, we have constructed an estimator, $\tilde{\theta}_{1T}$, from $(\gamma(S_T), \tilde{\Omega}_T)$ such that $\tilde{\theta}_{1T} \xrightarrow{p} \theta_0$ as $T \to \infty$.

We now iterate this minimum distance estimator in the obvious way by computing $\gamma(\tilde{\Omega}_T)$ and then a new covariance matrix estimator from the new residuals, etc. It is easy to show that lemmas 4.2 and 4.3 can be applied at each step to prove consistency of the resulting estimator of θ_0 at each step. As Malinvaud (1970b, p. 340) has observed, we can expect that this procedure will converge, and in fact, we assume that it does. Furthermore, as the number of iterations increases, we assume that the convergence is uniform in T. Since our likelihood functions will be seen to be very "regular", with unique and precisely defined optima, this assumption appears reasonable. For example, we would expect that at any T the procedure will have converged to any measurable degree of precision after 10^{10} iterations.

As Malinvaud (1970b, p. 340) has proved, if the procedure converges, then its limit is a critical point of the likelihood function. This is a generalization of a well-known result in linear models, equating the maximum likelihood estimator with an iterated generalized least squares estimator. In the remainder of this argument we shall act as if we were using the postulated algorithm. But of course if the critical point is unique, as it is in all of our cases, any method we may use to locate the MLE will converge to the same limit.

During this postulated generalized least squares iterative procedure, we have generated a sequence of random variables, $\tilde{\theta}_{mT}$, where m is the iteration number. By our assumption of uniform convergence, $\tilde{\theta}_{mT} \xrightarrow{a.s.} \hat{\theta}_T$ uniformly in T as $m \to \infty$, where $\hat{\theta}_T$ is a solution to the likelihood equation. Furthermore, we have proved that for any m, $\tilde{\theta}_{mT} \xrightarrow{p} \theta_0$ as $T \to \infty$. So by lemma 4.3 $\hat{\theta}_T = \theta_0 + o_p(1)$. We state this result for future reference.

Result 4.1. Under our accepted regularity conditions, the iterated generalized least squares procedure converges to a solution of the likelihood function, $\hat{\theta}_T$, such that $\hat{\theta}_T = \theta_0 + o_p(1)$.

The above proof probably could be strengthened to a proof of strong consistency by relating our approach to the nonlinear ordinary least squares work of Jennrich (1969), rather than the generalized least squares work of Malinvaud. But since we need only weak consistency, we shall not attempt that less direct extension. Note that our result does not assert that we have located the maximum likelihood estimate, but only a consistent root of the likelihood equations, where the likelihood equations are the first-order conditions for maximization of the likelihood function. All of our subsequent results will be based upon that root. We shall use the term ML estimator rather than MLE (or maximum likelihood estimator) to refer to $\hat{\boldsymbol{\theta}}_T$. But in all of our applications the realization of the likelihood function over which we search will have a unique and well-defined critical point. Since our sample size is large, we have evidence that the likelihood equations may have a unique root for all sufficiently large T. But there are no guarantees. The uniqueness of the root of the current realization of the likelihood equations for the current T demonstrates that our estimate is the maximum likelihood estimate, but we do not know whether our estimator is a maximum likelihood estimator.

Although it is reasonable to believe that a stronger result could be proved (see, for example, Wald, 1949), which would permit us to characterize the global maximum likelihood estimator, we must insist that our estimator is defined by the convergence of our postulated generalized least squares iteration. We shall imagine that if at some future T we were to locate two roots by our actual search method, we would revert to our postulated generalized least squares iteration to discriminate between them. The iterated generalized least squares (Aitken) estimator is available from Harvard's TSP program package.

Observe that we not only have proved the existence of a consistent root, but we have determined a means of locating it. Also observe that we could extend our argument to prove that our generalized least squares iteration converges to a consistent root for any initial positive definite covariance matrix estimate (i.e. not just our initial identity matrix); but we cannot claim the converse. We have not proved that a starting matrix exists such that the algorithm will converge to the maximum likelihood estimate.

Note that result 4.1 obtains without the assumption of normality of the error structure. For notational convenience we frequently drop the subscript T from $\hat{\boldsymbol{\theta}}_T$.

4.3. Lemmas and properties

In this section we present lemmas, properties, and assumptions that will be needed in our proofs. When we refer to a matrix valued function, say $f(\boldsymbol{A})$, we will frequently write $f^{-1}(A)$ to mean $[f(A)]^{-1}$. Since we shall not be dealing with the inverses of functions, this notation will always denote the inverse of the matrix $f(A)$.

Let S be any positive definite symmetric matrix, and let Z_t be the matrix $\partial g_t(\gamma)/\partial \gamma'|_{\gamma=\gamma_0}$. Then we define $M_T(S)$ by

$$M_T(S) = \frac{1}{T} \sum_{t=1}^{T} Z_t' S Z_t.$$

We accept the following assumptions from Malinvaud (1970b, p. 332).

Assumption 4.1. For any positive definite symmetric matrix, S, the matrix $M_T(S)$ is nonsingular and converges to a nonsingular matrix $M(S)$ as $T \to \infty$.

Assumption 4.2. The first three derivatives of each element of the vector $g_t(\gamma)$ are bounded uniformly in t and γ.

Assumption 4.2 will permit efficient proofs, although it possibly can be weakened to apply only to a neighborhood of γ_0. In fact Malinvaud (1970b, pp. 293 and 301) has speculated that his various boundedness conditions can be weakened substantially to assumptions such as the existence of higher-order moments of the ε_{ti} values. We accept assumption 4.2 in its present form as a useful, although not necessary, analytical simplification.

Assumption 4.1 is another "stationarity" assumption on the exogenous variables. It is a familiar sort of stationarity assumption having its analogs in the asymptotic theory of linear models, and it is a considerably weaker assumption than the stationarity assumption we already have accepted.

Malinvaud (1970b, p. 335) has shown that the following result follows easily from assumptions 4.1 and 4.2.

Lemma 4.4. If the random matrix S_T tends in probability to a positive definite matrix S, then $M_T(S_T) \xrightarrow{p} M(S)$ as $T \to \infty$.

On the same page (p. 335) he also showed that the next result follows from assumption 4.2.

Lemma 4.5. If $\tilde{\gamma}_T = \gamma_0 + o_p(1)$, then for $i = 1, \ldots, n$, $\max_{t \leq T} |g_{ti}(\gamma_0) - g_{ti}(\tilde{\gamma}_T)| = o_p(1)$, as $T \to \infty$.

We now define some matrices that will be used repeatedly. Define the likelihood function

$$L(\theta|y, x) = \prod_{t=1}^{T} f(y_t|\theta, x_t),$$

where $y = (y_1', \ldots, y_T')'$ and $x = (x_1', \ldots, x_T')'$. Observe that L depends upon T through (y, x) and that L is three times differentiable by the corresponding assumption on f. Now let $E_\theta(\cdot)$ and $\text{var}_\theta(\cdot)$ denote the expectation and variance respectively with respect to the law of y for given θ and the known x. We can then define the information matrix

$$I_T(\theta) = -E_\theta\left[\frac{\partial^2 \log L(\theta|y, x)}{\partial \theta \partial \theta'}\right].$$

Also define

$$\mathcal{I}_T(\theta) = -E_\theta\left[\frac{\partial^2 \log L(\theta|y, x)}{\partial \gamma \partial \gamma'}\right].$$

Malinvaud (1970b, p. 341) has proved that $I_T(\theta)$ is block diagonal with two diagonal blocks and with $\mathcal{I}_T(\theta)$ as the upper left diagonal block. So we can define a matrix $\mathcal{J}_T(\theta)$ such that

$$I_T(\theta) = \begin{bmatrix} \mathcal{I}_T(\theta) & 0 \\ 0 & \mathcal{J}_T(\theta) \end{bmatrix}.$$

On his pp. 338–341, Malinvaud (1970b) has derived a number of useful properties of the likelihood function. Since they will be used repeatedly in the following proofs, they are listed below for future reference.

Property 4.1. $\mathcal{I}_T(\theta) = TM_T(\Omega^{-1})$.

Property 4.2. There exists a nonsingular matrix valued transformation Q such that $\mathcal{J}_T(\theta) = (T/2)Q(\Omega)$.

Property 4.3.

$$d^2 \log L(\theta|y, x) = -\frac{T}{2}\text{tr}\left[(\Omega^{-1}d\Omega)^2(2\Omega^{-1}N(\gamma) - I)\right]$$
$$+ T\text{tr}\left[\Omega^{-1}d\Omega\Omega^{-1}dN\right] - \frac{T}{2}\text{tr}(\Omega^{-1}d^2N),$$

where $d^i N$ is the ith differential of the function $N(\gamma)$.

Property 4.4.

$$dN = -\frac{1}{T}\sum_{k=1}^{q}\sum_{t=1}^{T}\left[\varepsilon_t \frac{\partial g'_t(\gamma)}{\partial \gamma_k} + \frac{\partial g_t(\gamma)}{\partial \gamma_k}\varepsilon'_t\right]d\gamma_k.$$

Property 4.5.

$$d^2N = \frac{1}{T}\sum_{t=1}^{T}\sum_{j,k=1}^{q}\left[2\frac{\partial g_t(\gamma)}{\partial \gamma_j}\frac{\partial g'_t(\gamma)}{\partial \gamma_k}\right.$$
$$\left. - \varepsilon_t \frac{\partial^2 g'_t}{\partial \gamma_k \partial \gamma_j} - \frac{\partial^2 g_t}{\partial \gamma_k \partial \gamma_j}\varepsilon'_t\right]d\gamma_j d\gamma_k.$$

Observe that property 4.5 corrects two errors in sign contained in Malinvaud's expression.

Property 4.6. $E_\theta d^2 \log L(\theta|y,x) = -(T/2)\mathrm{tr}(\Omega^{-1}d\Omega)^2 + Td\gamma' M_T(\Omega^{-1})d\gamma$.

Property 4.7. $d \log L(\theta|y,x) = -(T/2)\{\mathrm{tr}[\Omega^{-1}d\Omega(I - \Omega^{-1}N(\gamma))] + \mathrm{tr}(\Omega^{-1}dN)\}$.

Property 4.8. $E_\theta(dN) = 0$.

Property 4.9. $\hat{\gamma}$ is the maximum likelihood estimate of γ_0 if and only if it minimizes $|N(\gamma)|$.

Property 4.10. If $\hat{\gamma}$ is the maximum likelihood estimate of γ_0, then $N(\hat{\gamma})$ is the maximum likelihood estimate of Ω_0.

Property 4.11. $\log L(\theta|y,x) = C - (T/2)[\log|\Omega| + \mathrm{tr}(\Omega^{-1}N(\gamma))]$, where C is a constant.

We will also have use for the following general property of stochastic convergence. The property is proved on p. 372 of Malinvaud (1970b).

Property 4.12. If the random variables z_t (where $t=1,2,\ldots$) are independent and identically distributed with zero mean, and if the scalars a_{tT} are bounded (where $t=1,2,\ldots,T$; $T=1,2,\ldots$), then

$$\frac{1}{T}\sum_{t=1}^{T} a_{tT} z_t \xrightarrow{p} 0, \quad \text{as } T\to\infty.$$

Now in order to relate the matrices $\mathcal{I}_T(\theta)$ and $\mathcal{J}_T(\theta)$ to assumption 4.1, we shall need the following lemma. In Appendix C, section C2, we show that the lemma follows from assumption 4.1 and properties 4.1 and 4.2.

Lemma 4.6. The matrices $(1/T)\mathcal{I}_T(\theta)$, $(1/T)\mathcal{J}_T(\theta)$, and therefore $(1/T)I_T(\theta)$ converge to nonsingular matrices as $T\to\infty$.

We can now define

$$\mathcal{I}(\theta) = \lim_{T\to\infty} \frac{1}{T}\mathcal{I}_T(\theta),$$

$$\mathcal{J}(\theta) = \lim_{T\to\infty} \frac{1}{T}\mathcal{J}_T(\theta),$$

$$I(\theta) = \lim_{T\to\infty} \frac{1}{T}I_T(\theta).$$

We shall have frequent use for the Hessian matrix

$$B_T(\theta) = -\frac{\partial^2 \log L(\theta|y,x)}{\partial\theta\partial\theta'},$$

which we assume to be nonsingular for all θ with probability 1 as $T\to\infty$. We also need the vector of efficient scores

$$a_T(\theta) = \frac{\partial \log L(\theta|y,x)}{\partial\theta}.$$

We define the function $h_{trk}(\gamma)$ such that $h_{trk}(\gamma) = \partial g_{tr}/\partial \gamma_k$.

The following simple lemma, proved in Appendix C, section C2, will be used repeatedly.

Lemma 4.7. Let X_t and Y_t be sequences of random variables such that $0 \leq |X_t| \leq Y_t$, and let $Y_T = o_p(1)$. Then $X_t = o_p(1)$.

Before seeking the limiting distribution of $\sqrt{(T)}(\hat{\theta}-\theta_0)$, we derive a valuable result permitting computationally efficient estimation of the information matrix. The result is needed at this point since it will be required during the derivation of the limiting distribution of $\sqrt{(T)}(\hat{\theta}-\theta_0)$. We begin by presenting two useful lemmas. In Appendix C, section C2, we show that the two lemmas follow from assumption 4.2, lemmas 4.4, 4.5, 4.7, and 4.8, and properties 4.3, 4.4, 4.5, and 4.12.

Lemma 4.8. Let S_T be a sequence of random matrices such that $S_T \xrightarrow{p} \Omega_0^{-1}$, and let $\tilde{\gamma}_T$ be a sequence of random vectors such that $\tilde{\gamma}_T \xrightarrow{p} \gamma_0$.

Then

$$\frac{1}{T}\sum_{t=1}^{T}\frac{\partial g'_t}{\partial \gamma_k}\bigg|_{\gamma=\tilde{\gamma}} S_T \frac{\partial g_t}{\partial \gamma_j}\bigg|_{\gamma=\tilde{\gamma}} \xrightarrow{P} \left[M(\Omega_0^{-1})\right]_{kj},$$

as $T\to\infty$ for $k, j = 1,\ldots, q$.

Recalling the definition of $N(\gamma)$ above, we prove the following lemma in Appendix C, section C2. The proof depends upon lemmas 4.1, 4.5, 4.7, and 4.8, properties 4.3, 4.4, 4.5, and 4.12, and assumption 4.2.

Lemma 4.9. Let $\tilde{\gamma}_T$ be a sequence of random vectors and S_T a sequence of random matrices such that $\tilde{\gamma}_T = \gamma_0 + o_p(1)$ and $S_T = \Omega_0 + o_p(1)$. Define $\tilde{\theta}_T$ in terms of $\tilde{\gamma}_T$ and S_T in the usual manner. Then

$$-\frac{1}{T} \mathrm{d}^2 \log L(\theta \mid y, x)\big|_{\theta=\tilde{\theta}} = \tfrac{1}{2} \mathrm{tr}\left[\Omega_0^{-1} \mathrm{d}\Omega\right]^2 + \mathrm{d}\gamma' M(\Omega_0^{-1}) \mathrm{d}\gamma + o_p(1).$$

4.4. Convergence in distribution

4.4.1. The asymptotic covariance matrix

The reader may observe that we are using the classical statistical approach to these proofs rather than the considerably simpler approach used by Malinvaud (1970b, pp. 334–336) in his analogous proof for the generalized least squares estimator. The reason is that we shall require the asymptotic distribution of all of $\hat{\theta}$ in our later proofs, while Malinvaud's approach provides the asymptotic distribution only of his estimator of γ_0. Finally, we can prove our first theorem. The proof, presented in Appendix C, section C2, depends upon property 6 and lemma 4.9.

Theorem 4.1. Let $\tilde{\theta}_T = \theta_0 + o_p(1)$. Then $TB_T^{-1}(\tilde{\theta}) = I^{-1}(\theta_0) + o_p(1)$.

Corollary 4.1. $TB_T^{-1}(\theta_0) = I^{-1}(\theta_0) + o_p(1)$.

As mentioned earlier, theorem 4.1 will be needed in the proof of the asymptotic normality of $\hat{\theta}$. However, it is a valuable result on its own. It tells us that given the ML estimator $\hat{\boldsymbol{\theta}}$ of $\boldsymbol{\theta}_0$, we can acquire a consistent estimator of $\boldsymbol{I}^{-1}(\boldsymbol{\theta}_0)$ from $T\boldsymbol{B}_T^{-1}(\hat{\boldsymbol{\theta}})$. We can use this result in acquiring asymptotic standard errors for $\hat{\boldsymbol{\theta}}$. Observe that, contrary to popular opinion, no sufficiency assumptions are needed.

The advantage of using $T\boldsymbol{B}_T^{-1}(\hat{\boldsymbol{\theta}})$ rather than $T\boldsymbol{I}_T^{-1}(\hat{\boldsymbol{\theta}})$ as an estimator of $\boldsymbol{I}^{-1}(\boldsymbol{\theta}_0)$ is that the computation of $\boldsymbol{B}_T^{-1}(\hat{\boldsymbol{\theta}})$ does not involve the integration contained in the definition of $\boldsymbol{I}_T(\boldsymbol{\theta})$, and the Hessian $\boldsymbol{B}_T(\hat{\boldsymbol{\theta}})$ is immediately available at the last iteration by a Newton's method solution for $\hat{\boldsymbol{\theta}}$. For this reason $T\boldsymbol{B}_T^{-1}(\hat{\boldsymbol{\theta}})$ is used widely to estimate $\boldsymbol{I}^{-1}(\boldsymbol{\theta}_0)$ in nonlinear models. Goldfeld and Quandt (1972, p. 161) state that deleting the expectation leads to "the standard variance approximation for nonlinear maximum likelihood estimators, generally known as the Cramer–Rao variances". According to Goldfeld and Quandt (1972, pp. 65–66) the justification for dropping the expectation is found in a result from Kendall and Stuart (1961). See also Dhrymes (1970, pp. 134–136) and Huzurbazar (1948).

Those results were derived for a random sample from a fixed distribution. But the y_t are not identically distributed, since $E(y_t)$ depends upon x_t in any regression model. In addition, the Kendall and Stuart result requires the existence of a nontrivial sufficient statistic. But it has been proved that in nonlinear regression models a nontrivial sufficient statistic exists if and only if the model is "essentially linear" in a sense rarely encountered in nonlinear models. See Hartley (1964, p. 349). Clearly, this problem does not arise in the full information maximum likelihood estimation of linear models, which of course are "essentially linear". So we are left with the puzzling fact that one of the most widely used theorems in nonlinear estimation is not applicable to nonlinear models. Theorem 4.1 solves this problem.

It might be interesting to consider whether other methods might exist to justify the use of $T\boldsymbol{B}_T^{-1}(\hat{\boldsymbol{\theta}})$ as an estimator of $\boldsymbol{I}^{-1}(\boldsymbol{\theta}_0)$. A common argument is that "it is well known that ...". One might easily be led to that belief, if he were to observe that the result follows immediately from Khintchine's theorem, if he knew the value of $\boldsymbol{\theta}_0$, and if the y_t are i.i.d. But of course the y_t are not i.i.d., and our lack of knowledge of $\boldsymbol{\theta}_0$ is more serious than it may appear. For example, our knowledge of corollary 4.1 to theorem 4.1 follows easily from theorem 4.1, but the converse is not true. We cannot simply substitute a consistent estimator of $\boldsymbol{\theta}_0$ into $\boldsymbol{B}_T(\boldsymbol{\theta}_0)$ on the grounds that $\boldsymbol{B}_T$ is a continuous function of $\boldsymbol{\theta}$, because it is *not* a continuous function of $\boldsymbol{\theta}$. It is a *sequence* of functions of $\boldsymbol{\theta}$. So we shall return to our theorem 4.1 when we seek to estimate $\boldsymbol{I}^{-1}(\boldsymbol{\theta}_0)$.

4.4.2. Asymptotic normality

We now proceed to prove the asymptotic normality of $\hat{\theta}$. We shall need the following lemmas, proved in Appendix C, section C2. The proofs depend upon assumption 4.2 and properties 4.4, 4.7, and 4.8.

Lemma 4.10. $E_{\theta_0} a_T(\theta_0) = 0.$

Lemma 4.11.

$$E_{\theta_0}\left[\frac{\partial \log f_t(y_t|\theta)}{\partial \theta}\right]_{\theta=\theta_0} = 0.$$

Let $\|\cdot\|$ be the Euclidean norm of a vector. Let $F_{\theta,t}(z)$ be the distribution function of $\partial \log f_t / \partial \theta$, so that $F_{\theta,t}(z) = P_\theta[\partial \log f_t / \partial \theta \leq z]$. In Appendix C, section C2, we prove the following lemma, which shows that the multivariate Lindeberg–Feller condition is satisfied. Recall that the Lindeberg–Feller condition prevents a random sum from being dominated by a single random element as $T \to \infty$.

Lemma 4.12. Let δ be any positive real number. Then

$$\frac{1}{T}\sum_{t=1}^{T}\int_{[\|z\|>\delta\sqrt{T}]} \|z\|^2 \, dF_{\theta_0,t}(z) \to 0, \text{ as } T \to \infty.$$

The following lemma and then theorem 4.2 can now be proved, as shown in Appendix C, section C2.

Lemma 4.13. $(1/\sqrt{T}) a_T(\theta_0) \xrightarrow{\mathcal{L}} N(0, I(\theta_0))$, as $T \to \infty$.

Theorem 4.2. $\sqrt{T}(\hat{\theta} - \theta_0) \xrightarrow{\mathcal{L}} N(0, I^{-1}(\theta_0))$, as $T \to \infty$.

In the next chapter, we shall be particularly interested in the first element of γ. So let that first element be α. The following two corollaries are proved in Appendix C, section C2.

Corollary 4.2. $\sqrt{T}(\hat{\alpha} - \alpha_0) \xrightarrow{\mathcal{L}} N(0, [I^{-1}(\theta_0)]_{11})$, as $T \to \infty$.

Corollary 4.3. $\sqrt{T}(\hat{\gamma} - \gamma_0) \xrightarrow{\mathcal{L}} N(0, \mathcal{J}^{-1}(\theta_0))$, as $T \to \infty$.

It appears that it might be possible to derive some of our results under weaker regularity conditions through the use of powerful theorems proved by Weiss (1971, 1973), rather than through our use of Malinvaud's work. However, our use of Malinvaud's work appears to lead to a more direct and cumulative derivation of our results. Verification of Weiss's conditions leads to proof of corollary 4.1 to our theorem 4.1. But to permit convenient computation of standard errors, we need theorem 4.1 itself as well as the particular asymptotic covariance matrix of theorem 4.2. Verification of Weiss's conditions neither provides these results nor does it provide a means of locating a consistent root of the likelihood equations with currently available computer programs. Furthermore, the verification of Weiss's conditions in this case requires much work and careful consideration of such problems as multicollinearity, which Malinvaud (1970b) has eliminated through (iii) and (iv) on his p. 331. In addition, Weiss's asymptotic efficiency criterion is not widely used in econometrics.

4.5. Asymptotic efficiency

From theorem 4.2 and Bahadur (1964, pp. 1550–1552), we can conclude that $\hat{\boldsymbol{\theta}}$ is an essentially BAN (best asymptotically normal) estimator of $\boldsymbol{\theta}$. Bahadur's regularity conditions relevant to our case of nonidentically distributed observations and a vector of parameters are easily verified from properties of the likelihood function presented above. In accordance with this asymptotic efficiency criterion, we find that if $V(\boldsymbol{\theta})$ is the covariance matrix of the limiting distribution of $T^{1/2}(\tilde{\boldsymbol{\theta}} - \boldsymbol{\theta}_0)$ for any other consistent asymptotically normal estimator, $\tilde{\boldsymbol{\theta}}$, of $\boldsymbol{\theta}$, then $V(\boldsymbol{\theta}) - I^{-1}(\boldsymbol{\theta})$ is positive semidefinite for all $\boldsymbol{\theta}$ except on a subset of the parameter space of Lebesgue measure zero. Observe that we have proved the asymptotic efficiency of $\hat{\boldsymbol{\Sigma}}$ as well as of $\hat{\boldsymbol{\gamma}}$.

Alternatively we could use Bahadur (1964) to support use of Rao's Best CUAN (consistent uniformly asymptotically normal) efficiency criterion. But little can be gained by further restricting the class of competing estimators (although perhaps reasonably) solely to eliminate pathological superefficient cases of measure zero. However, a preferred asymptotic efficiency criterion would result if the competing class of consistent estimators were to include those uniformly or continuously convergent in law but *not* necessarily asymptotically normal. While such results exist for the common random sampling case (see, for example, Rothenberg, 1973, and Weiss, 1975), the generalization to nonidentically distributed observations currently is available only for Markov processes. Useful discussions of asymptotic efficiency criteria can be found in Phillips (1976, pp. 350–351), Rao (1973, pp. 11–13), and Wolfowitz (1965, pp. 207–219).

Having found the asymptotic distribution of $\hat{\theta}$, the tools of asymptotic inference by classical likelihood methods are readily at hand. In particular we shall be needing the limiting distribution of $-2\log\lambda$, where λ is the relevant likelihood ratio for testing a composite nonlinear hypothesis.[1] Most available asymptotic results on inference by likelihood methods are formulated for use with a random sample or with a linear model. But our results are sufficiently strong to permit easy extension of those methods to our cases of nonidentically distributed observations from a nonlinear model.

4.6. The asymptotic likelihood ratio test

4.6.1. The hypothesis

We now proceed to acquire the limiting distribution of the asymptotic likelihood ratio test statistic, $-2\log\lambda$. Our result will follow easily from the following lemmas. The proofs, provided in Appendix C, section C2, depend upon theorem 4.2 and lemma 4.13.

Lemma 4.14. $(1/\sqrt{T})a_T(\theta_0)$ has the same limiting distribution as $I(\theta_0)[\sqrt{(T)}(\hat{\theta} - \theta_0)]$ as $T \to \infty$.

Lemma 4.15. $I^{-1}(\theta_0)[(1/\sqrt{T})a_T(\theta_0)]$ has the same limiting distribution as $\sqrt{(T)}(\hat{\theta} - \theta_0)$.

Recall that in the formulation of our model we imbedded our maintained parameter restrictions into the function $g_t(\theta_0)$. We now construct a hypothesis test defined by the imposition of k additional parameter restrictions. Our hypothesis will be

$$H_0: R_i(\gamma_0) = 0, \quad \text{for } i = 1, \ldots, k,$$

where the functions R_i are continuously differentiable, but need not be linear. Also observe that even if H_0 defines a unique solution for γ_0, H_0 leaves Ω completely unrestricted. So H_0 is a composite hypothesis.

---

[1] The fact that this limiting distribution is not known for nonlinear systems was observed by Blackorby, Boyce, and Russell (1978, p. 19), who credit the observation to Ernst Berndt.

Now let $A = \{\gamma: R_i(\gamma) = 0, i = 1, \ldots, k\}$, so that H_0 is true if and only if $\gamma_0 \in A$. Furthermore, define a set Δ such that the alternative hypothesis can be described by $\gamma_0 \in \Delta - A$. Observe that Δ may be defined by parameter restrictions on γ, so that the k restrictions defining A are additional restrictions on γ. We now can say that we are testing H_0 versus H_1 where each is defined by

$$H_0: \gamma_0 \in A \quad \text{and} \quad H_1: \gamma_0 \in \Delta - A.$$

4.6.2. The test statistic

We now define the likelihood ratio criterion that we shall use to test H_0 against H_1. Let us assume that Δ is a subspace of a finite dimensional space defined by a finite number of maintained parameter restrictions. Following the procedure described in this chapter, we can eliminate the maintained restrictions by substitution and estimate the remaining parameters with the iterated minimum distance algorithm postulated in our proofs. Let us denote the resulting estimator of θ by $\hat{\theta}_\Delta$. We can then repeat that procedure after further imposing the k restrictions defining H_0. Denote the resulting estimator of θ by θ_A. The likelihood ratio will be defined to be

$$\lambda_T = \frac{L(\hat{\theta}_A | y, x)}{L(\hat{\theta}_\Delta | y, x)}.$$

Now define λ^* such that

$$\lambda^* = \frac{\sup_{\gamma \in A, \Omega \in B} L(\theta | y, x)}{\sup_{\gamma \in \Delta, \Omega \in B} L(\theta | y, x)},$$

where B is the space of all symmetric positive definite $n \times n$-dimensional matrices. Since the realization of the likelihood function has a unique critical point in all of our applications, the realizations of λ^* and λ_T are the same in all of our applications, and in fact we shall compute λ^* without the use of iterated minimum distance estimates. But in the following theory we shall be using the random variable λ_T, which we have not proved to be equal, in general, to the random variable λ^*. In fact, contrary to popular opinion, computed likelihood ratios can, in principle, exceed one. Although this is not possible with λ^*, it is conceivable, although improbable, with λ_T.

We can prove the following theorem immediately. The proof, depending upon theorem 4.2 and lemmas 4.6 and 4.15, appears in Appendix C, section C2.

Theorem 4.3. If $\theta_0 \in A$, then $-2 \log \lambda_T \xrightarrow{\mathcal{L}} \chi^2(k)$ as $T \to \infty$.

Theorem 4.3 provides the asymptotic justification for the use of the test statistic $-2 \log \lambda_T$. However, it should be observed that tests based upon that statistic are unreliable when the sample size is not very much larger than the number of equations. See Laitinen (1978) and Meisner (1979a).

The key to proving theorem 4.3 is found in the results of theorem 4.2 and lemma 4.13. Lemmas 4.14 and 4.15 themselves follow easily from theorem 4.2 and lemma 4.13. We now find a simplified formula for computing λ_T. Since we know that $\lambda_T = \lambda^*$ for our data (y, x), we can base our derivation on λ^*.

4.6.3. Simplification of the test statistic

By property 4.10, we know that we can find the concentrated likelihood function in γ, by substituting $\Omega = N(\gamma)$ into $L(\theta | y, x)$. We denote the resulting concentrated likelihood function by $L^*(\gamma | y, x)$. Then by property 4.11 we find that $\log L^*(\gamma | y, x) = C - (T/2)[\log |N(\gamma)| + n]$. Hence, the likelihood ratio we seek is equal to

$$\lambda^* = \frac{\sup_{\gamma \in A} L^*(\gamma | y, x)}{\sup_{\gamma \in \Delta} L^*(\gamma | y, x)}.$$

Now

$$L^*(\gamma | y, x) = C_0 \exp\left(-\frac{T}{2} \log |N(\gamma)|\right)$$
$$= C_0 |N(\gamma)|^{-T/2},$$

where C_0 is a constant. So

$$\lambda^* = \frac{\sup_{\gamma \in A} |N(\gamma)|^{-T/2}}{\sup_{\gamma \in \Delta} |N(\gamma)|^{-T/2}}$$

follows at once. But it is easy to see that

$$\sup_{\gamma \in A} |N(\gamma)|^{-T/2} = \sup_{\gamma \in A} \frac{1}{|N(\gamma)|^{T/2}} = \frac{1}{\inf_{\gamma \in A} |N(\gamma)|^{T/2}}$$

$$= \frac{1}{\left[\inf_{\gamma \in A} |N(\gamma)|\right]^{T/2}} = \left[\inf_{\gamma \in A} |N(\gamma)|\right]^{-T/2}.$$

The analogous result obtains for the denominator of λ^*.

Hence, it follows that

$$\lambda^* = \left[\frac{\inf_{\gamma \in A} |N(\gamma)|}{\inf_{\gamma \in \Delta} |N(\gamma)|} \right]^{-T/2}.$$

Now let $\hat{\gamma}_\Delta$ be the maximum likelihood estimate of γ with γ restricted to lie in Δ, and let $\hat{\gamma}_A$ be the maximum likelihood estimate of γ with γ restricted to lie in A. In all of our applications the maximum will be attained for a feasible value of γ. Hence, it follows that

$$\lambda^* = \left[\frac{|N(\hat{\gamma}_A)|}{|N(\hat{\gamma}_\Delta)|} \right]^{-T/2}.$$

So finally we can determine that our test criterion is

$$-2\log \lambda_T = -2\log \lambda^* = T\log \frac{|N(\hat{\gamma}_A)|}{|N(\hat{\gamma}_\Delta)|}.$$

By theorem 4.3 we can compute the limiting tail area of H_0 by computing λ_T for our data (x, y) and then computing $P[\chi^2(k) > -2\log \lambda_T]$.[2] Observe that $N(\hat{\gamma}_A)$ and $N(\hat{\gamma}_\Delta)$ are easily computed from the residuals of the corresponding regressions. In the single equation case, Gallant (1975a) has investigated the power of this test for testing the simple hypothesis $\gamma = \gamma^*$ against $\gamma \neq \gamma^*$.

---

[2] Although most of our inferences will be based upon asymptotic likelihood ratio tests, we shall use confidence regions in one case in Chapter 5. The theoretical foundations for confidence regions are controversial, but rigorous measure theoretic foundations are now available from Barnett (1979a).

4.7. Asymptotic standard errors with nuisance parameters

4.7.1. The problem

We now seek standard errors for our estimators. First observe that if we seek standard errors for $\boldsymbol{\theta}$, we can appeal to theorems 4.1 and 4.2 to justify the use of the square roots of the diagonal elements of $\boldsymbol{B}_T^{-1}(\hat{\boldsymbol{\theta}})$. Now in one case in Chapter 5 we shall seek a standard error solely for $\hat{\alpha}$. By theorem 4.1 and corollary 4.1 to theorem 4.2, we could use $\sqrt{([\boldsymbol{B}_T^{-1}(\hat{\boldsymbol{\theta}})]_{11})}$; but computing and inverting the entire matrix $\boldsymbol{B}_T(\hat{\boldsymbol{\theta}})$ to acquire a scalar standard error is computationally highly inefficient. Since we will not use Newton's method in the next chapter, we will not have immediate access to $\boldsymbol{B}_T(\hat{\boldsymbol{\theta}})$. We seek a means to deal with this nuisance parameter problem.

We now manipulate an expression for $[\boldsymbol{B}_T^{-1}(\hat{\boldsymbol{\theta}})]_{11}$ analytically to provide a simplified formula for computation. An approach to simplifying the partitioned inverse of the Hessian of the log likelihood function was used successfully by Koopmans, Rubin, and Leipnik (1950, pp. 151–153) in the elimination of nuisance parameters from the full information maximum likelihood covariance matrix estimator for linear models. Although their result is derived and stated specifically for a well-defined class of linear models, the following use of a variant of their method indicates that their approach is not limited in applicability to linear models. A further generalization of our result is contained in Barnett (1976, sect. 5).

The method uses the concentrated likelihood function to eliminate parameter estimators the asymptotic distribution of which is of no interest. The validity of the use of the concentrated likelihood to simplify the computation of the maximum likelihood estimate itself is trivially valid, but its use to reduce the dimension of the information matrix requires rigorous theoretical support.

The following proof usually parallels the Koopmans, Rubin, and Leipnik proof, but without any linearity assumption. Our proof indicates that the use of the concentrated likelihood function for this purpose is valid whenever the relevant concentrated likelihood function exists and is twice differentiable. While the class of linear models that they consider guarantees the satisfaction of those existence and differentiability conditions, those conditions are undoubtedly satisfied by many widely used likelihood functions. It should, perhaps, be observed that their result is not precisely the same as ours. They are evaluating the information matrix, rather than the Hessian of the log likelihood function. But the approach appears to work for similar reasons in our case.

4.7.2. The concentrated likelihood function

We first must define the relevant concentrated likelihood function and some related functions. So let ϕ be the vector of all elements of θ (including the elements of Ω) other than α. Then let $k(\alpha|\,y,x)$ be the value of ϕ at which $L(\theta|\,y,x)$ is maximized conditionally upon α. Since the model that we shall be using in Chapter 5 is linear in β at any fixed α, the maximum likelihood estimate of ϕ conditionally upon α is the linear model maximum likelihood estimate of ϕ at α. It is known that in most linear models the maximum likelihood estimate exists and is unique. In our cases in Chapter 5, existence and uniqueness will be verified by extensive searches of the likelihood function. Hence, the function $k(\alpha|\,y,x)$ exists. In addition, since all of our maximum likelihood estimates were at the unique critical point of the relevant likelihood function, the estimate of ϕ at α satisfies the first- and second-order conditions for a local interior optimum, so

$$\left.\frac{\partial \log L(\theta|\,y,x)}{\partial \phi}\right|_{\phi=k(\alpha|\,y,x)} = 0, \quad \text{for all } \alpha \in R \tag{4.2}$$

and

$$\left.\frac{\partial \log L(\phi|\,y,x)}{\partial \phi' \partial \phi}\right|_{\phi=k(\alpha|\,y,x)} \text{ is negative definite.} \tag{4.3}$$

Now let $e(\theta|\,y,x) = \partial \log L(\theta|\,y,x)/\partial \phi$. Then by (4.2) and (4.3), it follows that

$$e(\alpha, \phi|\,y,x) = 0 \text{ at } \phi = k(\alpha|\,y,x), \quad \text{for all } \alpha \tag{4.4}$$

and

$$\left|\frac{\partial e}{\partial \phi'}\right|_{\phi=k(\alpha|\,y,x)} \neq 0. \tag{4.5}$$

Now at each α, $\phi = k(\alpha|\,y,x)$ is the unique solution for ϕ to the system of equations (4.4). So by (4.5) and the implicit function theorem, the functions k are differentiable in α. We assume that in fact k is twice differentiable.

We define the relevant concentrated likelihood function by $L^*(\alpha|\,y,x) = L(\alpha, k(\alpha|\,y,x)|\,y,x)$. Since L and k are both twice differentiable, so is L^*.

4.7.3. Asymptotic standard error

We can now state the theorem we intend to prove

Theorem 4.4.

$$\left[B_T^{-1}(\hat{\theta})\right]_{11} = -\frac{1}{\left.\dfrac{\partial^2 \log L^*(\alpha| y, x)}{\partial \alpha^2}\right|_{\alpha=\hat{\alpha}}},$$

where $\hat{\theta}$ and $\hat{\alpha}$ are the maximum likelihood estimates of θ_0 and α_0, respectively.

Recall that although our estimator may not be a global maximum likelihood estimator, our acquired estimates below will be maximum likelihood estimates. So to acquire our asymptotic standard error we need only compute the square root of minus the reciprocal of $\partial^2 \log L^*(\alpha| y, x)/\partial \alpha^2|_{\alpha=\hat{\alpha}}$. During the iterative procedure by which we shall find $\hat{\gamma}$, we shall compute the maximum likelihood estimate $k(\alpha| y, x)$ of ϕ at various α in the vicinity of $\hat{\alpha}$. So at each such α we can readily compute $L^*(\alpha| y, x) = L(\alpha, k(\alpha| y, x))$ to get points on the concentrated likelihood function in the vicinity of its maximum. Then $\partial^2 \log L^*(\alpha| y, x)/\partial \alpha^2|_{\alpha=\hat{\alpha}}$ can be computed by fitting a cubic spline to the points found on $\log L^*$ in the vicinity of $\hat{\alpha}$ and then by numerically differentiating the fitted spline twice.[3]

---

[3] This procedure is especially computationally simple using the commands INTERPOLATE and DIFFERENTIATE available in the Argonne Laboratory's SPEAKEASY language.

CHAPTER 5

DATA AND RESULTS

In this chapter we provide the empirical results for Part I of the book. We use the economic theory of Chapter 2, the specifications of Chapter 3, and the statistical theory of Chapter 4 to model consumer expenditure allocation jointly with leisure demand in accordance with the objectives defined in Chapter 1.

5.1. Description of the data

The data sources for Part I are provided in detail in Appendix D, section D1. We now briefly outline the data sources. Commodity consumption data was acquired from Kuznets (1961). The four categories of consumption expenditure are perishables, semidurables, durables, and services. Each will be viewed as a single "good". The data is annual and covers the years 1890–1955.

We used an implicit price deflator as the durables' price, although a rental price would have been theoretically preferable. Furthermore, all of our data terminates in 1955. Both of these difficulties were accepted to satisfy a more central objective: the acquisition of long-run data. Our objective is to capture long-run trends in leisure demand. The long-run trend towards increased leisure consumption is reputed to have been most dramatic during the earliest decades of this century and least evident after the Second World War. To prevent the cyclical behavior of leisure demand from obscuring the trend, we required data extending back to the start of the century. Kuznets' data provides the only consumption data available for both prices and quantities during those early decades. Unfortunately his data is not available after 1955 (although post-1955 data reputedly would carry only limited information about long-run leisure trends).

In addition, Kuznets' data contains neither rental price information nor the components required to construct such an index adequately or to decompose durables expenditures into their investment and rental (consumption) parts. With the available data, we could construct such series only under extremely strong and entirely unconvincing assumptions (on depreciation rates, etc.). Hence, we have adopted the widely used (if inelegant) alternative practice of fully depreciating all durables within one year. In effect we treat durables, semidurables, and perishables as if their lifetimes decreased in that order without ever exceeding one year. In fact this latter approach has been used widely even in cases in which data sources were less limited, since the alternative approaches are themselves controversial. See, for example, Theil (1975) and Abbott and Ashenfelter (1976). It nevertheless should be admitted that rental price and stock adjustment approaches are theoretically more elegant.

The years 1942–1945 were deleted from all of our data, since government-enforced rationing existed during those years. No First World War data was deleted, since no governmentally enforced rationing existed in this country during that war. However, it should be observed that informal private quantity rationing by retailers existed. So we shall investigate our First World War residuals with care.

The price of leisure data, appearing in table D1 of Appendix D, was computed as follows. First α was set equal to 2.3. As will be seen below, that is the maximum likelihood estimate under conditions that will be accepted in most of the work to follow. Then we computed a price of leisure series from $\hat{w} = wE^\alpha$. Finally, each of those prices was divided by the corresponding price in 1929 in accordance with our convention of deflating by 1929 prices. The resulting leisure index can be found in table D1.

Finally, it was necessary to generate a per capita leisure consumption series. Recall from eq. (2.4) of Chapter 2 that we have defined per capita leisure for the representative household to equal $\Gamma k_0 - (r_0/N_h)\bar{L}$. Since in table D1 we have not yet divided through by population to convert to a per capita basis, we seek aggregate leisure, which equals $zN_h\Gamma k_0 - zr_0\bar{L}$, where z is the number of households in the economy. Now zN_h is total population, while $zr_0\bar{L}$ is man-hours employed.

The value of k_0 was set to equal 4056 hours per year. It was computed as follows. Kuznets (1952, p. 64) estimated that the total number of hours per week available for work per able-bodied individual is 78 hours. So we set k_0 equal to 78×52, where 52 is the number of weeks in a year.

It remains only to determine Γ. Recall that in most applications, we shall not use a nonunitary scale factor, Γ, but will set Γ equal to 1. However, in some applications we shall set Γ equal to an upper bound on the labor force participation rate out of total population, in order to test for robustness in the definition of leisure. We now determine such an upper bound.

From Dewhurst et al. (1955, table 306, p. 725) we were able to compute the labor force participation rate out of total population up to the Second World War. For recent decades, that rate was computed from the *Economic Report of the President* (1973, tables B-21 and B-22). The rate was found to peak during the Second World War. It reached 0.477 in 1944, although it was 0.425 in 1940 and 0.423 in 1948. During recorded economic history, the rate has rarely exceeded 0.420, and in 1970 it stood at the relatively very high level of 0.419. The upper bound, Γ, will be set at 0.480.

The two "leisure consumption" series presented in table D1 were computed from the expression $zN_h\Gamma k_0 - zr_0\bar{L}$, with $\Gamma=1.0$ or $\Gamma=0.480$. The "leisure quantity" data in table D1 was valued at index year (1929) prices by multiplying leisure consumption (with $\Gamma=1.0$) by the 1929 wage rate.

5.2. The price of leisure

5.2.1. Estimation

In this section we present the results of our work with the CSE model (defined in Chapter 3). The objectives of that work relate to the investigation of our price of leisure equation, $\hat{w}=wE^\alpha$, the estimation of its parameter α, and the generation of the price of leisure data series presented in table D1.

In estimating the CSE model we define the $n+1$st of the $n+1$ goods to be leisure, and we eliminate the $n+1$st price by the substitution of the equation $p_{n+1}=wE^\alpha$. This introduces parameter nonlinearity into the CSE model in its price of leisure term and in its income term. The Divisia real income index, used both with the CSE and Rotterdam models, depends upon all prices, including the price of leisure.

During estimation we accepted the simplifications to the CSE model made possible by the elimination of constraints by substitution, as described in section 3.2. We then derived the likelihood function and eliminated all remaining parameter restrictions by substitution into the likelihood function. Since the restrictions can be solved for more than one subset of the parameters, we can effect this substitution in various ways.

We did so to acquire estimates and standard errors for our estimators of each of the model's coefficients.

The theory relevant to our estimation procedure was presented in Chapter 4. As described in that chapter, our theory relates to the maximum likelihood estimate whenever it is unique. If it were not unique, we would have to use our postulated iterative generalized least squares procedure to find a consistent root of the likelihood equation, in accordance with result 4.1 in section 4.2. But during searches of the likelihood function, we invariably located a unique local optimum. Hence, all Chapter 4 results apply immediately.

At any given value of α, our model is linear in all remaining parameters. Furthermore, our theory tells us that α is positive. So a reasonable procedure is to set α iteratively at various positive values and compute the resulting maximum likelihood estimates of the remaining parameters conditionally upon α to acquire the concentrated likelihood function. We seek the value of α resulting in the largest conditional maximum of the likelihood function. For this purpose we initially used the data generated without the scaling factor Γ in the definition of the price of leisure (or equivalently we set $\Gamma = 1$). We then ran a course search on α (including $\alpha = 0$, as a check on our theory).

Recall from Chapter 4 that the maximum likelihood estimates can be located by minimizing the generalized variance of the fit, $|N(\gamma)|$, where $N(\gamma)$ is defined in eq. (4.1). Fig. 5.1 presents the values of $|N(\gamma)|$ for various preset values of α (the first element of γ), with the rest of the parameters set at their maximum likelihood estimates conditionally upon α. Fig. 5.1 is then inversely related to the concentrated likelihood function (concentrated in α) defined in section 4.7.

We see that $|N(\gamma)|$ is rising very steeply in the vicinity of $\alpha = 0$, so that the likelihood function is dropping rapidly in that vicinity. Similarly, we see that the likelihood function has dropped to a relatively very low value for α greater than 10. In fact searches for α as high as 60 verified that the likelihood function continues dropping for α in excess of 10. There is no point in searching at higher values of α. For such high levels of α the price of leisure is effectively zero for all E. Observe that in our data the employment rate is defined in such a manner that it never attains one, so that $\hat{w} = wE^\alpha$ is approximately zero for all E at sufficiently high α. Hence, we would expect that if the likelihood value is very low for large α, then the maximum likelihood estimate could not lie at an even higher α. A fine search in the vicinity of the optimum was used to determine that $\hat{\alpha} = 2.26$, which we generally round off to be 2.3.

As discussed earlier, estimates of the other parameters of the CSE model will be used largely to verify conclusions later reached with the Rotterdam model. The maximum likelihood estimates of the CSE model are presented in table 5.1.[1] To provide comparability with our Rotterdam Model results, the standard errors were computed conditionally upon $\alpha = 2.3$. In accordance with theorem 4.1 of Chapter 4, we can determine standard errors by computing the square roots of the diagonal elements of the reciprocal of minus the Hessian of the relevant log likelihood function. Since we are conditioning upon α, we are using a linear model maximum likelihood estimator, so we could appeal directly to Koopmans, Rubin, and Leipnik (1950, pp. 151–153) for our standard errors. As they proved, the relevant likelihood function for use in computing the Hessian is that which has been concentrated to eliminate the elements of the unknown covariance matrix. We do not seek standard errors for our estimator of the unknown covariance matrix.

In table 5.1 observe the low income elasticity of leisure and the low own price Slutsky elasticity of leisure. This is in agreement with conventional views on the demand for leisure and tends to support our contention that our price of leisure adjustment theory has permitted us to identify the long-run leisure demand function. However, observe that the Slutsky elasticity of the demands for durables and for semidurables with respect to the price of leisure are larger and have high t-ratios. Their positive signs indicate that leisure is a substitute for durables and for semidurables. This interaction is in agreement with one's intuition about the relationship between leisure and time-saving goods. As would be expected, the effect is larger for durables than for semidurables, both in terms of the size of the cross price elasticity and of its t-ratio (the ratio of the estimate to its standard error). Cross elasticities between the demand for leisure and the prices of goods are very low. But the precision (t-ratios) of their estimates

---

[1] In all instances in which maximum likelihood estimation is used in Part I, the parameter estimates and standard errors are acquired through the use of the Newton method iteration available from the Chapman and Fair FIML program described in Fair (1972). This is a very powerful and highly efficient program. However, the potential user should be aware of certain difficulties in its coding. The formula used by the program to compute the standard errors of restricted parameters is wrong, except in the case of a restriction imposing equality between two parameters. However, the standard errors for estimators of unrestricted parameters are correct. Since the restrictions can be rearranged to restrict different parameters, one can usually rearrange the parameter restrictions and rerun the regression enough times to acquire valid standard errors for all parameter estimators. That procedure was followed in this research. On should also be aware that the program's ability to read in data by observations appears to be impaired. It is considerably safer to use the program's unlimited ability to read in data by variables. The computational efficiency of the algorithms and coding techniques used in the program is very high.

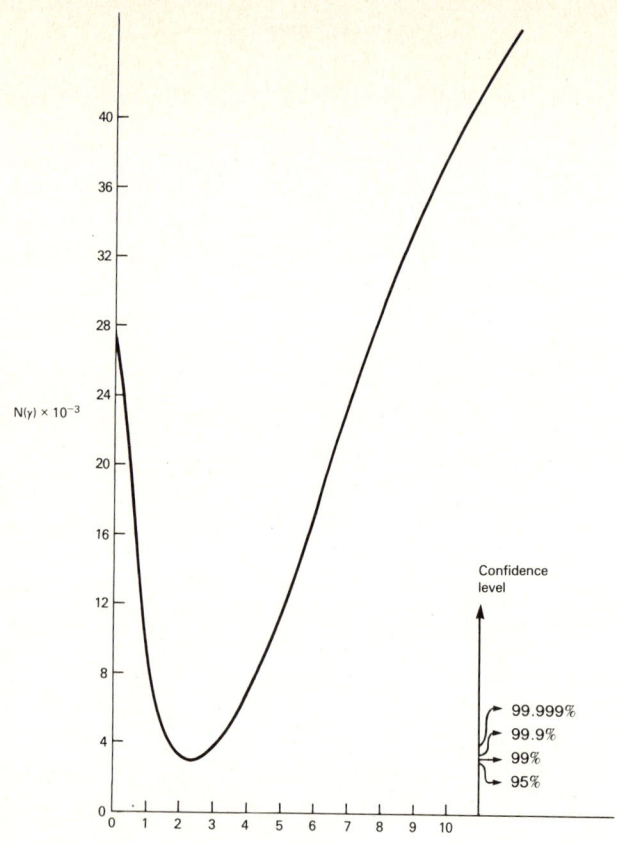

Figure 5.1. Generalized variance of the fit as α is varied.

Table 5.1
Maximum likelihood estimates of the CSE model (no intercept, $\alpha = 2.3$, $\Gamma = 1$).

Equation	Income elasticity	Slutsky price elasticities					D.W.
		Perishables	Semidurables	Durables	Services	Leisure	
Perishables	2.187	−0.302	0.073	0.068	0.032	0.130	2.097
	(0.377)	(0.057)	(0.023)	(0.029)	(0.037)	(0.054)	
Semidurables	1.074	0.220	−0.625	−0.075	0.075	0.405	2.193
	(0.442)	(0.068)	(0.071)	(0.052)	(0.052)	(0.063)	
Durables	3.938	0.282	−0.103	−0.877	−0.108	0.806	2.201
	(0.923)	(0.120)	(0.071)	(0.113)	(0.102)	(0.123)	
Services	3.296	0.035	0.027	−0.028	−0.172	0.138	2.310
	(0.341)	(0.041)	(0.019)	(0.026)	(0.047)	(0.046)	
Leisure	0.299	0.022	0.023	0.033	0.022	−0.101	2.117
	(0.087)	(0.009)	(0.004)	(0.005)	(0.007)	(0.014)	

Note: Standard errors computed conditionally upon $\alpha = 2.3$ are in parentheses.

is large in the cases of the interactions with respect to durables and semidurables.

The general properties of the model are as desired. All income elasticities are positive and are estimated with satisfactory precision. All own price elasticities are negative, and they are all estimated with considerable precision. Observe that in every equation, the largest Slutsky elasticity (in absolute value) is that with respect to the price of leisure.

5.2.2. Robustness to rescaling of leisure

In table 5.2 we have repeated the above process using our scale factor, Γ. With the resulting redefined leisure series, the maximum likelihood estimate of α increased to 3.1. All of our observations about table 5.1 are equally as applicable to table 5.2. Since Γ leads to a large rescaling of leisure, we see that our inferences are robust to the definition of leisure. This is particularly evident from a comparison of the t-ratios between the two tables. However, the changes in the estimates are large, as would be expected from the large changes in the leisure and income data resulting from the use of Γ. However, the information we seek is contained in the signs of the coefficients, the *relative* sizes of the coefficients, and the magnitude of the t-ratios. Our inferences are unchanged by the use of Γ. Since there are no apparent gains from scaling down leisure, we shall formulate our model without Γ (that is, with $\Gamma = 1$) to include the full value of leisure and to avoid the use of a relatively arbitrary constant.

It is interesting to consider the effect of Γ on our estimate of α. Considering the size of the rescaling of leisure, the change in α from 2.3 to

Table 5.2
Maximum likelihood estimates of the CSE model (no intercept, $\alpha = 3.1$, $\Gamma = 0.48$).

Equation	Income elasticity	Slutsky price elasticities					D.W.
		Perishables	Semidurables	Durables	Services	Leisure	
Perishables	1.142	−0.298	0.075	0.078	0.042	0.102	2.101
	(0.186)	(0.052)	(0.022)	(0.027)	(0.035)	(0.041)	
Semidurables	0.640	0.229	−0.617	−0.043	0.105	0.325	2.250
	(0.224)	(0.066)	(0.070)	(0.051)	(0.051)	(0.048)	
Durables	2.200	0.331	−0.060	−0.819	−0.063	0.611	2.251
	(0.465)	(0.116)	(0.072)	(0.112)	(0.100)	(0.093)	
Services	1.736	0.046	0.038	−0.016	−0.159	0.092	2.280
	(0.171)	(0.039)	(0.018)	(0.026)	(0.045)	(0.036)	
Leisure	0.432	0.059	0.062	0.083	0.049	−0.252	2.223
	(0.130)	(0.024)	(0.009)	(0.013)	(0.019)	(0.031)	

Note: Standard errors computed conditionally upon $\alpha = 3.1$ are in parentheses.

3.1 is not large. Now observe that with Γ, leisure's share is smaller than without Γ. Yet the increase in α indicates that the response of the price of leisure to employment changes has *increased*. By setting Γ to 1, we tend to minimize the response of the price of leisure series to the employment rate and to maximize its agreement with the wage rate.

5.2.3. Conclusions

Figure 5.2 presents the resulting price of leisure series along with the wage rate series. They are scaled so that percentage changes, but not levels, are comparable between series. In agreement with our data conventions, the price of leisure and the wage rate (as well as all other prices) equal one in

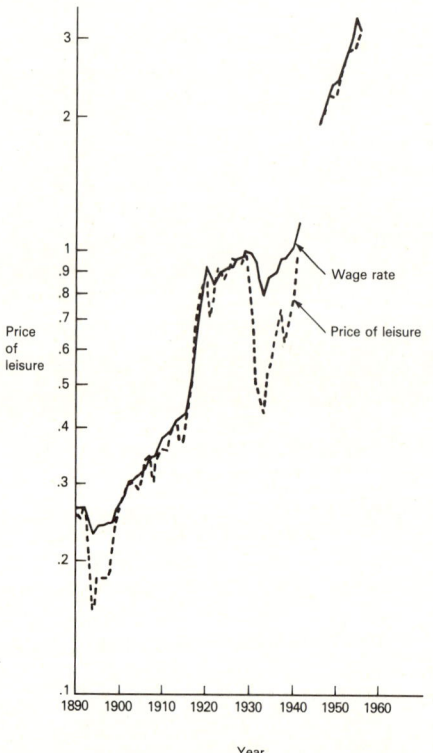

Figure 5.2. Comparison of the wage rate and the shadow price of leisure.

1929. Observe that both series tend to experience similar percentage changes during nondepression years. Discrepancies occurred during the depressions of the 1890s and the 1930s. Also, observe that both series rose sharply during the two world wars.

The substitution between leisure time and durables appears to be a household analog to the substitution between labor time and capital in the theory of the firm. In production studies it has been found that labor's and capital's shares tend to remain constant. Figs. 5.3 and 5.4 indicate that leisure's and durables' shares tend to remain constant. Fig. 5.3 presents leisure's share (without Γ). Although there is some evidence of an increase after the Second World War, the series evidences little long-run trend. Fig. 5.4 presents durables' share both in total expenditure (full income) and in goods expenditure (excluding leisure). Observe that the stability of the share is greater when computed relative to full income, as we would hope. Large fluctuations in either of the series can be traced to wars or depressions.

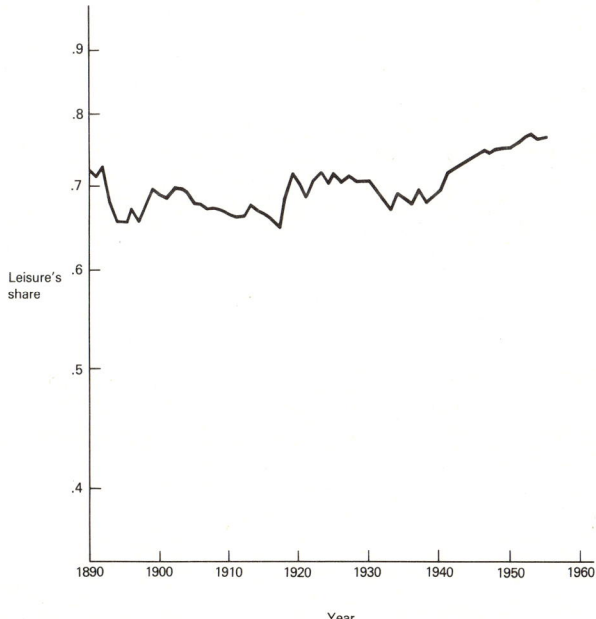

Figure 5.3. Stability over time of leisure's share of full income.

Figure 5.4. Stability of durables' share in full and in ordinary income.

5.3. Further discussion of price of leisure results

5.3.1. Precision

Since all of the standard errors above were computed conditionally upon α, we have no indication of the precision of our estimator of α. To acquire an asymptotic standard error for that estimator, we use theorem 4.4 of Chapter 4 and the numerical procedures described below that theorem. The result is a numerically computed standard error equal to 0.1. Since the maximum likelihood estimate was 2.26, the t-ratio is 22.6. The precision of our estimator is very high.

Since the standard error of our estimator of α was computed numerically, it would be desirable to have another indicator of the estimator's precision. We can do so by using the asymptotic likelihood ratio test criterion for testing $\alpha_0 = c$, for some c, to construct the corresponding confidence region. This procedure was used to construct a family of confidence regions for various confidence levels. Prior to constructing the confidence regions, the likelihood ratio tests of $\alpha = 0$ and of $\alpha = 1$ were computed. The relevant statistical theory is presented in section 4.6. In testing $\alpha=0$, the value of $-2\log\lambda$ was 135.96. Now with one degree of freedom, we can find from a table of the χ^2 distribution that $P[\chi^2(1)>21] = 10^{-6}$. So the tail area of the hypothesis is far below 10^{-6}. This is in agreement with our theory and leads to rejection of the hypothesis that the price of leisure equals the wage rate.

Christensen's (1968) and Grossman's (1973) method of acquiring price of leisure data is generated by setting $\alpha=1$ in our price of leisure equation. The value of $-2\log\lambda$ for that hypothesis test was 40.82. Again the tail area is less than 10^{-6}.

Now it is known that confidence regions generated using the asymptotic likelihood ratio criterion have boundaries of constant likelihood value, and in fact it is easily seen that our family of confidence regions for α can be found by horizontally sectioning the graph of the function in fig. 5.1 at various heights. The confidence levels associated with a few of such sections were computed and are displayed at the right-hand side of fig. 5.1. For example the 95 percent confidence interval is [2.23, 2.45].

As is now clear, the likelihood function not only discriminates strongly against values of α in the neighborhood of zero, but it also discriminates strongly against large values of α. The confidence levels tabulated in fig. 5.1 would suggest, for example, that the evidence against an α exceeding 4 is very great. But all of the models we shall be using, including the Rotterdam model, will converge to the corresponding model without leisure as $\alpha\to\infty$. This is easily seen from the fact that as $\alpha\to\infty$, the leisure price term disappears and full income converges to ordinary income. Hence, the likelihood function reflects unfavorably upon those values of α at which our model tends to approximate the CSE model without leisure. It is clear from the confidence levels displayed in fig. 5.1 that our numerically computed standard error of α does not overestimate the precision of our estimator.

5.3.2. Properties of the likelihood function

In fig. 5.5 we have plotted some ridge lines of the likelihood function. We have varied α and computed the maximum likelihood estimate of the Slutsky cross price elasticity of each good with respect to the price of leisure. These ridge lines were automatically generated by our search for $\hat{\alpha}$, in which we computed the maximum likelihood estimate of all other coefficients conditionally upon α at various α. It is interesting to observe that the cross price elasticities tend to be greatest in the vicinity of $\alpha=1$,

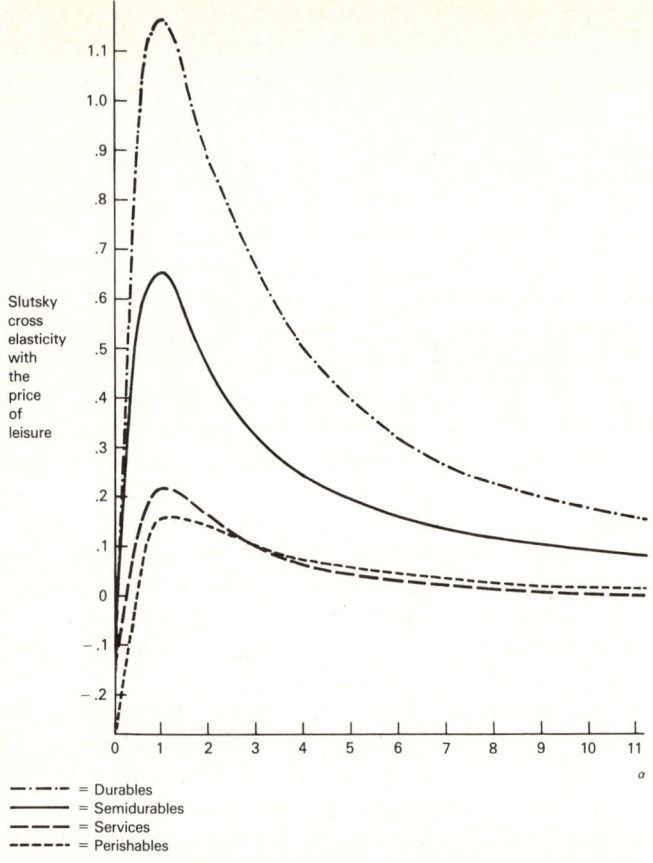

Figure 5.5. Slutsky cross elasticity of each good with the price of leisure.

which was Christensen's (1968) implicit choice. Also, observe that everywhere except in the vicinity of $\alpha = 0$ our conclusions about durables and semidurables obtain. Durables and semidurables remain Hicks–Allen substitutes for leisure, and the magnitude of that substitutability increases with increasing durability. Since the time saving characteristics of goods tend to increase with increasing durability, such results are as one might expect.

5.3.3. Relation to economic theory

Since we now have much information about α, it is interesting to consider the relation of our estimate of α to our price of leisure theory. Considering the size and precision of our estimate of α, the evidence against a zero value for α is great. In addition, the robustness of our conditional estimates of the Slutsky cross price elasticities to variation in α declines explosively as α approaches zero, and an implausible Hicks–Allen complementarity arises between leisure and each other good. Similarly, our economic theory excludes the possibility of $\alpha=0$. Furthermore, $\hat{\alpha}$ is positive, as our theory predicts.

Now consider the fact that an α of 2.3 in $\hat{w}=wE^{\alpha}$ leads to a rapid decrease in the price of leisure below the wage rate as the employment rate decreases. To relate this result to our price of leisure theory, suppose that the full-employment equivalent full-income level, $\hat{m}$, were not a function of the (shadow) price of leisure. Then the price of leisure would be the supply price of labor. But the wage rate is the demand price of labor. So if the supply of labor is inelastic, as is commonly believed and as is indicated by our estimated elasticities, the gap between the demand and supply price of leisure would tend to grow rapidly as the excess supply of labor increased. But in fact $\hat{m}$ *is* a function of the price of leisure.

To consider the effect of $\hat{m}$, recall that $\hat{m}=m-\ell(w-\hat{w})$. Hence, as the employment rate decreases, the decline in the price of leisure decreases the value of $\hat{m}$. Although we are holding m and w constant, $\bar{\ell}=k_0-\bar{L}$ will increase as the employment rate and hours of work decrease. This will further decrease $\hat{m}$. Now we have assumed, and our estimated income elasticities demonstrate, that leisure is a normal good. Thus, a decrease in income will increase the supply of labor. But the price of leisure is the supply price of labor with income adjusted to its equivalent full-income level. So with $\hat{m}$ dropping below m, we find that the price of leisure drops to a level that is even lower than the one we postulated in the previous paragraph. Hence, our price of leisure theory suggests that the price of leisure should tend to drop rapidly as the employment rate decreases. Our estimate of $\alpha=2.3$ is in agreement with our theory.

5.3.4. Extraneous estimation

In the next section we shall use the price of leisure series acquired in the current section but not the same demand model. Since we shall be conditioning upon our price of leisure series as data, it is useful to reconsider its properties. The great precision of our estimator of the parameter α in our price of leisure formula results from the severity of the unique optimum of the highly regular concentrated likelihood function, L^*. By comparison, Owen's (1964) single equation approach resulted in a very shallow optimum requiring an essentially arbitrary choice of the parameter of his linear leisure price specification. Although our current estimator of α must be treated as an extraneous estimator in the following sections, our extraneous estimator appears to be very good. In fact, the entire current section could be viewed as simply presenting an extremely elaborate data correction procedure permitting adjustment of the wage rate closer to the theoretical shadow price of leisure. Observe that $\hat{w}$ and w are competing indices of the price of the same good: nonmarket time; and w is nested within our formula for $\hat{w}$, since $\hat{w}=w$ when $\alpha=0$. Our approach is not subject to the methodological problems involved in the use of "shadow prices" in the household production function approach to demand modeling, in which goods prices and shadow prices are imputed to fundamentally different quantity constructs (see Chapter 8).

The use of an extraneous estimator for α is necessary in our case, since the Rotterdam model (to be used in the rest of this chapter), in its usual form, does not exist with α unknown. This results from the fact that all prices, including the price of leisure, are imbedded in the model's endogenous variables. An endogenous variable, by definition, cannot be a function of an unknown parameter. If we were to redefine the endogenous variables in a manner avoiding this difficulty, the model would become a nonlinear structural form extremely deeply nonlinear in its endogenous variables (as well as in its parameters). Furthermore, the Jacobian would become nonunitary, thereby destroying invariance of the maximum likelihood estimator to the equation deleted. In addition, "income" would become a function both of endogenous variables and of unknown parameters, rather than just itself being a predetermined variable (see Theil, 1976, ch. 8). Clearly, when prices are exogenous, the use of the left-hand side of the Rotterdam model's specification as its endogenous variable is inherent to the existing econometric foundations of our model. In fact, it also is inherent to the model's theoretical foundations which are based upon the explanation of share transitions.

The use of our specification of the shadow price of leisure as the "price of leisure" raises only minor empirical difficulties. Recall that our price of leisure data was computed from the formula $\hat{w}=wE^\alpha$. Since both E and w are exogenous, the price of leisure remains predetermined. Since our extraneous estimator for α possessed extremely high asymptotic precision, the "data" on $\hat{w}$ is good. Nevertheless, the robustness of our inferences to α will be explored below and will be found to be high. Of course, we condition upon all of our data (including $\hat{w}$) with the sobering knowledge that potentially serious data problems always exist.

Observe that a price of leisure adjustment such as ours is necessitated by our unwillingness to impose weak separability in leisure. Commonly one adjusts leisure consumption, rather than $\hat{w}$ and m, by adjusting employment to a "labor force" value and employed hours per worker to a "desired" hours per worker. But without weak separability in leisure, such an adjustment invalidly would alter preferences in other goods. Also note that without weak separability in leisure, we must keep leisure consumption in the utility function during our analysis of commodity consumption allocation, even when leisure consumption is determined involuntarily. Otherwise variations in leisure consumption would appear to shift preferences in other goods.

5.3.5. Empirical objectives of rest of chapter

Conventionally, labor economists have modeled a decision problem in which full income is allocated over leisure and aggregate goods consumption, while demand modelers have estimated systems consistent with the allocation of aggregate goods consumption expenditure over individual goods. This dichotomized approach requires the consumer to allocate full income over goods and leisure in two stages. But recently the literature on the allocation of time has motivated ongoing research on the joint modeling of leisure and goods demand. That research has been directly linked with concerns regarding the efficiency and allocative effects of wage and commodity taxes. This relationship has been considered at length by Abbott and Ashenfelter (1976), with particular emphasis on the negative income tax. Furthermore, if the two-stage decision should not satisfactorily approximate reality, leisure could be the "shift variable" causing the apparent taste change found in many second stage (goods-only expenditure allocation) goods demand models.

In addition a model of joint goods and leisure consumption could result in significant differences in forecasts of the cyclical behavior of durables consumption; we shall find that substitutability with leisure is important in explaining the behavior of time-saving durables demand. Similarly, changes in the allocation of goods expenditure could be the "shift variable" responsible for the apparent post-Second World War structural shift in the long-run trend in leisure consumption in first stage labor supply models (aggregating over all goods). We shall test the separability conditions necessary for consistency of the two-stage decision. In addition, our model of leisure and goods consumption will be explored for trends in tastes, for robustness (to our shadow price of leisure index and our leisure quantity index), and for satisfactory error structure properties. Our model will be found to have excellent properties and to evidence no unexplained structural shifts.

Since our objectives require the use of long-run time series data, our weak separability test must be carried out at the aggregate level. But current widely used demand systems acquire a link with theory at the aggregate level only if a community utility function exists, and such aggregate utility functions now are known to exist only under unacceptably strong assumptions. We shall use the version of the Rotterdam model derived in Chapter 3 under assumptions considerably weaker than those necessary for the existence of a community utility function. We shall derive results needed to implement that theory in practice. We will also test for the statistical significance of the (probably small) additive remainder term that appeared in the derivation in Chapter 3.

In section 5.4 we present our version of the aggregate absolute price version of the Rotterdam model, and we derive theorems permitting computation of elasticities from the model and providing a test for our separability conditions. In section 5.5 we present our estimates and explore the properties of our estimated model. In section 5.6 we present our separability test, and in section 5.7 we estimate the relative price version of the Rotterdam model. An extensive residual analysis and an information theoretic investigation of fit are contained in sections 5.8 and 5.9, respectively. In section 5.10 we summarize.

5.4. The specification

5.4.1. The model

We will estimate jointly a complete system of commodity and leisure demand functions. We then explore the gains provided by this approach relative to the conventional two-stage approach (presented in Chapter 1) dichotomizing consumer demand from labor supply studies. The system of demand functions that will be used to model the full joint decision is the version of the Rotterdam model derived in Chapter 3. The use of the Rotterdam model with leisure included involves treating leisure as another good. Although (full) income itself depends upon the price of leisure, the form of the Rotterdam Model (or of any other demand model) is not changed by the inclusion of leisure, since the existence of nonlabor sources of full current expenditure ("income") ensures that income can be varied independently of the price of leisure. We now briefly summarize relevant results from Chapter 3 on our specification.

The symbol D will denote the log change operator. That is, $Da_t = \log a_t - \log a_{t-1}$. Let k be an arbitrarily chosen "good" from the $n+1$ goods (including leisure). Define the set $S = \{1, \ldots, n+1\} - \{k\}$, and define $\hat{p}$ to be the vector $(p', \hat{w})'$. We now apply theorem 3.2 to eq. (3.29) to obtain our specification

$$W_{it}^* DQ_{it} = \bar{\mu}_i D\overline{M}_t + \sum_{j \in S} \bar{\pi}_{ij}(D\hat{p}_{jt} - D\hat{p}_{kt}) + \varepsilon_{it}, \quad i = 1, \ldots, n+1, \quad (5.1)$$

where $\hat{p}_t$ is the tth observation on $\hat{p}$; Q_{it}, $i = 1, \ldots, n+1$, is a quantity index of aggregate per capita consumption of the ith good during period t (where the $n+1$st "good" is leisure); $\overline{M}_t$ is a Divisia index of aggregate per capita real income during period t; and W_{it}^* is an index of the average per capita expenditure share of good i during the transition between periods $t-1$ and t. The formulae for computing these indices are discussed in Theil (1976, chs. 3 and 4). The model's parameters are the $\bar{\mu}_i$ and the $\bar{\pi}_{ij}$ values. We accept the assumptions used in Chapter 3 to derive (5.1). The constants $\bar{\pi}_{ij}$ ($i, j = 1, \ldots, n+1$) are called the model's aggregate Slutsky coefficients, and the constants $\bar{\mu}_i$ ($i = 1, \ldots, n+1$) are called the model's aggregate marginal budget shares.

Furthermore, we know from theorem 3.2 that

$$\sum_{i=1}^{n+1} \bar{\mu}_i = 1, \quad (5.2)$$

$$\bar{\pi}_{ij} = \bar{\pi}_{ji}, \quad \text{for } i, j = 1, \ldots, n+1, \quad (5.3)$$

the matrix $[\bar{\pi}_{ij}]$ is negative semidefinite and of rank n, (5.4)

$$\sum_{j=1}^{n+1} \bar{\pi}_{ij} = 0, \quad \text{for } i = 1, \ldots, n+1. \quad (5.5)$$

The disturbance terms ε_t are assumed to be distributed independently and identically as $N(\mathbf{0}, \Omega)$. It can be shown that Ω must be singular. However, Barten (1969) has proved that with given price data, one equation is redundant, and the maximum likelihood estimates of the parameters are invariant to the equation deleted. Restriction (5.2) implicitly is imposed when we delete an arbitrary equation. In acquiring (5.1) from (3.29), we already have imposed restrictions (5.5) by substitution. So in estimating the remaining equations the only equality restrictions we need impose are the symmetry conditions, (5.3). Restrictions (5.4) will not be imposed, although we shall check them.

5.4.2. Further model properties

Our theoretical foundations (5.1), (5.2), (5.3), (5.4), and (5.5) have already been derived in Chapter 3. But in our applications of that theory below, we shall also require elasticity estimates and a weak separability test. We now derive the theoretical results needed to satisfy those objectives. The following results are based upon those of Barnett (1979b).

We begin by deriving a condition on the macroparameters necessary for weak separability in leisure of each consumer's utility function. We use the notations $E(\cdot)$, $\text{cov}(\cdot)$, and $\text{var}(\cdot)$ to designate the expectation, covariance, and variance, respectively, over the population of consumers at a given point in time. More rigorously defined, they are computed with respect to the joint distribution of taste-determining variables and income. Let us assume that each consumer's utility function is weakly separable in leisure, and let us define $\bar{k}$ to equal Ek_c, where k_c is consumer c's value of $c(m, \hat{p})$ defined in eq. (1.2) of Chapter 1. Define ρ_i to equal the correlation coefficient between k_c and μ_{ic}^*, where $\mu_{ic}^* = m_c \mu_{ic}/Em_c$. For any random variable X_c, we shall define $\bar{V}(X_c)$ to be the coefficient of variation of X_c. That is, $\bar{V}(X_c) = (\text{var}\, X_c)^{1/2}/EX_c$. We now prove the following theorem.

Theorem 5.1. If each consumer's utility function is weakly separable in leisure ("good" number $n+1$), then

$$\bar{\pi}_{i,n+1} = \bar{k}\bar{\mu}_i(1+\Delta_i), \quad \text{for all } i=1,\ldots,n, \tag{5.6}$$

where $\Delta_i = \rho_i \bar{V}(k_c)\bar{V}(\mu_{ic}^*)$.

Proof. From eq. (1.2) of Chapter 1, we easily can determine that $\pi_{i,n+1,c} = k_c \mu_{ic}$ for all $i=1,\ldots,n$, where $\pi_{i,n+1,c}, k_c$, and μ_{ic} are each functions of $(m_c, \hat{p})$. Multiplying through by m_c/Em_c and taking the expectation of each side, we get that $\bar{\pi}_{ij} = \bar{k}\bar{\mu}_i + \phi_i$, where $\phi_i = \text{cov}(k_c, \mu_{ic}^*)$. But $\phi_i = \rho_i(\text{var}\, k_c)^{1/2}(\text{var}\, \mu_{ic}^*)^{1/2} = \rho_i \bar{V}(k_c)\bar{V}(\mu_{ic}^*)\bar{k}\bar{\mu}_i$. Hence eq. (5.6) follows immediately. Q.E.D.

We now briefly discuss the plausible magnitude of the expression $\Delta_i = \rho_i \bar{V}(k_c)\bar{V}(\mu_{ic}^*)$ appearing in eq. (5.6). First observe that necessarily

$|\rho_i| \leq 1$. Furthermore, consideration of its definition suggests that high $|\rho_i|$ would correspond to an extreme special case. Subjectively we would expect $\frac{1}{2}$ to represent a very conservative upper bound on the value of $|\rho_i|$ for all $i = 1, \ldots, n$.

Now observe that k_c is likely to have the same sign for a very large percentage of the consumers, c. So if, for example, k_c were assumed to be normally distributed (prior to the random drawing of a consumer), we would expect $|\overline{V}(k_c)|$ to be less than $\frac{1}{3}$. In fact, examination of eq. (1.2) of Chapter 1 suggests the use of $\frac{1}{3}$ as a plausible upper bound on $|\overline{V}(k_c)|$ regardless of any distributional assumptions.

Similarly, μ_{ic}^* is likely to have the same (positive) sign for the vast majority of consumers for each of the highly aggregated (plausibly normal) goods, $i = 1, \ldots, n$, in our data. By the analogous argument to that on $|\overline{V}(k_c)|$, we would expect $|\overline{V}(\mu_{ic}^*)|$ to be small. However, available income distribution data and the role of m_c in μ_{ic}^* suggests that $|\overline{V}(\mu_{ic}^*)|$ could be as high as $\frac{1}{2}$ (as opposed to our tighter $\frac{1}{3}$ bound on $|\overline{V}(k_c)|$). More detailed speculations on the magnitude of $\overline{V}(\mu_{ic}^*)$ can be found in Theil (1975, p. 158), and Theil's conclusions are in agreement with our $\frac{1}{2}$ bound over the range of $\bar{\mu}_i$ values encountered in our results.

Combining our conclusions above, we find for any $i = 1, \ldots, n$ that $|\Delta_i| = |\rho_i| |\overline{V}(k_c)| |\overline{V}(\mu_{ic}^*)| \leq \frac{1}{2} \times \frac{1}{3} \times \frac{1}{2} = \frac{1}{12}$.

Hence, the variable Δ_i typically will be globally small in absolute value (perhaps less than $\frac{1}{12}$). Hence, eq. (5.6) can be approximated globally by

$$\bar{\pi}_{i,n+1} = \bar{k}\bar{\mu}_i, \quad \text{for all } i = 1, \ldots, n. \tag{5.7}$$

We have our test for weak separability.

Observe that under our assumptions in Chapter 3, the results (5.2), (5.3), (5.4), and (5.5) all obtain exactly. Unfortunately, similar elegance (without additional assumptions) was not possible in acquiring (5.7), and further investigation into the properties of that approximation could be useful. It also should be observed that (5.6) is necessary but not sufficient for weak separability of each consumer's utility function in leisure. Rejection of (5.6) (through rejection of (5.7)) implies rejection of weak separability. But our assumptions are far too weak to provide any criterion sufficient for acceptance of weak separability in leisure of every consumer's preferences. At most, we have one necessary (but not sufficient) condition for acceptance of weak separability, although in fact we shall end up rejecting weak separability.

We require a means of deducing elasticity aggregates from our estimated macroparameters. Let $M = (1/N)\sum_{c=1}^{N} m_c$, and let $W_i = \hat{p}_i Q_i / M$. Throughout this discussion we will suppress the time subscript, t, although it should be understood to exist. Also, let $\eta_{ij} = (\hat{p}_i / Q_i)(\partial Q_i / \partial \hat{p}_j)$ with the differentiation performed while each consumer's utility level is held constant. Then η_{ij} is the aggregate Hicks–Allen (Slutsky) cross price elasticity of good i with respect to the price of good j. Observe that each factor in η_{ij} is aggregated separately over the complete consumer population. A different aggregate elasticity index would be acquired if we averaged over each consumer's complete elasticity function to get

$$\frac{1}{N} \sum_{c=1}^{N} (\hat{p}_j / q_{ic}) \frac{\partial q_{ic}}{\partial \hat{p}_j}\bigg|_{u_c}.$$

In the proof of the following theorem we shall be using the population expenditure share $\bar{w}_i = \hat{p}_i E(q_{ic}) / E m_c$. In the conventional manner, we use the notation $X_N = \theta + o_p(1)$ in our proof to indicate that X_N converges in probability to θ as $N \to \infty$.

Theorem 5.2. The absolute value of $\eta_{ij} - \bar{\pi}_{ij} / W_i$ converges in probability to zero as the number of consumers, N, goes to infinity for all $i, j = 1, \ldots, n+1$.

Proof. Let

$$\bar{\eta}_{ij} = (\hat{p}_j / E q_{ic}) E\left(\frac{\partial q_{ic}}{\partial \hat{p}_i}\bigg|_{u_c}\right).$$

Then we see that

$$\bar{\pi}_{ij} = \frac{E(m_c \pi_{ijc})}{E m_c} = \frac{\hat{p}_i \hat{p}_j}{E m_c} E\left(\frac{\partial q_{ic}}{\partial \hat{p}_j}\bigg|_{u_c}\right) = \bar{\eta}_{ij} \bar{w}_i. \tag{5.8}$$

By Khintchine's theorem and assumption 3.1 of section 3.5, we also know that $Q_i = E q_{ic} + o_p(1)$, $M = E m_c + o_p(1)$, and

$$\frac{\partial Q_i}{\partial \hat{p}_j} = \frac{1}{N} \sum_{c=1}^{N} \frac{\partial q_{ic}}{\partial \hat{p}_j}\bigg|_{u_c} = E\left(\frac{\partial q_{ic}}{\partial \hat{p}_j}\bigg|_{u_c}\right) + o_p(1).$$

So by Slutsky's theorem (on weak convergence), we find that $\eta_{ij} W_i = \bar{\eta}_{ij} \bar{w}_i + o_p(1)$. Hence, by (4.10), it follows that $\eta_{ij} W_i = \bar{\pi}_{ij} + o_p(1)$. Thus, $|\eta_{ij} - \bar{\pi}_{ij} / W_i| = o_p(1)$. Q.E.D.

Hence we find that for sufficiently large N we can approximate η_{ij} globally by $\bar{\pi}_{ij}/W_i$ arbitrarily well with arbitrarily high probability, and of course N is indeed extremely large. We now seek a comparable result for aggregate income elasticities.

Let $f(m_c) = m_c / \sum_{a=1}^{N} m_a$, and then define the income weighted average of the income derivatives $\partial q_{ic}/\partial m_c$, $c = 1, \ldots, N$, for arbitrary good i by

$$Q_m^*(i) = \sum_{c=1}^{N} f(m_c) \frac{\partial q_{ic}}{\partial m_c}.$$

Define $\eta_{i0} = (M/Q_i) Q_m^*(i)$. Through the income weighting within $Q_m^*(i)$, our aggregated income elasticity, η_{i0}, for good i is weighted towards the rich. Also, note that each factor in η_{i0} is aggregated over consumers separately (as in our price elasticity indices). If aggregation were carried out directly over elasticities rather than over each individual factor in the elasticity, and if the index were not weighted towards the rich, we would get

$$\frac{1}{N} \sum_{c=1}^{N} \frac{m_c}{q_{ic}} \frac{\partial q_{ic}}{\partial m_c}$$

as the theoretical population index. We shall prove the following theorem.

Theorem 5.3. The absolute value of $\eta_{i0} - \bar{\mu}_i/W_i$ converges in probability to zero as the number of consumers, N, goes to infinity for all $i, j = 1, \ldots, n+1$.

Proof. Let

$$\bar{\eta}_{i0} = E\left(m_c \frac{\partial q_{ic}}{\partial m_c}\right) \bigg/ Eq_{ic}.$$

Then from the definition of $\bar{\mu}_i$, we see that

$$\bar{\mu}_i = \hat{p}_i \frac{E\left(m_c \dfrac{\partial q_{ic}}{\partial m_c}\right)}{Em_c} = \bar{w}_i \bar{\eta}_{i0}. \tag{5.9}$$

By Khintchine's theorem and Slutsky's theorem (on weak convergence), it follows under assumption 3.1 of Chapter 3 that $W_i = \bar{w}_i + o_p(1)$, $Q_i = Eq_{ic} + o_p(1)$, and

$$\frac{1}{N} \sum_{c=1}^{N} m_c \frac{\partial q_{ic}}{\partial m_c} = E\left(m_c \frac{\partial q_{ic}}{\partial m_c}\right) + o_p(1).$$

But we can rearrange η_{i0} to get that

$$\eta_{i0} = (1/N) \left[\sum_{c=1}^{N} m_c \frac{\partial q_{ic}}{\partial m_c} \right] / Q_i.$$

Hence, if follows from Slutsky's theorem that $W_i \eta_{i0} = \bar{w}_i \bar{\eta}_{i0} + o_p(1)$. Thus, by (5.9) we have that $W_i \eta_{i0} = \bar{\mu}_i + o_p(1)$, and therefore that $|\eta_{i0} - \bar{\mu}_i / W_i| = o_p(1)$.   Q.E.D.

Therefore we can approximate η_{i0} very well by $\bar{\mu}_i / W_i$. Cross section studies have tended to indicate that Engel curves frequently are concave. Hence, the income weighted index η_{i0} may frequently tend to be lower than the corresponding unweighted index. Thus tests for aggregate normality of goods based upon η_{i0} may tend to be conservative. However, in fact η_{i0} itself may be a more informative aggregate index than an unweighted population aggregate, since the income weighted index is likely to more accurately approximate the response of aggregate per capita demand to variations in aggregate per capita income. This follows from the fact that aggregate income increases are commonly distributed in greater absolute amounts to members of higher income groups.

5.5. Estimates (absolute price version)

In this section we estimate our version of the absolute price version of the Rotterdam model. We also explore some of the properties of the estimates and of our model.

5.5.1. The joint model

Recall that our data is annual US data covering the years 1890–1955. The data includes four "goods" in addition to leisure: perishables, semidurables, durables, and services. Our model consists of (5.1) subject to (5.2) and (5.3), and we use the system to model the solution to the full joint decision, in which leisure is treated as the $n+1$st good. Having constructed price of leisure data for both $\alpha = 3.1$ and $\alpha = 2.3$ to support our leisure quantity data with and without the scale factor, Γ, we now can proceed to estimate our version of the absolute price version of the Rotterdam model.

As we indicated in Chapter 3, the Rotterdam model in absolute prices is linear in its parameters. We shall seek maximum likelihood estimates using the Chapman–Fair FIML program. But we first need initial estimates of the parameters at which our Newton method iterations can begin. We use the usual two-step generalized least squares estimator available from the widely used Zellner Three Stage Least Squares program. In the first step we compute the restricted generalized least squares estimates with Ω set equal to the identity matrix. We then use the residuals to re-estimate Ω in the usual manner and recompute the restricted generalized least squares estimates using the new covariance matrix estimate. See Theil (1971, sect. 6.8 and ch. 7) for relevant statistical theory. The resulting coefficient estimates using data without the Γ scale factor are displayed in table 5.3. Using those estimates as initial values, we then compute the maximum likelihood estimates, which are displayed in table 5.4. The Koopmans, Rubin, and Leipnik (1950) standard errors were used in the computation of the t-ratios in table 5.4.

Table 5.3
Two-step generalized least squares estimates of the absolute price version of the Rotterdam model ($\alpha=2.3$, $\Gamma=1$, no intercept).

		Price coefficients				
Equation	$\bar{\mu}_i$	Perishables	Semidurables	Durables	Services	Leisure
Perishables	0.297	−0.039	0.011	0.007	0.003	0.017
Semidurables	0.060	0.011	−0.028	−0.004	0.003	0.017
Durables	0.093	0.007	−0.004	−0.022	−0.005	0.023
Services	0.358	0.003	0.003	−0.005	−0.020	0.018
Leisure	0.192	0.017	0.017	0.023	0.018	−0.075

Table 5.4
Maximum likelihood estimates of the absolute price version of the Rotterdam model (no intercept, $\alpha=2.3$, $\Gamma=1$).

		Price coefficients					
Equation	$\bar{\mu}_i$	Perishables	Semidurables	Durables	Services	Leisure	D.W.
Perishables	0.292	−0.039	0.010	0.008	0.002	0.018	2.149
	(0.047)	(0.008)	(0.003)	(0.004)	(0.004)	(0.007)	
Semidurables	0.056	0.010	−0.028	−0.003	0.003	0.018	2.206
	(0.018)	(0.003)	(0.003)	(0.002)	(0.002)	(0.003)	
Durables	0.098	0.008	−0.003	−0.023	−0.004	0.023	2.171
	(0.027)	(0.004)	(0.002)	(0.003)	(0.003)	(0.004)	
Services	0.357	0.002	0.003	−0.004	−0.019	0.017	2.291
	(0.039)	(0.004)	(0.002)	(0.003)	(0.006)	(0.005)	
Leisure	0.197	0.018	0.018	0.023	0.017	−0.076	2.076
	(0.061)	(0.007)	(0.003)	(0.004)	(0.005)	(0.009)	

Note: Standard errors are in parentheses.

Although it is known that the asymptotic efficiency of the two-step Aitken (generalized least squares) estimator is the same as that of the maximum likelihood estimator, the maximum likelihood estimates will be used. The author's prejudices on the subject lead him to believe that the small sample properties of the maximum likelihood estimator may be superior to those of the two-step procedure, and the asymptotic likelihood ratio criterion provides a particularly convenient hypothesis-testing technique. But, more significantly, the maximum likelihood estimator, unlike the two-step Aitken estimator, is invariant to the equation deleted (through imposition of the budget constraint). Since we do have a large sample (60 years of data), we should expect the estimates from the two procedures to be similar. Comparison of tables 5.3 and 5.4 verifies that fact and gives further substantial support to our use of large sample methods.

Observe that the results have the same favorable properties as those acquired for the CSE model. The first column provides the $\bar{\mu}_i$ values, which are the (aggregated) marginal budget shares. They are all positive and estimated with satisfactory precision, so all goods, including leisure, are normal goods. All own price coefficients are negative and estimated with considerable precision. Durables and semidurables remain Hicks–Allen substitutes for leisure and the corresponding cross price Slutsky coefficients are estimated with great precision. Observe that tables 5.1, 5.2, 5.3, and 5.4 all indicate complementarity between durables and both semidurables and services. This result is in striking contrast to the expected substitutability between durables and leisure that we have confirmed with large and precisely estimated Slutsky coefficients.

Recall that the matrix $[\bar{\pi}_{ij}]$, which is a square matrix of dimension $n+1$, should be negative semidefinite of rank n. We have imposed the rank n condition by deleting an equation during estimation. Hence, one characteristic root must be zero. But we have not forced the other roots to be negative, and hence we should check that negativity condition. The characteristic roots of our estimate of the matrix $[\bar{\pi}_{ij}]$ are $(-0.0948, -0.0481, -0.0261, -0.0152, 0)$. So our estimated matrix is negative semidefinite of rank $n=4$.

From the previous section we know that η_{ij} can be approximated by $\bar{\pi}_{ij}/w_i$, and η_{i0} can be approximated by $\bar{\mu}_i/w_i$, where the η_{ij} values are the aggregate Slutsky elasticities and the η_{i0} values are the aggregate income elasticities. In the Rotterdam model the $\bar{\pi}_{ij}$ and the $\bar{\mu}_i$ values are constant, but the shares, W_i, are not. So elasticities are not constant. However, if we compute the average shares, $\overline{W}_i$, over the observations, then $\hat{\bar{\pi}}_{ij}/\overline{W}_i$ and $\hat{\bar{\mu}}_i/\overline{W}_i$ provide estimates of average elasticities. They are presented in table

Table 5.5
Average elasticities from maximum likelihood estimation of the absolute price version of the Rotterdam model ($\alpha=2.3$, no intercept, $\Gamma=1$).

Equation	Income elasticity	Slutsky price elasticities				
		Perishables	Semidurables	Durables	Services	Leisure
Perishables	2.416	−0.322	0.086	0.066	0.020	0.151
	(0.392)	(0.062)	(0.023)	(0.031)	(0.040)	(0.055)
Semidurables	1.394	0.259	−0.700	−0.082	0.080	0.443
	(1.394)	(0.070)	(0.073)	(0.053)	(0.052)	(0.062)
Durables	3.364	0.274	−0.113	−0.797	−0.143	0.780
	(0.922)	(0.127)	(0.073)	(0.118)	(0.105)	(0.122)
Services	3.188	0.021	0.029	−0.037	−0.165	0.152
	(0.346)	(0.042)	(0.019)	(0.027)	(0.049)	(0.046)
Leisure	0.282	0.026	0.025	0.032	0.024	−0.108
	(0.087)	(0.010)	(0.004)	(0.005)	(0.007)	(0.013)

Note: Standard errors are in parentheses.

5.5. Since these elasticities are the parameters of the CSE model, we now have a direct comparison of the results from the two models. Comparing tables 5.3 and 5.5 we see that the agreement is close, both in terms of the coefficient estimates and their t-ratios. Some difference exists in the conclusions about interactions between perishables and services, but the precision of the corresponding Slutsky coefficient estimators was very low in both models. Observe that all goods have positive aggregate income elasticities estimated with considerable precision, so that all goods are normal goods, including leisure. Also observe that in the semidurables, durables, and services equations, the most important Slutsky cross elasticity, both in terms of the size and precision of its estimate, is that with leisure. By inspection of the diagonal of the matrix of aggregate Slutsky elasticities, we see that all aggregate own price Slutsky elasticities (including leisure's) are negative and are estimated with high precision. Leisure demand behaves like any other demand function.

This conclusion is in agreement with the relevant theory when full income rather than nonlabor income is our income variable. We have used full income as our income variable since its use is dictated by the intertemporal separability assumption required to acquire a single period decision in a multiperiod world (see Theil, 1976, ch. 8). Abbott and Ashenfelter's (1976) use of nonlabor income is consistent with their single period model only in a world in which lifetimes literally never exceed one year. In addition, their resulting version of the Rotterdam model depends jointly upon three different income concepts. Despite Abbott and Ashenfelter's interpretation, the log change income concept on which they concentrate most directly does not appear to be identifiable with the rate of change of any meaningful component of any nominal or real income index. It should, however, be observed that their approach does succeed in avoiding the need to select a value for the constant Γk_0.

As is commonly believed (from the postwar stability of workweek data), the leisure demand function is highly inelastic in all of its explanatory variables, including income and its own price. The use of the full-employment-equivalent (shadow) leisure price concept was intended to permit identification of a stable long-run leisure demand function. Our low leisure elasticities suggest that we have estimated such a function. Also, note that the precision of the estimator of leisure's own price aggregate Slutsky elasticity is very high.

5.5.2. Robustness

Since our results with the Rotterdam model are conditional upon prices, it is interesting to consider the robustness of our inferences to variations in the value of α imbedded in the price of leisure data adjustment. Most of our inferences are related to the signs of our coefficient estimates and the absolute values of the *t*-ratios. Since the (signed) values of the *t*-ratios carry all of that information, we can investigate the robustness of our inferences to variations in our price of leisure parameter, α, by plotting the *t*-ratio of each price and income coefficient estimate against α. This procedure is followed in figs. 5.6–5.10, with each such price and income coefficient estimated by its maximum likelihood estimate computed conditionally upon α.

Observe that for values of α greater than our estimate of 2.3, our inferences tend to remain unchanged. Precisely estimated coefficients tend to retain the same signs and to remain precisely estimated. But for α less than 1, the robustness of our inferences deteriorates rapidly. Recall that our price of leisure theory predicts the existence of an identification problem in the vicinity of $\alpha=0$, where the price of leisure equals the wage rate uniformly in the unemployment rate. See in particular, fig. 5.10. The precision of the estimator of the own price Slutsky coefficient remains very high for large α, and its sign remains negative. But as α drops towards zero, precision drops off drastically, and in the vicinity of $\alpha=0$ the sign of the *t*-ratio changes. This change in sign and low precision near $\alpha=0$ is dramatic evidence of the postulated identification problem. The sign

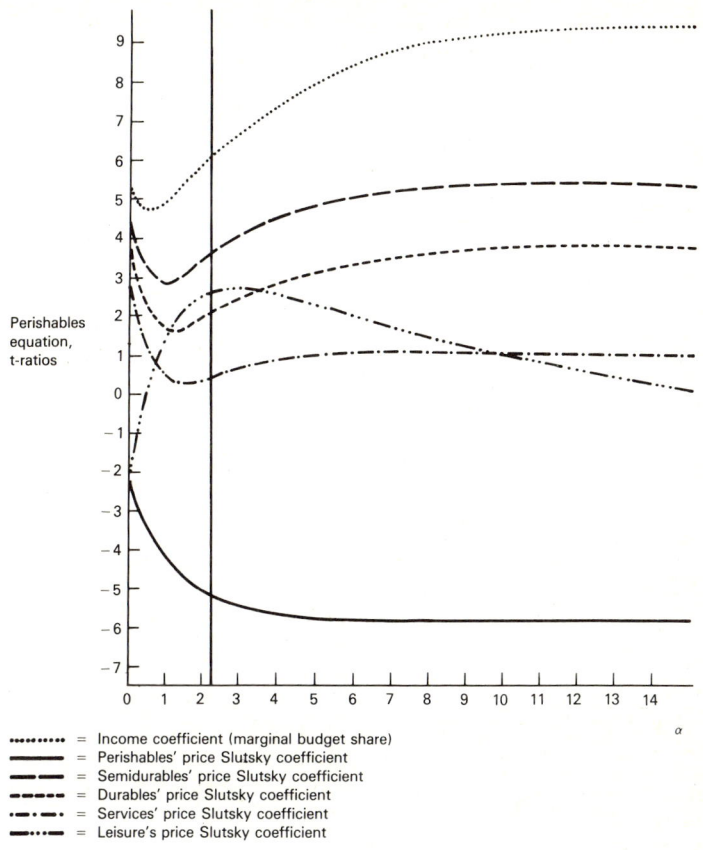

Figure 5.6. Each parameter's *t*-ratio in the perishables equation.

reversal reflects the properties of the demand for labor rather than those of its supply. The low precision indicates that supply and demand have been confounded. This is as we had expected. Hence, on empirical as well as theoretical grounds we see that the employment unadjusted wage rate is not the leisure price relevant to the joint estimation of a system of single period leisure and commodity demand functions.

Observe that the sign and precision of the estimators of the Slutsky cross effects with durables and semidurables remain high over all α greater than one. Also, observe the stability of the *t*-ratio of the marginal budget share estimator for all α greater than $\frac{1}{2}$; leisure is a normal good. Similar observations apply to figs. 5.6–5.9.

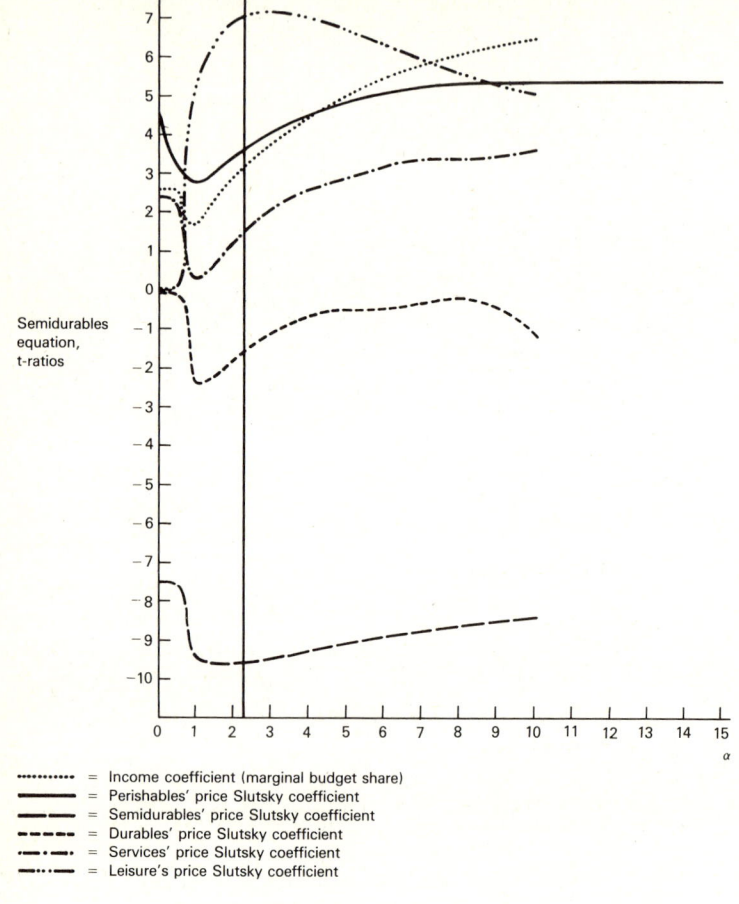

Figure 5.7. Each parameter's *t*-ratio in the semidurables equation.

Our results at (or near) $\alpha = 0$ strongly resemble Abbott and Ashenfelter's results with the Rotterdam model, all of which were acquired with wage rate data used directly as the price of leisure. Their estimates sometimes are puzzling and generally possess low precision. For example, their Slutsky compensated own price elasticity for housing was positive, and virtually their entire Slutsky matrix was statistically insignificant. We suspect that the use of the wage rate by Darrough (1977) as the price of leisure in his translog study (which did not test for separability in leisure)

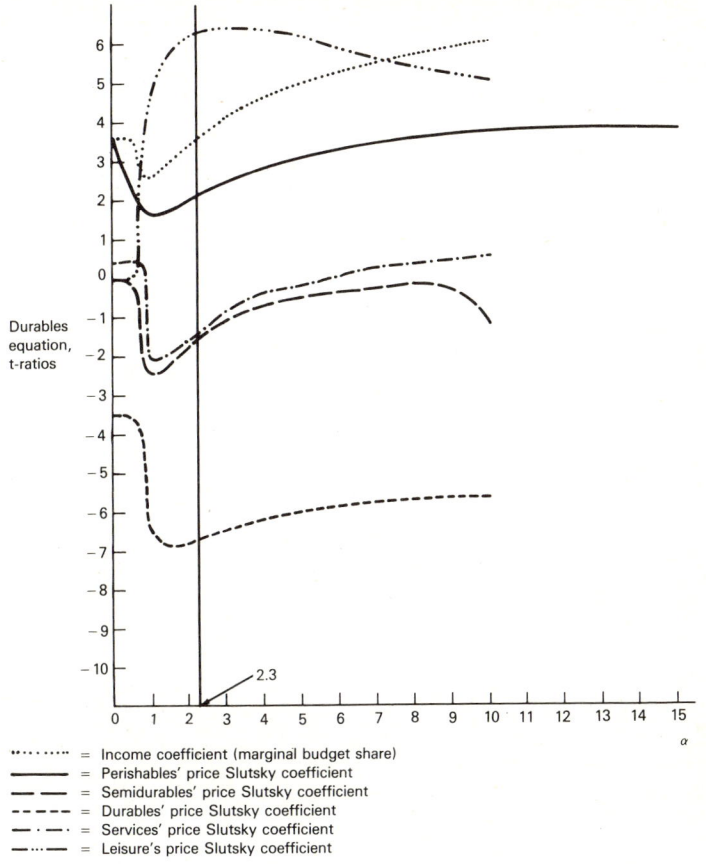

.... = Income coefficient (marginal budget share)
———— = Perishables' price Slutsky coefficient
— — = Semidurables' price Slutsky coefficient
- - - - - = Durables' price Slutsky coefficient
— · — · = Services' price Slutsky coefficient
— ··· — = Leisure's price Slutsky coefficient

Figure 5.8. Each parameter's t-ratio in the durables equation.

may be the source of his sign reversal problems. In his research, monotonicity and curvature conditions on the utility function were violated everywhere. His "representative consumer" maximized monotonically *decreasing* utility over a feasible set having the budget constraint as a *lower* bound. Similar difficulties also appear to exist in Kiefer (1975), although a source of particular interest in that paper lies in his use of a model within which both the Generalized Leontief and translog models are nested. Using Abbott and Ashenfelter's data and model, Kiefer (1977) acquired more plausible results using Bayesian methods to introduce prior theoretical information stochastically.

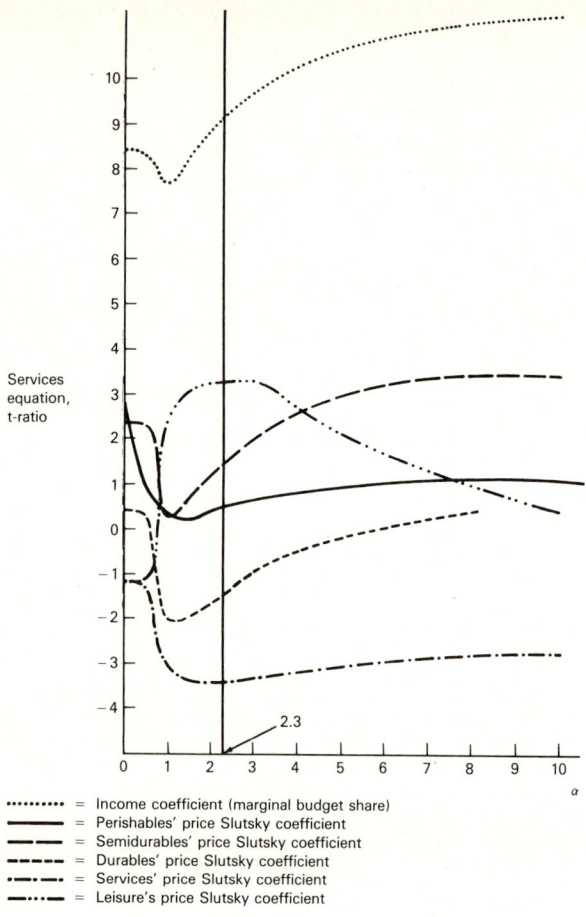

Figure 5.9. Each parameter's *t*-ratio in the services equation.

It is interesting to observe the way in which the *t*-ratios are affected by changes in the scaling of leisure. In addition to exploring the robustness of our leisure price data, we thereby can consider the robustness to our leisure quantity data. In the generation of leisure quantity data, the total number of annual hours available to consumers for work had to be selected. Recall that our leisure data is based upon the value of available hours chosen by Kuznets (1952, p. 64). But we also considered a plausible alternative scaling based upon the presumption that an upper bound, Γ,

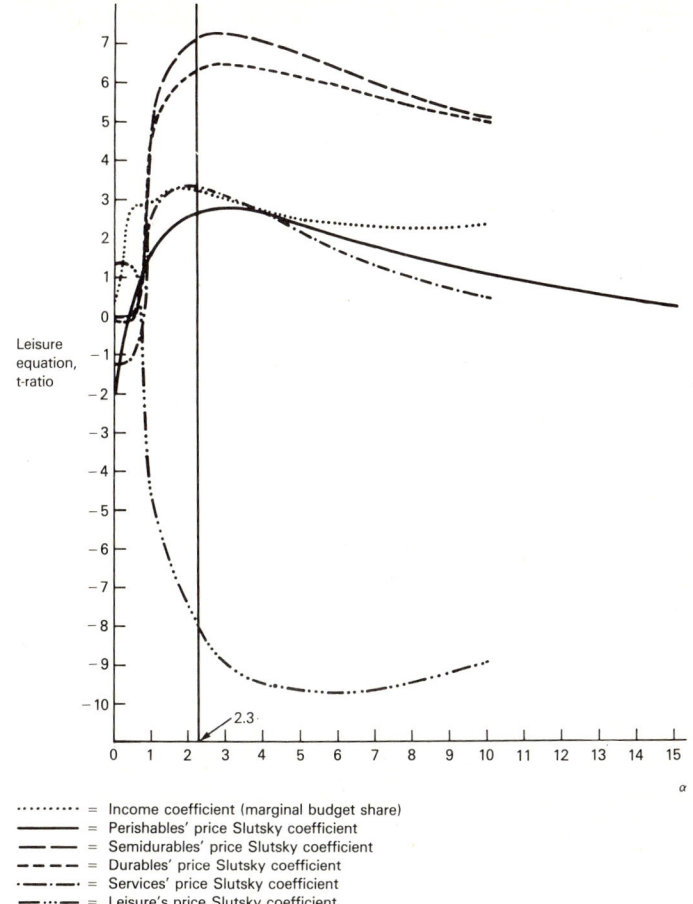

Figure 5.10. Each parameter's *t*-ratio in the leisure equation.

exists to the labor force participation rate. The use of Γ decreases leisure's share in aggregate expenditure by about 50 percent.

To explore the robustness of our inferences to variations in the definition of leisure, we reran our regressions using this substantially rescaled data. In section 5.2 we began this task by re-estimating α within Goldberger's model (the CSE model). We found that the maximum likelihood estimate of α had shifted from 2.3 to 3.1. So when we now pass to the Rotterdam model (conditionally upon α), the price of leisure data also has changed. Table 5.6 presents t-ratios with and without the use of Γ at various values of α between 0 and 10. But the t-ratios of the Rotterdam model's parameter estimates changed only slightly in magnitude (rarely by more than 10 percent), and never changed sign. In addition, at given values of α between 0 and 10 the shift in t-ratios accompanied by the introduction of (nonunitary) Γ was uniformly entirely negligible.

It appears that whatever changes in t-ratios can be attributed to the use of Γ are a result of the shift of the maximum likelihood estimate of α

Table 5.6
t-Ratios from maximum likelihood estimation of the absolute price version of the Rotterdam model ($\alpha = 0, 2.3, 3.1, 10$; no intercept).

Equation	Assumptions	$\bar{\mu}_i$	Price coefficients				
			Perishables	Semidurables	Durables	Services	Leisure
Perishables	$\alpha=0, \Gamma=1$	5.511	−2.292	4.552	3.801	2.770	−1.996
	$\alpha=0, \Gamma=0.48$	5.475	−2.302	4.518	3.788	2.712	−1.963
	$\alpha=2.3, \Gamma=1$	6.166	−5.191	3.693	2.151	0.496	2.728
	$\alpha=2.3, \Gamma=0.48$	6.068	−5.167	3.543	2.216	0.525	2.714
	$\alpha=3.1, \Gamma=0.48$	6.664	−5.404	3.960	2.583	0.773	2.743
	$\alpha=10, \Gamma=1$	9.477	−5.868	5.639	3.826	1.041	0.970
	$\alpha=10, \Gamma=0.48$	8.896	−5.740	5.045	3.626	1.115	1.173
Semidurables	$\alpha=0, \Gamma=1$	2.576	4.552	−7.548	−0.098	2.357	0.022
	$\alpha=0, \Gamma=0.48$	2.476	4.518	−7.549	−0.161	2.289	0.088
	$\alpha=2.3, \Gamma=1$	3.181	3.693	−9.633	−1.545	1.527	7.108
	$\alpha=2.3, \Gamma=0.48$	2.886	3.543	−9.629	−1.387	1.548	7.178
	$\alpha=3.1, \Gamma=0.48$	3.465	3.960	−9.517	−0.839	2.209	7.316
	$\alpha=10, \Gamma=1$	6.475	5.369	−8.409	−0.123	3.582	5.087
	$\alpha=10, \Gamma=0.48$	5.087	5.045	−9.047	0.464	3.828	5.916
Durables	$\alpha=0, \Gamma=1$	3.592	3.801	−0.098	−3.525	0.435	−0.114
	$\alpha=0, \Gamma=0.48$	3.530	3.788	−0.161	−3.550	0.415	−0.069
	$\alpha=2.3, \Gamma=1$	3.650	2.151	−1.545	−6.739	−1.364	6.391
	$\alpha=2.3, \Gamma=0.48$	3.727	2.216	−1.387	−6.689	−1.353	6.282
	$\alpha=3.1, \Gamma=0.48$	4.199	2.583	−0.839	−6.405	−0.886	6.288
	$\alpha=10, \Gamma=1$	6.035	3.826	−0.123	−5.619	0.550	5.022
	$\alpha=10, \Gamma=0.48$	5.566	3.626	0.464	−5.511	0.411	4.819
Services	$\alpha=0, \Gamma=1$	8.308	2.770	2.357	0.435	−1.177	−1.257
	$\alpha=0, \Gamma=0.48$	8.140	2.712	2.289	0.415	−1.167	−1.206
	$\alpha=2.3, \Gamma=1$	9.206	0.496	1.527	−1.364	−3.394	−3.277
	$\alpha=2.3, \Gamma=0.48$	9.196	0.525	1.548	−1.353	−3.333	3.194
	$\alpha=3.1, \Gamma=0.48$	9.816	0.773	2.209	−0.886	−3.232	2.875
	$\alpha=10, \Gamma=1$	11.335	1.041	3.582	0.550	−2.768	0.441
	$\alpha=10, \Gamma=0.48$	11.095	1.115	3.828	0.411	−2.762	0.206
Leisure	$\alpha=0, \Gamma=1$	0.286	−1.996	0.022	−0.114	−1.257	1.357
	$\alpha=0, \Gamma=0.48$	0.359	−1.963	0.088	−0.069	−1.206	1.292
	$\alpha=2.3, \Gamma=1$	3.242	2.728	7.108	6.391	3.277	−8.060
	$\alpha=2.3, \Gamma=0.48$	3.395	2.714	7.178	6.282	3.194	−8.013
	$\alpha=3.1, \Gamma=0.48$	3.206	2.743	7.316	6.288	2.875	−8.882
	$\alpha=10, \Gamma=1$	2.284	0.970	5.087	5.022	0.441	−9.023
	$\alpha=10, \Gamma=0.48$	2.575	1.173	5.916	4.819	0.206	−8.299

(acquired in section 5.2) from 2.3 to 3.1. The shift from 2.3 to 3.1 is seen not to be sufficiently large to change any of our conclusions. Hence, our inferences are robust to leisure's scaling, and we need consider only our results with $\Gamma = 1$ (i.e. no use of the scale factor Γ). Observe that with our arbitrary $\Gamma = 1$ choice, our data imputes to leisure the largest share of "full income" of any of our "goods."

5.5.3. The intercept

In the derivation of our version of the Rotterdam model specification, we dropped an additive remainder term taking the form of a covariance. We did so on theoretical grounds which suggest that the term is globally small. Yet in some empirical studies with the Rotterdam model, large statistically significant intercept terms have been encountered. While these intercepts commonly are attributed to systematic trends in preferences, it is conceivable that they may be evidence of an unexpectedly large remainder term in our stationary-preferences model. We shall investigate this possibility. Observe that an intercept in our specification can model a change in demand independent of income and prices.

If a consumer's utility function is not weakly separable in leisure, then his preferences over goods alone would appear to shift as leisure consumption varies. By including leisure in his utility function and modeling leisure demand jointly with goods demand, we have eliminated that source of apparent "taste change" by internalizing it. To see the effect upon the troublesome intercept, we have estimated the model with such an intercept. It can be shown that the constant terms must sum to zero, but since we are eliminating an equation during the estimation process, we need not impose that restriction during estimation. We use the restriction in estimating the constant term of the deleted equation.

The results are given in table 5.7. Observe that the t-ratio corresponding to each constant term is low in absolute value relative to the t-ratio of most other parameter estimates (especially of the important income and own price coefficients). Furthermore, the realizations and t-ratios of all other coefficient estimators are not appreciably different from those of table 5.4, in which no constant term was used. The hypothesis of no intercepts can be tested using the asymptotic likelihood ratio statistic $-2\log \lambda$, where λ is the relevant likelihood ratio (having a limiting chi-square distribution under the null hypothesis). The value of that statistic for our null hypothesis is 5.00. With four degrees of freedom, the tail area of the hypothesis is 0.24, and we can accept the hypothesis. We shall delete the

Table 5.7
Maximum likelihood estimates of the absolute price version of the Rotterdam model with intercept ($\Gamma=1$, $\alpha=2.3$).

Equation	$\bar{\mu}_i$	Price coefficients					Constant	D.W.
		Perishables	Semidurables	Durables	Services	Leisure		
Perishables	0.289	−0.040	0.011	0.008	0.002	0.018	0.004	2.140
	(0.051)	(0.008)	(0.003)	(0.004)	(0.004)	(0.007)	(0.068)	
Semidurables	0.071	0.011	−0.028	−0.004	0.003	0.018	−0.043	2.298
	(0.019)	(0.003)	(0.003)	(0.002)	(0.002)	(0.002)	(0.022)	
Durables	0.104	0.008	−0.004	−0.023	−0.004	0.023	−0.022	2.206
	(0.030)	(0.004)	(0.002)	(0.003)	(0.003)	(0.004)	(0.035)	
Services	0.365	0.002	0.003	−0.004	−0.019	0.017	−0.029	2.306
	(0.042)	(0.004)	(0.002)	(0.003)	(0.006)	(0.005)	(0.054)	
Leisure	0.171	0.018	0.018	0.023	0.017	−0.076	0.090	2.099
	(0.065)	(0.007)	(0.002)	(0.004)	(0.005)	(0.009)	(0.084)	

Note: Standard errors are in parentheses.

constant terms. By contrast, Abbott and Ashenfelter's (1976) results were virtually dominated by highly significant intercepts. Prices generally had negligible explanatory power.

Our results suggest that the significant intercepts encountered in some other Rotterdam model studies were not evidence of a theoretical remainder term but may have reflected seeming taste change, perhaps induced by variations in nonweakly-separable leisure consumption.[2] Those studies ignored leisure demand and thereby implicitly assumed weak separability in leisure. In the next section we shall test directly for and reject weak separability in leisure.

5.6. Separability in leisure

A primary objective of this chapter (and of all of Part I of this book) is to test for the consistency of the two-stage decision that is implicit in the usual dichotomy between consumer goods expenditure allocation studies and labor supply studies. Recall that a weak separability condition and a homotheticity condition are necessary and sufficient for the consistency of the two-stage decision. The weak separability condition is of particular importance, since without it a conditional utility function in goods alone does not even exist. We shall test for the weak separability condition in this section, and we shall briefly consider the homotheticity condition. Since we shall reject weak separability, which is necessary for consistent two stage budgeting, we need not pursue the homotheticity condition in depth.

First we compute the joint maximum likelihood estimates of the parameters of our model subject to the separability restrictions (4.9). We do so by imposing the linear restrictions (4.9) iteratively for various values of the constant $\bar{k}$ until we find that $\bar{k}$ at which the restricted maximum likelihood estimate attains the highest likelihood value. At that value of $\bar{k}$ the corresponding estimates of the other parameters are the maximum likelihood estimates subject to the weak separability restrictions.

The results are presented in table 5.8. The value of the asymptotic likelihood ratio statistic, $-2\log\lambda$, for the hypothesis that (4.9) holds was 20.04. From the χ^2 distribution with three degrees of freedom, we find that the tail area of the test is less than 10^{-5}. Clearly we cannot accept

---

[2] In some of those cases the apparent statistical significance of the intercepts alternatively may have resulted from the use of an asymptotic test with an insufficient sample size. See Laitinen (1978).

Table 5.8
Maximum likelihood estimates of the absolute price version of the Rotterdam model with weak separability in leisure imposed ($\alpha=2.3$, $\Gamma=1$, no intercept).

Equation	$\bar{\mu}_i$	Price coefficient					D.W.
		Perishables	Semidurables	Durables	Services	Leisure	
Perishables	0.232	−0.048	0.015	0.014	−0.007	0.025	2.090
	(0.026)	(0.005)	(0.003)	(0.003)	(0.004)	(0.003)	
Semidurables	0.099	0.015	−0.025	−0.004	0.003	0.011	2.207
	(0.011)	(0.003)	(0.003)	(0.002)	(0.002)	(0.001)	
Durables	0.145	0.014	−0.004	−0.023	−0.003	0.016	2.214
	(0.017)	(0.003)	(0.002)	(0.003)	(0.003)	(0.002)	
Services	0.266	−0.007	0.003	−0.003	−0.023	0.029	2.325
	(0.025)	(0.004)	(0.002)	(0.003)	(0.006)	(0.003)	
Leisure	0.258	0.025	0.011	0.016	0.029	−0.082	2.002
	(0.037)	(0.003)	(0.001)	(0.002)	(0.003)	(0.004)	

Note: Standard errors are in parentheses.

restrictions (4.9). But (4.9) closely approximates (4.8), which is necessary for weak separability in leisure. Furthermore, weak separability in leisure is necessary for the very existence of a utility function in goods alone and therefore certainly for the consistency (or even existence) of the conventional two-stage consumer decision. Hence, we reject the two-stage decision.

Nevertheless, our estimates remained plausible after imposition of the restrictions (4.9). Although those restrictions resulted in some large changes in coefficient estimates, all coefficient estimates retained the signs expected from theory, and the coefficients of greatest interest continued to be estimated with the highest precision. In this sense our rejected weak separability hypothesis performs considerably better than our rejected $\alpha=0$ "hypothesis".

If we were to accept weak separability in our model, which we have not, we would next seek to test for the linear homogeneity of the utility function in goods alone. But without weak separability, a utility function in goods alone does not exist. Nevertheless, we estimated the Rotterdam model in goods alone, since we will be needing it later. The result is given in table 5.9.

We could compute estimates of average income elasticities to permit us to test whether all goods in the goods-alone model have an income elasticity of exactly unity. Recall that unitary income elasticities in all goods are necessary and sufficient for linear homogeneity. But observe that the precision of the estimators of the marginal budget shares in table 5.9 is very great. No test of unitary income elasticities was attempted, since it is

Table 5.9
Maximum likelihood estimates of the absolute price version of the Rotterdam model without leisure (no intercept).

		Price coefficients			
Equation	$\bar{\mu}_i$	Perishables	Semidurables	Durables	Services
Perishables	0.347	−0.121	0.058	0.057	0.007
	(0.027)	(0.016)	(0.009)	(0.010)	(0.014)
Semidurables	0.121	0.058	−0.077	−0.003	0.023
	(0.015)	(0.009)	(0.010)	(0.007)	(0.008)
Durables	0.187	0.057	−0.003	−0.063	0.010
	(0.022)	(0.010)	(0.007)	(0.011)	(0.011)
Services	0.345	0.007	0.023	0.010	−0.039
	(0.032)	(0.014)	(0.008)	(0.011)	(0.018)

Note: Standard errors are in parentheses.

immediately clear that the hypothesis does not stand a chance of being accepted.

5.7. The Rotterdam model in relative prices

5.7.1. Introduction

In this chapter we have established conventional Hicks–Allen substitutability between leisure and both durables and semidurables, and through the Slutsky equation we could easily verify Cournot substitutability. But to investigate utility-based interactions, we would have to consider the cardinal concept of "specific" substitutability. Such specific interactions can be investigated through the use of an alternative variant of the Rotterdam model called the "relative price" version, which we have defined in section 3.3. In addition, the relative price version, unlike the absolute price version, permits convenient testing for complete or blockwise strong separability. In this section we shall estimate the relative price version of the Rotterdam model to acquire the information about preference structures available from that model.

It should be observed that the concept of specific interactions, whether specific substitutability or specific complementarity, is inherently cardinal, and all cardinal concepts are controversial. However, our tests for strong separability are not subject to that difficulty since, by definition, strong separability is invariant to monotonic transformations of utility functions. Another difficulty arises from the fact that our aggregation theory derived in section 3.4 applies directly only to the absolute price version of the

Rotterdam model. We have not attempted the difficult task of applying our aggregation approach to the relative price version. Hence, we base our use of the relative price version upon the aggregation theory in Theil (1975, ch. 4). Since Theil's assumptions are considerably stronger than those used in our section 3.4, we should understand that the strong inferences that we acquire with the relative price version are acquired at the cost of strong assumptions and occasionally (when exploring specific interactions) at the cost of cardinal reasoning.

5.7.2. Estimation

Recall from section 3.3 that the parameters $\bar{v}_{ij}$ of the relative price version of the Rotterdam model provide direct and highly useful information about preferences. We now proceed to estimate that relative price version. We shall be particularly interested in checking whether durables and semidurables are specific substitutes for leisure as well as Hicks–Allen substitutes. Since the functional form of Theil's aggregated relative price version is identical to the disaggregated version in section 3.3, we shall use the same notation for aggregated variables and parameters as we did in section 3.3 for the corresponding disaggregated values. Although Theil's aggregation theory does not depend upon the existence of a "representative consumer", we nevertheless could view the model as notationally (but not theoretically) equivalent to one in which a representative consumer exists. Our notations for macroparameters and microparameters will be used interchangeably in this chapter.

As mentioned in Chapter 3, the relative price version of the Rotterdam model is not estimable unless an additional restriction is imposed on the matrix $[\bar{v}_{ij}]$. This is generally accomplished by imposing additivity (strong separability) in one good. Additivity in good r is imposed by setting $\bar{v}_{ir} = 0$ for all $i \neq r$. The need for such a normalization is dictated by the ordinal nature of utility. The normalization selects a single utility function from the equivalence class of monotonic transformations of an index utility function defining a consumer's preferences. We should expect that perishables would be a reasonable candidate for an additive good. Clearly with respect to leisure we would not expect to observe significant interactions with perishables. Perishables are not likely to be either time-saving or time-using to any appreciable degree. Similarly, the useful interactions captured earlier between durables and other goods did not extend to perishables. So for our purposes the imposition of additivity in perishables would appear to result in a minimal loss of useful information.

Prior to the imposition of additivity in perishables, it would be desirable to be able to appeal to a hypothesis test. Our absolute price version of the Rotterdam model does not provide any direct test of additivity, but, as we have seen, it does permit testing for weak separability. If weak separability in a good were rejected, then additivity in that good would also be rejected. However, the converse is not true: acceptance of weak separability does not lead to acceptance of additivity. So the best we can do is to check whether a lack of weak separability dictates rejection of additivity.

Recall that our test for weak separability of good k from the rest consists of seeking constancy of $\bar{\pi}_{ik}/\bar{\mu}_i$ over i for all $i \neq k$ (assuming that the $\bar{\mu}_i$ values are nonzero). Using the absolute price version of the Rotterdam model, these ratios were computed from table 5.6 to check for weak separability in each individual good. Although a formal test was not constructed, inspection of those ratios along with the related t-ratios can be informative. Weak separability in perishables appeared to be more plausible than weak separability in any other good or in leisure. Weak separability in services also appeared plausible.

We have considered only weak separability between one good and all the rest. But it is possible to encounter weak separability between two sets of goods, of which neither is a singleton set. In that case the marginal rate of substitution between any two goods in one set must be independent of the quantity consumed of any good in the other set. By extending our previous result, it can be shown that if the goods subscripts are separated into two mutually exclusive and exhaustive sets, S_1 and S_2, then an individual consumer's utility function is weakly separable in the partition $\{S_1, S_2\}$ if and only if $\bar{\pi}_{ij}/\bar{\mu}_i\bar{\mu}_j$ is constant for all $i \in S_2$ and all $j \in S_2$ (assuming that the $\bar{\mu}_i$ values are nonzero). These ratios were computed using the analogous macroparameters, but our impressions were unchanged. Additivity in perishables appears to be the most reasonable initial assumption.

In Table 5.10 we display our estimates of the relative price version of the Rotterdam model with the imposition of additivity in perishables. The procedure used was the two-step generalized least squares estimation procedure previously used for the absolute price version. Now recall that the relative price version of the Rotterdam model is nonlinear in the parameters. As a first step we follow Theil in linearizing the model by substituting into the factors $A_{it}(\bar{\mu})$ the estimate of the aggregate marginal budget shares, $\bar{\mu}$, acquired from the absolute price version. The asymptotic justification of the procedure is available in Theil (1971, sect. 11.9).

Standard errors for parameters omitted during estimation are not immediately available. In section 3.3 we have described a means for acquir-

Table 5.10
Two-step generalized least squares estimates of the first blocking of the relative price version of the Rotterdam model ($\alpha = 2.3$, $\Gamma = 1$, no intercept).

Equation	$\bar{\mu}_i$	Price coefficients				
		Perishables	Semidurables	Durables	Services	Leisure
Perishables	0.338	−0.049	0.0	0.0	0.0	0.0
	(0.049)	(0.012)				
Semidurables	0.038	0.0	−0.022	−0.003	0.002	0.018
	(0.019)		(0.003)	(0.002)	(0.003)	(0.003)
Durables	0.085	0.0	−0.003	−0.022	−0.009	0.021
	(0.024)		(0.002)	(0.005)	(0.003)	(0.003)
Services	0.380	0.0	0.002	−0.009	−0.052	0.005
	(0.044)		(0.003)	(0.003)	(0.011)	(0.007)
Leisure	0.159	0.0	0.018	0.021	0.005	−0.067
	(0.053)		(0.003)	(0.003)	(0.007)	(0.010)

$$\hat{\bar{\phi}} = -0.144 \, (0.037)$$

Note: Standard errors are in parentheses.

ing those standard errors. During estimation by the two-step generalized least squares procedure, the parameters estimated are those listed across the top of table 5.11 while the parameters omitted are listed along the left-hand side. Then table 5.11 presents the matrix $D(\gamma)$ described in section 3.3, and table 5.12 presents the usual estimate of the asymptotic covariance matrix of $\hat{\gamma}$.[3] We have denoted that estimate by $(1/T)\hat{V}$. As described in section 3.3, we need only substitute our estimate, $\hat{\gamma}$, of γ from table 5.10 into $D(\gamma)$ and compute $D(\hat{\gamma})[(1/T)\hat{V}]D(\hat{\gamma})$ to acquire our estimate of the asymptotic covariance matrix of the omitted parameters. Estimates of the omitted parameters were computed by substituting the available estimates into the restrictions; that is to say, we computed $\hat{\beta} = \hat{\beta}(\hat{\gamma})$. Table 5.10 contains the resulting estimates of all of the model's parameters along with the associated standard errors.

Observe that the $\hat{\bar{\nu}}_{ij}$ values relating durables and semidurables to leisure are positive and are estimated with considerable precision. Hence, durables and semidurables are specific substitutes for leisure. Also, observe that our new estimates of the marginal budget shares are reasonably close to those from table 5.4 that were used to linearize the model. Recall that the marginal budget shares, $\bar{\mu}$, appear both as arguments of the functions $A_{it}(\bar{\mu})$ in the relative price version and as coefficients of the log changes in

---

[3] We used the asymptotic covariance matrix estimator derived by Theil (1971, pp. 590–595). That estimator is subject to a slight error. See Theil and Laitinen (1979).

Table 5.11
Derivatives of the derived parameters in two-step generalized least squares estimation of the first blocking.

	$\bar{\mu}_1$	$\bar{\mu}_2$	$\bar{\mu}_3$	$\bar{\mu}_5$	$\bar{\phi}$	$\bar{\nu}_{23}$	$\bar{\nu}_{24}$	$\bar{\nu}_{25}$	$\bar{\nu}_{34}$	$\bar{\nu}_{35}$	$\bar{\nu}_{54}$
$\bar{\mu}_4$	-1	-1	-1	-1	0	0	0	0	0	0	0
$\bar{\nu}_{11}$	$\bar{\phi}$	0	0	0	$\bar{\mu}_1$	0	0	0	0	0	0
$\bar{\nu}_{22}$	0	$\bar{\phi}$	0	0	$\bar{\mu}_2$	-1	-1	-1	0	0	0
$\bar{\nu}_{33}$	0	0	$\bar{\phi}$	0	$\bar{\mu}_3$	-1	0	0	-1	-1	0
$\bar{\nu}_{44}$	$-\bar{\phi}$	$-\bar{\phi}$	$-\bar{\phi}$	$-\bar{\phi}$	$\bar{\mu}_4$	0	-1	0	-1	0	-1
$\bar{\nu}_{55}$	0	0	0	$\bar{\phi}$	$\bar{\mu}_5$	0	0	-1	0	-1	-1

Table 5.12
Estimated covariance matrix of two-step generalized least squares coefficient estimators of the Rotterdam model's first blocking.[a]

$\bar{\mu}_1$	$\bar{\mu}_2$	$\bar{\mu}_3$	$\bar{\mu}_5$	$\bar{\phi}$	$\bar{\nu}_{23}$	$\bar{\nu}_{24}$	$\bar{\nu}_{25}$	$\bar{\nu}_{34}$	$\bar{\nu}_{35}$	$\bar{\nu}_{54}$	
23.62	56.28	36.44	-1504	692.3	7.522	14.55	9.548	29.13	19.56	79.26	$\bar{\mu}_1$
	347.1	-24.4	-229.3	-60.82	-14.51	7.462	-15.25	-1.527	4.626	-8.669	$\bar{\mu}_2$
		558.7	-400.7	-109.8	10.38	-6.876	-1.13	14.54	-13.88	-15.24	$\bar{\mu}_3$
			2790	-151.1	1.587	-11.34	11.38	-9.099	-9.88	31.51	$\bar{\mu}_5$
				1385	15.05	29.1	19.1	58.28	39.13	158.6	$\bar{\phi}$
					5.549	-1.332	-0.1851	-0.2208	-1.738	3.129	$\bar{\nu}_{23}$
						6.209	-1.435	1.069	1.76	1.829	$\bar{\nu}_{24}$
							6.896	1.366	0.361	1.276	$\bar{\nu}_{25}$
								10.79	-1.455	4.384	$\bar{\nu}_{34}$
									10.04	3.81	$\bar{\nu}_{35}$
										39.96	$\bar{\nu}_{54}$

[a] All entries are to be multiplied by 10^{-6}.

real income. We have linearized the model by substituting into $A_{it}(\bar{\mu})$ the value of $\bar{\mu}$ from table 5.4, but we have re-estimated $\bar{\mu}$ from its appearance as the coefficients of the log change in real income.

We now compute the maximum likelihood estimates using the estimates in table 5.10 as initial values in the Chapman–Fair program. The result is in the first column of table 5.13, headed "No iteration". The iteration to which we refer is an iteration on the arguments of the $A_{it}(\bar{\mu})$ functions. We have not computed estimates of the omitted parameters, and in general we shall do so only for initial two-stage generalized least squares results.

The second column of table 5.13 presents the results following an iteration on the arguments of the $A_{it}(\bar{\mu})$ functions. The iteration proceeded in the obvious way. The new estimates of $\bar{\mu}$ tabulated in table 5.10 were substituted into the $A_{it}(\bar{\mu})$ functions in place of those from table 5.4, and

Table 5.13

Maximum likelihood estimates of the relative price version of the Rotterdam model ($\alpha=2.3$, $\Gamma=1$, no intercept).

	First blocking		Final blocking	
	No iteration	After convergence	No iteration	After convergence
$\bar{\mu}_1$	0.337	0.357	0.347	0.354
	(0.049)	(0.049)	(0.046)	(0.047)
$\bar{\mu}_2$	0.035	0.031	0.032	0.028
	(0.017)	(0.017)	(0.016)	(0.016)
$\bar{\mu}_3$	0.085	0.082	0.107	0.109
	(0.024)	(0.024)	(0.024)	(0.024)
$\bar{\mu}_5$	0.151	0.141	0.146	0.131
	(0.057)	(0.057)	(0.058)	(0.060)
$\bar{\phi}$	−0.148	−0.102	−0.127	−0.105
	(0.037)	(0.031)	(0.023)	(0.021)
$\bar{\nu}_{23}$	−0.003	−0.002	−0.002	−0.002
	(0.003)	(0.003)	(0.002)	(0.003)
$\bar{\nu}_{24}$	0.001	0.003		
	(0.002)	(0.003)		
$\bar{\nu}_{25}$	0.019	0.020	0.020	0.022
	(0.002)	(0.002)	(0.002)	(0.002)
$\bar{\nu}_{34}$	−0.010	−0.008		
	(0.004)	(0.004)		
$\bar{\nu}_{35}$	0.022	0.024	0.019	0.020
	(0.003)	(0.003)	(0.003)	(0.003)
$\bar{\nu}_{45}$	0.005	0.006		
	(0.007)	(0.007)		

Note: Standard errors are in parentheses.

the resulting linearized model was estimated using the Chapman–Fair program. The new estimates of $\bar{\mu}$ were substituted back into $A_{it}(\bar{\mu})$ and the procedure repeated. Iteration continued until convergence. As can be seen from table 5.13, the converged estimates do not differ substantially from those acquired without iteration, and neither differs appreciably from those acquired from the two-step procedure in table 5.10.

Recall from Chapter 3 that the matrix of price coefficients $[\bar{\nu}_{ij}]$ is negative definite. Although we did not impose that restriction, we now verify it. The eigenvalues of our estimate of that matrix in table 5.10 are (−0.082, −0.052, −0.049, −0.017, −0.011). So the matrix is negative definite.

Now observe from table 5.10 that the specific price interactions with services are estimated with only fair precision. In particular, observe the *t*-ratio of 0.710 for the interaction between services and leisure. It would appear that we can reasonably impose additivity in services as well as in perishables. So we now set $\bar{\nu}_{4i} = 0$ for all $i \neq 4$ and repeat our estimation procedures. Table 5.14 contains the results for the two-step generalized least squares procedure, while tables 5.15 and 5.16 display the matrices needed to acquire our estimate of the asymptotic covariance matrix of the asymptotic distribution of the omitted estimators. The last two columns of table 5.13 present the results from maximum likelihood estimation with and without iteration on the arguments of the $A_{it}(\bar{\mu})$ functions. Again the

Table 5.14
Two-step generalized least squares estimates of the final blocking of the relative price version of the Rotterdam model ($\alpha = 2.3$, $\Gamma = 1$, no intercept).

Equation	$\bar{\mu}_i$	Price coefficient				
		Perishables	Semidurables	Durables	Services	Leisure
Perishables	0.342	−0.047	0.0	0.0	0.0	0.0
	(0.047)	(0.009)				
Semidurables	0.034	0.0	−0.021	−0.003	0.0	0.019
	(0.017)		(0.003)	(0.002)		(0.002)
Durables	0.108	0.0	−0.003	−0.031	0.0	0.019
	(0.025)		(0.002)	(0.005)		(0.003)
Services	0.367	0.0	0.0	0.0	−0.050	0.0
	(0.038)				(0.009)	
Leisure	0.149	0.0	0.019	0.019	0.0	−0.059
	(0.055)		(0.002)	(0.003)		(0.009)

$$\hat{\bar{\phi}} = -0.136 \; (0.021)$$

Note: Standard errors are in parentheses.

Table 5.15
Derivatives of the derived parameters in two-step generalized least squares estimation of the final blocking.

	$\bar{\mu}_1$	$\bar{\mu}_2$	$\bar{\mu}_3$	$\bar{\mu}_5$	$\bar{\phi}$	$\bar{\nu}_{23}$	$\bar{\nu}_{25}$	$\bar{\nu}_{35}$
$\bar{\mu}_4$	−1	−1	−1	−1	0	0	0	0
$\bar{\nu}_{11}$	$\bar{\phi}$	0	0	0	$\bar{\mu}_1$	0	0	0
$\bar{\nu}_{22}$	0	$\bar{\phi}$	0	0	$\bar{\mu}_2$	−1	−1	0
$\bar{\nu}_{33}$	0	0	$\bar{\phi}$	0	$\bar{\mu}_3$	−1	0	−1
$\bar{\nu}_{44}$	$-\bar{\phi}$	$-\bar{\phi}$	$-\bar{\phi}$	$-\bar{\phi}$	$\bar{\mu}_4$	0	0	0
$\bar{\nu}_{55}$	0	0	0	$\bar{\phi}$	$\bar{\mu}_5$	0	−1	−1

Table 5.16
Estimated covariance matrix of two-step generalized least squares coefficient estimators of the Rotterdam model's final blocking.[a]

$\bar{\mu}_1$	$\bar{\mu}_2$	$\bar{\mu}_3$	$\bar{\mu}_5$	$\bar{\phi}$	$\bar{\nu}_{23}$	$\bar{\nu}_{25}$	$\bar{\nu}_{35}$	
2186	34.61	261.3	−1913	227	4.242	5.524	11.72	$\bar{\mu}_1$
	282.1	−21.92	−223.4	−40.76	−11.19	−11	2.935	$\bar{\mu}_2$
		623.6	−509.7	−74.12	9.993	−3.797	−5.882	$\bar{\mu}_3$
			3071	−163.5	−4.007	8.018	−11.43	$\bar{\mu}_5$
				454.2	8.488	11.05	23.45	$\bar{\phi}$
					4.584	−0.5306	−1.463	$\bar{\nu}_{23}$
						5.411	0.6477	$\bar{\nu}_{25}$
							8.994	$\bar{\nu}_{35}$

[a] All entries are to be multiplied by 10^{-6}.

estimation procedures lead to similar conclusions, and durables and semidurables remain specific substitutes for leisure. Precision has been improved somewhat.

5.7.3. Strong separability

In applications, the most widely used model permitting the separate modeling of labor supply and goods demand has been Stone's linear expenditure system. It satisfies both the weak separability and the linear homogeneity conditions for the two-stage decisions, and since it is formulated in terms of supernumerary quantities, the model retains empirical merit despite the linear homogeneity property. Stone's model has most frequently been used with highly aggregated data such as ours; it is completely additive. The precisely estimated specific interactions we have encountered between durables and leisure and between semidurables and leisure should lead us to be very skeptical about an assumption of complete additivity, but the hypothesis will be tested as a result of its historical importance.

Since we already have rejected weak separability in leisure, we know that complete strong separability will be rejected. Nevertheless, the imposition of weak separability did not result in particularly unreasonable changes in the properties of our model, and we believe that weak separability, although formally rejected, may be a reasonable assumption in some

Table 5.17
Conditional maximum likelihood estimates of the fully additive relative price version of the Rotterdam model ($\alpha = 2.3$, $\Gamma = 1$, no intercept, no iteration on $A_{it}(\bar{\mu})$).

Equation	$\bar{\mu}_1$	D.W.	R^2
Perishables	0.320 (0.048)	2.157	0.554
Semidurables	0.071 (0.021)	2.395	0.355
Durables	0.118 (0.028)	1.945	0.343
Leisure	0.129 (0.065)	1.881	0.346
	$\hat{\hat{\phi}} = -0.180\ (0.027)$		

Note: Standard errors are in parentheses.

cases and for some purposes. We now investigate the potential usefulness of the assumption of complete strong separability.

Table 5.17 presents the results of the maximum likelihood estimation of the relative price version with full additivity imposed. We have not iterated on the arguments of the functions $A_{it}(\bar{\mu})$, as explained earlier, since such iteration leads to no gain in asymptotic efficiency and destroys our ability to use an asymptotic likelihood ratio test. However, our estimates must be viewed as conditional maximum likelihood estimates. The services equation was deleted during estimation. Observe that the correlation coefficients are very low in all equations, with the highest being for the perishables equation. Recall (with only heuristic relevancy) that we had originally accepted additivity in perishables. The value of the asymptotic likelihood ratio criterion, $-2\log\lambda$, was 78.13. With additivity in perishables accepted as a maintained hypothesis, the tail area of the hypothesis is computed using the χ^2 distribution with six degrees of freedom. The tail area is far below 10^{-6}.

Our evidence on the imposition of weak separability was considerably less negative than that on the imposition of complete additivity. Although the tail areas of both hypotheses are very low, that of complete additivity is much lower. It appears that the imposition of complete additivity, even with highly aggregated data, should be approached with considerable caution. However, when estimators are found to have inadequate precision, the imposition of weak separability in leisure appears to be worthy of consideration.

5.8. Residual analysis

5.8.1. Orthogonally transformed disturbances

Having completed our estimation of both the absolute and relative price versions of the Rotterdam model, we seek to test our assumptions on the error structure. Statistics well suited to testing the zero mean assumption, the homoscedasticity assumption, and the assumption of no autocorrelation have been developed in Theil (1975, ch. 5). Those tests will now be used. We will also present and use a Kolmogorov–Smirnov test for the normality assumption. We shall use our maximum likelihood results for the absolute price version and for the final blocking of the relative price version with both perishables and services additive. In the relative price version we shall use the results without iteration on the arguments of the $A_{it}(\bar{\mu})$ functions. For testing purposes using the likelihood ratio criterion, the iteration on the marginal budget shares introduces unnecessary complications by changing the definition of the data on which we condition in acquiring the maximum likelihood estimate. Since the iteration does not increase the asymptotic efficiency of the estimator, we shall not use the iterated estimates in this section.

We begin by computing orthogonally transformed disturbances. The stochastic error term in our regression during the tth observation is ε_t. Let C be the orthogonal 4×4 matrix the columns of which are the characteristic vectors of Ω, and let Λ^2 be the 4×4 diagonal matrix the diagonal elements of which are the latent roots of Ω. Then $\Omega = C\Lambda^2 C$. Let Λ be a matrix the elements of which are the positive square roots of the corresponding elements of Λ^2. We now define the transformed disturbances ξ_t, $t = 1, \ldots, T$, by

$$\xi_t = C\Lambda^{-1}C'\varepsilon_t.$$

It is easily demonstrated that the elements of ξ_t are uncorrelated random variables with zero mean and unit variance for all t. By our normality assumption on the ε_t values we can apply standard normal theory to the ξ_t values.

Since we cannot observe ε_t, we follow Theil in approximating the stochastic errors, ξ_t, using the residuals for the ε_t values. For Ω, we substitute its maximum likelihood estimate. A large sample justification exists for those approximations in the tests to follow. We use the same symbol ξ_t both for the transformed disturbances and for their asymptotic residual approximation. The usage will be evident from the context.

Now to compute our approximation to the vectors ξ_t, $t=1,\ldots,T$, we need the maximum likelihood estimate of Ω and the residuals. Our estimate of Ω for the absolute price version is:

$$\begin{bmatrix} \text{(Perishables)} & \text{(Semidurables)} & \text{(Durables)} & \text{(Services)} \\ 0.191 & 0.013 & 0.014 & -0.033 \\ 0.013 & 0.024 & 0.002 & -0.004 \\ 0.014 & 0.002 & 0.059 & -0.022 \\ -0.033 & -0.004 & -0.022 & 0.144 \end{bmatrix} \begin{matrix} \text{(Perishables)} \\ \text{(Semidurables)} \\ \text{(Durables)} \\ \text{(Services)} \end{matrix}$$

The maximum likelihood estimate of Ω for the relative price version is as follows:

$$\begin{bmatrix} \text{(Perishables)} & \text{(Semidurables)} & \text{(Durables)} & \text{(Leisure)} \\ 0.249 & 0.005 & 0.030 & -0.233 \\ 0.005 & 0.025 & 0.001 & -0.030 \\ 0.030 & 0.001 & 0.064 & -0.066 \\ -0.233 & -0.030 & -0.066 & 0.400 \end{bmatrix} \begin{matrix} \text{(Perishables)} \\ \text{(Semidurables)} \\ \text{(Durables)} \\ \text{(Leisure)} \end{matrix}$$

Observe that in the absolute price version we have deleted the leisure equation, while in the relative price version we have deleted the services equation.

Having computed our transformed residuals, we plotted their empirical distribution function on normal graph paper. The result for the absolute price version is displayed in fig. 5.11 and for the relative price version in fig. 5.12. During this procedure it was observed that of the seven transformed residuals that exceeded 2.5 in absolute value, four occurred during the years 1916–1919. Recall that while we have deleted data for the Second World War, we have not deleted First World War data since governmentally enforced rationing did not exist during that war. However, uncleared markets were common, and informal quantity rationing by retailers existed. The other three large transformed residuals all occurred during depressions early in the century.

5.8.2. The tests

We now test the normality assumption using a Kolmogorov–Smirnov test. Let $F(x)$ be the cumulative distribution function of the standard normal distribution. We need its value at each ξ_{ti}, $i=1,\ldots,4$ and $t=1,\ldots,60$. This can be accomplished by integrating the standard normal density numerically using the trapezoidal rule. The numerical integration was checked against a table of the normal distribution and found to be very accurate. Now let $F_{n_0}(x)$ be the empirical distribution function of the pooled transformed residuals, where n_0 is the size of the pooled sample, so that

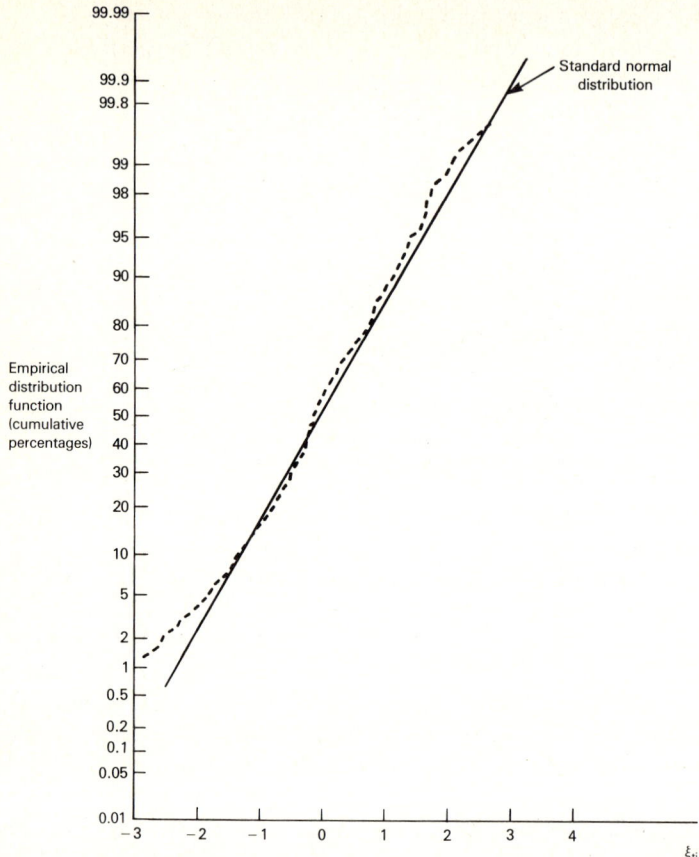

Figure 5.11. Empirical distribution function of the transformed residuals for the absolute price version model.

$n_0 = 4 \times 60 = 240$. Letting $D_{n_0}^* = \max_{x \in R} |F(x) - F_{n_0}(x)|$, we compute the test statistic $n_0^{1/2} D_{n_0}^*$.

First consider the absolute price version. The value of $D_{n_0}^*$ is 0.085, so that the value of $n_0^{1/2} D_{n_0}^*$ is 1.32. The tail area of the test is 0.067. We cannot reject normality at the 0.05 level. Considering the large sample size, we accept normality. With the relative price version, $D_{n_0}^* = 0.044$ and $n_0^{1/2} D_{n_0}^* = 0.677$. The resulting tail area is 0.75. Normality is strongly acceptable, as is evident from fig. 5.12.

We now test the hypothesis that ε_t has zero mean for all t. For this purpose, Theil derived the test statistic $U_1 = T \bar{\xi}' \bar{\xi}$, where $\bar{\xi} = (1/T) \sum_{t=1}^{T} \xi_t$.

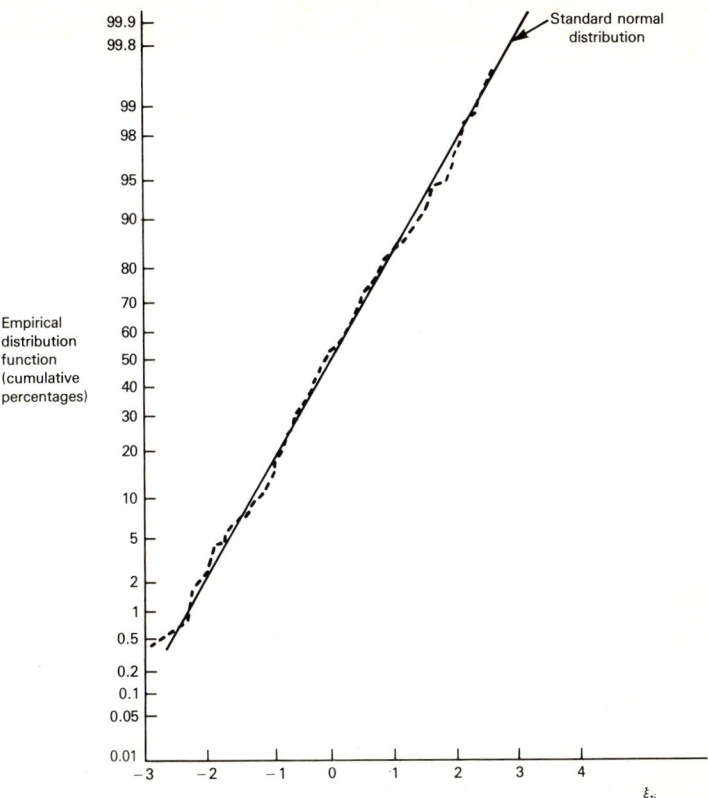

Figure 5.12. Empirical distribution function of the transformed residuals for the relative price version model.

It can be shown that if $E\varepsilon_t = 0$, then U_1 is distributed as a χ^2 with four degrees of freedom. Since U_1 is a measure of the distance from the origin, we reject our hypothesis if U_1 is large. For the absolute price version we find that $U_1 = 3.81$, so the tail area of the zero mean hypothesis is 0.43. For the relative price version, $U_1 = 2.30$ and the tail area is 0.68. The zero mean hypothesis clearly is accepted in both cases.

To test the hypothesis of no serial correlation, Theil derived the statistic

$$U_2 = \frac{1}{T-1} \sum_{t=2}^{T} (\xi_t - \xi_{t-1})'(\xi_t - \xi_{t-1}).$$

Under the null hypothesis of no serial correlation, it follows from the law of large numbers that for large T, this average should be near $E(\xi_t - \xi_{t-1})'(\xi_t - \xi_{t-1}) = E(\xi_t'\xi_t) + E(\xi_{t-1}'\xi_{t-1}) = 4 + 4 = 8$. Alternatively, suppose there is first-order autocorrelation. Then $U_2 = 8(1-\rho)$, where $\rho \in [-1, 1]$, and it follows that $U_2 \in [0, 16]$. We now compute U_2 to determine whether it is close to 8, at the center of the potential range of 0–16.

For the absolute price version we find that $U_2 = 8.96$. This is close to 8 and far from the limits of 0 and 16. Furthermore, the implied estimate of ρ for first-order autocorrelation is -0.1, which is reasonably approximated by zero. In the relative price version we find that $U_2 = 9.41$, which implies an estimate of -0.176 for ρ. Again U_2 is considerably closer to 8 than to 0 or 16, and $\rho = 0$ appears to be a reasonable approximation. But the evidence of negative autocorrelation is somewhat more pronounced than for the absolute price version.

It should be observed that the evidence from the Durbin–Watson statistics, labeled D.W. in some of the tables of this chapter, is similar. The hypothesis of no autocorrelation cannot be rejected in any case, but whatever evidence of autocorrelation that does exist appears to favor negative autocorrelation. It is known that first differencing data tends to induce negative autocorrelation.

For a four-equation system, Theil's test statistic for testing the homoscedasticity assumption is

$$U_3 = \frac{\sum_{t=1}^{T_1} \xi_t'\xi_t / 4T_1}{\sum_{t=T_1+1}^{T} \xi_t'\xi_t / 4T_2}.$$

In defining this statistic we must divide the transformed residuals into two groups. We select T_1 to equal the number of observations up to and including 1915, and we let T_2 equal the number of observations after 1915. Then $T = T_1 + T_2$. We seek to check whether Ω may have shifted during the First World War. The motivation for the choice of 1915 is clear from fig. 5.4. There appears to be evidence of larger fluctuations in shares after 1915, and we seek to determine whether that phenomenon has been explained by our model's exogenous variables.

It is easily shown that under the homoscedasticity assumption, U_3 is distributed as $F(4T_1, 4T_2)$ or $F(100, 140)$. Furthermore, we can show that $\xi_t'\xi_t = \varepsilon_t'\Omega^{-1}\varepsilon_t$. Hence, if Ω has remained unchanged, we would expect the average values in the numerator and denominator of U_3 to be about the same. Thus, we accept homoscedasticity if U_3 is near one. In other words we seek a two-sided test.

With the absolute price version we found that $U_3 = 0.84$. Now the upper and lower 5 percent points of the $F(100, 140)$ distribution are 0.73 and 1.35. Hence, any two-sided 0.05 level acceptance region must contain [0.73, 1.35]. Any two-sided 0.05 level test would lead to acceptance of homoscedasticity.

With the relative price data, we got $U_3 = 0.72$. Hence, any two-sided test that allocated any reasonable percentage of the 0.05 to the right tail would lead to acceptance of homoscedasticity. Observe that the larger number of explanatory variables contained in the absolute price version appears to assist in explaining the greater variability in the shares after 1915. Also, observe that 240 is a very large sample size and that we have chosen the year 1915 *after* looking at the data. We should be very cautious about rejecting homoscedasticity.

5.9. Model fit

5.9.1. Information inaccuracies

The Rotterdam model was originally derived as a means of forecasting value shares. It can be shown that the model's dependent variables are the quantity components of the changes in the value shares of each good; and at time t, the model's implied prediction, $\hat{W}_{i,t+1}$, of the share of the ith good is simply $\hat{W}_{i,t+1} = W_{it} - e_{it}$, where W_{it} is the actual income share of the ith good during period t, and e_{it} is the period t residual of the model's equation for the ith good. See Theil (1971, pp. 329 and 647). Since the shares are positive and sum to unity, the shares may be viewed as probabilities. Information theory provides a powerful and elegant means of evaluating the fit of such decomposition models. In that approach, we evaluate model fit by viewing the model's implicit ex-post share predictions (fitted values) as prior probabilities and determining the expected gain in information acquired from the actual shares, viewed as posterior probabilities. In this context, the term "forecast" is synonymous with "fitted value". The information measure has the desirable property of being additive over time and over goods, so we easily can acquire information indices of the model's success in explaining the consumption of any combination of goods during any time interval.

If our implied forecasts for the shares during period t are $\hat{W}_{it}, \ldots, \hat{W}_{N+1,t}$, while the actual shares are $W_{it}, \ldots, W_{N+1,t}$, then the information inaccuracy of the predictions is measured by

$$I_t = \sum_{i=1}^{N+1} W_{it} \log_e \left(\frac{W_{it}}{\hat{W}_{it}} \right).$$

We then measure the system's performance over the years from t_1 to t_2 using the average information inaccuracy

$$\bar{I} = \frac{1}{t_2 - t_1 + 1} \sum_{t=t_1}^{t_2} I_t.$$

It should be observed that we use the information indices to measure fit, not to test hypotheses. In our case the models we compare frequently are not only not nested but do not even have the same endogenous variables. Neither the likelihood function nor the generalized variance of the fit is comparable between models.

To provide comparability of information measures between competing models, a degrees of freedom correction has been developed to compensate for differing numbers of explanatory variables in different systems. See Theil (1971, pp. 651–652). We use the correction whenever $\bar{I}$ is computed over all equations and all years. Then the correction leads to the multiplication of $\bar{I}$ by a factor equal to $60M/(60M - k_u)$, where M is the number of equations jointly estimated, 60 is the number of years in our data, and k_u is the number of unrestricted unknown coefficients. Observe that $60M$ is the number of observations in the jointly estimated data and k_u is the number of parameters freely adjusted. The analogy to the well-known degrees of freedom adjustment of the correlation coefficient is obvious.

The formulae presented above provide joint system measures. To acquire a single equation measure for good i alone, we simply group all other goods together to get the information measure

$$I_t = W_{it} \log_e \left(\frac{W_{it}}{\hat{W}_{it}} \right) + (1 - W_{it}) \log_e \left(\frac{1 - W_{it}}{1 - \hat{W}_{it}} \right).$$

Then $\bar{I}$ is computed as before. It is known that information measures are unreliable when shares do not sum to one with considerable precision. The proper procedure is to divide all shares by their sum over goods to assure that the shares sum exactly to one.

5.9.2. Model with leisure

Table 5.18 presents the relevant average information inaccuracies for the models we have estimated jointly with leisure. To provide a means of

Table 5.18
Information inaccuracies with leisure included[a] ($\alpha=2.3$, $\Gamma=1$, no intercept).

	Absolute prices	Relative prices First blocking	Relative prices Final blocking	Relative prices Fully additive	Naive
System results					
Uncorrected info. inaccuracy	2.948	3.183	3.416	4.433	9.792
Info. inaccuracy with d.f. correction	3.131	3.336	3.534	4.527	
Percent reduction from naive	68.02%	65.93%	63.91%	53.76%	
Pre-WWI info. inaccuracy	3.033				10.607
Percent reduction from naive	71.40%				
Post-WWI info. inaccuracy	2.468				5.172
Percent reduction from naive	52.29%				
Single equation results					
Perishables info. inaccuracy	0.851	1.128	1.122	1.156	2.872
Percent reduction from naive	70.39%	60.73%	60.95%	59.74%	
Semidurables info. inaccuracy	0.318	0.340	0.331	0.675	0.509
Percent reduction from naive	37.39%	33.05%	34.87%	−32.68%	
Durables info. inaccuracy	1.031	1.013	1.124	1.625	1.248
Percent reduction from naive	17.43%	18.84%	9.96%	−30.19%	
Services equation	0.725	0.690	0.834	0.932	4.772
Percent reduction from naive	84.81%	85.54%	82.53%	80.47%	
Leisure equation	0.844	0.907	0.946	1.211	4.412
Percent reduction from naive	80.86%	79.46%	78.57%	72.56%	

[a] The information inaccuracies are to be multiplied by 10^{-4}.

assessing these average information inaccuracies, a norm is needed. For that purpose we shall compute the average information inaccuracies resulting from a no-change forecast of the value shares. The resulting implied forecast $\hat{W}_{i,t+1}$ was computed from $\hat{W}_{i,t+1} = W_{it}$ for all $i = 1, \ldots, n+1$ and for all t during the relevant time span. The results for the no change extrapolation are tabulated in the last column as "naive". We can then judge our models by the percentage reduction in average information inaccuracy that they provide relative to the no-change extrapolation.

It should be observed that the no-change extrapolation is not as naive as it may appear. Parks (1969) computed information measures for the Rotterdam model and for three competing models, including Houthakker's Indirect Addilog Model and Stone's Linear Expenditure System with and without a time trend. He used a century of Swedish data. Although the absolute price version of the Rotterdam model tended to achieve percentage reductions of about 34 percent, he was unable to detect any appreciable improvements over the no-change extrapolation with any of the other models.

We computed the average information inaccuracies in table 5.18 using our maximum likelihood estimates of the absolute price version and our maximum likelihood estimates of the relative price versions without iteration on the arguments of the $A_{it}(\bar{\mu})$ functions. Observe that using the degrees of freedom adjustment we have achieved a 68 percent reduction with the absolute price version. Although the relative price version with perishables additive has fewer parameters, that version achieved a 66 percent reduction. When we also imposed additivity in services, the reduction dropped slightly to 64 percent. But the imposition of full additivity led to a drop in the percentage reduction to 54 percent. Also note that when we computed the system information inaccuracies separately for the years prior to and after the First World War, we found that we had acquired somewhat better model performance prior to the war. Recall that the shares appear to fluctuate more widely after the First World War.

Now let us turn to the single equation results at the bottom of table 5.18. The success of the leisure demand function is clear. Its 81 percent reduction is very large; but the durables equation only achieved a 17 percent reduction from the no-change extrapolation. Since durables' share in full income has tended to remain relatively constant over time (recall fig. 5.4), the no-change extrapolation is difficult to beat.

Observe the extremely poor performance of the fully additive model in fitting both durables and semidurables consumption shares. The performance (fit) of those equations was more than 30 percent worse than that of the no-change extrapolation. Also, observe that the imposition of additivity in perishables led to negligible changes in performance relative to the absolute price version. Only the perishables equation itself did appreciably worse. The further imposition of additivity in services led to detectable deterioration only in the durables equation, and observe that we are not using a degrees of freedom correction to compensate for the decreased number of unknown parameters.

5.9.3. Model without leisure

It would be interesting to acquire a direct comparison between the performance of our models and that of the Rotterdam model fitted, in the usual manner, to expenditure on goods alone. Recall that we have displayed the goods-alone regression in table 5.9. Our models explain shares in full income while the model tabulated in table 5.9 explains shares in ordinary income. To provide comparability we must use our models to fit the shares of goods alone in ordinary income.

We generated the necessary implied forecasts from our models by computing the implied forecasts (fitted values) of the share of each good in

Table 5.19
Information inaccuracies with leisure deleted.[a]

	Extended	Usual	Naive
System Results			
Uncorrected info. inaccuracy	7.042	8.166	17.38
Info. inaccuracy with d.f. correction	7.478	8.596	
Percent reduction from naive	56.97%	50.54%	
Percent reduction from usual	13.01%		
Single equation results			
Perishables info. inaccuracy	2.070	2.264	6.352
Percent reduction from naive	67.41%	64.35%	
Percent reduction from usual	8.57%		
Semidurables info. inaccuracy	1.026	1.369	2.093
Percent reduction from naive	50.98%	34.61%	
Percent reduction from usual	25.05%		
Durables info. inaccuracy	3.406	3.902	5.304
Percent reduction from naive	35.78%	26.44%	
Percent reduction from usual	12.70%		
Services info. inaccuracy	2.981	3.425	11.036
Percent reduction from naive	72.99%	68.96%	
Percent reduction from usual	12.98%		

[a] The information inaccuracies are to be multiplied by 10^{-4}.

full income and then multiplying that implied forecast by the ratio of full income (expenditure on goods and leisure) to ordinary income (expenditure on goods alone). Then we computed the average information inaccuracies displayed in table 5.19.

The results termed "extended" in that table are the results from our absolute price version with share forecasts transformed to shares in ordinary income. The results called "usual" were generated from the model in table 5.9. Under the system results in table 5.19, our model does 13 percent better than the usual version. Under single equation results in table 5.19, our model does uniformly better than the usual version in forecasting the demand for each good. Our improvement is particularly good for the semidurables equation in which our model's performance is 25 percent better than that of the usual approach. It is interesting to observe that the percentage reduction from the naive for our extended durables equation is 36 percent, while the percentage reduction was only 17 percent in table 5.18. This result again reflects the merits of the no-change extrapolation for durables' share in table 5.18.

5.10. Conclusions

We have tested an aggregation condition necessary for the conventional separation of the consumer's decision into a labor supply and a dichotomized commodity consumption allocation decision. The condition is rejected. We use information theory to compare the degrees of freedom adjusted fit of our model estimated with and without leisure. Joint estimation of the full system of leisure and commodity demand functions resulted in uniform gains in fit, as measured both by single equation and system information indices. These gains appear to result from highly significant non-weakly-separable (inconsistent with a separability group norm) substitution between both durables and semidurables and leisure. This substitutability appears to be a household analog to the substitutability of capital for labor time in the theory of the firm.

It frequently is asserted that leisure consumption has experienced a long-run trend interrupted by a postwar structural change. All of our consumption quantities are measured as shares in full income. By that allocation measure, leisure's, durables', and semidurables' shares all have tended to remain *unchanged* over the long run. No unexplained structural shifts were observed. In addition, the autonomous time trends (or intercepts in first differenced models such as ours) which have plagued demand studies did not appear, and all properties of the estimated equations were plausible, precisely estimated, and in agreement with theory. Our inferences were acquired with a model derived under weaker conditions than those implicit in other aggregate demand models.

PART II

NEW MODELS AND APPROACHES

INTRODUCTION TO PART II

In Part I we used widely known models and techniques to analyze in depth, both theoretically and empirically, a single economic issue: the merits of modeling consumer goods expenditure allocation jointly with labor supply. In Part II we leave that issue and present and explore new demand models, approaches, and methodologies.

CHAPTER 6

RECURSIVE SUBAGGREGATION AND A GENERALIZED HYPOCYCLOIDAL DEMAND MODEL

6.1. Introduction

In recent years much progress has been made in the systems approach to modeling consumption expenditure allocation. Yet, in practice that approach rarely has been used in price forecasting. In this chapter we build upon and extend the systems approach to generate a highly flexible recursive methodology for demand price forecasting, and we construct the food price forecasting sector of a version of such a model. Unlike Part I, Chapter 6 will use an approach that requires the existence of a community utility function.

Our utility function will contain interaction terms at all levels of the utility tree, and our utility tree is only blockwise weakly separable between groups. By contrast, Brown and Heien's (1972) S-Branch contains no interaction terms at any level of the utility tree, either within or between branches. In addition, our model will permit testing for groupwise strong separability either within or between branches. We shall test for and impose such subgroupings to improve estimator precision. In fact, our estimator frequently will select such subgroupings automatically. Finally, we shall postulate a generalized hypocycloidal (g-hypo) model as a special case. We shall see that g-hypo provides substantial simplification in estimation, and our empirical results will lead to acceptance of g-hypo at all levels and in branches of our full utility tree.

In conjunction with the well-known utility tree concept, there exists a less widely used literature on dual price and quantity subindices. We shall utilize the relevant theory of quantity indices to formulate and recursively to estimate conditional demand models at successive levels of aggregation. The approach will facilitate the recursive construction and linking of inverse demand models of various economic sectors at various levels of aggregation, and thereby will simplify greatly our estimation task. In addition to providing recursive aggregation over goods, our model satisfies Gorman's conditions for aggregation over consumers.

Unlike most globally integrable demand systems, our model will be an inverse demand model having endogenous prices and predetermined quantities. The direct translog has endogenous prices, but except in the Cobb–Douglas case we cannot a priori impose upon translog either global integrability or even local integrability over *finite* regions. Without any such imposed functional regularity, the model's behavior is not adequately controllable for our forecasting purposes. For example, we would be uncomfortable about the properties of any forecast found to lie in a region in which "community" utility is being locally minimized, as occurs in those regions of translog in which preference convexity is violated. This possibility is not removed by the existing ability to impose integrability of translog at a single infinitesimal point. Since our model is an inverse demand model, it is conveniently designed for price forecasting. We shall compute the matrix of elasticities of the full inverse demand system, and we shall use a duality relationship between direct and inverse demand systems to compute the matrix of all expenditure and Hicks–Allen (Slutsky) price elasticities of the implied direct demand system.

During estimation we shall pay particular attention to the inequality constraints imposed on the parameters by theory. Such inequality constraints exist on the parameters of all integrable demand models, but the empirical implications of such constraints have not been recognized. Whether or not binding, the existence of inequality constraints truncates the distribution of the parameter estimators. This fact invalidates the statistical theory usually used to support the construction of standard errors in most demand models. We shall transform the parameter space in such a manner as to free all parameters from such inequality constraints, and we shall estimate the unrestricted transformed parameters. Since our approach implicitly imposes all available theoretical restrictions, our estimates are certain always to lead to a globally integrable model. We also test for the gains from joint versus separate estimation of collections of conditional demand systems. Joint estimation of all of our model's disaggregated consumption sectors is accomplished using a substantially expanded and extended version of the Eisenpress and Greenstadt (1966) nonlinear FIML program.

6.2. The model

6.2.1. Two-step maximization

We consider ten goods grouped into three groups, and we correspondingly partition the "representative consumer's" ten-dimensional current period consumption expenditure vector, x, such that $x = (x_1', x_2', x_3')'$, where $x_r = (x_{r1}, \ldots, x_{rn_r})'$ for $r = 1, 2, 3$. Let $b_r = (b_{r1}, \ldots, b_{rn_r})'$ be a vector of constants for each $r = 1, 2, 3$, and let $y = (y_1', y_2', y_3')'$, where $y_r = x_r - b_r$. Let $B_r = [B_{rij}]$ be a symmetric matrix of constants, and let ρ_r be less than $\frac{1}{2}$ for $r = 1, 2, 3$. Following convention, we refer to y as the vector of supernumerary consumption quantities, although we do not restrict $b = (b_1', b_2', b_3')'$ to be non-negative, and we do not interpret b to be subsistence consumption quantities. When b can contain negative elements in such affine transformations (from x to $x - b$), Solari (1971, p. 59) has interpreted the negative elements in terms of a hierarchical ordering of superior goods. We call b the affine origin.

We now define an aggregate supernumerary quantity index for group r by

$$Q_r = Q_r(y_r) = \left(\sum_{i=1}^{n_r} \sum_{j=1}^{n_r} B_{rij}^2 y_{ri}^{\rho_r} y_{rj}^{\rho_r} \right)^{1/2\rho_r}.$$

The properties of the function $Q_r(y_r)$ have been considered by Kadiyala (1972), Denny (1974), and Blackorby, Primont, and Russell (1977).

We then define a utility function on the aggregates $q = (Q_1, Q_2, Q_3)'$ by

$$u(q) = \left[\sum_{k=1}^{3} \sum_{\ell=1}^{3} A_{k\ell}^2 Q_k^\rho Q_\ell^\rho \right]^{1/2\rho},$$

where $A = [A_{kl}]$ is a symmetric matrix of constants, and $\rho < \frac{1}{2}$ is a constant scalar. Then the composite function

$$v(x) = u(Q_1(x_1 - b_1), Q_2(x_2 - b_2), Q_3(x_3 - b_3))$$

defines a strictly concave monotonically increasing utility function on quantities, x, and v is weakly separable in the subvectors $\{x_1, x_2, x_3\}$. We refer to v as the WS-branch utility function. It reduces to S-branch when both A and all of the B_r matrices are diagonal. The generalization to q groups and n goods is obvious. We use the term WS-branch to emphasize its blockwise weak separability (WS).

We could further generalize our model by replacing q in $u(\cdot)$ by $q - \gamma$, where γ would translate the origin in the aggregate supernumerary quantity indices. Although b already has imbedded within q an analogous translation of the disaggregated quantities, x, the introduction of a nonzero γ vector would not violate the homothetic separability conditions on which our derivation will be based. But a nonzero γ vector would complicate the interpretation of our quantity indices at higher levels of recursive subaggregation, and an attempt at introducing nonzero γ led to statistically insignificant estimates of all of its elements and to negligible changes in the estimates of all other parameters. The t-ratios of the γ estimators varied between 0.53 and 1.3 for WS-branch (defined below) and between 0.76 and 1.2 for g-hypo (defined below).

We assume that the "representative consumer" selects his annual consumption vector, x, to

$$\text{maximize } v(x) \text{ subject to } x'p = m, \qquad (6.1)$$

where $m > 0$ is total annual expenditure on the ten goods. The vector of prices, $p > 0$, of the ten goods is partitioned into three subvectors, p_r, $r = 1, 2, 3$, corresponding to the three groups of goods such that $p = (p'_1, p'_2, p'_3)'$, where $p_r = (p_{r1}, \ldots, p_{rn_r})'$. We let $M = m - \sum_{r=1}^{3} p'_r b_r$, which we call total supernumerary consumption expenditure. Strictly speaking we should call M augmented supernumerary expenditure, since we permit the affine origin b to have negative elements. See Solari (1971, p. 59).

We restrict consideration to values of (m, p) in a set S defined such that on S the values of m, p, and M are strictly positive, and the solution for x to problem (6.1) and resulting value of $y = x - b$ are strictly positive. We see that for (m, p) on S the solution to problem (6.1) must satisfy

$$x > b. \qquad (6.2)$$

We now define two auxiliary decision problems.

In the first problem, q is selected to

$$\text{maximize } u(q) \text{ subject to } q'p^* = M, \qquad (6.3)$$

where $p^* = (P_1, P_2, P_3)'$ is a vector of aggregate price indices corresponding to the quantity aggregates q. The restrictiveness in this problem of the homotheticity of u would be great if Q_r were an aggregator of x_r. But recall that Q_r actually is an aggregator of the supernumerary consumption quantities y_r. The determination of the indices p^* will be considered below. In the second auxiliary decision problem, y_r is selected for each $r = 1, 2, 3$ to

$$\text{maximize } Q_r(y_r) \text{ subject to } y'_r p_r = Q_r P_r. \qquad (6.4)$$

Now let us suppose that a consumer were to select q to solve problem (6.3) and then were to solve problem (6.4) to determine y. Finally, in a third stage, suppose he were to select x such that $x = y + b$. It can then be shown that there exists aggregate price indices $p^* > 0$ which are functions solely of $p > 0$ such that the solution for x to the above three-stage decision is identical to the solution to the consumer's actual decision problem (6.1) for all $(m, p) \in S$. Referring to theorem 4 of Green (1964, p. 25), we see that v satisfies the necessary and sufficient conditions for our conclusion to obtain. This result is a generalization of the result in section 1.3. This mathematical equivalency between problem (6.1) and the three-stage decision permits us to specify our model in terms of the implications of the three-stage decision.

Observe that we view (6.1) as the decision problem actually solved by the consumer. We only prove that he acts *as if* he solved the three-stage decision. No need exists to rationalize b in the three-stage decision in terms of a budgeting process. Also, note that the homotheticity of our functions Q_r in y_r is necessary for our use of Green's theorem 4. Since this assumption implies only marginal homotheticity with respect to x, there is no implication of unitary income elasticities for the demand for x. However, there is such an implication with respect to the demand for supernumerary quantities, y. That implication also could be eliminated by introducing two price indices jointly, as in Theil (1976). We do not pursue that possibility here.

6.2.2. Solution to the nested maximization problems

From the first-order conditions for the solution to problem (6.3), we can determine that

$$W_r = \frac{\sum_{k=1}^{3} A_{kr}^2 Q_k^\rho Q_r^\rho}{\sum_{k=1}^{3} \sum_{\ell=1}^{3} A_{k\ell}^2 Q_k^\rho Q_\ell^\rho} \tag{6.5}$$

for $r=1,2,3$ where $W_r = P_r Q_r / M$. However, from the budget constraint in problem (2.3) we know that $P_r Q_r = p_r' y_r$. Hence, we see that

$$W_r = p_r' y_r / M. \tag{6.6}$$

Observe that the unknown price index P_r has been eliminated from (6.5).

Similarly, from the first-order conditions for the solution to problem (6.4) and from the equality $y = x - b$ we can determine that for $r=1,2,3$ and $i=1,\ldots,n_r$,

$$w_{ri} = \frac{x_{ri}(x_{ri} - b_{ri})^{\rho_r - 1} \sum_{j=1}^{n_r} B_{rji}^2 (x_{rj} - b_{rj})^{\rho_r}}{\sum_{j=1}^{n_r} \sum_{k=1}^{n_r} B_{rjk}^2 (x_{rj} - b_{rj})^{\rho_r} (x_{rk} - b_{rk})^{\rho_r - 1} x_{rk}}, \tag{6.7}$$

where $w_{ri} = p_{ri}x_{ri}/m_r$ with $m_r = Q_r P_r + p'_r b_r$. But from the budget constraint to problem (2.4) observe that $Q_r P_r + p'_r b_r = x'_r p_r$. Hence,

$$w_{ri} = p_{ri}x_{ri}/p'_r x_r \tag{6.8}$$

and we have removed the unknown price index P_r from (6.7).

6.2.3. Side restrictions on the parameters

In (6.2) we have imposed an upper bound on the affine origin b. Although (6.2) could be weakened to a weak inequality, the WS-branch utility function would not be defined if x_{ri} were less than b_{ri} for any (r, i). Hence (6.2) is a basic part of the model. But we now also impose a lower bound on b, although no such lower bound is necessarily dictated by the model.

Since q is linearly homogeneous in y, it follows immediately that the solution to problem (6.4) is of the form

$$y_{ri} = F_{ri}(p_r)(Q_r P_r) \quad (i = 1, \ldots, n_r), \tag{6.9}$$

for some functions F_{ri}, $i = 1, \ldots, n_r$. Then by definition of y_{ri} and by the budget constraint of problem (6.4), it follows that

$$x_{ri} = b_{ri} + F_{ri}(p_r)\mu_r,$$

where $\mu_r = y'_r p_r$. Now on the set S we know that $x_r > 0$ so that

$$F_{ri}(p_r)\mu_r > -b_{ri} \tag{6.10}$$

for all $i = 1, \ldots, n_r$. From (6.9) it follows that the F_{ri}, $i = 1, \ldots, n_r$, are non-negative. Furthermore, supernumerary expenditure on group r, μ_r, is positive for $(m, p) \in S$, and we would expect μ_r to be positive in any application. So if b_r were non-negative, (6.10) would pose no problems. But if b_{ri} were negative for any $i = 1, \ldots, n_r$, then (6.10) would require that

$$\mu_r > \max\left\{\frac{|b_{ri}|}{F_{ri}(p_r)} : b_{ri} < 0, i = 1, \ldots, n_r\right\}. \tag{6.11}$$

Condition (6.11) is a nontrivial implication of our assumption that $(m, p) \in S$. If actual and supernumerary expenditure on group r were positive but (6.11) were not satisfied, then the solution to problem (6.1) would be a corner solution in which $x_{ri} = 0$ for some $i \in \{1, \ldots, n_r\}$.

The level of aggregation over goods and consumers in our data is such that we would find corner solutions to be implausible, and our results (6.5) and (6.7) obtain only for regular interior solutions. For forecasting purposes we would wish our model to be applicable over as large a range of prices as possible. But we see from (6.11) that the restrictiveness of set S tends to increase as values of b_{ri} ($i = 1, \ldots, n_r$) become increasingly negative. The nature of the problem can be seen geometrically by translating the origin upwards into a field of indifference curves. The new axes will intersect the indifference curves at greater angles than the original axes. In our case the indifference curves are tangent to the original axes when they meet, so that corner solutions are impossible with $(m, p) > 0$ when $b = 0$.

In addition, very negative values of b_{ri} frequently characterize goods having very high own price elasticities and expenditure elasticities. See Solari (1971, pp. 54–63) for a detailed description of some implications of such affine transformations. Pollak and Wales (1969) have used such implausible elasticities as a basis for imposing the far stronger restriction (on the linear expenditure system) that the affine origin must be strictly non-negative. Furthermore, negative components of our estimates of b usually will be seen to have only moderate to low precision. This fact alone gives us little confidence in very negative estimates of b_{ri} values. Hence, we impose a lower bound on the affine origin, b. In particular we strengthen (6.2) to the symmetric restriction on b:

$$|b_{ri}| < x_{ri}, \tag{6.12}$$

for all $r = 1, 2, 3$ and $i = 1, \ldots, n_r$.

6.3. Estimation

6.3.1. Recursive estimation procedure

We shall utilize a recursive estimation scheme in which we ourselves construct all aggregate quantity indices from results of the previous estimation stage at a lower level of aggregation. Although we shall carry the procedure through only two stages, the approach clearly can and should be pursued sequentially through the complete utility tree characterizing the consumer's current and intertemporal consumption allocation preferences. A dual approach has been proposed by Keller (1976) and used by Hasenkamp (1975). They use direct rather than inverse demand functions. But with prices exogenous, they required knowledge of an analytic expression for the price indices, p^*. That expression is known only for utility functions considerably less flexible than the WS-branch. A related approach in the production literature has been considered by Mundlak and Razin (1969).

We begin by adding a stochastic error term u_{ri} onto (6.7) for each $r=1,2,3$ and each $i=1,\ldots,n_r$. We make the usual assumptions of homoscedasticity, no autocorrelation, etc. and we compute the joint maximum likelihood (FIML) estimates of eqs. (6.7) with the quantities, x, exogenous and the expenditure shares, w_{ri}, endogenous. We shall test whether the errors are correlated across branches. As we shall see, they are correlated, and we shall estimate all conditional demand systems in (6.7) jointly. We shall use an extensively expanded and improved version of the Eisenpress nonlinear FIML program. We will then use our estimate of B_r ($r=1,2,3$), of b, and of (ρ_1, ρ_2, ρ_3) to compute the aggregate supernumerary quantity indices q and the supernumerary expenditure shares $w=(W_1,W_2,W_3)'$. We use those estimated indices as data in the estimation of (6.5) with additive stochastic errors ε_r, $r=1,2,3$. We assume that ε_r is uncorrelated with u_{ri} for all (r,i), so that our FIML estimator of q also is uncorrelated with $\varepsilon=(\varepsilon_1,\varepsilon_2,\varepsilon_3)'$. Hence, we can treat our estimator of q as predetermined in (6.5). We take w as endogenous. Of course, an errors-in-the-variables problem exists in the use of estimated (w,q) as data. But then any aggregate index is an estimate, and to use a prior published index as data simply is to ensure that one's aggregators are inconsistent with one's theory. The appropriate aggregators are dictated by one's estimated utility tree.

It is well known that demand systems tend to have strongly positive autoregressive error structures, and we could estimate the parameters of such an error structure. But in estimating the parameters of demand equations themselves, Kiefer and MacKinnon (1976) have shown that the small sample properties of one's estimator are good, if one acts as if no serial correlation existed; we follow that procedure here. Estimates of the parameters of the actual autoregressive error structure are needed only in forecasting.

Throughout our estimation we shall treat prices as endogenous and quantities as predetermined. We implicitly assume that food supply is a function of lagged prices, and that the stochastic errors in supply are uncorrelated with those in demand. The resulting block recursiveness leads to endogenous prices and predetermined quantities in the demand block. This form of block recursiveness is widely assumed in agricultural economics, since long lags exist between planting and harvest. Through joint use of the model's first and second aggregation levels, eqs. (6.5) and (6.7), our model is designed to provide disaggregated food price forecasts conditionally upon quantities supplied and aggregate food expenditure. By continuing our recursive modeling procedure, aggregate food expenditure could be replaced by aggregate total consumption expenditure.

6.3.2. Normalization of parameters

In (6.5) and (6.7) the matrices B_r ($r = 1, 2, 3$) and A are identified only up to an arbitrary multiplicative constant. Eqs. (6.5) and (6.7) are homogeneous of degree zero in B_r and in A. Hence, the matrices must be normalized. It should be observed that the choice of normalization has no theoretical implications and is totally arbitrary. No normalization can be more "general" than any other. In fact, if we estimate our model subject to one normalization, we can always transform our estimates directly into those that would have been acquired subject to any other normalization. We need only multiply our estimated matrices by the appropriate constant. We shall follow precisely that procedure.

Initially we shall estimate (6.7) subject to the normalization $B_{rij} = 1$ for $i = j = n_r$ and $r = 1, 2, 3$, and we shall report those estimates. This normalization is convenient during estimation. But prior to estimating the aggregate model (6.5), we shall renormalize our estimate $\hat{B}_r$ of B_r by dividing $\hat{B}_r$ by

$$\left[\sum_{i=1}^{n_r} \sum_{j=1}^{n_r} \hat{B}_{rij}^2 \right]^{1/2}.$$

The newly transformed estimator of B_r will satisfy the normalization

$$\sum_{i=1}^{n_r} \sum_{j=1}^{n_r} \hat{B}_{rij}^2 = 1,$$

and the new estimates are identical to those that we would have acquired if we had imposed the normalization

$$\sum_{i=1}^{n_r} \sum_{j=1}^{n_r} B_{rij}^2 = 1$$

initially. We use the newly normalized estimates in computing the aggregate quantity data used in (6.5). The Euclidean distance restriction on B_r is attractive at this stage, since the aggregate quantity index Q_r then becomes a mean of order $\rho_r/2$ in the disaggregated supernumerary quantities, y_r; hence, Q_r is a form of "average" of the elements of y_r. A common alternative quantity index normalization would have resulted if we had divided Q_r in each year by Q_r at its value in some index year. When we estimate (6.5), we impose the normalization $A_{33} = 1$. If we were recursively to estimate an even higher level of aggregation at a following stage, we then would renormalize A to satisfy

$$\sum_{i=1}^{n_r} \sum_{j=1}^{n_r} A_{ij}^2 = 1$$

before computing an aggregate food quantity index.

6.3.3. Imposition of parameter restrictions

Since we have squared the elements of the matrices A and B_r, $r = 1, 2, 3$, the matrices are subject to no inequality constraints. If they had not been squared, they would have been subject to a non-negativity constraint. But (ρ_1, ρ_2, ρ_3), ρ, and b are still subject to inequality constraints. If we estimated them directly, the distribution of our estimators would be truncated, whether or not the inequality constraint was binding. For example, the parameter b_{ri} must satisfy (6.12). Constraint (6.12) defines the parameter space in which b must lie. But an admissible estimator must take values solely in the parameter space. Since our estimator cannot impute positive density to regions not satisfying (6.12), an estimator of b cannot be asymptotically normal, and the available statistical theory is not relevant to direct estimation of b. We shall transform the parameter space into an unconstrained Euclidean space.

Constraint (6.12) restricts b to an open set. Hence, corner solutions never can be attained, and the existence of a maximum of the likelihood function is in doubt. We replace (6.12) with the weak inequality $|b_{ri}| \leq x_{ri} - \delta$, where δ is a small number. In practice we shall use $\delta = 0.01$. Define x_{rit} to be the tth observation on x_{ri}. Now define $\phi = (\phi_1', \phi_2', \phi_3')'$, where $\phi_r = (\phi_{r1}, \ldots, \phi_{rn_r})'$ and where

$$b_{ri} = \left(\min_t x_{rit} - \delta \right) \sin \phi_{ri}. \tag{6.13}$$

By substituting (6.13) into (6.5) and (6.7) we eliminate the constrained parameters b, and we introduce the unconstrained parameters ϕ. We shall estimate ϕ. By the invariance property of the MLE we could then compute the maximum likelihood estimate of b from (6.13) and from the maximum likelihood estimate of ϕ.

We also have inequality constraints on ρ, ρ_1, ρ_2, and ρ_3. Each must be strictly less than $\frac{1}{2}$ to ensure strict quasiconcavity of v. To convert that restriction into a weak inequality that can be imposed, we use $\rho, \rho_1, \rho_2, \rho_3 \leq (\frac{1}{2}) - \delta$, where $\delta > 0$. We have excluded $\delta = 0$, since when $\delta = 0$ the WS-branch utility function need not be strictly quasiconcave. If indifference curves are linear, then demand is not determined from a unique interior optimum, and our model is not applicable. Our model is applicable in theory for any positive δ, but for very low δ the elasticity of substitution between goods can become implausibly high. This prior view could be imposed more elegantly through Bayesian or mixed estimation, but our estimation task already is formidable. We select $\delta = \frac{1}{6}$ to impose that nonstochastic prior information. We thereby have restricted the theoretically admissible region $(-\infty, \frac{1}{2})$ to $(-\infty, \frac{1}{3})$. We believe that use of a smaller value of δ would increase the model's generality only slightly, but at great cost in lost plausibility. Then we have that

$$\rho, \rho_1, \rho_2, \rho_3 \leq \tfrac{1}{3}. \tag{6.14}$$

To impose $\rho \leq \frac{1}{3}$ we could substitute $(4/3) - \cosh \theta$ for ρ and estimate θ, but in fact we shall find that (6.14) always will be binding: the likelihood function always will be maximized at $\rho = \rho_1 = \rho_2 = \rho_3 = \frac{1}{3}$. We refer to that special case of the WS-branch as the g-hypo (generalized hypocycloidal) model. In mathematics, a (two-dimensional) hypocycloid of four cusps (or an astroid) is the graph of the function $x^{2/3} + y^{2/3} = a^{2/3}$, or equivalently it is the set $\{(x, y): x = a\cos^3 \theta, y = a\sin^3 \theta, 0 \leq \theta \leq 2\pi\}$. Its form is that of a diamond with center at the origin having vertices on the x and y axes at distances of a from the origin, but with the sides bowed in towards the origin. If the off-diagonal (interaction) elements of A and $B_r(r=1,2,3)$ are zero, our model becomes hypocycloidal with indifference surfaces which are hypocycloids (in the non-negative orthant) in supernumerary quantities. The generalized hypocycloidal utility function is acquired by introducing nonzero off-diagonal interaction coefficients into the hypocycloidal utility function.

6.3.4. Data

Our data consists of annual data on ten food goods, blocked into three categories. The first group $(r = 1)$ is a "protein group" containing the four goods (i) meats, (ii) poultry, (iii) eggs, and (iv) dairy (including butter). The second group $(r = 2)$ is an "other foods" group containing (i) fresh fruits and vegetables, (ii) processed fruits and vegetables, and (iii) cereals (including flour, as well as rice, cornmeal, etc.). The third group is a "miscellaneous goods" group containing (i) sugar and sweeteners, (ii) beverages (including only coffee, tea, and cocoa), and (iii) fats and oils (excluding butter). The data covers the years 1935–1974, but we deleted the war years of 1942–1945.

The United States Department of Agriculture (USDA) quantity data is adjusted civilian domestic disappearance acquired from table 1 of *Food: Consumption, Prices, Expenditures* (1968a, 1968b). The categories are as defined in that table 1, except for fresh and processed fruits and vegetables. We aggregated those categories from a finer classification in table 1 using index year prices as weights. The resulting indices are as follows. Fresh fruits and vegetables equal 0.310 (fresh fruits) + 0.513 (fresh vegetables) + 0.177 (potatoes and sweet potatoes). Processed fruits and vegetables equal 0.689 (processed fruits) + 0.181 (processed vegetables) + 0.130 (beans, peas, nuts, soya products). The price data was constructed from the Bureau of Labor Statistics sources in tables 96 and 97 of the same publication. Those consumer price indices were reaggregated to correspond with the ten USDA quantity categories discussed above. The price data were converted to a 1957–1959 base, and each quantity index then was rescaled by a constant factor such that expenditure in the 1957–1959 base period on that good equaled actual expenditure, given in column 8 of table 3 of United States Department of Agriculture (1968a).

6.4. Results

6.4.1. Separate estimation of the three disaggregated branches

Modeling of the disaggregated allocation stage requires the estimation of the ten equations in (6.7). Those equations are divided into three groups corresponding to the grouping of goods described above. We began our estimation process by estimating each of the three groups of equations separately, although the equations within each group were estimated jointly. Since joint estimation of all three groups is expensive, we sought to acquire initial inferences through blockwise estimation to provide carefully selected initial conditions for iterative full joint estimation. In the usual manner, the last equation in each group was deleted during estimation to prevent the covariance matrix singularity otherwise induced by the budget constraint.

Such estimates for reduced form demand systems are known to be invariant to the equation deleted. Throughout our discussion below, we refer to A and B_r, $r = 1, 2, 3$, as the coefficient matrices. We refer to the diagonal elements of those matrices as the own effects and the off-diagonal elements as the cross (or interaction) effects.

As observed earlier, we have normalized the coefficient matrices during estimation by setting the last own effect equal to one, and hence no estimates appear for those own effects in the tables. The values in parentheses in the tables are t-ratios. The notation $(-)$ in place of a t ratio designates a parameter constrained to equal some value (0 to $\frac{1}{3}$) in advance. An estimate of ϕ_{ri} is $\pm \pi/2$ if and only if the constraint $|b_{ri}| \leq x_{ri} - \delta$ is binding on b_{ri}. The standard errors were computed using Barnett's (1976) theorem 4, which is the matrix analog of theorem 4.4 in Chapter 4 above. The asymptotic properties of these standard errors are provided by theorems 4.1 and 4.2.

We began our blockwise estimation of the three branches by estimating them with no constraints imposed on (ρ_1, ρ_2, ρ_3). All other inequality constraints were imposed through the use of the transformations described above. The results are contained in the first column of each of tables 6.1, 6.2, and 6.3. Observe that our maintained restriction (3.2) is violated in all cases. From the first column of table 6.2 we see that permitting ρ_2 to rise to 0.968 clearly has led to entirely implausible results. While we have normalized a diagonal element of B_2 to equal one, the estimates of all free elements have risen to implausibly high numbers. Furthermore, their corresponding t-ratios are so small that even the largest of these implausible estimates is statistically insignificant from zero. In two cases (the first two branches) the violation of (6.14) is large both in the size of the exponents' estimates and in the statistical "significance" induced by the high precision of the exponents' estimators. We should not be surprised by unfavorable empirical evidence on quasiconcavity, since aggregate demand functions are integrable only under entirely implausible conditions. Nevertheless, quasiconcavity is a useful regularity condition. If it were our intention to test quasiconcavity of the utility function, we would have to reject it. But that is not our intention. We maintain (6.14) as nonstochastic prior information, not subject to testing. This is equivalent to the limiting case in which the inherently arbitrary test size (frequently set at 0.05) for testing concavity goes to zero. Hence, we are saying, in effect, that the test size appropriate to our purposes is so small that we can reasonably approximate it by zero and thereby delete the test.

Table 6.1
Parameter estimates of the protein block (group 1).

Parameter	Separate estimation		Joint estimation (g-hypo)		
	WS-Branch	G-hypo	1st blocking	2nd blocking	3rd blocking
B_{111}	1.306	1.541	1.436	1.377	1.225
	(4.339)	(6.189)	(5.419)	(5.670)	(6.847)
B_{112}	1.031	0.609	0.509	0.514	0.622
	(4.686)	(4.087)	(2.532)	(2.888)	(6.193)
B_{113}	6.01	0.0	0.0	0.0	0.0
	(2.414)	(0.0)	(0.0)	(—)	(—)
B_{114}	0.0	0.0	−0.001	0.0	0.0
	(0.0)	(0.0)	(0.0)	(0.0)	(—)
B_{122}	0.0	0.0	0.001	0.0	0.0
	(0.0)	(0.0)	(0.002)	(0.0)	(0.0)
B_{123}	0.265	0.0	0.0	0.0	0.0
	(0.688)	(0.0)	(0.0)	(—)	(—)
B_{124}	1.315	0.779	0.686	0.618	0.0
	(3.704)	(2.305)	(1.96)	(1.948)	(—)
B_{133}	1.425	1.267	1.174	1.129	1.027
	(8.143)	(6.812)	(5.671)	(5.850)	(6.760)
B_{134}	0.975	0.0	0.0	0.0	0.0
	(3.176)	(0.0)	(0.0)	(—)	(—)
ϕ_{11}	$\pi/2$	$-\pi/2$	−1.568	$-\pi/2$	$-\pi/2$
	(12.983)	(0.631)	(0.827)	(0.640)	(0.912)
ϕ_{12}	1.386	−1.535	−0.433	−0.409	−0.151
	(1.577)	(0.105)	(0.935)	(0.899)	(0.510)
ϕ_{13}	0.065	$-\pi/2$	$-\pi/2$	$-\pi/2$	$-\pi/2$
	(0.054)	(0.430)	(1.371)	(1.345)	(1.243)
ϕ_{14}	1.328	0.707	0.617	0.574	0.719
	(5.355)	(3.367)	(1.719)	(2.974)	(1.237)
ρ_1	0.760	1/3	1/3	1/3	1/3
	(11.585)	(—)	(—)	(—)	(—)

Notes: Numbers in parentheses are *t*-ratios. The goods subscripts refer to meats (good 1), poultry (good 2), eggs (good 3), and dairy (good 4).

As a means of controlling the behavior of the model and acquiring plausible regularity in our results, we now impose constraint (6.14). We treat unconstrained estimation only as the first stage in a two-step approach to constrained estimation. Since constraint (6.14) clearly will be binding in the maximization of the likelihood function, imposition of (6.14) is equivalent to setting $\rho_1 = \rho_2 = \rho_3 = \frac{1}{3}$ and estimating g-hypo. We shall do so. The second column of each of tables 6.1, 6.2, and 6.3 contains the resulting estimates for each branch. Observe that the order of magnitude of all parameter estimates now is plausible. We no longer see estimates in the

Table 6.2
Parameter estimates of the other foods block (group 2).

Parameter	Separate Estimation			Joint estimation (g-hypo)		
	WS-branch	G-hypo	Additive g-hypo	1st blocking	2nd blocking	3rd blocking
B_{211}	615.08	1.559	0.887	0.848	0.846	0.843
	(0.009)	(0.687)	(11.827)	(20.683)	(20.89)	(21.08)
B_{212}	851.46	0.439	0.0	0.0	0.0	0.0
	(.009)	(.282)	(—)	(—)	(—)	(—)
B_{213}	805.43	1.928	0.0	0.0	0.0	0.0
	(.009)	(.414)	(—)	(—)	(—)	(—)
B_{222}	0.0	2.254	0.899	0.881	0.881	0.881
	(0.0)	(.529)	(11.987)	(176.2)	(203.9)	(204.6)
B_{223}	343.86	0.0	0.0	0.0	0.0	0.0
	(.009)	(0.0)	(—)	(—)	(—)	(—)
ϕ_{21}	0.252	0.324	0.617	0.712	0.728	0.743
	(4.0)	(.682)	(7.092)	(3.940)	(4.022)	(4.198)
ϕ_{22}	−4.712	$-\pi/2$	$-\pi/2$	$-\pi/2$	$-\pi/2$	$-\pi/2$
	(3.175)	(1.628)	(1.759)	(2.009)	(2.046)	(1.835)
ϕ_{23}	$\pi/2$	0.100	−0.851	−1.577	$-\pi/2$	$-\pi/2$
	(6.714)	(0.169)	(0.581)	(0.573)	(0.410)	(0.672)
ρ_2	0.968	1/3	1/3	1/3	1/3	1/3
	(19.48)	(—)	(—)	(—)	(—)	(—)

Notes: Numbers in parentheses are t-ratios. The goods subscripts refer to fresh fruits and vegetables (good 1), processed fruits and vegetables (good 2), and cereals (good 3).

Table 6.3
Parameter estimates of the miscellaneous goods block (group 3).

Parameter	Separate estimation		Joint estimation (g-hypo)		
	WS-branch	G-hypo	1st blocking	2nd blocking	3rd blocking
B_{311}	2.565	1.891	1.365	1.167	1.176
	(1.177)	(3.940)	(3.730)	(18.178)	(21.826)
B_{312}	1.820	1.400	0.815	0.657	0.640
	(1.222)	(3.104)	(2.470)	(5.054)	(5.524)
B_{313}	0.0	0.0	0.516	0.0	0.0
	(0.0)	(0.0)	(1.030)	(—)	(—)
B_{322}	0.0	0.0	0.0	0.0	0.0
	(0.0)	(0.0)	(0.0)	(0.0)	(0.0)
B_{323}	2.068	1.301	0.0	0.0	0.0
	(0.866)	(2.126)	(0.0)	(—)	(—)
ϕ_{31}	−0.355	−0.460	$-\pi/2$	$-\pi/2$	$-\pi/2$
	(0.307)	(0.428)	(0.682)	(0.559)	(0.387)
ϕ_{32}	$-\pi/2$	$-\pi/2$	0.687	0.763	0.888
	(0.884)	(0.572)	(0.707)	(0.832)	(1.006)
ϕ_{33}	$\pi/2$	$\pi/2$	$\pi/2$	$\pi/2$	$\pi/2$
	(3.586)	(3.174)	(2.713)	(2.737)	(2.597)
ρ_3	0.40	1/3	1/3	1/3	1/3
	(2.930)	(—)	(—)	(—)	(—)

Notes: Numbers in parentheses are t-ratios. The goods subscripts refer to sugar and sweets (good 1), beverages (good 2), and fats and oils (good 3).

hundreds (or even exceeding 2.5). But the precision of our estimates of the coefficient matrix of the second branch remains very poor. In the third column of table 6.2 we have imposed complete additivity within the second branch (we have set all off-diagonal elements of B_2 equal to zero). The precision (t) of the remaining own effect estimators has risen dramatically to very high levels.

We used an asymptotic likelihood ratio test to test the additivity of the second branch. The relevant asymptotic statistical theory for our class of models has been derived in Chapter 4. We implicitly condition all of our inferences on the regularity conditions in that chapter. It then follows from theorem 4.3 that the test statistic $-2\log\lambda$, where λ is the relevant likelihood ratio, has a limiting χ^2 distribution with three degrees of freedom. The tail area of the test equals 0.37, which is sufficiently far above 0.05 to lead to an unambiguous acceptance of additivity within the second branch. In the third branch, the interactions with fats and oils appear to be estimated with only fair precision. We attempted imposing block additivity with sugar-and-sweeteners and beverages in one block and with oils strongly separated into its own block. But the tail area of the test was 0.00005, and we could not accept that further blocking at this point.

Observe that our estimator automatically has imposed block additivity on the first branch. Boundary solutions for interaction terms with eggs have led to strong separability in eggs. Such automatic blockings also are automatically accepted by an asymptotic likelihood ratio test. The maximum of the likelihood function would be unchanged if we imposed the blocking initially. Also, observe that poultry's own effect is zero. Poultry enters that utility function solely through its cross effects, and primarily through its precisely estimated interaction with meats. Any utility tree which is completely additive (strongly separable) within branches would seriously mis-specify our protein branch. A similar phenomenon occurs in the third branch. A corner solution has set the own effect for beverages equal to zero. Beverages enter the utility function largely through an interaction with sugar and sweeteners; this is not surprising for commonly sweetened coffee and tea. Our speculations on dominant interactions above will be validated by our further results below.

6.4.2. Joint estimation of all disaggregated branches

Having exhausted the potentially useful inferences available from separate estimation of the three branches, we now proceed to joint estimation of all three branches. We begin by accepting our previous selection of complete additivity within the second group and of no restrictions on the other groups, and we use the previous blockwise estimates as initial conditions in the full joint estimation iterations. Subsequent testing verified additivity of the second group through joint estimation as well. We began the full joint estimation with our final results from blockwise estimation to conserve on the expensive joint estimation costs. The resulting estimates are contained in tables 6.1, 6.2, and 6.3 in the columns headed "joint estimation" and "1st blocking". The estimates of the first two groups have not changed appreciably. The precision of the own effects estimators in the second branch has increased, despite the fact that we are estimating more parameters during joint estimation through the fuller error covariance matrix.

Blockwise estimation of the three branches is equivalent to full joint estimation with a correspondingly blocked block-diagonal covariance matrix. Hence, we can treat blockwise estimation as following from restrictions on the specification used during full joint estimation. We constructed the appropriate asymptotic likelihood ratio test for this hypothesis. The test statistic has 16 degrees of freedom, and the tail area of the test is 5×10^{-5}. Block diagonality and, hence, blockwise estimation are rejected. We continue with joint estimation.

Inspecting our joint estimates of the third branch, we see that strong separability in fats and oils looks very plausible. Although we were unable to accept that blocking during separate branch estimation, we try it again in the columns labeled "2nd blocking". The tail area of the hypothesis defined by the restrictions added in the second blocking exceeded 0.75. This is far in excess of 0.05, and we now accept the joint second blocking.

Having rejected block diagonality of the disturbance covariance matrix, our inferences acquired during separate estimation no longer have any statistical meaning. Our results during blockwise estimation now are usable only (but very successfully) as initial conditions for our iterative joint estimation; separate estimation also was required to construct the likelihood ratio statistic for testing covariance matrix block diagonality itself. Also, observe that the final blockwise estimates provide a respectable approximation to the joint estimates. Some potential users of this model may find our established empirical gains from joint estimation to be insufficient to justify the additional computing cost, especially when the number of goods is large.

Inspecting the estimates and standard errors of the second joint blocking, we observe that in the first branch the interactions with dairy appear to be small and imprecisely estimated. We further impose additivity in dairy products within the first category to obtain the third joint blocking in the last column of tables 6.1, 6.2, and 6.3. The tail area of the asymptotic likelihood ratio test of the new restrictions is 0.49. We accept the third blocking as our final blocking. Two interactions remain. In the protein group we have a precisely estimated interaction between meats and poultry. In the third group we have a precisely estimated interaction between beverages and sugar and sweetners. All other interactions within groups are gone. We do not consider hypothesis nesting, and we do not allocate test size over successive tests. We treat tail areas as a form of information rather than as a mechanical decision-making device.

We have given no particular consideration to the estimates of $\phi_r, r = 1, 2, 3$, during this selection process. Yet their precision frequently has been low. However, we see no merit in setting a ϕ_{ri} equal to zero. Doing so would not delete any explanatory variable, but would only arbitrarily estimate a parameter to equal zero. Having imposed our prior knowledge through (6.13), we generally shall accept the maximum likelihood estimate of ϕ_r, regardless of the estimator's precision. It is possible that the introduction of proportional habit formation might have been beneficial, but habit formation results in current supernumerary quantity indices q which depend upon lagged consumption. Although this presents no problems in theory, we sought a more transparently understandable current quantity index at this stage of our research.

6.4.3. Recursive estimation of the aggregate stage

Having completed the estimation of (6.7), we renormalize the coefficient matrices, construct the indices q and W_r, and estimate (6.5), as discussed earlier. The results are shown in table 6.4. The last two columns were constructed from our final joint estimates of (6.7). In the third column we impose no restrictions on ρ. The resulting ρ estimate of 0.719 is inadmissable, and we impose (6.14). This implies that $\rho = \frac{1}{3}$, and our estimates of g-hypo at the aggregate level are contained in the fourth column. Observe that in the third column the estimates are implausibly high relative to our normalization $A_{33} = 1$, and the precision of our estimators is extremely low. In the fourth column, complete additivity has resulted automatically from corner solutions for estimates of the non-negative interaction coefficients $A_{ij}^2 (i \neq j)$. The remaining direct effects have plausible magnitudes and are estimated with immense precision.

Table 6.4
Parameter estimates of the aggregate model.

Parameter	Separate estimation		Joint estimation (3rd blocking)	
	WS-branch	G-hypo	WS-branch	G-hypo
A_{11}	71.312	1.361	40.130	1.374
	(0.026)	(136.1)	(0.051)	(147.842)
A_{12}	96.353	0.0	35.699	0.0
	(0.026)	(0.0)	(0.050)	(0.0)
A_{13}	93.8	0.0	35.507	0.0
	(0.0003)	(0.0)	(0.050)	(0.0)
A_{22}	48.7	1.118	32.483	1.155
	(0.0003)	(159.7)	(0.050)	(296.8)
A_{23}	0.0	0.0	22.996	0.0
	(0.0)	(0.0)	(0.051)	(0.0)
ρ	0.823	1/3	0.719	1/3
	(6.858)	(—)	(2.864)	(—)

Notes: Numbers in parentheses are *t*-ratios. Aggregate goods (group) subscripts refer to protein goods (group 1), other foods (group 2), and miscellaneous goods (group 3).

This result could be viewed as reflecting favorably upon our original a priori (blockwise weakly separable) grouping of the goods. We have just accepted blockwise strong separability in the same grouping, and blockwise strong separability implies blockwise weak separability. In any applications in which such a test of blockwise strong separability leads to rejection, it might be reasonable to select that initial utility tree the blockwise weakly separable grouping of which yields the highest tail area for the hypothesis test of the corresponding blockwise strongly separable grouping. However, it should be observed that, strictly speaking, no rigorously conclusive formal test for the original weakly separable blocking is possible, since we inherently must condition upon that blocking as a maintained hypothesis in all of our inferences.

As a test of the robustness of the aggregate model estimates to our inferences at the disaggregated level, we reconstruct the index numbers in (6.5) from the last estimates of (6.7) acquired from separate estimation of the three branches. We then re-estimate (6.5), and we present the results in columns 1 and 2 of table 6.4. Permitting ρ to be free led to results as unacceptable as those in column 3, but the g-hypo results of column 2 are very similar to those in column 4. Robustness is high. Subject to our renormalization of $\hat{B}_1$, $\hat{B}_2$, and $\hat{B}_3$, our final model consists of the las column of tables 6.1, 6.2, 6.3, and 6.4.

Looking back over first step (WS-branch) results in tables 6.2 and 6.4, we now can observe the gains from imposing strict quasiconcavity of the utility function in our second (g-hypo) step (through the imposition of (6.14)). When we did not impose integrability conditions in advance, we acquired entirely unacceptable estimates both at the aggregate level and in the second branch at the disaggregate level. Yet the integrability-constrained (g-hypo) estimates always were reasonable. Our results illustrate the risks involved in the widespread related practice of estimating second-order unconstrained local approximations to an arbitrary cardinal utility function. Without maintaining adequately strong functional regularity conditions (such as convexity of community preferences), the behavior of a richly parameterized nonlinear model can be very strange indeed.

For forecasting purposes, our final model was altered slightly by changing our estimate of ϕ_{23} to equal zero. The t-ratio of our estimator of ϕ_{23} was a very low 0.67 and the sign of the estimate suggested a higher expenditure elasticity than expected for cereals demand. Rather than just changing our final estimate of ϕ_{23} to zero, it would have been preferable to re-estimate all parameters subject to the side constraint $\phi_{23}=0$. But our admittedly inelegant change resulted in joint estimates of all parameters that would lie well within any reasonable confidence region, and the computing costs involved in an additional constrained joint estimation of the disaggregated equations are out of proportion to the very small empirical gain attributable to the negligible increase possible in the likelihood function.

Although our final model contains only two interactions, they were selected empirically. The precision with which interactions can be captured depends upon sample size and the level of aggregation. Strong separability never should be imposed a priori. It is a very strong condition which can lead to serious specification error when the relevant interactions could have been captured with sufficient precision.

6.5. Elasticities and duality

6.5.1. Duality between direct and inverse demand

In this section we derive expressions for two matrices of elasticities which relate to each other as duals, and we compute all expenditure and Hicks–Allen price elasticities. As has been argued by Katzner (1970, p. 44) and by Pearce (1964, pp. 57–64), the relevant demand concept to the planner (or price forecaster), rather than to the producer, is the inverse demand system explaining prices in terms of planned output (or expected quantity supplied). Hence, the local forecasting properties of our model could be summarized in terms of the quantity elasticities of that inverse demand system. An independent objective in computing elasticities commonly is to provide a convenient basis for comparing one's results with those acquired from other demand models. For that purpose, the matrix of expenditure and Hicks–Allen price elasticities of the implied direct demand system is useful. We seek these direct demand elasticities since they provide information on substitutes, complements, superior goods, etc.

As Katzner (1970) and Pearce (1964) have shown, direct and inverse demand systems are dual concepts, residing in mutual shadow worlds possessing remarkably analogous properties. In addition, bijective passage between the two worlds is possible through simple inversion of corresponding matrices. For example, the Slutsky matrix of direct demand is just the inverse of the Antonelli matrix of inverse demand. See Katzner (1970, pp. 49 and 50). Even when an explicit closed form expression for the direct demand system does not exist, estimation of the inverse demand system, which always exists in closed form, is sufficient to permit estimation, through duality, of all income, Cournot, and Slutsky price elasticities of direct demand. Theoretical results on these duality relationships also are available in Samuelson (1947, pp. 125–129; 1950) and Lange (1942). We shall use that bijective relationship to permit immediate computation of the elasticities of direct demand from the easily computed elasticities of inverse demand.

We begin by defining the inverse demand system. We select an arbitrary good as numeraire, and we rearrange the groups such that the numeraire good is the last good in the last group. In the general case of N groups with n_r goods in the rth group ($r = 1, \ldots, N$), we can say that good (N, n_N) in our two-dimensional array of grouped goods is the numeraire. Good (r, ℓ) designates the ℓth good in the rth group. The elasticities to be derived below are invariant to the choice of numeraire.

For forecasting purposes, cereals may be a convenient numeraire, since usable independent price forecasts for that category can be deduced from the information contained in the market prices of relevant commodities futures contracts and in price support programs. The need for an independent forecast of a numeraire price would be eliminated if a prior forecast of m existed. When such a prior forecast of m exists, the most convenient forecasting form of our model is the system comprised of (6.5) and (6.7). When an independent numeraire price forecast exists, the most convenient forecasting form of our model is system (6.17), derived below. In either case, prices are forecasted conditionally upon quantities.

Denote the marginal rate of substitution between good (r, ℓ) and the numeraire by

$$g_{r\ell}(x) = \frac{\partial v / \partial x_{r\ell}}{\partial v / \partial x_{Nn_N}}$$

for $r = 1, \ldots, N$ and $\ell = 1, \ldots, n_r$. Note that $g_{r\ell}(x) = 1$ for the case $(r, \ell) = (N, n_N)$, which we do not exclude. It then follows that

$$\frac{p_{r\ell}}{p_{Nn_N}} = g_{r\ell}(x). \tag{6.15}$$

From the budget constraint and (6.15) it also follows that

$$\frac{m}{p_{Nn_N}} = \sum_{r=1}^{N} \sum_{\ell=1}^{n_r} g_{r\ell}(x) x_{r\ell}. \tag{6.16}$$

Let $k = \sum_{r}^{N} n_r$ be the total number of goods in all groups, and define the normalized price vector $\bar{p} = (\bar{p}_1, \ldots, \bar{p}_k - 1)'$, such that $(\bar{p}', 1)' = (1/p_{Nn_N})p$. Also, define deflated food expenditure, $\bar{m}$, by $\bar{m} = m/p_{Nn_N}$. Finally, define the vector valued function $f(x) = (f_1(x), \ldots, f_k(x))'$ as follows. Let $f_k(x)$ equal the right-hand side of (6.16). Let $(f_1(x), \ldots, f_{k-1}(x))'$ be defined such that $(f_1(x), \ldots, f_{k-1}(x), 1)' = (g_1'(x), \ldots, g_N'(x))'$, where $g_r(x) = (g_{r1}(x), \ldots, g_{rn_r}(x))'$ for $r = 1, \ldots, N$. Then it follows from (6.15) and (6.16) that

$$(\bar{p}', \bar{m})' = f(x). \tag{6.17}$$

The system of equations (6.17) is the inverse demand system.

The solution to problem (6.1) can be written as $x = d(\bar{p}, \bar{m})$, where $d = (D_1, \ldots, D_k)'$ is the vector of direct demand functions. Hence, it immediately is evident that f is just the inverse of the mapping d. The relationship between f and d is bijective, and the mappings d and f are duals. Although the duality relationships between d and f have found little, if any, use in the empirical demand literature, Pearce (1964, pp. 57–64) and Katzner (1970, p. 51) have shown that the duality between d and f is one of the strongest and most informative in economic theory. But while no closed form expression need exist for d, an explicit expression for f always is easily derivable from any differentiable utility function, v.

6.5.2. Elasticity matrices

We define

$$\xi_{ij} = \frac{\partial \log f_i(x)}{\partial \log x_j}$$

for $i, j = 1, \ldots, k$. Observe that here we use the singly subscripted notation x_j to refer to the jth component of the full vector of all consumption quantities, $x = (x'_1, \ldots, x'_N)'$. When we previously have used the doubly subscripted notation $x_{r\ell}$, we have referred to the ℓth component of the subvector x_r. Then define the $k \times k$ matrix E such that $E = [\xi_{ij}]$. The easily computed matrix E is the matrix of elasticities of inverse demand. For price forecasting purposes the first $k-1$ rows of E are of particular interest, since they provide the values of $\xi_{ij} = \partial \log \bar{p}_i / \partial \log x_j$ for $i = 1, \ldots, k-1$ and $j = 1, \ldots, k$. The last row of E provides $\xi_{kj} = \partial \log \overline{m} / \partial \log x_j$ for $j = 1, \ldots, k$.

Having derived the elasticities of inverse demand, we now seek the elasticities of direct demand. Define $\eta_{ij} = \partial \log D_i / \partial \log \bar{p}_j$ for $i = 1, \ldots, k$ and $j = 1, \ldots, k-1$, and define $\eta_{ik} = \partial \log D_i / \partial \log \overline{m}$ for $i = 1, \ldots, k$. Then define the $k \times k$ matrix R such that $R = [\eta_{ij}]$. Clearly, R is the complete matrix of all expenditure and Cournot normalized-price elasticities of direct demand, with the expenditure elasticities lying in the last column of R.

We shall need to compute R, although we do not have an explicit expression for d. By the known duality relationships between d and f, it follows immediately that $R = E^{-1}$. Equivalently, this result could be derived directly from theorem 23 in Buck (1965, p. 278). Now price elasticities with respect to normalized prices, $\bar{p}$, equal price elasticities with respect to nominal prices, p. Hence, in its first $k-1$ columns, R provides all ordinary Cournot (nominal) price elasticities of demand, except for those with respect to the numeraire price, p_k. But the numeraire price elasticities are easily computed from R using the well-known fact that the sum of all Cournot price elasticities of good i equals minus the expenditure elasticity of good i.

Having computed all expenditure and Cournot price elasticities of direct demand, we seek Hicks–Allen (Slutsky) price elasticities to permit us to explore complementarity and substitutability between goods. These elasticities are easily computed from the above elasticities and the Slutsky equation. Alternatively, the Hicks–Allen price elasticities could have been

Table 6.5
Estimated Hicks – Allen price elasticities.

	Meat	Poultry	Eggs	Dairy	Fresh fruits and vegetables	Processed fruits and vegetables	Cereals	Sugar and sweets	Beverages	Fats and oils
Meats	−2.23	0.02	0.42	0.39	0.16	0.28	0.26	0.48	0.13	0.11
	(−2.48)	(0.002)	(0.48)	(0.49)	(0.22)	(0.26)	(0.28)	(0.52)	(0.12)	(0.11)
Poultry	0.08	−1.46	0.26	0.25	0.10	0.17	0.16	0.30	0.08	0.07
	(0.01)	(−1.51)	(0.29)	(0.29)	(0.13)	(0.16)	(0.17)	(0.32)	(0.07)	(0.06)
Eggs	2.77	0.33	−5.11	0.44	0.18	0.31	0.29	0.53	0.14	0.12
	(2.50)	(0.27)	(−4.75)	(0.48)	(0.22)	(0.26)	(0.28)	(0.52)	(0.12)	(0.11)
Dairy	0.57	0.07	0.10	−1.05	0.04	0.06	0.06	0.11	0.03	0.03
	(0.61)	(0.07)	(0.12)	(−1.16)	(0.05)	(0.06)	(0.07)	(0.13)	(0.03)	(0.03)
Fresh fruits and vegetables	0.54	0.06	0.09	0.09	−1.05	0.06	0.06	0.10	0.03	0.02
	(0.64)	(0.07)	(0.12)	(0.12)	(−1.28)	(0.07)	(0.07)	(0.13)	(0.03)	(0.03)
Processed fruits and vegetables	1.79	0.21	0.30	0.28	0.11	−3.41	0.19	0.34	0.09	0.08
	(1.81)	(0.19)	(0.34)	(0.35)	(0.16)	(−3.59)	(0.20)	(0.38)	(0.09)	(0.08)
Cereals	1.49	0.18	0.25	0.24	0.10	0.17	−2.84	0.29	0.08	0.07
	(1.44)	(0.15)	(0.27)	(0.28)	(0.12)	(0.15)	(−2.84)	(0.30)	(0.07)	(0.06)
Sugar and sweeteners	2.18	0.26	0.37	0.35	0.14	0.24	0.23	−3.69	−0.17	0.10
	(2.18)	(0.23)	(0.41)	(0.42)	(0.19)	(0.23)	(0.24)	(−3.79)	(−0.21)	(0.09)
Beverages	0.80	0.10	0.13	0.13	0.05	0.09	0.08	−0.60	−0.81	0.04
	(0.83)	(0.09)	(0.16)	(0.16)	(0.07)	(0.09)	(0.09)	(−0.64)	(−0.89)	(0.04)
Fats and oils	1.04	0.12	0.18	0.17	0.07	0.12	0.11	0.20	0.05	−2.05
	(0.86)	(0.09)	(0.16)	(0.17)	(0.07)	(0.09)	(0.10)	(0.18)	(0.04)	(−1.76)

Notes: Numbers in parentheses are elasticities computed at average quantities. All other elasticities are at 1974 quantities.

Table 6.6
Estimated expenditure elasticities.

Commodity	Elasticity at 1974 quantities	Elasticity at average quantities
Meats	1.54	1.59
Poultry	0.97	0.96
Eggs	1.73	1.58
Dairy	0.35	0.39
Fresh fruits and vegetables	0.33	0.40
Processed fruits and vegetables	1.12	1.14
Cereals	0.93	0.91
Sugar and sweeteners	1.36	1.38
Beverages	0.50	0.53
Fats and oils	0.65	0.54

computed from the duality relationship between the Slutsky matrix and the Antonelli matrix. The matrix of all Hicks–Allen price elasticities of demand for our final forecasting model are displayed in table 6.5. All expenditure elasticities, acquired from the last column of R, are displayed in table 6.6. All elasticities were computed both at 1974 quantities (which are the most relevant for forecasting) and at average quantities. In table 6.5 the elasticities at average quantities are in parentheses. Standard errors were not computed for any elasticities. Since elasticities are not parameters in our model, no asymptotic statistical foundations exist to support such a computation. The population values of elasticities at average or most recent quantities vary as sample size increases.

From tables 6.5 and 6.6 we see that all Hicks–Allen own price elasticities are negative, and all expenditure elasticities are positive. Expenditure elasticities exceeded one for meats, eggs, processed fruits and vegetables, and sugar and sweeteners. Hence, as total food expenditure increases, the share of those goods in the food budget will tend to increase. The most own-price-elastic foods are eggs and sugar-and-sweeteners. All foods were found to be more own price elastic than had been found in previous studies. We believe that the reason relates to the endogeneity of quantities in those studies. The forecasting properties of a price forecasting model (with endogenous prices) are more easily seen from the matrix E of elasticities of inverse demand. From E we found that the own quantity elasticities of normalized prices (inverse demand) varied between -0.179 and -1.25 at 1974 quantities and between -0.192 and -1.154 at average quantities. Such modest elasticities of inverse demand tend to imply highly elastic direct demand, and vice versa. If direct demand had been less own price elastic, our price forecasts would have responded very widely to variations in supply. Since simultaneous bias exists in all econometric models, elasticity estimates ultimately must be conditioned upon the choice of endogenous variables appropriate to one's purposes.

As just observed, our relatively high own price elasticities of demand imply relatively modest responsiveness of equilibrium prices to (supply) quantity variations; this may suggest that food market prices respond to supply variations with a distributed lag on quantities. We view the introduction of lags (habit formation, etc.) into the model to be a logical next step in this research. All foods are Hicks–Allen substitutes except for beverages and sugar-and-sweeteners, which are complements. It is interesting to observe that this highly plausible complementarity between only two goods in a three-goods group would be impossible in S-branch, in which all goods within any branch are either mutual substitutes or mutual complements.

CHAPTER 7

AGGREGATION OF MONETARY ASSETS

7.1. Introduction

Monetary policy is related to the behavior of indices of the quantity, "price", and velocity of money. Yet, for such aggregates to be useful, they must have meaning and must be measurable. This raises troublesome methodological questions. What is money? Is it a "good" whose quantity can be measured, or is it just a vector of different characteristics (liquidity, means of payment, etc.)? Do currency and time deposits possess identical "moneyness" so that they can be summed linearly and with equal weights to acquire a meaningful quantity aggregate? If money is a meaningful good, then what is its price? Can more than one monetary aggregate jointly have meaning? In sections 7.2–7.11, we shall explore these issues using the general theory of economic aggregates. Economic indices are also called functional, true, or exact indices. The other well-known class of indices, used in section 7.12, consists of statistical indices, which are intended to approximate functional indices.

Although not previously applied to money demand, the literature on aggregation theory exists *precisely* for the purpose of providing rigorous and unique answers to the above questions in terms of a single internally consistent approach. That approach builds upon the aggregation implications of the multistage decision theory introduced in sections 1.3, 5.6, and 6.2. In this chapter we discuss the potential usefulness of the theory of aggregates to the joint construction of theoretically meaningful quantity and price indices at multiple levels of aggregation. We shall apply aggregation theory to the aggregation of passbook accounts across institution types and then to nested aggregation over transaction balances. The approach is the analog to that used in Chapter 6, but in terms of direct demand. This chapter, based upon Barnett (1980a), realizes objectives defined in Friedman and Schwartz (1970, pp. 151–154).

We shall show that passbook accounts at different types of institutions are close substitutes and hence can be aggregated linearly. But aggregation by simple summation is rejected, since the coefficients of the linear function are unequal. Substitutability between passbook savings and transaction balances is found to be low. Hence, nonlinear aggregation is required to approximate the economic index over savings and transaction balances. Our results also suggest that passbook accounts at commercial banks possess greater "moneyness" than passbook accounts in savings and loans or mutual savings banks, since the economic index weights passbook accounts at commercial banks more heavily than passbook accounts at savings and loans or at mutual savings banks. Similarly, transaction balances are far more heavily weighted than our economic passbook account aggregate. We provide similar empirical results relative to time deposits and large certificates of deposit.

Since the beginning of this century, a highly respected and increasingly sophisticated literature has been under development on statistical index number theory. While aggregation theory results in exact aggregator functions depending upon unknown (but estimable) parameters, statistical index number theory results in *parameter-free* approximations to aggregator functions. Index number theory provides the basis for the index numbers published by almost every governmental agency in the world (other than the central banks). In the latter sections of this chapter we explore the implication of statistical index number theory for the construction of monetary quantity index numbers.

During the past decade there has been much concern about the apparent destabilization of velocity. In fact, the problem arose primarily because of the long-run substitution effect resulting from rising own rates on unregulated monetary assets relative to the own rate on rate-regulated monetary assets. But the value of an *economic* aggregate (by its definition) *cannot* change as a result of internal substitution effects. Hence, the money market substitution effects' destabilizing velocity should be completely internalized by aggregation over the money market.

When *any* reputable index number formula is used, we find that the velocity of money *is* increasingly stabilized as the level of aggregation is increased, but the velocity of the usual simple sum index is destabilized by aggregation beyond an intermediate level. Furthermore, we use information theory to compare the information content of Divisia versus simple sum monetary aggregates. We find that the Divisia index dominates the simple sum index, regardless of the monetary components of the index and regardless of the choice of final targets. The gains in information from the simple sum to Divisia index (over the same components) frequently is very large. The simple sum index is *severely* defective.

7.2. Objectives

7.2.1. Theoretical and actual practices

Functional (economic) indices can be constructed at multiple levels of monetary aggregation in such a manner that the multiple indices are fully and uniquely nested. As a result, internal contradictions cannot arise at varying levels of aggregation. The functional index number generation process is inherently linked with a money market modeling procedure, so that a full system model of liquid asset demand would result as a byproduct of the nested index number generation procedure.

Suppose we should wish to construct a monetary quantity index as some function of currency, demand deposits, and consumer-type savings and time deposits at commercial banks. We call the resulting index M_2. In economic aggregation theory, consumers then must be able to treat M_2 as the quantity of a meaningful single good in their decisions. By the definition of a consumer good, consumers must be able to select their desired aggregate quantity of M_2 without regard to its composition. The allocation of M_2 over its component elements could be accomplished in a later second stage decision, conditionally upon the prechosen aggregate level of M_2. Varying the relative quantities of currency and time deposits within M_2 while holding the aggregate M_2 level constant must not affect consumers' preferences over any other goods. If this condition is satisfied, consumers can possess stable preferences over M_2 and other goods. If M_2 is not a good in this fundamental sense, then consumer preferences over M_2 and other goods will appear to shift whenever the relative proportions of the components of M_2 change.

It can be shown that when a meaningful functional quantity index exists for a consumer, that index itself must possess the known properties of a utility function, and that utility function must possess certain additional special properties (homotheticity and weakly separable nesting within the consumer's full utility function). Then, when the aggregate quantity index is held constant, the "utility of money" is necessarily held constant independently of its composition. As has been observed by Samuelson and Swamy (1974, p. 568): "The fundamental point about an economic quantity index, which is too little stressed by writers, Leontief and Afriat being exceptions, is that it must itself be a cardinal indicator of ordinal utility."

The functional quantity index cannot be known exactly without knowledge of the representative consumer's utility function, since the functional quantity index depends upon and is defined in terms of consumer preferences. Conventional accounting practices generate meaningful indices only to the degree that those indices imply plausible preference orderings over components. Yet, all current monetary quantity indices are constructed from simple addition of components. This means that *if* those indices have any economic (as opposed to accounting) meaning at all, the indices have been generated by a utility function for financial assets possessing the same simple unweighted summation form used in constructing the index. But such a utility function requires the goods over which it is defined to be perfect substitutes in identical ratios. In other words, the components of the quantity index must be indistinguishable to the consumer. In the existing simple sum M_2, for example, the consumption characteristics of one dollar of currency must be *identical* to those of one dollar of long-term time deposits. The violation of aggregation theory increases as the level of aggregation increases, since the higher the level of aggregation the less substitutable the components of the aggregates become.

Velocity can have no more meaning than the quantity aggregates relative to which velocity is defined. If we have no theory treating M_1, M_2, and M_3, for example, as goods related behaviorally, then what do we conclude when M_1 goes down, M_2 goes up, and M_3 remains unchanged? We have ambiguously conflicting information.

We frequently seek information about the "price" of money. In various studies the price of money has been viewed as an interest rate, an index of interest rates, the rate of change of prices, the price level, or an index of some subset of those subindices. But we shall prove that the literature on economic quantity indices and on user costs (equivalent rental prices) can be utilized to derive a unique dual theory of implied monetary rental price indices. Once a monetary aggregate has been operationalized, the consumer's decision modeled, and the consumer's preference structure estimated, the "price" and the quantity of the aggregate are simultaneously implied. These indices satisfy the accounting identity of equality between expenditure and the product of quantity and price, and the consumer can be shown to behave in a rational manner relative to the good whose price and quantity have been defined. This rationality obtains both relative to the aggregates and relative to their components, and consumers' decisions at all levels of aggregation are consistent with a single joint rational choice criterion.

Fisher (1922) provided a list of desirable properties for economic price and quantity indices. Frisch (1930) proved that when the number of goods exceeds unity, no index number formula can satisfy all of those properties. However, Samuelson and Swamy (1974, p. 566) have shown that if price and per capita quantity data is assumed to fall on neoclassical demand functions (rather than to be unrestricted independent variables, as assumed by Frisch), then the economic quantity and dual price indices "do meet the spirit of all of Fisher's criteria in the only case in which a single index number of the price of cost of living makes economic sense – namely the ("homothetic") case of unitary income elasticities in which at all levels of living the calculated price change is the same". We use such economic quantity indices.

We see that the theory of quantity and dual price indices can provide unique and meaningful quantity and price indices. But we seek indices corresponding to more than one level of aggregation. Can this be accomplished in an internally consistent manner? In fact, this can be done using a theory of functional structure which has been developed along with and attached to the recent theory of quantity and dual price indices. Under certain assumptions (weakly separable nesting) on preferences, a hierarchy of aggregates is dictated by that theory. Hence, everything we sought above becomes available under appropriate assumptions on preferences. No contradictions arise, and all becomes understandable jointly within a single recursively nested model of consumer portfolio allocation.

In Chapter 6 we provided a means of applying the theory of aggregation to modeling, recursively aggregating, and estimating a food demand sector. The demand model derived and applied in that chapter is the most flexible of the globally integrable demand models currently available. However, the dual price indices implied by that model are not known, and a closed form solution does not exist for the demand functions. In modeling the money market, we should prefer a simpler specification permitting use of the entire theory of functional structure. We adopt such a simpler specification and use the recursive approach presented in Chapter 6.

While exact aggregator functions form the basis for economic aggregation theory, they contain unknown parameters that must be estimated. We use aggregator functions for hypothesis testing and other research purposes and to reveal the implications of aggregation theory in money markets. However, for data construction purposes, parameter-free "statistical" index numbers are preferable. Hence, we also present results with the use of statistical index numbers, and those results lead us to advocate the use of Divisia monetary quantity indices.

7.2.2. Structural change and the utility approach to money demand

The theory of functional structure (see, for example, Blackorby, Primont and Russell, 1978) possesses a known link with the otherwise unrelated theory of consumption characteristics. Lancaster and Becker postulated that consumer preferences are more revealingly understood in terms of preferences for certain properties (consumption characteristics) of goods (such as nutrition, flavor, etc.) rather than in terms of the market goods themselves (such as candy, yogurt, etc.). Advocates of that approach argue that the production of consumption characteristics (as through internal household activities) from market goods and the consumption of the resulting characteristics produced are distinguishable phenomena which should not be confounded by modeling market goods demand directly, without regard to characteristics production.

This approach is particularly relevant when one suspects that structural changes are occurring in the mode of transformation of goods into characteristics, since structural (or quality) change need not imply changes in preferences for the resulting characteristics. Hence, the demand for characteristics may be stable, although changes in the transformation between goods and consumption characteristics may result in the appearance of unstable goods demand if the characteristics production and consumption processes are not separated. A rigorous and systematic approach to modeling such decision shifts is provided in Chapter 8.

This theory is relevant to our understanding of money markets. The properties of various money market instruments have been changing. Denominations of Treasury bills have varied; changing regulations have varied the properties of savings deposits and resulted in the introduction of certificates of deposit; NOW accounts (negotiable orders of withdrawal) are changing the consumption characteristics of demand deposits – and then there are electronic funds transfer, repurchase agreements, and money market funds.[1] Yet, consumers' tastes for liquidity, means of payment, store of value, and other such monetary characteristics may not have changed. Only their mode and efficiency of production may have changed. When we seek stability of money demand we frequently think in terms of the demand for these underlying monetary characteristics; we must therefore remove complicating structural shifts in the transformation of monetary instruments into characteristics.

It has been shown that certain assumptions on the Lancaster–Becker theory of consumption characteristics are sufficient to imply the function structure necessary for our recursive money market modeling and index number theory. Hence, under those assumptions all of the theories we have

---

[1] In the United States, NOW accounts are defined to be interest-bearing demand deposits (checking accounts).

discussed above become unified. Shifts in our index numbers have specific meaning in terms of consumption characteristics, and structural change becomes an index number problem rather than an apparent shift in consumer behavior. It can be shown that under those assumptions increasing amounts of structural change in money markets are internalized into index numbers as the level of aggregation is increased. Hence, if the recursive theoretical aggregation approach is carried to relatively high levels of aggregation within the money market, money demand becomes dependent solely upon the demand for consumption characteristics, which are likely to be stable. At each level of aggregation, shifts or trends in the parameters of economic quantity aggregator functions relate to conditional (upon lower level indices) structural change at the corresponding level of aggregation within the money market.

It perhaps is worth noting that the utility approach to money demand modeling (on which the above results depend) is currently the basis for rapidly expanding empirical research in the literature. Consider, for example, Chetty (1969), Bisignano (1974), Diewert (1974b), Parkin, Cooper, Henderson and Danes (1975), Clements (1976), Donovan (1978), Phlips (1978), Offenbacher (1979), and Clements and Nguyen (1979). Early advocates of the utility approach include Friedman and Patinkin. The utility approach is based upon implicit modeling rather than the explicit modeling used in the transactions demand or portfolio analysis approaches. In an economic (rather than empirical) sense, the utility approach is a reduced form approach which models, restricts, and characterizes the results of the consumer's decisions without the need to consider the explicit structure of the decision. While the "true" utility function does not contain money, a derived utility function containing money generally can be acquired, and it is with this derived utility function that we begin. Regarding its existence in the general case, see Arrow and Hahn (1971, p. 350) and Quirk and Saposnik (1968, p. 97).

In conventional utility modeling of consumer goods demand, the structure of household transformation of goods into ultimate consumption characteristics is absorbed into (and lost within) the utility function. Alternative approaches must be used when we seek explicitly to model structural change within that internal household transformation. Similarly, in the utility modeling of money demand we absorb the transactions technology and other aspects of the structure of the consumer's decision within his utility function. The resulting approach has the merit of unifying the modeling of the demand for all money market instruments within a single framework without the need to explore the detailed and different structures of the consumer's decisions within each sector of the money market. If the structure shifts, then the model's parameters will shift.

We need to incorporate explicit structural economic modeling techniques into our approach only when we require explanation or modeling of large parameter shifts. Considering the surprisingly high precision of our estimators, we shall be content in this chapter with the assumption that our model's underlying structure is stable, and we do not test explicitly for parameter variation.

In this chapter we postulate the existence of a representative consumer, although we argued against that practice in Chapter 3. We use a community utility function because of its usefulness as an approximation, rather than out of any conviction that such a community utility function actually exists. However, there is some empirical and theoretical evidence that under some conditions the behavior of aggregate consumption data may be approximated by a consistent and transitive preference preordering. See Dixon (1975), Maks (1978), and Donovan (1978).

7.2.3. The velocity function

The concept of velocity becomes particularly meaningful when a velocity function can be factored out of the money demand function. Under the assumption of homotheticity of preferences, velocity will be factorable as a nontautological entity within our model. At any level of aggregation the appropriate velocity function will depend upon the dual prices of the corresponding quantity aggregate and of other quantity aggregates within the same branch of the utility tree. Since those price aggregates previously have never been computed for monetary aggregates, the explanatory variables in the factored velocity function are not currently available. Yet, the theory of nested aggregates automatically would generate the factored velocity function *along with* its dual price arguments at each level of aggregation. The theory has the potential to simplify and unify our understanding of phenomena which otherwise appear to be complex and puzzling.

However, it should be understood that the resulting velocity functions are not equatable with the usual concept of velocity. The "income" concept relevant to our velocity function is the right-hand side of the budget constraint. Depending upon the level of aggregation and our separability assumptions, that "income" could be total expenditure on monetary assets, total expenditure on monetary assets plus consumption goods, or total wealth, but not an index of national income or product.

7.3. The consumer's decision

7.3.1. Intertemporal allocation

In this section we derive the Jorgensonian user cost (equivalent rental price) of monetary assets from a rigorous Fisherine intertemporal consumption expenditure allocation model. Since the model is formulated in discrete time, a structure of assumptions is required regarding the timing of interest rate and price changes and of portfolio transactions. Although we shall not fix the time interval, it could be set at one day, since interest on savings deposits rarely is paid more frequently than daily. For our purposes a daily discrete time model could be viewed as approximating a continuous time model, since our average quarterly data corresponds to a substantially longer period.

We define time period t to be the time interval $[t, t+1)$, closed on the left and open on the right. Hence, the instant of time t is included in interval t, but the instant $t+1$ is not. We assume that the consumption of goods can proceed continuously throughout any time interval, although our model will use only the total (integral) of that consumption for any time period. Stocks of monetary assets and bonds are constant during each period, and can change only at the end of an interval. Hence, during period t any changes in holdings occurring at instant $t+1$ are not seen until the initial instant of interval $t+1$. In short, all portfolio transactions take place at the boundaries between intervals.

Interest on bonds and on monetary assets is paid at the end of each period. Since the end (right-hand boundary) of period t is included in period $t+1$, but not in period t, interest paid for asset holdings during period t cannot be consumed until period $t+1$. Interest rates, prices, and wage rates remain constant within the interior of each period, but can change discretely at the boundaries of periods. Hence, capital gains (or losses) resulting from changes in market bond yields can take place only at the boundaries of periods.

We treat labor supply as exogenously determined, and we assume that labor supplies, $(L_t, \ldots, L_{t+T})$, during all periods of the consumer's planning horizon are blockwise weakly separable from all other arguments of his utility function, so that we can use the subutility function defined only over the other arguments.

Let t be the current period (or equivalently the instant of time at the start of the period). Let T be the length of the planning horizon, so that the consumer currently plans through all periods, s, in $\{s: t \leqslant s \leqslant t+T\}$.

We now define our variables:

x_s = vector of per capita (planned) consumption of goods and services (including those of durables) during period s;

p_s = vector of goods and services expected prices and of durable goods expected rental prices during period s;

m_{is} = planned per capita real balances of monetary asset i during period s ($i = 1, \ldots, n$);

r_{is} = the expected nominal holding period (including capital gains and losses) yield on monetary asset i during period s ($i = 1, \ldots, n$);

A_s = planned per capita real "bond" holdings during period s;

R_s = the expected one-period holding yield on "bonds" during period s;

L_s = per capita labor supply during period s; and

w_s = the wage rate during period s.

As will be seen in the formulation of the consumer's decision problem below, R_s is the expected one-period holding (including realized or unrealized capital gains or losses) yield (during period s) on assets accumulated to transfer wealth between multiperiod planning horizons rather than to yield liquidity or other services during the current period. As a result, A_s will enter the consumer's utility function only during period $s = t + T$, and A_s need not necessarily be bond holdings. We use the word "bonds" (also sometimes referred to as the benchmark asset in this context) to simplify exposition. The benchmark asset's one-period holding yield during period s is defined to contain all market premiums available for forgoing the services provided by monetary assets. Observe that the holding period used in defining R_s must equal that of r_{is}, which is a short rate.

We let u_t be the representative consumer's current intertemporal, T-period, utility function. We assume that u_t is weakly separable in each period's consumption of goods and monetary assets, so that u_t can be written in the form

$$u_t = u_t(m_t, \ldots, m_{t+T}; x_t, \ldots, x_{t+T}; A_{t+T})$$
$$= U_t(v(m_t), v_{t+1}(m_{t+1}), \ldots, v_{t+T}(m_{t+T});$$
$$V(x_t), V_{t+1}(x_{t+1}), \ldots, V_{t+T}(x_{t+T}); A_{t+T}) \qquad (7.1)$$

for some monotonically increasing, linearly homogeneous, strictly quasiconcave functions, $v_{t+1}, \ldots, v_{t+T}, V, V_{t+1}, \ldots, V_{t+T}$. The function v is monotonically increasing and strictly quasiconcave, but not necessarily linearly homogeneous. The function U_t also is monotonically increasing.

Dual to the functions V and V_s $(s=t+1,\ldots,t+T)$, there exist current and planned true cost of living indices, $p_t^* = p(p_t)$ and $p_s^* = p_s^*(p_s)$ $\cdot (s=t+1,\ldots,t+T)$.[2] Those indices will be used to deflate all nominal quantities to real quantities, as in the definitions of m_{is} and A_s above.

Assuming replanning at each t, we write the consumer's decision problem during each period $s(t \leq s \leq t+T)$ within his planning horizon so as to choose $(m_t,\ldots,m_{t+T}; x_t,\ldots,x_{t+T}; A_{t+T}) \geq 0$ to

maximize $\quad u_t(m_t,\ldots,m_{t+T}; x_t,\ldots,x_{t+T}; A_{t+T})$

subject to $\quad p_s' x_s = w_s L_s + \sum_{i=1}^{n} \left[(1+r_{i,s-1}) p_{s-1}^* m_{i,s-1} - p_s^* m_{is} \right] \quad (7.2)$

$\qquad\qquad + \left[(1+R_{s-1}) p_{s-1}^* A_{s-1} - p_s^* A_s \right].$

The real value of assets carried over (endowed) from the prior planning period is

$$\sum_{i=1}^{n} (1+r_{i,t-1}) m_{i,t-1} + (1+R_{t-1}) A_{t-1},$$

and the real value of the consumer's provisions for later planning periods is

$$\sum_{i=1}^{n} (1+r_{i,t+T}) m_{i,t+T} + (1+R_{t+T}) A_{t+T}.$$

Let

$$\rho_s = \begin{cases} 1, & \text{for } s=t, \\ \prod_{u=t}^{s-1} (1+R_u) & t+1 \leq s \leq t+T. \end{cases}$$

Then ρ_s is the discount factor for discounting period s transactions. Observe that $\rho_s \neq \prod_{u=t}^{s} (1+R_u)$, since R_s is not paid during $[s,s+1)$, but rather at the start of $[s+1,s+2)$. In problem (7.2), (m_t, x_t) is actual consumption of goods and monetary assets during period t, while $(m_{t+1},\ldots,m_{t+T}; x_{t+1},\ldots,x_{t+T})$ is planned consumption of goods and monetary assets.

Since we assume replanning at each period and permit u_t to vary over time, the consumer's behavior is bound only by his decisions regarding current period consumption. Actual consumption patterns need not evolve

---

[2] For a discussion of the relevant duality theory, see section 7.5. The true cost of living index for a weakly separable block of goods equals expenditure on those goods divided by the (category) indirect utility function for those goods.

in agreement with prior plans. However, further restrictions (stationary preferences, intertemporal strong separability, and constant rate of time preference) could be imposed upon u_t to ensure that the sequence of current consumption quantities evolves over time in agreement with plans whenever correct expectations exist for all variables that are not under the consumer's control. Agreement between actual and planned consumption paths is not necessary to the estimation of our model.

Solve (7.2) for A_s and write the resulting equation for each s between t and $t+T$. Then back substitute for A_s starting from A_{t+T} and working down to A_t, always substituting the lower subscripted equation into the next higher one. Completion of the sequence of back-substitutions results in the single wealth constraint:

$$\sum_{s=t}^{t+T}(p_s'/\rho_s)x_s + \sum_{s=t}^{t+T}\sum_{i=1}^{n}\left[\frac{p_s^*}{\rho_s} - \frac{p_s^*(1+r_{is})}{\rho_{s+1}}\right]m_{is}$$
$$+ \sum_{i=1}^{n}\frac{p_{t+T}^*(1+r_{i,t+T})}{\rho_{t+T+1}}m_{i,t+T} + \frac{p_{t+T}^*}{\rho_{t+T}}A_{t+T}$$
$$= \sum_{s=t}^{t+T}(w_s/\rho_s)L_s + \sum_{i=1}^{n}(1+r_{i,t-1})p_{t-1}^*m_{i,t-1} + (1+R_{t-1})A_{t-1}p_{t-1}^*.$$
(7.3)

The consumer can now be viewed as maximizing utility subject to the single wealth constraint, (7.3).

The left-hand side of the constraint is the discounted value of goods consumption plus the discounted user-cost evaluated monetary asset holdings plus the discounted cost of passing on $m_{t+T} = (m_{1,t+T},\ldots,m_{n,t+T})'$ to the next planning period plus the discounted cost of passing on A_{t+T} to the next planning period. The right-hand side is discounted total labor income plus the value of monetary assets passed to this planning period from the last one plus the value of bonds passed on to the start of this planning period from the end of the last planning period.

7.3.2. The user-cost of monetary assets

From (7.3) we see immediately that the user cost (equivalent rental price) of m_{is} is

$$\pi_i^s = \frac{p_s^*}{\rho_s} - \frac{p_s^*(1+r_{is})}{\rho_{s+1}}.$$
(7.4)

Finally, the current period user cost, π_{it}, of m_{it} reduces to

$$\pi_{it} = \frac{p_t^*(R_t - r_{it})}{1 + R_t}.$$

It can be shown that π_{it} is the monetary asset analog of the well-known Jorgensonian user cost (rental price) of durable consumer goods (see Donovan, 1978). Correcting the formula for taxation, we obtain

$$\pi_{it} = \frac{p_t^*(R_t - r_{it})(1 - \tau_t)}{1 + R_t(1 - \tau_t)}, \qquad (7.5)$$

where τ_t is the marginal income tax rate. Observe that financial asset i is a free good if $r_{it} = R_t$, and observe that the current period user costs of financial assets are independent of expectations. We shall use formula (7.5) to compute the user costs of financial assets.

User costs commonly are viewed as the prices of the services of durables rather than of their stocks (see Donovan, 1978). In that interpretation services are assumed to be proportional to stocks, and units of quantities and prices are assumed to have been chosen such that the proportionality constants are one. Hence user-cost evaluated stocks (stocks multiplied by corresponding user costs) are expenditures *on the services* of the stocks.

It is interesting to observe that although (7.5) does not depend directly upon inflation rates, the nominal interest rates within the formula can be expected to respond to expected inflation rates. Furthermore, since the well-known user-cost formula for nonmonetary durables services does depend inversely upon the expected inflation rate, it follows that the user cost of monetary assets relative to durables increases as the expected inflation rate increases. Hence, consumers will respond to increased inflationary expectations by substituting consumer durables for monetary assets.

7.3.3. Supernumerary quantities

We have not assumed linear homogeneity of v since that assumption would be unnecessarily strong for our purposes and would imply unitary income elasticities. However, in this subsection we assume a form of marginal homogeneity that will be required for aggregation.

We assume that v depends upon m_{t-1} as well as upon m_t. This assumption introduces no complications into the earlier sections, since the consumer selected m_{t-1} during the prior planning horizon and hence m_{t-1}

is given and fixed during the current horizon. We further assume that there exist constants, $\boldsymbol{\delta} = (\delta_1, \ldots, \delta_n)'$, and a linearly homogeneous function, u, such that $v(\boldsymbol{m}_t; \boldsymbol{m}_{t-1}) = u(\boldsymbol{y}_t)$, where $\boldsymbol{y}_t = (y_{1t}, \ldots, y_{nt})'$ and $y_{it} = m_{it} - \delta_i m_{i,t-1}$. In short, we assume the existence of proportional habit formation in current (but not future planned) consumption. In the language of the habit formation literature, y_t is supernumerary consumption of monetary assets and $\delta_i m_{i,t-1}$ is the quantity of monetary asset i consumed out of habit (independently of current interest rates or income) during period t. The theoretical implications of habit formation have been considered by Pollak (1976).

From (7.1), (7.3), (7.4), and (7.5), we see that the consumer's intertemporal decision problem can be rewritten as to choose $(\boldsymbol{y}_t, \boldsymbol{m}_{t+1}, \ldots, \boldsymbol{m}_{t+T}; \boldsymbol{x}_t, \ldots, \boldsymbol{x}_{t+T}; A_{t+T}) \geqslant \boldsymbol{0}$ to maximize

$$U_t(u(\boldsymbol{y}_t), v_{t+1}(\boldsymbol{m}_{t+1}), \ldots, v_{t+T}(\boldsymbol{m}_{t+T});$$
$$V(\boldsymbol{x}_t), V_{t+1}(\boldsymbol{x}_{t+1}), \ldots, V_{t+T}(\boldsymbol{x}_{t+T}); A_{t+T}) \tag{7.6}$$

subject to the single wealth constraint

$$\sum_{s=t}^{t+T} (\boldsymbol{p}_s'/\rho_s)\boldsymbol{x}_s + \sum_{i=1}^{n} \pi_{it} y_{it} + \sum_{s=t+1}^{t+T} \sum_{i=1}^{n} \pi_i^s m_{is}$$

$$+ \sum_{i=1}^{n} \frac{p_{t+T}^*(1 + r_{i,t+T})}{\rho_{t+T+1}} m_{i,t+T} + \frac{p_{t+T}^*}{\rho_{t+T}} A_{t+T}$$

$$= \sum_{s=t}^{t+T} (w_s/p_s)L_s + \sum_{i=1}^{n} \left[(1 + r_{i,t-1})p_{t-1}^* - \delta_i \pi_{it} \right] m_{i,t-1}$$

$$+ (1 + R_{t-1})A_{t-1}p_{t-1}^*. \tag{7.7}$$

We have now established the model and assumption structure needed to apply aggregation theory to monetary aggregation. If we must use aggregates, a case can be made for accepting whatever assumptions are required to render economic aggregates meaningful. If we cannot accept the assumptions, we have no economic aggregates at all. As Samuelson and Swamy (1974, p. 592) conclude, "one must not expect to be able to make the naive measurements that untutored common sense always longs for;

we must accept the sad facts of life, and be grateful for the more complicated procedures economic theory devises".

7.4. Conditional current period allocation

Our assumptions on the homogeneous blockwise weakly separable structure of the intertemporal utility function, eq. (7.6), are sufficient for consistent two-stage budgeting. Hence by Green's (1964) theorem 4 it follows that the consumer can maximize utility (7.6), subject to the wealth constraint (7.7), in two stages. In the first stage the consumer selects aggregate monetary asset expenditure (supernumerary expenditure for the current period) and aggregate consumer goods expenditure for each period within his planning horizon and his terminal bond (or other benchmark asset) holdings, A_{t+T}. The chosen bond holdings are to be carried forward to the start of his next planning horizon. In the second stage he allocates current aggregate monetary asset expenditure and current aggregate consumer goods expenditure over individual current period monetary assets and consumer goods.

The second stage allocation decision over individual current period supernumerary monetary assets is to select y_t to

$$\text{maximize} \quad u(y_t)$$
$$\text{subject to} \quad \pi_t^{*\prime} y_t = M_t^*, \tag{7.8}$$

where $\pi_{it}^* = \pi_{it}/p_t^*$ is the real current period user cost of monetary asset i, $\pi_t^* = \pi_{1t}^*, \ldots, \pi_{nt}^*$, and M_t^* is the real value of aggregate supernumerary monetary asset holdings allocated to the current period in the consumer's first stage decision. Observe that $\pi_{it}^* = (R_t - r_{it})(1 - \tau_t)/[1 + R_t(1 - \tau_t)]$ independently of p_t^*.

The choice between the real values, π_{it}^* and M_t^*, and the corresponding nominal values, π_{it} and M_t, is arbitrary, since p_t^* can be canceled out of each side of the budget constraint in the nominal case. This observation is just a restatement of the well-known homogeneity of demand. We further could multiply the budget constraint through by $[1 + R_t(1 - \tau_t)]/(1 - \tau_t)$ in order to use $R_t - r_{it}$ as prices. The simplified formulation then would correspond with that of Klein (1974) and Offenbacher (1979).

We model the conditional current period monetary asset allocation decision, (7.8), in sections 7.5–7.9, and we explore its implications for aggregation.

7.5. Preference structure over financial assets

7.5.1. Blocking of the utility function

Suppose that y_t contains only total transaction balances and passbook savings deposits at three institution types, and we seek to aggregate passbook savings deposits over institution types and to nest that aggregate within an aggregate of all of the components of y_t. We partition the vector y_t such that $y_t = (y_{1t}, y'_{2t})'$, where y_{1t} is per capita real supernumerary transaction balances and y_{2t} is a vector of per capita real supernumerary passbook account deposits. We correspondingly partition π_t^* and δ such that $\pi_t^* = (\pi_{1t}^*, \pi_{2t}^{*\prime})'$ and $\delta = (\delta_1, \delta'_2)'$.

We assume that the utility function, $u(y_t)$, can be written in the blockwise weakly separable form

$$u(y_t) = \mu(y_{1t}, u_2(y_{2t})), \tag{7.9}$$

with the function u_2 being linearly homogeneous. As discussed below, these conditions are both necessary and sufficient for the existence of the economic aggregates we seek. This conclusion, based upon Green's (1964) theorem 4, assumes that y_t is held exclusively by consumers. For firms, the analogous conditions would be applied to the production functions.

Backsubstituting (7.9) into (7.6), observe the way in which we have nested weakly separable blocks within weakly separable blocks. We have established a fully nested utility tree. As a result, we can acquire a rational multistage budgeting procedure in which the structured utility function itself defines the relevant theoretical quantity index at each stage, and duality theory defines the corresponding functional price index. Other financial assets (repurchase agreements, money market mutual funds, Treasury bills, commercial paper, etc.) could be included in the analysis by increasing the dimension of y_t, partitioning it into more than two subsectors, and blocking u into multiple blocks accordingly.

In the next subsection we elaborate on the multistage budgeting properties of decision (7.8) and the implications for quantity and price aggregation.

7.5.2. Multistage budgeting

Our assumptions on the properties of u are sufficient for the two-stage solution of the decision problem (7.8). We define that two-stage decision in this subsection. It should be observed that the homogeneity assumption on u could be deleted if we required only differential consistency of the two-stage decision (see Theil, 1980). However, we define and use global consistency below, as is done in economic aggregation theory.

Let $\Pi_{2t}^* = \Pi_2(\boldsymbol{\Pi}_{2t}^*)$ be a function of the user costs $\boldsymbol{\pi}_{2t}^*$. The first stage of the two-stage decision is to select y_{1t} and Y_{2t} to solve

$$\underset{(y_{1t}, Y_{2t})}{\text{maximize}} \mu(y_{1t}, Y_{2t}) \text{ subject to } \pi_{1t}^* y_{1t} + \Pi_{2t}^* Y_{2t} = M_t^*. \tag{7.10}$$

From the solution of problem (7.10), the consumer determines aggregate supernumerary consumption of real passbook account services, $\Pi_{2t}^* Y_{2t}$.

In the second stage, the consumer allocates $\Pi_{2t}^* Y_{2t}$ over consumption of the services of passbook accounts at individual institution types. He does so by solving the decision problem:

$$\underset{y_{2t}}{\text{maximize}}\, u_2(y_{2t}) \text{ subject to } \pi^{*'}_{2t} y_{2t} = \Pi_{2t}^* Y_{2t}. \tag{7.11}$$

It follows from Green's (1964) theorem 4 that there exists some function, Π_2, such that the solution for y_t to problem (7.8) is the same as the solution for y_t acquired from the two-stage decision, (7.10) and (7.11), for any theoretically admissible values of M_t^* and π_t^*. It furthermore can be shown that if we use that function Π_2 in (7.10) then $Y_{2t} = u_2(y_{2t})$ at the solution values for Y_{2t} and y_{2t} to the two-stage decision. We shall say that $Y_{2t} = u_2(y_{2t})$ is the economic (or functional) quantity aggregate (or index) corresponding (or dual) to the economic (or functional) user-cost aggregate (or index), $\Pi_{2t}^* = \Pi_2(\pi_{2t}^*)$. We shall call u_2 the quantity aggregator function, and we shall call Π_2 the user-cost (or price) aggregator function.

In general, the quantity aggregator function is the corresponding (category) utility function. We show in the next subsection that the corresponding price (user-cost) index is equal to expenditure, $\Pi_{2t}^* Y_{2t}$, divided by the (category) indirect utility function (induced by the direct utility function, u_2).

This two-stage decision process is two-stage budgeting, and can be extended to n-stage budgeting simply by nesting weakly separable blocks within weakly separable blocks, etc. in an analogous manner. The result that follows from such nesting is purely mathematical and need not be related to actual multistage decision processes. We need only observe that the consumer acts "as if" he were making his decision in stages if his preferences are nested. The approach is that previously used in sections 1.3, 5.6, and 6.2.

The price index, Π_{2t}^*, and the quantity index, Y_{2t}, are economic price and quantity indices. As can be seen from problem (7.10), those indices have all of the properties of quantities and prices of actual goods (whether or not aggregates). In particular, observe that the consumer acts as if actual aggregate goods existed. Also, observe that quantity indices depend exclusively upon quantities, and that price indices depend exclusively upon prices. Furthermore, the budget constraint of problem (7.11) shows that the product of a dual price index and its corresponding quantity index always equals actual expenditure on the goods within the aggregate.

7.5.3. Duality

A quantity aggregator function and its corresponding price aggregator function are duals. The mathematics of function duals is not the subject of this chapter and will not be discussed in detail. Nevertheless, the reader familiar with classical duality relationships will recognize the foundations for the following observation. We begin with the two-stage decision defined in the previous subsection.

Dual to the (quantity aggregator) function $u_p(y_{pt})$ exists the function $\Pi_p(\pi_{pt})$ such that the identity $u_p(y_{pt})\Pi_p(\pi_{pt}) = y'_{pt}\pi_{pt}$ will hold whenever y_{pt} is the solution to the dual problem

$$\underset{y_{pt}}{\text{minimize}}\, y'_{pt}\pi_{pt} \text{ subject to } u_p(y_{pt}) = k_1,$$

where k_1 is a positive constant.

This duality relationship demonstrates that knowledge of the function u is sufficient for determination of the function Π_p. Hence, we need only estimate the conditional demand system solving (7.11) to estimate Π_p and therefore to compute estimates of the passbook real user-cost index, $\Pi_{pt}^* = \Pi_p(\pi_{pt}^*)$. We thereby can acquire Π_{pt}^* without estimating the higher level utility function, μ, of eq. (7.9). Hence, we could treat Π_{pt}^* as given and recursively estimate the utility tree from the bottom up. In fact it can be shown that $\Pi_p(\pi_{pt}^*)$ is just real expenditure on passbook account services, $y'_{pt}\pi_{pt}^*$, divided by the indirect utility function corresponding to $u_p(y_{pt})$. Since preferences are assumed to be homogeneous of degree one, it follows that the resulting function, Π_p, depends only upon π_{pt}^* (and is independent of expenditure on passbook account services).

The function Π_p is homogeneous of degree 1. Hence $\Pi_p(\pi_{pt}^*) = \Pi_p(\pi_{pt})/p_t^*$. As a result, we can compute the real value of the user-cost price aggregate, $\Pi_p(\pi_{pt})/p_t^*$, by using real user costs, π_{pt}^*, as arguments for Π_p. Thus, our earlier observation that our estimates do not depend upon the use of p_t^* is verified.

It is interesting to observe that this nesting process immediately can be carried to a higher level to acquire a user-cost index for the economic aggregate over passbook accounts and transaction balances taken jointly. Since economic quantity aggregates always are utility functions, the quantity aggregate immediately is seen to be $u_t = \mu(m_{1t}, u_p(y_{pt})) = \mu(m_{1t}, u_{pt})$. We define the dual user-cost index by observing that dual to the function (quantity index) $\mu(m_{1t}, u_{pt})$ exists a function (price index) $\Pi(\pi_{1t}, \Pi_{pt}) = \Pi(\pi_{1t}, \Pi_p(\pi_{pt}))$ such that the identity

$$\mu(m_{1t}, u_{pt})\Pi(\pi_{1t}, \Pi_{pt}) = m_{1t}\pi_{1t} + u_{pt}\Pi_{pt} = m_{1t}\pi_{1t} + y'_{pt}\pi_{pt}$$

will hold whenever (m_{1t}, u_{pt}) is the solution to the dual problem

$$\underset{(m_{1t}, u_{pt})}{\text{minimize}} (m_{1t}\pi_{1t} + u_{pt}\Pi_{pt}) \text{ subject to } \mu(m_{1t}, u_{pt}) = k_2,$$

where k_2 is a positive constant.

By Fisher's factor reversal test (equality of expenditure to the product of the price and quantity index), the price (user-cost) index dual to a functional quantity index must equal total expenditure on the aggregated assets divided by the indirect category (conditional) utility function defined on those assets. Because of our linear homogeneity assumption on category utility functions, total expenditure cancels out of the quotient leaving a functional price index depending solely upon prices.

7.6. Recursive estimation approach

The consumer is viewed as making his budgeting decisions from the top of the tree down, as he decentralizes his budgeting to lower levels of aggregation; but we can estimate the entire implied model recursively from the bottom up. We begin at the bottom of the tree and estimate the most disaggregated demand decisions. We compute the implied price (user-cost) and quantity indices, based upon the utility functions we have estimated, and we then move up to estimate the next level using the just-computed price aggregates as instrumental variables. This approach to the recursive estimation of utility trees has been developed by Barnett (1977a), Fuss (1977), and Anderson (1979). Our data consists of quarterly average values from the first quarter of 1970 to the first quarter of 1978. The data sources are described in section 7.7.

Recall that the current period monetary asset allocation problem, (7.8), is defined conditionally upon the consumer price index, p_t^*, which is dual to (and therefore derivable from) the consumer goods current period utility function, V. Hence, to apply this instrumental variables approach most fully, we should estimate the function, V, defined over the consumer goods sector, prior to estimating u, defined over the monetary asset sector. But aside from p_t^*, we seek no other information from the consumption sector. Hence, the cost of strict adherence to the recursive instrumental variables approach is excessive in the case of computation of p_t^*.

As a result, we use a statistical index rather than a functional index for p_t^*. Statistical price indices can depend upon quantities as well as prices, but cannot depend upon unknown parameters.[3] We assume that $V(x_t) = (x_t' B x_t)^{1/2}$ locally for some square matrix B of unknown parameters. That specification can provide a quadratic approximation to any aggregator function. Diewert (1976b) has shown that if a representative consumer exists, then the Fisher Ideal statistical price index (geometric mean of the Laspeyres and Paasche indices) is always equal to the true value of the functional index, p_t^*, regardless of the values of the parameters in the matrix, B. We shall use the Fisher Ideal price index for p_t^*. In computing the Fisher Ideal index, we use the Bureau of Labor Statistics' CPI as the Laspeyres index and the Commerce Department's Implicit Price Deflator as the Paasche Index. Some approximation error exists in the use of the CPI as the Laspeyres index, although the error is small (see Triplett, 1976).

Having computed p_t^*, we begin our empirical ascent up the utility tree. Recalling the form of eq. (7.11), we begin by estimating u_2. Then $u_2(y_{2t})$ becomes the economic quantity index used with y_{1t} in the next (higher) stage. We compute the implied price index dual to u_2 and estimate the demand system generated by μ. The procedure could be carried to any level of aggregation, but will be terminated at μ.

7.7. Data

7.7.1. Data sources

Our data consists of quarterly average values from the first quarter of 1970 to the first quarter of 1978. The data sources follow.

In converting nominal balances to per capita balances, we used Census Bureau population data. For the maximum available yield, R_t, we used the

---

[3] Statistical indices are introduced more rigorously in section 7.12.

maximum of Moody's A seasoned corporate bond yield and the commercial paper rate. All yields and interest rates were divided by four to acquire quarterly rates of return. Our measure of R_t is consistent with the common convention. See, for example, Offenbacher (1979) and Klein (1974).

In addition to convention, two bodies of theory exist that are relevant to the measurement of R_t. Recall from section 7.3 that R_t is the maximum available expected one-period holding yield. Term structure theory, perfect arbitrage, and rational expectations theory jointly imply that R_t should be the maximum available short rate (plus a probably small "liquidity" premium). However, recent empirical research does not support that conclusion. For example, see Shiller (1979) whose results support our measurement method. Shiller found that when the yield curve is upward sloping, the expected one-period holding yield is at least as high as the long rate. In addition, our experiments with alternative measures of R_t indicated considerable robustness. The reason evidently is that R_t appears in all users costs, and hence relative prices are more sensitive to the own rates, r_{it}, than to R_t.

Commercial bank consumer passbook account deposits were acquired by subtracting Christmas club accounts, business savings, and domestic government savings, NOW accounts, and savings of banks and of foreign official institutions from savings deposits at all commercial banks based upon reported member bank data and estimated nonmember data. Unpublished internal daily average Board data was used to acquire quarterly averages.

Savings and loan association passbook deposits were acquired using Federal Home Loan Bank Board savings and loan association balance sheet data. Since passbook deposit data is available separately from time deposits only for Federally insured S&Ls, we multiplied the total of passbook deposits and time deposits for all S&Ls by the ratio of passbook deposits to the total of time plus passbook deposits at insured S&Ls to acquire an estimate of passbook deposits at all S&Ls. The data was monthly average data acquired by averaging end-of-month data from succeeding months. Quarterly averages were then constructed.

Passbook account deposit data at mutual savings banks were acquired from the National Association of Mutual Savings Banks' *Balance Sheet of Mutual Banks*. The data consists of monthly averages computed as averages of succeeding month-end values. Quarterly averages were constructed.

The commercial bank passbook account interest rate was acquired from the "Survey of Time and Savings Deposits" reported in the *Federal Reserve Bulletin*. The data reflects a one-day survey taken near the end of the first month of the quarter. The nature of the survey question is such that the data can be taken directly as quarterly averages.

The savings and loan association interest rate was acquired from the Home Loan Bank Board's *Interest and Dividend Practices* survey. The data reflects a one-day survey taken near the end of the first month of the quarter. The mutual savings banks passbook interest rate was acquired from the FDIC quarterly survey, reflecting end of the first month values.

The tax rate was acquired by dividing the sum of Federal personal income tax liability and state and local government personal income tax and nontax payments by the sum of that numerator plus disposable personal income (accrual basis). Although this provides an average rate rather than the marginal rate required by the theory, all of our results are invariant to the values used for the marginal tax rate. This conclusion follows from the homogeneity property of demand, or by dividing both sides of the budget constraint in (7.8) by $(1-\tau_t)/[1+R_t(1-\tau_t)]$ and redefining the resulting variable on the right-hand side.

Transaction balances were computed to equal M_1 plus NOW accounts (at all institution types) plus share drafts at credit unions plus demand deposits at mutual savings banks. Internal weekly average Board data was used to acquire quarterly averages.

7.7.2. Data transformations

Prior to estimation of the model, the data was transformed to provide normalized user-cost prices and to rescale the data to be closer to 1.0. In this subsection we present those elementary data transformations.

We took the fourth quarter of 1973 as the base quarter for our price indices. We divided each user cost, computed in accordance with eq. (7.3), by the user cost for passbook account services from the same institution type in the base quarter. The transformed user-cost price series thereby equaled 1.0 for each institution type in the base period. In order to ensure that the product of price and quantity remained unchanged by our rescaling, we correspondingly multiplied each of our per capita real passbook balance series by the original base period user cost for the same institution type. We thereby acquired new per capita "quantity" values, defined to equal expenditure evaluated in index period user-cost prices.

We then rescaled the newly transformed per capita quantity data by dividing all of those new quantity series by a common constant. The common constant was the average value of all of the transformed per capita passbook savings quantity values (averaged over all quarters and all institution types). It should be observed that these data rescalings have no effect on the economics of the model. The objective was to increase computing precision during estimation by avoiding unnecessarily large or small data values.

7.8. Estimation of passbook branch

7.8.1. CES specification

In the current subsection we present our specification for the conditional demand for passbook savings, which is the solution to decision (7.11). Since m_{2t} is a vector, we implicitly have segmented passbook deposits into categories. We let $m_{2t} = (m_{21t}, m_{22t}, m_{23t})'$, where m_{21t} = real per capita holdings of commercial bank passbook accounts, m_{22t} = real per capita holdings of savings and loan passbook accounts, and m_{23t} = real per capita holdings of mutual savings bank passbook accounts. We then write the tth period supernumerary real per capita holdings in passbook account category i as $y_{2it} = m_{2it} - \delta_{2i} m_{2i,t-1}$.

To clarify our notation, we replace the subscript 2 with p (for "passbook"). Then $u_p(y_{pt}) = u_2(y_{2t})$, etc. The CES specification for u_p is

$$u_p(y_{pt}) = \left[\sum_{i=1}^{3} \alpha_i y_{pit}^{\beta} \right]^{1/\beta}$$

$$= \left[\sum_{i=1}^{3} \alpha_i (m_{pit} - \delta_{pi} m_{pi,t-1})^{\beta} \right]^{1/\beta},$$

where $\alpha = (\alpha_1, \alpha_2, \alpha_3)'$ and β are parameters satisfying $\beta < 1$ and $\alpha \geq 0$. While more flexible utility functions exist than the CES, they did not appear to be appropriate to our objectives. Our approach estimates a demand system that is integrable to a marginally homothetic utility function and has known closed form representations both for the demand system and for the utility function. The model also should be a generalization of the simple sum utility function which provides the conventional quantity indices. The CES satisfies all of those objectives and is a very substantial generalization of the simple sum function. Since the simple sum aggregate is widely used, it could be impractical (at this stage of research) to consider a quantity index more general than the CES. Furthermore, the use of a common elasticity of substitution appears reasonable with our passbook savings data. At higher levels of aggregation, a more flexible functional form would be required.

In decision (7.11) we let $E_{pt}^* = \Pi_{2t}^* Y_{2t}$, which is total user-cost-evaluated expenditure allocated to passbook account services, determined from the prior allocation stage (one level higher in the utility tree).

The solution to (7.11) is the demand system

$$m_{pit} = \delta_{pi} m_{pi,t-1} + \frac{\bar{\alpha}_i \pi_{pit}^{*\bar{\beta}}}{\pi_{pit}^* \sum_k \bar{\alpha}_k \pi_{pkt}^{*\bar{\beta}}} \left(E_{pt}^* - \sum_k \pi_{pkt}^* \delta_{pk} m_{pk,t-1} \right), \qquad (7.12)$$

where $\bar{\alpha}_i = \alpha_i^{1/(1-\beta)}$ and $\bar{\beta} = \beta/(\beta-1)$, with $\bar{\alpha} = (\bar{\alpha}_1, \bar{\alpha}_2, \bar{\alpha}_3)' > 0$ and $\bar{\beta} < 1$.

The vector of parameters $\bar{\alpha}$ is not jointly identified, since the demand system is homogeneous of degree zero in $\bar{\alpha}$. Hence, we impose the identifying restriction $\sum_i \bar{\alpha}_i = 1$. We do so by estimating (7.12) with the normalization $\bar{\alpha}_3 = 1$, and then renormalizing the resulting estimates to get $\sum_i \bar{\alpha}_i = 1$. The choice of normalization is arbitrary; we can renormalize at will.

We seek to estimate (7.12) in a form that will impose all theoretical restrictions. We do so by transforming the parameters into other parameters that are free of inequality restrictions. We then impose our restrictions by substitution. We can acquire the maximum likelihood (MLE) estimates of the transformed parameters and then acquire the unique MLEs of the original restricted parameters by using the invariance property of the MLE. In particular, we substitute the transformation $\bar{\alpha}_j = \gamma_j^2$ ($j = 1, 2, 3$) to impose $\bar{\alpha}_j \geq 0$, and we estimate the unrestricted parameters $\gamma = (\gamma_1, \gamma_2, \gamma_3)'$. Since $\bar{\beta} < 1$ defines an open set, that restriction (or any other such strict inequality restriction) cannot be imposed. We replace $\bar{\beta} < 1$ with the approximation $\bar{\beta} \leq 0.9$. We then substitute the transformation $\bar{\beta} = 1.9 - \cosh \theta$ into (7.12) and estimate the unrestricted parameter θ.

Since $y_{pt} > 0$, it follows that for any i, we must have $m_{pit} > \delta_{pi} m_{pi,t-1}$ for all t. Since passbook deposits never changed by more than 20 percent between quarters in our data, a sufficient condition for that inequality would be $\delta_{pi} \leq 0.8$ for all $i = 1, 2, 3$. We shall impose that sufficient condition. In addition, we require that $\delta_p \geq 0$. Although theory does not require this restriction, the logic of the multistage budgeting process becomes more difficult to interpret when δ_p contains negative elements. In addition, our prior views on δ_p impute low probability to negative elements of δ_p, and we have seen in Chapter 6 that negative estimates of δ_p tend to have low precision and hence to be statistically indistinguishable from zero at conventional levels of significance. We jointly impose all of these restrictions on δ_p by substituting the transformations $\delta_{pit} = 0.4 (1 + \sin \phi_i)$ for $i = 1, 2, 3$ and estimating the unrestricted vector $\phi = (\phi_1, \phi_2, \phi_3)'$.

Multiplying (7.12) by π_{pit}^*/E_{pt}^* to acquire the desired expenditure shares, $w_{pit}^* = \pi_{pit}^* m_{pit}/E_{pt}^*$, and making all of the parameter substitutions described above, we acquire our model for the consumer's desired expenditure shares. Since adjustment costs may exist, we permit actual expenditure shares, w_{pit}, to differ from desired expenditure shares, w_{pit}^*, in accordance with the partial adjustment scheme $w_{pit} = \lambda w_{pit}^* + (1-\lambda)w_{pi,t-1}$, where $0 \leq \lambda \leq 1$. We use the same adjustment rate, λ, for each institution type to ensure that the budget constraint will be satisfied in actual expenditure shares as well as in desired budget shares. In addition, equality of adjustment rates appears plausible for passbook accounts at different institution types. Performing all of these transformations on (7.12), we have our passbook deposits allocation model. We take w_{pit}, $i=1, 2, 3$, as endogenous and E_{pt}^* and π_{pkt}^*, $i=1, 2, 3$, as exogenous. We adopt a conventional additive error structure without serial correlation. Serially correlated disturbances did not appear to be a potential problem, since our specification contains lagged values both of quantity demanded (through habit formation) and of expenditure shares (through partial adjustment).

7.8.2. Theoretical index number properties

We now consider the properties of the functional price and quantity index numbers for passbook savings, when aggregation over institution types is to be consistent with the CES consumer preferences specified in the previous subsection.

The functional quantity index is the utility level itself. Normalizing the index to equal 1.0 at the first observation, we acquire the normalized functional quantity index $Q_p(y_{pt}) = u_p(y_{pt})/u_p(y_{p1})$.[4] The nominal functional price index that is dual to our CES specification of u_p is

$$\Pi_p(\pi_{pt}) = \left(\sum_{i=1}^{3} \bar{\alpha}_i \pi_{pit}^{\bar{\beta}} \right)^{1/\bar{\beta}},$$

where $(\bar{\alpha}, \bar{\beta})$ are as defined in the previous section. The corresponding normalized nominal user-cost price index is $P_p(\pi_{pt}) = \Pi_p(\pi_{pt})/\Pi_p(\pi_{p1})$.

---

[4]A functional quantity index must be linearly homogeneous in its arguments. While u_p is linearly homogeneous in y_{pt}, u_p is not homogeneous in m_{pt} unless $\delta_{pi} = 0$ for all i. Hence, u_p cannot strictly be viewed as an aggregator function for m_{pt} when some δ_{pi} is nonzero, although $u_p(y_{pt})$ is always the functional quantity aggregate for the supernumerary quantities, y_{pt}.

The corresponding real price indices are $\Pi_p(\pi_{pt}^*)$ and $P_p(\pi_{pt}^*)$. If we were to require an index of *total* (rather than per capita) supernumerary nominal balances, we could compute $Q_p(y_{pt})$ using the total passbook deposit data in place of the per capita real balances, m_{pt}, in the definition of y_{pt}. The result would be identical to computing $Q_p(y_{pt})$ with population and p_t^* fixed at index year levels, since those fixed index year levels would be cancelled out of the numerator and denominator of $Q_p(y_{pt})$.

We seek to consider the limiting case in which $\alpha_1 = \alpha_2 = \alpha_3$ and $\beta = 1$. In that case the functional quantity index equals the simple sum of its components. Since the elasticity of substitution, σ, equals $1/(1-\beta)$, we see that $\sigma \to \infty$ as $\beta \to 1$. Hence, the special case we are considering is that of three "goods" (or, more appropriately, services) that are perfect substitutes in equal proportions, i.e. indistinguishable goods. When $\beta = 1$ (but the α_i values are not necessarily equal), the functional quantity index acquires the form of a Laspeyres-type (fixed weight linear) quantity index. The functional price index that is dual to the Laspeyres quantity index is the Leontief price index, $\pi_p(\pi_{pt}) = \min \{\pi_{pit}/\alpha_i: i = 1,2,3\}$. See Samuelson and Swamy (1974, p. 574). Hence, if the monetary quantity index is the usual simple sum index (so that $\alpha_1 = \alpha_2 = \alpha_3$), then the corresponding price index is just the minimum user cost.

7.8.3. Results with passbook savings

The parameter estimates for eqs. (7.12) using passbook data and joint maximum likelihood (FIML) estimation are displayed in table 7.1 with standard errors in parentheses and with γ_3 normalized to equal one. The estimates of ϕ_1 and (ϕ_2, ϕ_3) imply boundary solutions for δ_{p1} and $(\delta_{p2}, \delta_{p3})$ at their lower and upper bounds, respectively. Transforming back to the original parameters of $u_p(y_{pt})$, we find that the implied joint maximum likelihood estimates are $\beta = 0.62$ and $\alpha = (0.55, 0.26, 0.20)'$, where α has been renormalized such that $\Sigma_{i=1}^3 \alpha_i = 1$.

Precisions (t-ratios) are generally high. The implied elasticity of substitution, σ, equals 2.66, which is very high. This elasticity is the short-run

Table 7.1
Passbook branch parameter estimates.

θ	ϕ_1	ϕ_2	ϕ_3	γ_1	γ_2	λ
1.94	$-\pi/2$	$\pi/2$	$\pi/2$	3.83	1.43	0.206
(0.24)	(1.31)	(0.35)	(0.27)	(0.18)	(0.06)	(0.06)

Note: Standard errors are in parentheses.

elasticity of substitution, as is relevant to the aggregator function and hence to aggregation and index number theory. With regard to the long-run utility function, see Pollak (1976). We can see just how high that elasticity is by observing that σ is monotonically increasing in β, and β must lie between $-\infty$ and 1. Clearly, $\hat{\beta} = 0.62$ is very close to the upper bound of 1, at which the utility function (and hence the functional quantity index) is linear and demand functions become set valued correspondences. Observe from $\hat{\lambda}$ that the estimated quarterly adjustment rate from desired to actual shares is about 21 percent.

Thus, we see that passbook accounts at different institution types are highly substitutable, and a simple linear quantity index may be a reasonable approximation to the theoretical quantity index. However, the simple sum index requires equal weights in the linear index, and $\hat{\alpha}_1$ differs substantially from $\hat{\alpha}_2$, which does approximately equal $\hat{\alpha}_3$.[5] The tail area of the asymptotic likelihood ratio test of equal α_i values is less than 0.00001. Since that tail area is well below 0.05, we reject the hypothesis of equal α_i values. To test the hypothesis of a simple sum aggregate, we should test the hypothesis that $\beta = 1$ jointly with the hypothesis of equal intensity parameters (α_i's). However, the likelihood function is not uniquely defined when $\beta = 1$, since demand functions become set valued in that case. Hence, a likelihood ratio test is not applicable.

A functional quantity index measures the quantity of a properly aggregated economic "good". Since α_1 clearly exceeds α_2 or α_3, we see that commercial bank passbook accounts contribute more heavily to that meaningful economic "good" than mutual savings bank or savings and loan passbook accounts. An explanation may lie in the fact that commercial bank passbook accounts possess all of the basic consumption characteristics of the other two types, but greater liquidity through the "one-stop-banking" property made available during routine trips to the bank to deposit funds into checking accounts. Aggregation theory does not attach a name (such as "moneyness" or "liquidity") to the functional quantity index. However, our use of user costs dictates that the quantity index is the quantity of services provided by the components of the aggregate. Hence, it may not be unreasonable to deduce that commercial bank passbook accounts appear to provide greater "monetary services"

---

[5] If $\alpha_1 = \alpha_2 = \alpha_3$ with $\beta = 1$, then $u(y_{pt})$ is a linear function of the usual simple sum index, $\Sigma_{i=1}^{3} m_{pit}$. But with unequal α_i values, our economic quantity index is a linear function of $\Sigma_{i=1}^{3} \alpha_i m_{pit}$, not of the simple unweighted sum.

than passbook accounts at the other two institution types. If funds were transferred from savings and loan passbook accounts to commercial bank passbook accounts, our functional quantity index would increase, perhaps to reflect the economy's increased liquidity. The usual sum index would not change.

We also observed that computed values of the normalized functional quantity index, $Q_p(y_{pt})$, and the normalized user-cost price index, $P_p(\pi_{pt})$, tended to move in opposite directions, as would be expected from movement along a demand curve. This result is not surprising since Regulation Q cannot decrease the user cost of passbook account deposits to below the equilibrium price, although the regulation can raise the user cost to above the equilibrium level. Hence, an excess supply but not an excess demand can exist in the passbook account market. We therefore can expect the data always to lie on the demand function, even when the market is out of equilibrium. In addition, governmental rate setting tends to minimize simultaneous bias in estimators that condition upon exogenous user costs.

There appears to be information contained in the fact that δ_{p1} is at its lower bound, while δ_{p2} and δ_{p3} are large. Recall that $\delta_{pi} m_{pi,t-1}$ is a vector of quantities consumed out of habit (or for "subsistence") regardless of the variations in user costs or in total consumption expenditure within the sample period. Evidently commercial bank passbook accounts contain actively managed primary balances, while mutual savings bank and savings and loan passbook accounts contain a greater percentage of less actively managed secondary balances and saved consumer reserve funds. When integrability conditions are imposed, as we have done, it is common for some of them to be binding. Hence, the existence of binding regularity conditions is not surprising. Nevertheless, it is also possible that the boundary solutions on the habit formation parameters may have resulted from the joint use of habit formation dynamics and partial adjustment dynamics. Despite the fact that all of the model's parameters are identified, the data may not contain sufficient information to permit distinguishing adequately between the two sources of dynamic consumer behavior.

7.9. Transactions balances

7.9.1. Specification

We now progress to the next level of the utility tree in (7.8) to estimate μ. We again use a CES utility function. At this level of aggregation it no longer would be reasonable to assume that elasticities of substitution are constant between all monetary assets. But we now have only two "goods" and hence only one elasticity of substitution. The flexibility of the CES specification therefore still remains satisfactory for our purposes. Furthermore, a constant finite elasticity of substitution, even between all monetary assets, would be more reasonable than the uniformly infinite elasticities of substitution implied by the usual simple sum indices.

We specify μ to be CES in two goods: real per capital supernumerary transactions balances, y_{1t}, and the economic real per capita supernumerary passbook savings aggregate, $u_{pt} = u_p(y_{pt})$. We introduce no additional habit formation at this level of aggregation (in y_{1t} and the aggregate u_{pt}), since habit formation is already built into $u_p(y_{pt})$ through the specification of y_{pt}, and since we expect short-run Engel curves in m_{1t} to pass through the origin. Observe therefore that $y_{1t} = m_{1t}$ and that μ is homothetic in real per capita transaction balances and in aggregate real per capita supernumerary (not total) passbook savings deposits.

Offenbacher's (1979) results suggest that currency and demand deposits do not satisfy the conditions for aggregation by summation; however, separate treatment of those two components requires imputation of separate own rates to each. In this chapter we avoid such ambiguous and controversial imputations. Hence, we condition upon summed transaction balances as an elementary good.

We impute to m_{1t} the user-cost price, (7.5), with the own rate set equal to zero. We impute to the supernumerary passbook aggregate, $u_p(y_{py})$, the dual user-cost functional price index, $\Pi_{pt} = \Pi_p(\pi_{pt})$. We do not introduce adjustment dynamics at this level of aggregation. Since the turnover rates of transaction balances are high, we believe that adjustment to the desired transaction balances share in monetary asset consumption is rapid.

Combining both stages of the decision over transaction balances and passbook savings deposits, we find that consumers are viewed as allocating expenditure over transaction balances and passbook savings deposits (either jointly or through the equivalent two-stage decision) by utility maximization (with habit formation in passbook savings preferences) to acquire desired consumption levels. The desired level of transaction balances is then purchased without lags. In addition, the desired level is acquired of current total user-cost-evaluated expenditure on the services of passbook savings deposits, but its distribution over institution types differs from the desired allocation in accordance with the linear partial adjustment mechanism used in section 7.8.

The utility function is of the CES form

$$\mu(m_{1t}, u_{pt}) = \mu(m_{1t}, u_{pt}) = \left(\alpha_1 m_{1t}^\beta + \alpha_2 u_{pt}^\beta\right)^{1/\beta},$$

where $(\alpha_1, \alpha_2, \beta)$ are parameters satisfying $\beta < 1$ and $(\alpha_1, \alpha_2) \geqslant \mathbf{0}$.

The conditional decision problem at this level of aggregation is to choose (m_{1t}, u_{pt}) to

maximize $\mu(m_{1t}, u_{pt})$

subject to $m_{1t}\pi_{1t}^* + u_{pt}\Pi_p(\pi_{pt}^*) = E_t^*,$ (7.13)

where E_t is user-cost-evaluated expenditure allocated to the services of real transaction balances and of real supernumerary passbook savings deposits during the current period.

We define the expenditure share of transaction balances in E_t^* to be $w_{1t} = m_{1t}\pi_{1t}^*/E_t^*$. The share of supernumerary passbook deposits then is $w_{pt} = 1 - w_{1t}$. After employing parameter transformations analogous to those in section 7.8, we find that the solution to (7.13) can be written in the form

$$w_{1t} = \frac{\gamma_1^2 \pi_{1t}^{*(1.9-\cosh\theta)}}{\gamma_1^2 \pi_{1t}^{*(1.9-\cosh\theta)} + \gamma_2^2 \Pi_{pt}^{*(1.9-\cosh\theta)}}$$ (7.14)

and $w_{pt} = 1 - w_{1t}$, where $\Pi_{pt}^* = \Pi_p(\pi_{pt}^*)$.

Let $\hat{\Pi}_{pt}^*$ be the value of $\Pi_p(\pi_{pt}^*)$ with the parameters of Π_p replaced by their estimates acquired in section 7.8. We replace Π_{pt}^* with $\hat{\Pi}_{pt}^*$, normalize γ_2 to equal 1.0, and estimate (7.14) with an additive disturbance term. Fuss (1977) has considered the properties of such nested estimation procedures.

Letting $\varepsilon_t(t=1,\ldots,T)$ be the additive error in equation (7.14), we introduce first-order autocorrelation by specifying that $(\varepsilon_2,\ldots,\varepsilon_T)$ is a sample from a stationary scalar autoregressive stochastic process satisfying the stochastic difference equation $\varepsilon_t = \rho\varepsilon_{t-1} + u_t$, where the sequence $\langle u_t : t = 2,\ldots,T \rangle$ consists of independently and identically distributed normal random variables with mean zero. The same value, ρ, is used in defining the error structure for each of the two demand equations derived from (7.13). That procedure follows from Berndt and Savin (1975), when no serial correlation of disturbances exists across equations. The parameter ρ is subject to the constraint $-1 \leq \rho \leq 1$. To impose that restriction, we let $\rho = \sin\psi$. We eliminate that equality by substitution and estimate the unconstrained parameter, ψ.

To estimate (7.14) with the additive autoregressive disturbance, ε, we use the following transformation. Let the right-hand side of (7.14) be written as $f(\pi_{1t}^*, \Pi_{pt}^*; \gamma_1, \theta)$, so that

$$w_{1t} = \rho w_{1,t-1} + \left[f(\pi_{1t}^*, \Pi_{pt}^*; \gamma_1, \theta) - \rho f(\pi_{1,t-1}^*, \Pi_{p,t-1}^*; \gamma_1, \theta) \right].$$

If we add ε_t to the right-hand side of (7.14), it then follows that the

Table 7.2
Parameter estimates with transaction balances and aggregated savings.

θ	γ	ψ
0.597	1.20	1.29
(0.22)	(0.17)	(0.17)

Note: Standard errors are in parentheses.

disturbance to be added to the right-hand side of the transformed equation is $\varepsilon_t - \rho\varepsilon_{t-1} = u_t$. So we can estimate the transformed equation using maximum likelihood estimation with a conventional disturbance, u_t.

7.9.2. Estimates

The resulting maximum likelihood estimates of (γ_1, θ, ψ) are presented in table 7.2. Transforming back to the original parameters of u, we find that $\hat{\beta} = -2.53$, $\hat{\rho} = 0.96$, and $(\hat{\alpha}_1, \hat{\alpha}_2) = (0.77, 0.23)$, where (α_1, α_2) have been renormalized to sum to one. Our estimate of the intensity parameter, α_1, is more than three times our estimate of α_2. Hence, we might deduce that transaction balances, m_{1t}, contribute to our monetary asset economic quantity aggregate more heavily than our nested passbook deposits aggregate, u_{pt}. However, one should be cautious about viewing the intensity parameters as simple weights in this case, since μ is a nonlinear function rather than a linear weighted average.

The implied elasticity of substitution is $1/(1-\hat{\beta}) = 0.28$. Substitutability between transaction balances and passbook savings deposits is far lower than between passbook accounts at different institution types. The elasticity of substitution of 0.28 is too low and the precision of its estimator is too high to justify a linear approximation (requiring infinite elasticity of substitution) to μ.

7.9.3. Functional index numbers

In the present section our highest level aggregator function is μ. Hence, our highest level economic quantity aggregate is $u_t = \mu(m_{1t}, u_p(y_{pt}))$. The nominal dual user cost aggregate is

$$\Pi(\pi_{1t}, \Pi_{pt}) = \left(\bar{\alpha}_1 \pi_{1t}^{\bar{\beta}} + \bar{\alpha}_2 \Pi_{pt}^{\bar{\beta}}\right)^{1/\bar{\beta}},$$

where $\bar{\alpha}_i = \alpha_i^{1/(1-\beta)}$ and $\bar{\beta} = \beta/(\beta-1)$.

In summary, we have acquired the following nested pair of quantity and nominal dual user cost indices, with all indices normalized to equal 1.0 in the first quarter. For passbook accounts we have the maximum likelihood estimate of the normalized functional quantity index, $Q_p(y_{pt})$, and its nominal dual user cost index, $P_p(\pi_{pt})$. For our higher level (M_2-type) monetary asset aggregate, we have the maximum likelihood estimate of the normalized functional quantity index, $Q(m_{1t}, y_{pt}) = \mu(m_{1t}, u_p(y_{pt}))/\mu(m_{11}, u_p(y_{p1}))$, and its nominal dual user-cost index, $P(\pi_{1t}, \Pi_{pt}) = \Pi(\pi_{1t}, \pi_p(\Pi_{pt}))/\Pi(\pi_{11}, \Pi_p(\pi_{p1}))$.

7.9.4. Implications of estimates

While passbook accounts at different institutions are excellent substitutes, we find no evidence to support equal weighting of the accounts across institutions. Although a simple linear (Laspeyres-type) index of passbook deposits may be useful, the conventional unweighted sum index should be understood to be based upon accounting practice rather than upon any economically meaningful index number construct. If one sought no more than total dollar deposits in passbook accounts in all institution types, the use of simple summation would be dictated tautologically by an accounting identity.

The simple sum index in economics corresponds to the degenerate limiting special case of preferences having linear indifference curves at 45° angles, and the corresponding dual price index is the poorly behaved Leontief fixed coefficients index. In our case, consumers would use passbook accounts in only one institution type, unless all institutions paid the exact same interest rate. If all institutions did pay the exact same interest rate, then the budget constraint would lie on top of a linear indifference curve, and consumers would not care how they allocated funds over institution types. No unique solution would exist. But in fact commercial banks pay lower interest rates than the other two institution types yet acquire stable nonzero deposits. Since passbook accounts across institution types do provide very similar services, we should expect to find even poorer support for the simple sum index at higher levels of aggregation within the money market, and that conclusion generally is supported by our results with transaction balances at the next aggregation level.

When we pass to a higher level of aggregation to incorporate transaction balances into our monetary aggregate, the possibility of a useful linear approximation, even with unequal coefficients, disappears. Transaction balances and passbook savings are not perfect substitutes and possess an elasticity of substitution of only 0.28. The usual simple sum monetary quantity index is rejected. The current M_2 aggregate provides useful accounting information on commercial bank liability structure, but is not well designed as an economic monetary quantity index.

7.10. Empirical selection of blocking

7.10.1. Conditions on elasticities of substitution

In section 7.5 we selected our homogeneous weakly separable blocking of the current period conditional utility function, u, on a priori grounds. That blocking then dictated the components of each subindex and index at all levels of aggregation within our hierarchy of aggregates. Conditionally upon that blocking we determined, in sections 7.8 and 7.9, that the form of the aggregator function over the components of each index precludes the use of aggregation by simple summation. In the current subsection we briefly consider the possibility of formally testing for the blocking itself, rather than solely for the form of the preblocked utility (aggregator) function.

We begin with the current period monetary asset utility function, $u(y_t)$, for the vector of real supernumerary per capita holdings, y_t, of all monetary assets in the economy. We seek a partitioning, $y_t = (y'_{1t}, \ldots, y'_{Mt})'$, such that u can be written in the blockwise weakly separable form,

$$u(y_t) = \mu(u_1(y_{1t}), u_2(y_{2t}), \ldots, u_M(y_{Mt})), \quad (7.15)$$

with u_k linearly homogeneous for all $k = 1, \ldots, M$. The existence of such a homogeneous weakly separable blocking is necessary and sufficient for the existence of consistent quantity aggregation (to the functional quantity aggregates, $u_1(y_{1t}), u_2(y_{2t}), \ldots, u_M(y_{Mt}))$.[6] Clearly, our earlier a priori blocking, (7.9), was a special case of (7.15) with one-dimensional y_{1t} and with $M = 2$.

Necessary and sufficient conditions for that homogeneous weakly separable blocking are that the elasticity of substitution between any component of y_{kt} (for fixed $k = 1, \ldots, M$) and any (supernumerary) monetary asset *not in* y_{kt} be independent of the element of y_{kt} selected. We shall refer

---

[6] The conditions could be substantially weakened by dropping the homogeneity condition, if we permit Fisher's factor reversal test to be violated.

to those conditions on elasticities of substitution as the *aggregation conditions*. Systematic testing for those conditions with monetary assets has not yet been undertaken and is a promising area for future research. However, Appendix E contains elasticity of substitution estimates (without formal separability hypothesis tests) between many categories of monetary assets. The conclusions suggested (at unknown statistical significance levels) by comparisons of those elasticity of substitution estimates follow.

7.10.2. Empirical evidence

The estimates in Appendix E indicate the following. Over the past decade substitutability among passbook accounts at the three institution types (commercial banks, S&Ls, and MSBs) has risen substantially and to high levels. In addition substitutability is high between small time deposits at S&Ls and MSBs. However, substitutability is low between time deposits at commercial banks and at either of the two thrift institutions. Those individuals who purchase small time deposits at commercial banks evidently perceive them to possess properties that are, in some ways, significantly different from those of small time deposits at S&Ls or MSBs. This result is not surprising, since those individuals who purchase small time deposits at commercial banks generally are locked into the lower yields paid by the commercial banks, as a result of the penalty structure imposed on early redemption. In fact it would be difficult to understand why anyone would hold commercial bank small time deposits if he considered them to be close substitutes for small time deposits at thrift institutions. In general, substitutability within the many diverse groups of financial assets considered in Appendix E has tended to rise over the past decade. However, with the exception of the two cases just described, substitutability between financial assets has remained *very* low.[7]

We now consider the implications of those elasticity of substitution estimates for the selection of the components of aggregates. In Appendix E we find that the elasticities of substitution between passbook accounts at different institution types are far higher than the elasticities of substitution between passbook accounts at any one of those institution types and any

---

[7] Earlier published studies of substitutability between monetary assets have all indicated very low substitutability between monetary assets. Hence, our results are in general agreement with the earlier findings, and our finding of current high substitutability between passbook accounts at the three institution types and between small time deposits at thrift institutions are thereby strengthened by contrast.

other financial asset. Hence, any aggregate (such as the old M_2 index) which contained passbook accounts at some but not at all institution types would violate the *aggregation conditions*. Similarly, we find that any aggregate containing small time deposits at S&Ls must also contain small time deposits at MSBs. In short, the empirical evidence in Appendix E tends to support aggregation of like-assets over institution types, as proposed in Barnett, Beck, Ettin, Kalchbrenner, Lindsey, Porter, Simpson, and Tinsley (1979).

In sections 7.8 and 7.9 we considered the separate question of whether aggregation over *given* components can be accomplished by simple summation. Aggregation by summation is a special case of linear aggregation. The necessary and sufficient conditions on elasticities of substitution for linear aggregation are infinite elasticities of substitution between all components *within the aggregate*. We call those conditions the *linearity conditions*. The frequently very low elasticities of substitution found in Appendix E further strengthen our rejection of the *linearity conditions* in sections 7.8 and 7.9.

It should, however, be observed that our inferences drawn from Appendix E, without formal statistical testing, are highly tentative. Our conclusions in this subsection should be viewed as suggestive of areas for future research through systematic hypothesis testing with models specifically designed for that purpose.

7.11. Statistical index numbers

7.11.1. Definition

In previous sections we have been using aggregation theory. In aggregation theory, aggregator functions are utility functions for consumers and production functions for firms. Aggregator functions provide the foundations of aggregation theory, and hence their existence and properties are important in understanding aggregation. By estimating aggregator functions in previous sections, we have acquired information regarding the components of consistent aggregates, and we have determined that aggregator functions defined over financial assets cannot be adequately approximated by simple summation. Aggregation theory itself then would leave us with the alternative of using the actual nonlinear aggregator function in aggregating over monetary assets.

However, as we have seen, functional quantity aggregators depend upon the quantities of the component goods and upon *unknown* parameters. Estimates of the unknown parameters depend upon the specified model, the data, and the estimator. Hence, aggregator functions, although important in theory and in hypothesis testing, are not generally useful in constructing index numbers which are publishable as data by governmental agencies. For precisely that purpose, the theory of statistical index numbers has been developed. We introduce and then use that highly practical theory in this section.

A functional quantity aggregator depends only upon component quantities and unknown parameters. Functional quantity aggregators cannot depend upon prices, and the definition of a functional quantity aggregator does not depend upon maximizing behavior by economic agents. On the other hand, statistical index numbers do *not* depend upon any unknown parameters, but quantity index numbers can depend upon component prices as well as upon component quantities, and the definition of *exact* statistical index numbers does depend upon the maximizing behavior of economic agents. In brief, the introduction of prices (and maximizing behavior in the exact case) into index number theory permits us to dispense with the unknown parameters that exist in the aggregator functions. The merits of the resulting index numbers are not dependent upon any specialized properties of the aggregator function (such as linearity of the function).

A quantity index between periods $t-1$ and t, $Q(\pi_{t-1}, \pi_t; m_{t-1}, m_t)$, is a function of the vectors of prices (user costs) in periods $t-1$ and t, $\pi_{t-1} > 0$ and $\pi_t > 0$, and the corresponding quantity vectors, $m_{t-1} > 0$ and $m_t > 0$. Diewert defines such an index to be exact for a given aggregator function, f, if $Q(\pi_{t-1}, \pi_t; m_{t-1}, m_t) = f(m_t)/f(m_{t-1})$ whenever $m_t > 0$ is the value of $m > 0$ which maximizes $f(m)$ subject to $\pi_t' m \leq \pi_t' m_t$. In other words, a quantity index number is exact if it exactly equals the aggregator function whenever the data is consistent with microeconomic maximizing behavior. Since the aggregator function depends only upon quantities, the index number is a quantity index number despite the existence of prices in its formula. Given a quantity index, the corresponding price index then can be computed from Fisher's weak factor reversal test. See Diewert (1976b, p. 115).

The form of the index numbers does not depend upon whether the aggregator function is a utility function or a production function. If distributional data were available on shares held by firms (versus households) or by different categories of wealth holders, that information could be incorporated directly into the index number. See Theil (1967, ch. 5) for

an information theoretic interpretation of the resulting index numbers.
Two particularly noteworthy contributions exist in the recent literature on index numbers. Hulten (1973) has proved that in continuous time the Divisia index is always exact for *any* consistent (blockwise homothetically weakly separable) aggregator function. Hence, no index number can be better than the Divisia in continuous time. The Divisia index is the line integral defined by the differential $d\log Q = \Sigma_{i=1}^{N} s_i \, d\log q_i$, where $s_i = p_i x_i / \mathbf{p}'\mathbf{x}$. Although no always-exact index numbers are known in the discrete time case, Diewert (1976b) has constructed an elegant theory of superlative index numbers in discrete time. Diewert defines an index number to be "superlative" if it is exact for some aggregator function, f_s, which can provide a second-order approximation to any linearly homogeneous aggregator function. We call such an index number Diewert-superlative.

Fisher (1922) advocated the following quantity index number, called the Fisher Ideal index:

$$Q_t^F = Q_{t-1}^F \left[\frac{\left(\sum_{i=1}^{N} \pi_{it} m_{it}\right)\left(\sum_{i=1}^{N} \pi_{i,t-1} m_{it}\right)}{\left(\sum_{i=1}^{N} \pi_{it} m_{i,t-1}\right)\left(\sum_{i=1}^{N} \pi_{i,t-1} m_{i,t-1}\right)} \right]^{1/2}.$$

Törnquist (1936), and subsequently Theil (1967), advocated the following quantity index number, called the Törnquist–Theil Divisia index:

$$Q_t^T = Q_{t-1}^T \prod_{i=1}^{N} (m_{it}/m_{i,t-1})^{(1/2)(s_{it}+s_{i,t-1})},$$

where

$$s_{it} = \pi_{it} m_{it} \Big/ \sum_{k=1}^{N} \pi_{kt} m_{kt}.$$

Taking logarithms of each side, observe that

$$\log Q_t^T - \log Q_{t-1}^T = \sum_{i=1}^{N} s_{it}^* (\log m_{it} - \log m_{i,t-1}), \tag{7.16}$$

where $s_{it}^* = (1/2)(s_{it} + s_{i,t-1})$. The same index numbers result, regardless of whether the aggregator functions are utility functions or production functions.

Diewert (1976b) has proved that both the Fisher Ideal and Törnquist–Theil Divisia indices are Diewert-superlative. In addition, as can be seen from (7.16), the Törnquist–Theil Divisia index provides a discrete time approximation to the optimal continuous time Divisia index. In fact the Törnquist–Theil Divisia index can be derived by numerical integration of the Divisia line integral. The Törnquist–Theil Divisia index and the Fisher Ideal index are highly reputable throughout all segments of the current literature on index numbers, both for their statistical and economic properties.[8]

As a quantity index the Törnquist–Theil Divisia index is more widely used than the Fisher Ideal index, since eq. (7.16) permits a natural interpretation of the index. Observe that the growth rate of the index is a weighted average of the growth rates of the components. The weights are the share contributions of each component to the total value of the services of all components. Because of the availability of that transparently clear interpretation, we advocate use of the Törnquist–Theil Divisia index to measure the quantity of money at all levels of aggregation (at least at levels higher than M_1).

7.11.2. Example

In this section we consider the case of an aggregate having the following components: transaction balances, passbook savings at the three institution types and at credit unions, small time deposits at the three institution types, and negotiable and non-negotiable large CDs at commercial banks. The components were selected on the basis of ready availability of the data rather than as a proposal. The proper procedure for selecting components was described in section 7.10, but we seek only an example in the current section. The collection of components will be called M_3. Table 7.3 displays the GNP velocity of the Törnquist–Theil Divisia index, of the Fisher Ideal index, and of the simple sum index for seasonally adjusted data. Velocity is is normalized to be one in the first quarter. Observe that the velocities of the Fisher Ideal and Törnquist–Theil Divisia indices are *identical* to three decimal places, so that the choice between those two indices is of no importance.

This phenomenon resulted from the fact that each is a Diewert-superlative index number. Hence, if an aggregator function exists and if maximizing behavior obtains, then the two indices can differ only by a third-order remainder term. In addition, each of the indices should agree

---

[8] For further details on Divisia indices see Barnett (1980c).

Table 7.3
GNP velocities of three monetary quantity index numbers (seasonally adjusted data).

Quarter	Fisher Ideal	Törnquist–Theil Divisia	Simple sum
1968(1)	1.0000	1.0000	1.0000
1968(2)	1.0141	1.0141	1.0141
1968(3)	1.0131	1.0131	1.0094
1968(4)	1.0088	1.0088	1.0027
1969(1)	1.0174	1.0174	1.0188
1969(2)	1.0311	1.0312	1.0385
1969(3)	1.0524	1.0525	1.0713
1969(4)	1.0570	1.0571	1.0793
1970(1)	1.0626	1.0626	1.0825
1970(2)	1.0574	1.0574	1.0671
1970(3)	1.0473	1.0472	1.0412
1970(4)	1.0231	1.0229	1.0072
1971(1)	1.0219	1.0217	0.9975
1971(2)	1.0123	1.0121	0.9846
1971(3)	1.0041	1.0037	0.9726
1971(4)	0.9997	0.9993	0.9617
1972(1)	1.0031	1.0027	0.9611
1972(2)	1.0013	1.0009	0.9553
1972(3)	0.9919	0.9916	0.9419
1972(4)	0.9942	0.9939	0.9407
1973(1)	0.9998	0.9996	0.9365
1973(2)	0.9977	0.9976	0.9241
1973(3)	1.0061	1.0060	0.9205
1973(4)	1.0172	1.0171	0.9248
1974(1)	1.0104	1.0103	0.9065
1974(2)	1.0234	1.0233	0.9019
1974(3)	1.0348	1.0347	0.9043
1974(4)	1.0339	1.0338	0.8997
1975(1)	1.0170	1.0169	0.8823
1975(2)	1.0263	1.0262	0.8895
1975(3)	1.0517	1.0516	0.9116
1975(4)	1.0555	1.0554	0.9127
1976(1)	1.0670	1.0668	0.9209
1976(2)	1.0681	1.0680	0.9206
1976(3)	1.0661	1.0660	0.9163
1976(4)	1.0608	1.0607	0.9097
1977(1)	1.0709	1.0707	0.9164
1977(2)	1.0815	1.0814	0.9237
1977(3)	1.0801	1.0800	0.9197
1977(4)	1.0766	1.0765	0.9128
1978(1)	1.0733	1.0732	0.9057

with the unknown aggregator function equally as well as they agree with each other, since the remainder term is of the same order in either case.

However, the ordinary simple sum index differs *substantially* from the two Diewert-superlative indices. In addition, the range of values of the velocity of the sum index (0.201) is more than twice that of the superlative indices (0.089). The velocity of the simple sum index (labeled "M_3 simple sum") and of a Diewert-superlative (labeled "M_3 Diewert-sup") index are plotted in fig. 7.1. The Diewert-superlative indices are too close to be plotted separately.

The velocity of the simple sum index continues declining secularly from 1972(3), while the velocity of the Diewert-superlative index rises. Our aggregate does not include many money market instruments such as RPs, treasury bills, commercial paper, money market funds, etc. while our aggregate includes many assets subject to governmental rate regulation. Hence, we should expect substitution (disintermediation) to occur out of our aggregate and into such substitutes during periods of rising interest rates and high inflation, if our M_3 index approximates an economic monetary good. In such cases velocity should *rise*. Clearly the declining velocity of the simple sum index is very misleading.

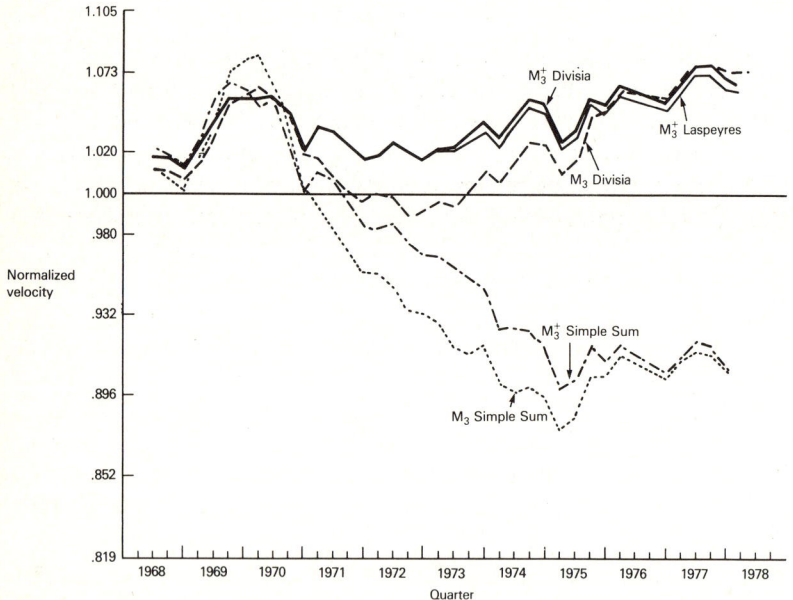

Figure 7.1. Seasonally adjusted velocity (normalized).

Aggregation of monetary assets 225

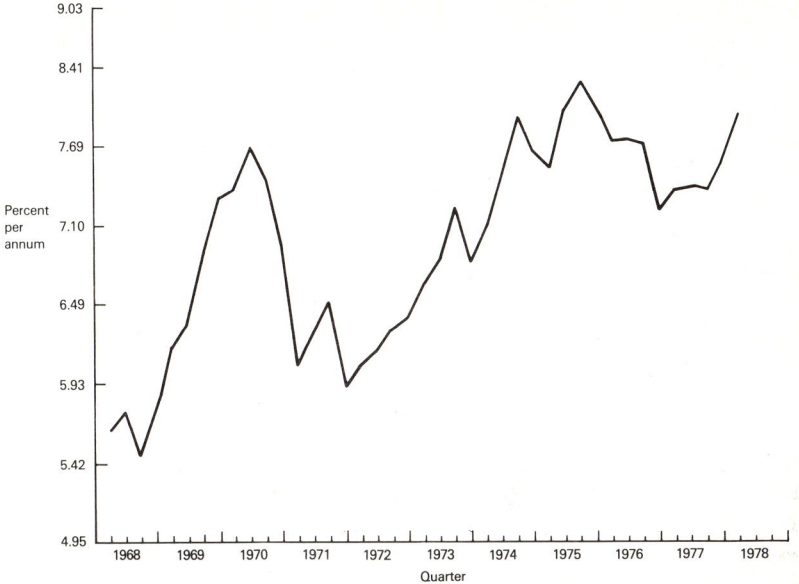

Figure 7.2. Ten-year government bond rate.

Comparing fig. 7.1 with the ten-year government bond rate in fig. 7.2, we see that variations in the velocity of the Diewert-superlative index make economic sense; the interest elasticity of money demand has the correct sign. Internalizing further money market substitution by aggregating over further money market instruments can be expected to further stabilize the velocity of the superlative index. The substitution effect (*defined* to hold utility constant) of a change in the relative prices of components *within* an aggregate *cannot* change the value of an economic quantity aggregate (utility level)!

In contrast, the trend in velocity of the simple sum index would suggest that, in response to rising interest rates and rising inflationary expectations, monetary asset holders have increased the fraction of GNP allocated to consumption of the services of the lowest yielding (largely rate controlled) sector of the market.[9] Disintermediation thereby would appear (misleadingly) to have proceeded within the money market in the wrong direction:

---

[9] Since GNP does not include the user-cost evaluated services of durables or of monetary assets, our conclusion is based upon the use of GNP as an approximation to the corresponding theoretical national product concept.

It is not surprising that simple sum aggregates frequently provide conflicting information.

It is tempting to conclude that the reason the velocity of the Diewert-superlative index tracks the government bond rate is the fact that the Diewert-superlative index depends upon interest rates. However, the index is constructed to approximate the aggregator function, which depends only upon quantities and therefore not upon R_t. The computational reason for the divergence between the Diewert-superlative and sum indices can be seen from eq. (7.16). The Törnquist–Theil Divisia index (or therefore, approximately, any Diewert-superlative index) weights transaction balances more heavily than any of the other components of the aggregates, since transaction balances provide the largest share of monetary services, s_{it}. An economic reason for the heavy weighting of transaction balances is that their liquidity contributes heavily to monetary services. But the velocity of transaction balances has been rising rapidly in recent years. Hence, the inadequate weighting of transaction balances in the simple sum M_3 has permitted velocity to be drawn down by the substitution effect of the increasing relative price (user cost) of transaction balances relative to less liquid monetary substitutes.

To further verify our interpretation, we now incorporate elements of the unregulated money market into M_3 to create M_3^+. We incorporate dealer and directly placed commercial paper, repurchase agreements (RPs) of commercial banks with the nonbank public, bankers' acceptances, and negotiable Treasury securities with less than one year remaining to maturity. In fig. 7.1 we plot the velocity of M_3^+, with M_3^+ computed as a simple sum index (labeled "M_3^+ simple sum"), as a Diewert-superlative index (labeled "M_3^+ Diewert-sup"), and as a chained Laspeyres index (labeled "M_3^+ Laspeyres"). We continue to normalize all velocities to equal 1.0 in the first quarter.

Clearly internalizing those additional segments of the money market has further stabilized the velocity of the Diewert-superlative index. The velocity of the simple sum index continues to trend in the wrong direction. The Laspeyres index is seen to provide a far better approximation than the simple sum index, despite the fact that the Laspeyres index provides only a first-order approximation to the value of the aggregator function. The slight variations remaining in the velocity of the Diewert-superlative index continue to correlate with the ten-year bond rate and to reflect the fact that some elements of the unregulated money market remain outside of the aggregate.

An entirely rigorous conclusion would be based upon the observation that the velocity of the Diewert-superlative index reveals (to the second

Aggregation of monetary assets 227

order) movements along the aggregator function and therefore movements of the underlying economic aggregate. Hence, fig. 7.1 indicates that the velocity of the simple sum index has been moving in the wrong direction, in the sense of moving in the direction opposite to that of the economic aggregate.

The simple sum index is a Laspeyres quantity index with the weights erroneously set to be equal. Clearly the erroneous weighting destroys the index's critical independence of substitution effects (within the aggregate), and hence the simple sum index *cannot* approximate the economic aggregate.

7.12. Information content of the index

In this section we apply information theory to compare (Törnquist–Theil) Divisia monetary quantity indices with the conventional sum indices. In each case we compute the information that the monetary aggregate provides about relevant common policy targets. The section is based upon Barnett and Spindt (1979).

Let the state of the economy in period t be summarized by the n-dimensional vector, s_t. Its components are defined to contain final policy target variables and the per capita growth rate of a monetary aggregate. At time $t-1$, s_t has not yet been generated by the economy and is a random vector, S_t, determined from the economy's reduced form. In this section only, we emphasize that distinction by using capital letters for random variables and corresponding lower case letters for realizations. Let S_t be partitioned such that $S_t = (X_t, Y_t')'$, where Y_t is the $n-1$-dimensional vector of policy target variables and X_t is the per capita growth rate of a monetary aggregate. Let $f(s_t)$ be the joint density of S_t, let $g(y_t)$ be the marginal density of Y_t, and let $h(y_t | x_t)$ be the conditional density of Y_t, given $X_t = x_t$.

We explore the information about Y_t that would be acquired by conditioning upon knowledge of X_t. The expected information content,

$$I_{Y_t|X_t} = H_{Y_t} - H_{Y_t|X_t},$$

about Y_t from knowledge of X_t, is the reduction in expected uncertainty (entropy). The reduction is from the unconditional values, H_{Y_t}, to the conditional value, $H_{Y_t|X_t}$, where $H_{Y_t} = E(-\ln g(Y_t))$ and $H_{Y_t|X_t} = E_{X_t}[E_{Y_t}(-\ln h(Y_t|X_t)|X_t)]$.[10] The information function, $I_{Y_t|X_t}$, is zero

---

[10] See Theil (1967). The subscript on the expectations operator identifies the random variables with respect to which the expectation is being taken.

valued if and only if Y_t and X_t are stochastically independent.[11] We assume that the marginal distribution of S_t is multivariate normal at each t.

Let $\sigma^2_{X_t X_t}$ be the variance of X_t, let $\Omega_{Y_t Y_t}$ be the contemporaneous covariance matrix of Y_t, and let $\Omega_{S_t S_t}$ be the contemporaneous covariance matrix of S_t. Then it follows, under our normality assumption, that

$$I_{Y_t|X_t} = \tfrac{1}{2} \log \frac{|\Omega_{Y_t Y_t}| \sigma^2_{X_t X_t}}{\Omega_{S_t S_t}} \tag{7.17}$$

at each t. We now estimate $I_{Y_t|X_t}$ under various definitions of Y_t and X_t and under two different assumptions on the stochastic process generating S_t.

7.12.1. Sample estimates

In this subsection we make the strongly simplifying assumption that the moments of S_t do not vary over time, so that the maximum likelihood estimate of $I_{Y_t|X_t}$ can be computed directly from the empirical distribution function of the data by using the corresponding sample moments in equation (7.17). We compute the resulting maximum likelihood estimates of the information content, $I_{Y_t|X_t}$, of several monetary quantity aggregates with respect to the three definitions of Y_t described in table 7.4. The six sets of components of the monetary aggregates considered are defined in table 7.5. For purposes of comparison, the monetary aggregate in each case is computed both as a conventional simple sum and as the (Törnquist–Theil) Divisia quantity index.

In table 7.6 the percentage gain in information content in going from the simple sum to the Divisia index are reported. Except in one case, the Divisia index *dominates* the sum index, *regardless* of the selection of targets, Y_t, or of the selection of components for the monetary aggregates.

7.12.2. Extensions

Two areas for further research are particularly promising. We could permit the state vector to contain intertemporal components. In addition we could weaken the constant-moments assumption contained in the previous sub-

---

[11] See Tinsley, Spindt and Friar (1980). Also, see their paper for an interpretation of such information theoretic applications in terms of MARL (minimum average risk linear) predictors and filters.

Table 7.4
Specifications of policy targets (Y_t).

Specification	Components of Y_t
I	1. Per capita GNP
II	1. Per capita GNP (deflated)
	2. Consumer price index
	3. Unemployment rate
III	1–11. Eleven components of GNP

Note: Data are quarterly proportionate rates of change of seasonally adjusted quantities. All items in specification III are per capita nominal quantities. Data span the period 1970(I)–1978(IV).

Table 7.5
Components of monetary aggregates.

Symbol	Components
M_i^c ($i=2,3$)	Current M_i
M_i^p ($i=2,3$)	Proposed M_i
M_{3a}^p	Proposed M_3 less large time
M_∞^p	Current M_5 plus nonbank public holdings of Eurodollars, money market mutual fund shares, short-term Treasury securities, municipal bonds, RPs, and commercial paper.

Note: The aggregates are computed as proportionate rates of change in per capita seasonally adjusted nominal quantities. See Barnett, Beck, Ettin, Kalchbrenner, Lindsey, Simpson, and Tinsley (1979) for the details of the current and proposed aggregates listed in this table.

Table 7.6
Sample estimates of percent information gain from summation to Divisia aggregation of monetary assets.

Components	Specification of Y_t		
	I	II	III
M_2^c	36.2	51.1	75.6
M_2^p	16.1	16.4	3.7
M_3^c	18.9	17.9	34.3
M_3^p	118.9	194.1	92.8
M_{3a}^p	6.7	0.0	4.3
M_∞^p	18.8	−1.0	66.9

Table 7.7
ARIMA estimates of percent information gain from summation to Divisia aggregation of monetary assets (per capita GNP growth rate target).

Components	Percent information gain
M_2^c	20.0
M_2^p	12.2
M_3^c	8.0
M_3^p	225.0
M_{3a}^p	8.2
M_∞^p	1000.0

section by using a model of the economy. While a full structural model of the economy would be particularly informative, we shall consider the simpler alternative of an elementary time series model. We model each component of S_t as a univariate ARIMA process under the assumption that the innovations have zero mean, are serially uncorrelated, and have a time-invariant contemporaneous covariance matrix. We estimate the parameters of the processes using ordinary single equation least squares.

We use the estimated ARIMA specifications in estimating the gains in information content in going from the simple sum index to the Divisia index relative to the GNP growth rate target. This procedure results in the covariances in eq. (7.17) becoming the population covariances of the ARIMA innovations, which then are estimated by the sample covariances of the residuals. The results are presented in table 7.7. The Divisia index *dominates* the sum index. The information gain is particularly dramatic at the highest level of aggregation. The evidence favoring Divisia over summation aggregation for monetary aggregates is substantial.

7.13. Conclusion

In computing monetary quantity indices the simple sum index number formula is not satisfactory. The aggregates should be computed as Törnquist–Theil Divisia indices. The components of the aggregates should be selected to satisfy the conditions for consistent aggregation described in section 7.10. These conclusions apply so long as the indices are to be used as quantity indices of monetary services, as required in economics. Simple summation would provide valid indices of the stock of nominal monetary wealth, as required in national accounting, or indices of bank liability structure, as required in bank accounting, but *not* valid structural economic variables.

The discussion in this chapter has related to the economic theories of aggregation and index numbers. However, there is also a statistical theory of index numbers which does not depend upon economic theory for its foundations. Statistical index number theory considers the ability of index numbers to pass certain classical tests, such as factor reversal and circularity tests. During the past decade, results from both approaches have converged on the Törnquist–Theil Divisia and Fisher Ideal indices as being clearly among the best, and advocates of both the economic and statistical approaches view the simple sum index as being among the very worst index numbers ever devised.[12]

According to Fisher, the two worst statistical properties that an index number can possess are called "bias" and "freakishness". Regarding the simple sum (or equivalently the arithmetic average) index, which Fisher called his formula 1, Fisher (1922, p. 363) observed that, "There are two objections to Formula 1, the simple arithmetic, viz.: (1) that it is 'simple,' and (2) that it is arithmetic! – that it is at once freakish and biased. In the case of Sauerbeck's index number, for instance, the bias alone reaches 36 percent!" In our case we found that much of the component information is lost unnecessarily when the components are aggregated by simple summation, and the simple sum index dismally failed to internalize the long-run substitution effects that have occurred within the money markets during the past decade. In addition, the economic restrictions on the aggregator functions necessary for simple sum aggregation were strongly rejected.[13] Fisher deduced correctly (1922, p. 361) that: "The simple arithmetic (Formula 1) should not be used under any circumstances."

We conclude with the following quotation from Fisher's (1922, p. 29) classical book, written over half a century ago:

> The simple arithmetic average is put first merely because it naturally comes first to the reader's mind, being the most common form of average. In fields other than index numbers it is often the best form of average to use. But we shall see that the simple arithmetic average produces one of the very worst of index numbers, and if this book has no other effect than to lead to the total abandonment of the simple arithmetic type of index number, it will have served a useful purpose.

---

[12] As we have observed, Hulten's and Diewert's work strongly supports the economic foundations of the Törnquist–Theil Divisia and Fisher Ideal indices. In addition, Fisher (1922) and Theil (1967) strongly support those same indices on the basis of their statistical index number properties.

[13] For further discussion of the failure of summation aggregation of monetary assets, see Barnett (1980b) and Barnett, Offenbacher, and Spindt (1981).

CHAPTER 8

DECISION STRUCTURE

8.1. Introduction

Conventional demand analysis and demand modeling can be viewed as a reduced form approach which models the ultimate effects of consumer and household decisions without exploring the underlying structure. The sources of preference orderings over market goods are collapsed into utility functions defined directly over those ultimate market goods. Nevertheless, introspection suggests that consumer and household preferences for market goods are derived from tastes for more elementary consumption characteristics.

In some cases the structure of the transformation between market goods and elementary consumption characteristics can be important. In such cases it can be useful to decompose the preference ordering over market goods into the underlying structure. Such cases include those in which change has occurred within household structure and those in which the underlying structure reveals informative properties of preferences.

In this chapter we shall explore two approaches which decompose preferences into underlying structure. In sections 8.2 and 8.3 we develop a rigorous and general method for modeling and jointly estimating the structure of household preferences and internal household technology. In section 8.4 we show that our approach is not subject to the limitations that Pollak and Wachter (1975) argue exist within other formulations and uses of the household production function approach. Sections 8.2 and 8.3 are based upon Barnett (1977a). In section 8.5 we present a related but different structural approach. That approach, developed by Brooks (1970) and Theil (1976), applies a preference independence transformation to preferences over market goods in order to reveal strongly separable preferences over more elementary and highly informative consumption characteristics. In section 8.6 we apply that approach to the estimates in Chapter 5. The results in section 8.6 are based upon Flinn (1978).

8.2. The household production function approach

8.2.1. Introduction

Let $x=(x_1,\ldots,x_n)'$ be a vector of market goods, and let $z=(z_1,\ldots,z_N)'$ be a vector of elementary "commodities" (or consumption characteristics) generated from goods by the household's production process. Let U be the household's utility function, which we shall assume is defined over commodity vectors, and let $p=(p_1,\ldots,p_n)'$ be the vector of goods prices. Pollak and Wachter (1975) have shown that a cost function $C(p,z)$ exists such that the household maximizes $U(z)$ subject to the constraint $C(p,z)=m$, where m is total expenditure available. The solution is a system of commodity demand equations $z=f(p,m)$. Translating U back into the goods space, we can also derive goods demand functions $x=h(p,m)$.

Assuming that household production is characterized by constant returns to scale, Pollak and Wachter have shown that the household equivalently can be shown to solve for that value, z^*, which will

$$\text{maximize } U(z) \text{ subject to } \pi'z=m, \tag{8.1}$$

where $\pi=(\pi_1,\ldots,\pi_N)'$ is the gradient of $C(p,z)$ with respect to z; π therefore is a function of (p,z). Then $\pi_i(p,z)$ is defined to be the shadow price of the ith commodity.

8.2.2. Basic constructs

Shadow prices usually are defined in terms of the normal to a separating hyperplane constructed at a solution point. That construction is dependent upon the location of the solution point, which need not be solely supply or technology determined. Now recall that $z^*=f(p,m)$ is the household's solution value for z. Define π^* by $\pi^*=\pi(p,z^*)$, and let us instruct the household to reselect z conditionally upon π^* to

$$\text{maximize } U(z) \text{ subject to } \pi^{*\prime}z=m. \tag{8.2}$$

To permit our prior computation of π^*, we assume that the household already has solved its full decision problem (8.1). Nevertheless, problem (8.2) can be defined formally, despite the seeming redundancy of its objectives.

The constraint in problem (8.2) *is* the hyperplane contemplated by the shadow price approach. The solution for z (in terms of (π^*,m)) can be denoted implicitly by $\tilde{g}(z, \pi^*, m) = 0$. Formally we could use the conventional notation $z = g(\pi^*, m)$, but we use the implicit function notation $\tilde{g}$ to emphasize the fact that an explicit closed form solution for g need not always exist, as can be seen from the models used in Chapters 6 and 9. By comparing the first-order conditions for the solution to problem (8.2) with those for the solution to the household's actual decision problem (8.1), we see immediately that $\tilde{g}(z^*, \pi^*, m) = 0$. We now can say that the household acts *as if* it were solving problem (8.2), and we see that $\tilde{g}$ has all of the known conventional properties of neoclassical (implicit) demand functions.

The function $\tilde{g}$ should not be confused with the composite function defined by the substitution of the function $\pi(p, z)$ for the value of the argument π^* in $\tilde{g}$. The fact that the function π depends upon z is not relevant to the properties of the function $\tilde{g}$. The function $\tilde{g}$ neither knows nor cares where the commodity shadow prices came from.

The question now is whether this merely definitional construct, $\tilde{g}$, can be incorporated into the household structural model in such a manner that *all* functions in the structure have known neoclassical properties and such that each function depends either solely upon tastes or solely upon technology.

8.2.3. The structure

Substitute $\pi(p, z)$ for π^* in $\tilde{g}$ to obtain that

$$\tilde{g}(z, \pi(p, z), m) = 0. \tag{8.3}$$

The constant-commodity-consumption goods demand functions, r_i, $i = 1, \ldots, n$, determine the cost minimizing goods consumption quantities at given (z, p). By Shephard's lemma we know that $r_i(z, p) = \partial C(p, z)/\partial p_i$. Defining r by $r = (r_1, \ldots, r_n)'$, we have that

$$x = r(z, p). \tag{8.4}$$

By the homogeneity of r in p and by Euler's theorem, we know that the cost function can be determined from r. Hence (8.4) fully defines the technology.

Adjoining (8.4) to (8.3), we acquire a complete system of $n + N$ simultaneous equations in the $n + N$ endogenous variables (x, z) and the $n + 1$ exogenous variables (p, m). We shall call this complete system (with any appropriate error structure) the household structural form. It utilizes only the functions g and (π, r), which each relate *solely* to preferences or to technology, respectively. Recall that $\tilde{g}$ lies in a one-to-one correspondence with preferences, while r lies in a one-to-one correspondence with technology. But $\pi(p,z)$ has z as an argument, and z depends upon preferences as well as technology. However, the *function* π itself depends solely upon the cost function. Furthermore, if we have theories of taste or technological change, we can incorporate them individually into the specification of g or of (π, r), respectively. Observe that *all* of the functions in ((8.3), (8.4)) have known conventional neoclassical properties. It is *this* structural form which we identify with the commodity shadow price approach.

To specify technology we could have used the production or cost function rather than our "factor" demand functions r. But whether alone or adjoined to (8.3), the resulting system would be incomplete (having an unequal number of endogenous variables and equations). An incomplete system does not define the joint distribution of the endogenous variables and, therefore, cannot define *any* model. An analogous use of factor demand equations to complete a system has been considered in a production context by Hall (1973).

Asymptotically efficient estimators of this system are available from FIML estimation. Consistent but not asymptotically efficient estimators are available at lower computing cost through nonlinear two-stage least squares or nonlinear three-stage least squares. See, for example, Amemiya (1974, 1975, 1977) and Gallant (1977). These latter estimators also are robust to specification and data errors. Relevant computer programs are contained in the TSP (Harvard) and TROLL (NBER) packages and in the Wymer (IMF) and Barnett–Eisenpress (Appendix C) programs.

Pollak and Wachter (1975) appear to advocate (or perhaps to impute to the household production function approach) a two-stage approach in which technology (perhaps (8.4)) is estimated separately in a first stage. This two-step estimator is not consistent (since the system is not block recursive) and has no known desirable properties. In fact it has no known properties (or available standard errors) at all.

We have not explicitly introduced an error structure into ((8.3), (8.4)), but a conventional additive error commonly would be a convenient choice. Observe that we can estimate the full system without deleting an arbitrary equation, since the usual disturbance covariance matrix singularity problem does not arise. Although the budget constraint $\sum p_k x_k = m$ does create a linear dependency between the equations of (8.4), the dependency does not generate singularity of the covariance matrix of the joint error vector added to ((8.3), (8.4)). This can be seen by applying to ((8.3), (8.4)) the usual singularity derivation (for conventional demand systems) while recalling that z is random on the right-hand side of (8.4). The proof is provided in the next subsection.

We solve the system of equations ((8.3), (8.4)) for (z, x) in terms of (p, m). The solution is

$$z = f(p, m) \tag{8.5}$$
$$x = h(p, m) \tag{8.6}$$

which provides the reduced form (closed form solution) corresponding to the structural household model ((8.3), (8.4)).

8.2.4. Nonsingularity of the disturbance covariance matrix

We have observed previously that the full disturbance covariance matrix is nonsingular so that we need not delete an arbitrary equation to establish nonsingularity. We prove this fact in this subsection.

Let us add a stochastic error vector $\varepsilon = (\varepsilon_1, \ldots, \varepsilon_N)'$ to the right-hand side of (8.3) and another stochastic error vector $u = (u_1, \ldots, u_n)'$ to the right-hand side of (8.4). We permit u_i and ε_j to be correlated for any $i = 1, \ldots, n$ and $j = 1, \ldots, N$, but we assume that ε and u have zero means. We delete the time subscript throughout. The budget constraint $\sum p_k x_k = m$ does indeed create a linear dependency between the equations of (8.4). But as we shall see, the covariance matrix of the error structure remains nonsingular. We also could relate a "budget constraint" to (8.1) in terms of shadow prices, but with a nonlinear cost function such a constraint could generate no linear dependencies within the error structure.

Multiplying each equation of (8.4) by the corresponding good price and summing over the equations, we get that

$$\sum_i p_i x_i = \sum_i p_i r_i(z, p) + \sum_i p_i u_i. \tag{8.7}$$

Although the left-hand side of (8.7) must sum to m, the first term on the right-hand side of (8.7) need not. This results from the randomness of z. Hence we have that

$$\sum_i p_i u_i = m - \sum_i p_i r_i(z, p). \tag{8.8}$$

Now define $v = (v_1, \ldots, v_{N+n})'$ such that $v = (\varepsilon', u')'$, multiply (8.8) through by v_j, and take the expectation of each side to get that

$$\sum_i p_i E(u_i v_j) = -\sum_i p_i E[v_j r_i(z, p)]. \tag{8.9}$$

To acquire an analog to the usual result in demand theory, we could treat z as stochastically independent of v_j so that the right-hand side of

(8.9) would equal zero. But to acquire singularity of the covariance matrix of v, we need the stronger result that $\Sigma_i p_i E(v_i v_j) = 0$, which does not follow. Furthermore, z need not be stochastically independent of v_j. The covariance matrix of v is not singular.

8.3. Identification of the structural form

8.3.1. Exclusion restrictions

The household production function approach can be viewed as predicated upon the ability of system ((8.3), (8.4)) to unscramble tastes from technology. The dependence of shadow prices both upon tastes and technology could pose a fundamental methodological problem only if that joint dependency resulted in an identification problem; furthermore, our own advocacy of ((8.3), (8.4)) as the household's structural model would be unsupportable if it were unidentified. To dispel in advance any truly serious potential doubts about the use of shadow prices, we shall disprove nonidentification by counterexample.

It is well known that nonlinear functions of exogenous variables can be viewed as new exogenous variables. Although the exogenous variables p may appear in all of the equations of ((8.3), (8.4)), some functions of the elements of p certainly will be missing from some equations. The result is exclusion restrictions on those equations whenever the functions do exist elsewhere in the system. Fisher (1966) has proved that terms involving endogenous variables can generate exclusion restrictions in a similar manner, and ((8.3), (8.4)) inherently is nonlinear in both its endogenous and exogenous variables. The fundamental difference between the structure of (8.3) and (8.4) ensures the existence of many such exclusion restrictions in the combined system ((8.3), (8.4)).

Furthermore, observe that m occurs in (8.3) but not in (8.4). Each occurrence of m alone or in an interaction with an endogenous or exogenous variable of (8.3) provides an exclusion restriction on (8.4). Such restrictions cannot hinder identification and usually help considerably. See Koopmans et al. (1950, p. 94), and Wegge (1965). Hence, our results are very conservative.

Also, observe that only system (8.4) depends upon tastes. Hence, if an identification problem should arise in a particular application (although we have been unable to construct such an example), further restrictions can be introduced into the system by postulating systematic taste or technological change. The literature on the new home economics is rich in household characteristics that can be appropriate choices as shift variables in tastes and technology.

We now illustrate our observations through an example chosen to be as simple as possible without excluding joint production. Our conclusions will be very conservative since we shall not introduce any form of taste or technological change, and we shall make no use of the numerous existing cross equation parameter restrictions. The structural form will be shown to be overidentified with or without joint production. The example will illustrate the manner in which joint production commonly *helps* us identify tastes and technology. The very large number of overidentifying restrictions will be shown to be decreased in every equation when production nonjointness is imposed. Jointness helps identification in the same manner as taste or technological change commonly can help. Virtually any such complication tends to increase the number of interactions between variables appearing in a subset of the system's equations. The result is an increase in the number of exclusion restrictions on the system. Similarly, we should expect that a more complicated specification of g would tend to introduce further exclusion restrictions upon our system. Interactions work in our favor!

8.3.2. Example

Consider a two-good, two-commodity household. We assume that the household's commodity demand functions are of the Bergson form, $z_i = \beta_i m/\pi_i$, with $\beta_i > 0$ for $i = 1, 2$. We do not impose the Cobb–Douglas restriction $\beta_1 + \beta_2 = 1$, since we are not utilizing our cross equation parameter restrictions. We assume that the household has a Hybrid Diewert joint cost function (see, for example, Hall). Using $a_{ijk\ell}$ ($i, j, k, \ell = 1, 2$) to denote parameters, we have that

$$C(z_1, z_2, p_1, p_2) = a_{1111}z_1p_1 + a_{1122}z_2p_1 + a_{2211}z_1p_2$$
$$+ a_{2222}z_2p_2 + 2a_{1211}z_1\sqrt{(p_1p_2)}$$
$$+ 2a_{1222}z_2\sqrt{(p_1p_2)} + 2a_{1112}p_1\sqrt{(z_1z_2)}$$
$$+ 2a_{2212}p_2\sqrt{(z_1z_2)} + 4a_{1212}\sqrt{(z_1z_2)}\sqrt{(p_1p_2)}.$$

Joint production is excluded if and only if $a_{1112} = a_{1212} = a_{2212} = 0$.

Before introducing the stochastic error term, we multiply each commodity demand equation by π_i to get $z_i\pi_i = \beta_i m$. We then differentiate $C(z, p)$

with respect to z_i to acquire π_i for $i = 1, 2$ and substitute those shadow price functions into the commodity demand functions. Adding the stochastic error terms, we get that

$$a_{11ii}p_1 z_i + a_{22ii}p_2 z_i + 2a_{12ii}\sqrt{(p_1 p_2)}z_i + a_{1112}p_1\sqrt{(z_1 z_2)}$$
$$+ a_{2212}p_2\sqrt{(z_1 z_2)} + 2a_{1212}\sqrt{(z_1 z_2)}\sqrt{(p_1 p_2)} - \beta_i m = \varepsilon_i, \qquad i = 1, 2. \tag{8.10}$$

Differentiating $C(z, p)$ with respect to z_i, $i = 1, 2$, we can derive the system

$$x_i - a_{ii11}z_1 - 2a_{ii12}\sqrt{(z_1 z_2)} - a_{ii22}z_2 - (p_1/p_2)^{1/2k}$$
$$(a_{1211}z_1 + 2a_{1212}\sqrt{(z_1 z_2)} + a_{1222}z_2) = u_i, \qquad i = 1, 2, \tag{8.11}$$

where $k = -1$ if $i = 1$ and $k = +1$ if $i = 2$. The system ((8.10), (8.11)) is our household structural form ((8.3), (8.4)).

Let $y = (z', x', p', m)'$. The first step in the verification of Fisher's identification conditions is to determine all linearly independent functions of y appearing in the structural form. Denoting the vector of such functions by $q(y)$, we find that

$$q(y) = (p_1 z_1, p_2 z_1, 2\sqrt{(p_1 p_2)}z_1, p_1\sqrt{(z_1 z_2)}, p_2\sqrt{(z_1 z_2)}, 2\sqrt{(z_1 z_2)}\sqrt{(p_1 p_2)},$$
$$-m, p_1 z_2, p_2 z_2, 2\sqrt{(p_1 p_2)}z_2, x_1, -z_1, -2\sqrt{(z_1 z_2)},$$
$$-z_2, -z_1\sqrt{(p_2/p_1)}, -2\sqrt{(p_2/p_1)}\sqrt{(z_1 z_2)},$$
$$-z_2\sqrt{(p_2/p_1)}, x_2, -\sqrt{(p_1/p_2)}z_1,$$
$$-2\sqrt{(p_1/p_2)}\sqrt{(z_1 z_2)} - \sqrt{(p_1/p_2)}z_2)'.$$

We then define the matrix of parameters and constants, A, such that the structural form ((8.10), (8.11)) can be written as $Aq(y) = v$, where $v = (\varepsilon', u')'$. Matrix A is displayed in table 8.1. Each zero entry in A defines an exclusion restriction on the corresponding equation. We see that there are exactly 14 exclusion restrictions on each equation. Inspecting A for parameters that appear in more than one equation, we can determine that the number of cross equation parameter restrictions is 15. Although these restrictions almost certainly assist in identification, we shall ignore them, since their precise effect on the order and rank conditions for identification is not known. However, if the system is identified when the cross equation parameter restrictions are not imposed, then the system certainly will be identified when they are imposed. Also, observe that an additional cross equation parameter restriction would exist if we imposed the Cobb-Douglas restrictions $\beta_1 + \beta_2 = 1$.

Table 8.1
Matrix A.

a_{1111}	a_{2211}	a_{1211}	a_{1112}	a_{2212}	B_1	0	0	0	0	0	0	0	0	0	0	0	0	0	0
0	0	0	a_{1112}	a_{2212}	a_{1212}	B_2	a_{1122}	a_{2222}	a_{1222}	0	0	0	0	0	0	0	0	0	0
0	0	0	0	0	0	0	0	0	1	a_{1111}	a_{1112}	a_{1122}	a_{1211}	a_{1212}	a_{1222}	0	0	0	0
0	0	0	0	0	0	0	0	0	0	a_{2211}	a_{2212}	a_{2222}	0	0	0	1	a_{1211}	a_{1212}	a_{1222}

We now must compute the matrix $\partial q(y)/\partial y'$, which we designate by Q. The matrix Q is displayed in table 8.2. In order to define the relevant rank and order conditions for identification, we must determine the number of linear dependencies that exist between the rows of Q. Hence, we seek the vectors of constants h that satisfy $h'Q = 0'$. We find that $h = 0$ is the only such vector. Verification of this result is tedious. From the third column of Q we have that $h_{11} = 0$. From the fourth column we have that $h_{18} = 0$. From the last column we have $h_7 = 0$. Letting m vary at successive fixed values of p, we can verify from the first column of Q that $h_1 = h_2 = h_3 = h_4 = h_5 = h_6 = h_{12} = h_{13} = h_{15} = h_{16} = h_{19} = h_{20} = 0$. By the same method we can determine from the second column of Q that $h_8 = h_9 = h_{10} = h_{14} =$

Table 8.2
Matrix Q.

p_1	0	0	0	z_1	0	0
p_2	0	0	0	0	z_1	0
$2\sqrt{(p_1 p_2)}$	0	0	0	$z_1\sqrt{(p_2/p_1)}$	$z_1\sqrt{(p_1/p_2)}$	0
$(1/2)p_1\sqrt{(z_2/z_1)}$	$(1/2)p_1\sqrt{(z_1/z_2)}$	0	0	$\sqrt{(z_1 z_2)}$	0	0
$(1/2)p_2\sqrt{(z_2/z_1)}$	$(1/2)p_2\sqrt{(z_1/z_2)}$	0	0	0	$\sqrt{(z_1 z_2)}$	0
$\sqrt{(z_2/z_1)}\sqrt{(p_1 p_2)}$	$\sqrt{(z_1/z_2)}\sqrt{(p_1 p_2)}$	0	0	$\sqrt{(z_1 z_2)}\sqrt{(p_2/p_1)}$	$\sqrt{(z_1 z_2)}\sqrt{(p_1/p_2)}$	0
0	0	0	0	0	0	-1
0	p_1	0	0	z_2	0	0
0	p_2	0	0	0	z_2	0
0	$2\sqrt{(p_1 p_2)}$	0	0	$z_2\sqrt{(p_2/p_1)}$	$z_2\sqrt{(p_1/p_2)}$	0
0	0	1	0	0	0	0
-1	0	0	0	0	0	0
$-\sqrt{(z_2/z_1)}$	$-\sqrt{(z_1/z_2)}$	0	0	0	0	0
0	-1	0	0	0	0	0
$-\sqrt{(p_2/p_1)}$	0	0	0	$(1/2)z_1\sqrt{(p_2)}p_1^{-3/2}$	$-(1/2)z_1(p_1 p_2)^{-1/2}$	0
$-\sqrt{(p_2/p_1)}\sqrt{(z_2/z_1)}$	$-\sqrt{(p_2/p_1)}\sqrt{(z_1/z_2)}$	0	0	$\sqrt{(z_1 z_2)}\sqrt{(p_2)}p_1^{-3/2}$	$-\sqrt{(z_1 z_2)}(p_1 p_2)^{-1/2}$	0
0	$-\sqrt{(p_2/p_1)}$	0	0	$(1/2)z_2\sqrt{(p_2)}p_1^{-3/2}$	$-(1/2)z_2(p_1 p_2)^{-1/2}$	0
0	0	0	1	$-(1/2)\sqrt{(1/p_1 p_2)}z_1$	$(1/2)z_1\sqrt{(p_1)}p_2^{-3/2}$	0
$-\sqrt{(p_1/p_2)}$	0	0	0	$-(p_1 p_2)^{-1/2}\sqrt{(z_1 z_2)}$	$\sqrt{(z_1 z_2)}\sqrt{(p_1)}p_2^{-3/2}$	0
$-\sqrt{(p_1/p_2)}\sqrt{(z_2/z_1)}$	$-\sqrt{(p_1/p_2)}\sqrt{(z_1/z_2)}$	0	0	$-(1/2)(p_1 p_2)^{-1/2}z_2$	$1/2\sqrt{(p_1)}p_2^{-3/2}z_2$	0
0	$-\sqrt{(p_1/p_2)}$	0	0			

$h_{17} = h_{21} = 0$. Hence, $h = 0$. Therefore we do not have to augment the matrix A in defining Fisher's rank and order conditions.

We now consider the rank condition for identifiability. Let A_i be the ith row of A, and let ϕ_i be the matrix of zeros and ones such that $A_i \phi_i = 0'$ defines all of the 14 exclusion restrictions on the ith equation. In our case, ϕ_i is a 21×14 matrix consisting of a 14×14 identity matrix bordered above by a 7×14 matrix of zeros. The rank (necessary and sufficient) condition for identification of the ith equation is rank $(A\phi_i) = M - 1$, where M is the number of equations in the system. See Fisher (1966, ch. 25). For $i = 1, \ldots, 4$, we can determine that rank $(A\phi_i) = 3$. Since $M = 4$, the system is identified.

We now consider the order (necessary) condition for identification. As shown by Fisher, the order condition is satisfied if rank $(\phi_i) \geq M - 1$. Now rank (ϕ_i) is equal to the number of exclusion restrictions in equation i, which we previously have determined to be 14 for each $i = 1, \ldots, 4$. Hence, each equation is overidentified. Furthermore, we have ignored the 15 available cross equation parameter restrictions. Therefore our results are very conservative. Of course, we have verified identification only for one specification of ((8.3), (8.4)), but our approach to verification is so conservative and our results are so strong that there can remain little reason for concern about an identification problem in ((8.3), (8.4)).

We now consider the effect of nonjointness on identification. To impose nonjointness on ((8.10), (8.11)), we set $a_{1112} = a_{1212} = a_{2212} = 0$. Eleven exclusion restrictions remain in the first or second rows of A while 13 remain in the third or fourth rows. We have *lost* three overidentifying restrictions in each of the equations (8.10) and one overidentifying restriction in each of the equations (8.11). Joint production helps in identification.

The results acquired from our counterexample reflect general properties of the theoretical structural form ((8.3), (8.4)) rather than properties specific to the chosen specification. The large number of exclusion restrictions results from the nonlinearity in the variables inherent to ((8.3), (8.4)) and from the fundamental difference between the structures of (8.3) and (8.4). Joint production does not hinder identification. In fact, it is known in general that such interactions and the nonlinearities which result do not hinder (and commonly assist) in identification. A rigorous proof in the case of nonlinearity in the variables is available in Fisher (1966, pp. 148–151).

8.4. The Pollak and Wachter critique

Pollak and Wachter (1975) argue that the household production function approach, or the use of shadow prices in that approach, is fundamentally methodologically flawed. The rigorously general version of that approach presented in the previous section possesses no such flaws, and we shall discuss that fact in this section.

8.4.1. Introduction

In "The Relevance of the Household Production Function and its Implications for the Allocation of Time", Pollak and Wachter (1975) have provided a valuable analytical interpretation of the theory underlying the "new home economics". In addition Pollak and Wachter have provided insights into serious potential abuses of the household production function approach. However, their identification of one such potential abuse led them to terminate their analysis prematurely with the rejection of the entire shadow price concept on which much of the new home economics is based. Their conclusion is unwarranted.

Pollak and Wachter maintain that joint production inherently is important in household technology, and they argue that joint production breaks the link between the existing household production function approach and the neoclassical theory on which that approach is based. They also argue that joint production results in the confounding of tastes and technology within shadow prices. But such "confounding" could pose a fundamental theoretical problem only if the postulated "confounding" can be translated into an identification problem. We have equated a particular theoretical structural model, ((8.3), (8.4)), with the household production function approach. We have demonstrated that *all* functions in the structural form *do* have known neoclassical properties, and we have discussed the identification of the structure. We have *derived* household structure and proved its identification when tastes are Bergson and technology is Hybrid Diewert. The structure has been shown to be overidentified, and joint production has been shown to *increase* the number of overidentifying restrictions. We have argued that in the general case joint production commonly tends to assist in identification without introducing *any* non-neoclassical theoretical complications.

Having rejected commodity shadow prices, Pollak and Wachter recommend an alternative. We shall equate that alternative with a reduced form approach not having capabilities comparable to those of the household production function approach.

Pollak and Wachter (1975, p. 258) maintain that if the constraint $\pi(p,z)'z = m$ in (8.1) is nonlinear in z, then the link with conventional theory is broken, since commodity demand functions derived from (8.1) would "correspond to those in a model in which consumers are monopsonists or are offered tie-in sales". But the commodity shadow prices $\pi(p, z)$ do depend upon z whenever household production exhibits jointness, which Pollak and Wachter maintain is inherently characteristic of household production processes. Hence, Pollak and Wachter (1975, p. 258) conclude that in the usual case the household production function approach must model a non-neoclassical decision problem for which "there are virtually no substantive results". On these grounds, which we have shown to be specious, they immediately reject the use of commodity shadow prices as arguments of commodity demand functions. When z is not measurable, they recommend the estimation of h. Otherwise they recommend estimation of f (perhaps preceded by a prior stage estimation of technology). In order to address these issues, we have *not* excluded joint production in the last section.

Observe carefully that the issue they raise is the availability of theoretical knowledge of the properties of the functions used in the household production function approach. This mathematical question about *nonstochastic function* properties is independent of the separate statistical question of the endogeneity of any *random variables*. For example, the endogeneity of the random variable $\pi(p, z)$ follows trivially from the direct functional dependency of $\pi(p, z)$ upon the endogenous random variable z. Yet this endogeneity is irrelevant to Pollak and Wachter's contention of the presumed unavailability of known theoretical properties of the *function* π or of any other function in household structure.

Pollak and Wachter have observed correctly that their function f does not have the known properties of conventional neoclassical demand functions. In addition, f and h depend both upon technology and preferences in a manner that provides little information about either. But as Pollak and Wachter (1975, p. 260) have explained, the primary objective of the new home economics is to avoid "confounding tastes and technology". We have shown that the use of commodity shadow prices permits us to isolate sources of taste and technological change while using *only* functions having known conventional neoclassical properties.

8.4.2. The issue

Systems (8.5) and (8.6) are the two equation systems that Pollak and Wachter have suggested we estimate, the first when z is measurable and second otherwise. From section 8.3 we see that the two models recommended to us by Pollak and Wachter consist of the two sets of equations defining the household's theoretical (exclusive of an error structure) reduced form.

The source of Pollak and Wachter's objections to the commodity shadow price concept now becomes clear. For forecasting purposes, the reduced form places solely "explanatory" (predetermined) variables on the right-hand side and permits direct interpretation of cause and effect relationships. In a structural form, the right-hand side can depend upon endogenous variables, and in our structural form, ((8.3), (8.4)), $\pi(p, z)$ does depend upon the endogenous variables z. It is the imputation of explanatory power to commodity shadow prices that Pollak and Wachter convincingly have warned us against. But to use the shadow price *function*, π, in the construction of ((8.3), (8.4)), we have *no need* to impute explanatory power to the value of the *variables* $\pi(p, z)$. Different households may have identical technologies and be "given" identical (p, m) without having identical shadow prices. In such a case we should conclude that shadow prices are different as the result of differing tastes. To view shadow prices as explanatory would reverse the direction of causation.

Each function in the reduced form can carry joint information *both* about preferences and technology. If we wish to investigate properties of the household's structure or to consider household structural change, we must use a structural parameterization permitting the unscrambling of tastes from technology. For example, without a structural parameterization we could not incorporate habit formation into the model without confounding tastes and technology. Prior estimation of technology would not help. Of course in the exceptional borderline case of exact identification, structural form parameters for a fixed structure can be computed from reduced form parameters. But structural change can be investigated only in terms of changes in structural form parameters. Furthermore, even if the structural form were exactly identified, nonlinearities that typically exist in both the structural and reduced form would severely complicate solution for the structural form parameters from the reduced form.

To investigate technological change, we can explore shifts in the parameters of the *function* π and the function *r*. We do not explore variations in the *value* of $\pi(p, z)$, since such variations depend upon preferences as well as technology. In brief, the merits of Pollak and Wachter's approach are precisely those of a reduced form system, while those of the shadow price approach are precisely those of a structural form. But the advantages of structural form estimation are well known. Furthermore, reduced form forecasts are easily computed numerically from an identified structural form, so that the objectives of the reduced form can be served by the structural form itself. No need exists ever to estimate directly or to solve analytically for the inherently less informative reduced form.

Also, observe that the household's structural form ((8.3), (8.4)) is well designed for deriving refutable theoretical results. The properties of all the functions in ((8.3), (8.4)) are restricted by neoclassical demand and production theory, regardless of whether or not joint production exists. Those restrictions imply restrictions upon the response of z to variations in tastes, technology, and (p, m). But such theoretical results are very weak unless further assumptions are made about tastes and technology. In this context it frequently is productive to exclude corner solutions and inferior commodities. Excluding joint production is neither necessary nor desirable. In contrast, observe that Pollak and Wachter's function f itself does not possess conventional neoclassical demand properties although its actual properties can be deduced from ((8.3), (8.4)).

When z is measurable, Pollak and Wachter advocate estimating (8.5) (perhaps preceded by the estimation of technology). The most general approach to modeling f would involve parameterizing f directly. The selection of such a direct reduced form parameterization preferably should be guided by a duality theory, although in practice we may be satisfied with a parameterization of f which only approximates the underlying theory. Each parameter of a direct reduced form parameterization could carry information both about preferences and technology, and untangling the two sources (whether or not technology is itself estimated in a prior stage) would rarely be feasible. This is truly a reduced form approach. Alternatively we could *structurally* parameterize (8.5) by selecting parameterizations of preferences and technology (rather than directly of f) and then deriving (8.5) in terms of those original structural parameters. But this approach would be of little practical value, since the resulting system would be derivable only in pathological cases, as we will now illustrate.

To complete the system, suppose we were to adjoin (8.4) to (8.5), as was advocated by Pollak and Wachter (1977). Then suppose we were to attempt to derive the resulting system from a prior parameterization of tastes and technology. We first could derive ((8.3), (8.4)), which indexes the equivalence class of structural forms consisting of all elementary transformations of ((8.3), (8.4)). To pass from the shadow price approach, defined (in the wide sense) by this equivalence class, to the Pollak and Wachter equations (8.5), we must be able to solve the structural equations (8.3) *explicitly* for a closed form representation of the reduced form equations (8.5).

As is true in general for nonlinear structures, this rarely is possible. As a simple example, consider Hybrid-Diewert technology and CES commodity preferences in the two-good, two-commodity case. Substituting into (8.3) for the two-good, two-commodity case, we obtain a two-equation system of the form:

$$\left[a_i(\boldsymbol{p})z_i + b_i(\boldsymbol{p})\sqrt{(z_i z_2)} \{ \alpha_1 [c(\boldsymbol{p}) + d(\boldsymbol{p})\sqrt{(z_2/z_1)}]^\beta \right.$$
$$\left. + \alpha_2 [e(\boldsymbol{p}) + f(\boldsymbol{p})\sqrt{(z_1/z_2)}]^\beta \} = \alpha_1 m [g_i(\boldsymbol{p}) + h_i(\boldsymbol{p})\sqrt{(z_2/z_1)}]^\beta \right.$$

for $i = 1, 2$, where α and β are parameters satisfying $1 < \beta < \infty$ and $1 < \alpha_i < \infty$, and where $a_i, b_i, c, d, e, f, g_i,$ and h_i are functions of goods prices, $\boldsymbol{p}$. Now let $z_0 = \sqrt{z_2}$, and let β be an arbitrary integer exceeding 4. Then apply the binomial expansion to the terms of order β in that equation, multiply out the resulting terms, and collect all terms onto the right-hand side. To separate the variables z_1 and z_2, we must be able to solve this polynomial for z_0. But the polynomial is full and of order $\beta + 1$, and it is well known in Galois theory that the general polynomial of degree exceeding 4 is not solvable.

In the usual mathematical sense we define "solvability" to be the ability to find a closed form solution by radicals. Polynomials of degree exceeding 4 have explicit solutions only in terms of elliptic and Fuchsian functions, which are not empirically implementable by any known techniques. See Conkwright (1957, p. 85). Hence, we see that to parameterize ((8.4), (8.5)) structurally we must back up to an implicit representation, i.e. into an element of the equivalence class defining the shadow price approach itself.

Even in the rare cases in which (8.5) can be derived with the original structural parameters preserved, the resulting system would be far more difficult to estimate than the original structure ((8.3), (8.4)). The sole such case of which we are aware (permitting both joint technology and a closed form representation of (8.5)) is the case of Cobb–Douglas preferences and Hybrid-Diewert technology. In that case ((8.4), (8.5)) is both nonlinear in the variables and deeply nonlinear in its parameters, while our system ((8.3), (8.4)) is nonlinear in the variables but fully linear in all of its parameters.

Pollak and Wachter maintain that the commodity shadow price approach dictates the use of a two-stage estimation procedure. In the first stage commodity prices are estimated from a specification depending solely upon technology. This procedure permits viewing commodity shadow prices as household "supply" determined. In the second stage, household commodity demand is estimated conditionally upon commodity shadow prices. Our presentation of the commodity shadow price approach postulates no such two-stage process. We assume that problem (8.1) is the one and only problem that the household actually solves, and the household solves that joint production and consumption decision in one step. Problem (8.2) is only a mathematical construct.

8.4.3. Conclusion

The household structural form that we have identified with the household production function approach does not and *need not* contain commodity shadow prices as predetermined or supply determined variables to which causality can be imputed, but rather as functions of both the exogenous variables, p, and the endogenous variables, z. The household's structural form contains *only* functions having conventional neoclassical properties, with each function related solely and identifiably either to preferences or to technology. Causality can be imputed to explainable taste and technological change and to variations in the *exogenous* variables (p, m). The existence of joint production poses *no* problems in the modeling of household structure.

Pollak and Wachter also discuss the formidable problems involved in defining and measuring commodity consumption quantities. Those issues are independent of Pollak and Wachter's more fundamental critique of the theory underlying the household production function approach, and we have abstracted from such measurement problems. Nevertheless, measurement problems cannot be ignored in practice, and they undoubtedly exclude many household decisions from the domain of attractive applications of the household production function approach.

The measurement and imputation problems in the household production function literature are greater than in most other areas of applied economic research. But the significance of this observation should not be exaggerated. Much of the household production function literature has dealt with issues previously viewed as lying within the domain of "softer" social sciences. Research on such issues inherently requires operationalizing vague concepts, and the available literature on these definitional problems in the social sciences is formidable. See, for example, Lazarsfeld and Rosenberg (1971).

We agree with Pollak and Wachter that some applications of that approach have (unnecessarily) imputed causation to shadow prices. But we do not believe that an approach should be rejected by identifying it definitionally with its abuses. The solution to the abuse of an approach is the proper use of the approach, and we have provided relevant foundations for such proper use in sections 8.2 and 8.3.

8.5. The preference independence transformation

In section 8.2 we presented a rigorous and explicit means of formulating and using the household production function approach. However, as we have observed, that approach requires one to operationalize and measure quantities consumed of elementary, nonmarket "commodities" or consumption characteristics. The approach is powerful in those cases in which such measurement is natural and practicable. All implications of internal household structure and consumer market demands become fully usable. However, in many cases the application does not dictate any natural operationalization of the elementary consumption characteristics. Nevertheless, in some such cases we can work in reverse to reveal information about the unknown elementary consumption characteristics from the available data on market goods consumption. In this section we present the Brooks-Theil method of revealing such information, and we present Flinn's (1978) results with that approach using the data and model from Chapter 5.

8.5.1. Introduction

We begin by deriving theoretical differential demand results for an individual consumer. As will be seen below, the derivation will closely parallel that in Chapter 3 for the Rotterdam model, and that relationship will motivate us to adopt the Rotterdam model parameterization. However, it is important to observe that the theory is completely general (whenever the utility function is strictly concave), and the resulting preference independence transformation can be applied with any regular neoclassical demand system.

As observed in section 8.2, the transformation, T, between market goods and elementary consumption commodities along with the utility function defined over those consumption commodities can be collapsed into a utility function defined directly over the market goods. We begin in this section with that collapsed utility function, $u(x)$, defined over the vector of n market goods, x. We seek an inverse transformation permitting us to transform locally from u back to the utility function, $U(z)$, over the N elementary consumption commodities, z.

In the Lancaster (1966) approach the transformation T could reflect properties of the internal structure of the individual consumer's preferences. In the Becker (1965) approach, T defines household technology. In this section we shall abstract from the question of the source of T. Our "individual consumer" would be viewed as a household or as a representative household member, if T were identified with Becker's household production function.

Without knowledge of T or measurability of z, we have no hope, in the general case, of revealing any properties at all of U from estimates of u and knowledge of x. However, Theil (1976) has shown that under certain axioms and under the central assumption that U is strongly separable, a unique local transformation then exists which reveals properties of U from estimates of u. In this section we apply that transformation to the results of Chapter 5.

8.5.2. Differential demand equations

In order to apply the preference independence transformation, we assume that U is strongly separable, so that

$$U(z) = f\left[\sum_{i=1}^{N} U_i(z_i)\right], \tag{8.12}$$

where $f' \geq 0$. An element of that equivalence class of functions is acquired by setting f equal to the identity mapping so that

$$U(z) = \sum_{i=1}^{N} [U_i(z_i)]. \tag{8.13}$$

Hence (8.13) is a sufficient (but not necessary) condition for (8.12). It suffices to transform goods preferences, u, into a function of the form (8.13) to reveal the strongly separable preference preordering over z. The preference independence transformation provides that transformation. The cardinal property (8.13) could be viewed as suggesting that the z_i values represent the consumer's basic wants, and is called preference independence. We let p be the vector of goods prices, we let x be per capita consumption of those goods, and we let $m = p'x$ be total expenditure available. Then the ith budget share is $w_i = p_i x_i / m$. The associated Divisia quantity index is defined to be the solution for Q to

$$d(\log Q) = \sum_{i=1}^{n} w_i d(\log x_i). \tag{8.14}$$

The function u is assumed to be twice continuously differentiable, monotonically increasing, and strictly quasiconcave. We shall normalize preferences to select a specific element from the equivalence class of monotonic transformations of utility functions. We therefore can impute the further cardinal property of strict concavity to that element. Hence, the Hessian matrix of u is negative definite. We let $[u_{ij}]$ be that Hessian matrix.

The representative consumer then maximizes $u(x)$ subject to $p'x = m$.[1] Theil's (1975, 1976) differential approach to demand analysis can be applied to acquire

$$w_i d(\log x_i) = \mu_i d(\log Q) + \phi \sum_{j=1}^{n} \theta_{ij} d\left(\log \frac{p_j}{P^*}\right), \tag{8.15}$$

where the coefficients, ϕ, $\mu = (\mu_1, \ldots, \mu_n)'$, and $[\theta_{ij}]$ depend upon income and prices. Eq. (8.15) is entirely general, when applied to an individual consumer, as was our eq. (3.14) in Chapter 3.

The left-hand variable is the contribution of the ith good to (8.14) and is also the quantity component of the change in the ith budget share. The first term on the right is the real income component, with real income measured by the Divisia quantity index. Equivalently real income is m divided by the price index determined by Q and Fisher's (1922) factor reversal test. As in section 3.5, $\mu_i = p_i \partial x_i / \partial m$, and hence from (3.15) it follows that

$$\sum_{i=1}^{n} \mu_i = 1. \tag{8.16}$$

The last term in (8.15) is the substitution component, where ϕ is the income flexibility (the reciprocal of the income elasticity of the marginal utility of income). The differentials in the substitution component consist of changes in relative prices. The deflator is the Frisch price index,

$$d(\log P^*) = \sum_{i=1}^{n} \mu_i d(\log p_i). \tag{8.17}$$

---

[1] We postulate the existence of a representative consumer, since in this section we use a version of the relative price version of the Rotterdam model. As mentioned in Chapter 3, we do not deal directly with aggregation over consumers with the relative price version in this book.

Observe that $d[\log(p_j/P^*)] = d(\log p_j) - d(\log P^*)$.

The coefficient θ_{ij} in (8.15) is defined as

$$\theta_{ij} = \frac{\lambda}{\phi m} p_i u^{ij} p_j, \tag{8.18}$$

where λ is the marginal utility of income and u^{ij} is the (i,j)th element of $[u_{ij}]^{-1}$ (the inverse of the Hessian matrix of the utility function). The $n \times n$ matrix $[\theta_{ij}]$ is symmetric positive definite, because $\phi < 0$ and $[U_{ij}]$ (and hence its inverse) is symmetric negative definite. Also, the θ_{ij} values in each equation add up to the corresponding marginal share.

$$\sum_{j=1}^{n} \theta_{ij} = \mu_i, \quad i = 1, \ldots, n. \tag{8.19}$$

By summing (8.19) over i and using (8.16), we obtain $\Sigma_i \Sigma_j \theta_{ij} = 1$, which is expressed by referring to the θ_{ij} values as the normalized price coefficients of the differential demand system (8.15). The θ_{ij} values are the $\bar{\nu}_{ij}$ values of section 3.3 after they have been normalized to add up to 1.[2] Hence $\theta_{ij} = \bar{\nu}_{ij} / \Sigma_i \Sigma_j \bar{\nu}_{ij}$.

Assume that eq. (8.13) obtains, so that the marginal utility of each good is independent of the quantities of all others. In that case the Hessian $[u_{ij}]$ and its inverse both become diagonal, and the same holds for $[\theta_{ij}]$ in view of (8.18), while (8.19) takes the form $\theta_{ii} = \mu_i$. When there is preference independence in the sense described above, (8.15) becomes

$$w_i d(\log x_i) = \mu_i d(\log \dot{Q}) + \phi \mu_i d \log\left(\frac{p_i}{P^*}\right), \tag{8.20}$$

which is a differential demand equation with only one relative price. Although (8.20) holds only under preference independence, the preference independence transformation can always transform (8.15) into the form (8.20). We shall apply this transformation when the system (8.15) for $i = 1, \ldots, n$ has been defined to include a demand equation for leisure.

8.5.3. The preference independence transformation

The preference independence transformation diagonalizes the Hessian matrix $[u_{ij}]$, and hence also the normalized price coefficient matrix, $[\theta_{ij}]$, subject to the constraint that the Divisia price and quantity indices and

---
[2] See Theil (1976, ch. 12).

total expenditure, m, remain invariant. The transformation maps u into a strongly separable function, U, over the unknown characteristics, z. The preference independence transformation may be viewed as a constrained principal component transformation. The constraint ensures that the transformation is unique subject to a qualification on latent roots. This uniqueness result does not apply to the conventional (unconstrained) principal component transformation, which depends on the units of the variables prior to the transformation.

We write Θ for $[\theta_{ij}]$ and W for the $n \times n$ diagonal matrix with the budget shares $(w_1, \ldots, w_n)$ on the diagonal. The transformation involves a diagonalization of Θ relative to W,

$$(\Theta - \lambda_i W) y_i = 0, \qquad i = 1, \ldots, n, \tag{8.21}$$

where $\lambda_1, \ldots, \lambda_n$ are latent roots and $y_1, \ldots, y_n$ are characteristic vectors normalized so that $[y_i' W y_j]$ is the identity matrix. We can implement (8.21) conveniently in the form

$$(D^{-1} \Theta D^{-1} - \lambda_i I) D y_i = 0, \qquad i = 1, \ldots, n, \tag{8.22}$$

where D is the diagonal matrix with the square roots of the budget shares $(\sqrt{w_1}, \ldots, \sqrt{w_n})$ on the diagonal. Both diagonalizations, (8.21) and (8.22), are unique when the roots $\lambda_1, \ldots, \lambda_n$ are all distinct. The roots are real and positive because $D^{-1} \Theta D^{-1}$ in (8.22) is a symmetric positive definite matrix.

It can be shown that the λ_i values are the *income elasticities* of the transformed goods, z (i.e. of the revealed elementary commodities or consumption characteristics).[3] Thus, the statement that the transformation is unique when the λ_i values are distinct is equivalent to the proposition that the transformed goods are identified by their income elasticities. The luxury or necessity character of a transformed good ($\lambda_i > 1$ or $\lambda_i < 1$) is one tool for the interpretation of this good. Another tool is the matrix

$$C = (Y^{-1} \iota)_\Delta Y^{-1}, \tag{8.23}$$

where Y is the matrix $[y_1 \, y_2 \cdots y_n]$ of characteristic vectors, ι is the column vector consisting of n unit elements, and $(Y^{-1} \iota)_\Delta$ stands for the vector $Y^{-1} \iota$ written in the form of a diagonal matrix. The matrix (8.23) is called the *composition matrix* of the transformation. The column sums of C are the budget shares of the observed goods, and the row sums are the budget shares of the transformed goods. Each row of C displays the composition

---

[3] It follows from (8.15) that μ_i / w_i is equal to the elasticity $\partial(\log x_i)/\partial(\log m)$.

of a transformed good in terms of the n observed goods; each column of C displays the contribution of an observed good to the n transformed goods, z.

If we linearize the translation from goods space to transformed goods (commodity) space in Becker's household production approach, we get the relation $z = Gx$, where z is the vector of transformed goods, x is the vector of goods purchased in the market (including time inputs of the household members), and G is a matrix of constants. Lancaster's exposition adds an intermediate stage consisting of activities, although we can eliminate this step by assuming that the number of transformed goods is equal to the number of market goods, and that there are also the same number of activities. In this case, Becker's and Lancaster's specifications are observationally equivalent, since Lancaster's model can then be written as $z = Ba$ and $x = Aa$, so that $z = BA^{-1}x$ or $z = Gx$, where $G = BA^{-1}$ and a is the vector of household activities. The composition matrix, C, is analogous to G, but the elements of C are dimensionless, so that the results of the transformation applied to different data sets can be compared.

In addition to the invariance constraints imposed on the Divisia indices and on m, several other invariance properties exist. The Frisch price index, (8.17), is invariant under the independence transformation, as is the income flexibility, ϕ. Also, when the prices of all observed goods change proportionately, the price of each transformed good changes in the same proportion. The quantities of the two sets of goods have the same desirable property.

8.6. Application to Chapter 5 estimates

8.6.1. The transformation

Implementing the transformation requires estimates of the θ_{ij} values. Hence, we must replace eq. (8.15), which is in infinitesimal changes, by a parameterized estimable model. The simplest choice is the relative price version of the Rotterdam model used in section 5.7. In that specification we substitute finite changes for the infinitesimal changes in (8.14), (8.15), and (8.17), replace w_i in (8.14) and (8.15) by the arithmetic average of the ith budget share in two successive periods, postulate that the θ_{ij} values are constants, and preserve the model's form after aggregating over consumers.

In Chapter 5 we used annual per capita US data on five goods for the period 1890–1955. The goods were perishables, services, semidurables,

durables, and leisure. Including leisure implies that m must be interpreted as full income, including the value of the household's time, and that w_i becomes the share of the ith good in full income. In Chapter 5 we deleted the war years 1942–1945 during which there was rationing, but we did not delete the First World War years of 1916–1919, since no governmental rationing existed during that war. However, the residuals during 1916–1919 were conspicuously large, probably as a result of the informal nongovernmental rationing that existed during the First World War. This fact induced Flinn (1978) to re-estimate our model with the 1916–1919 years deleted. In addition, in our definition of per capita leisure in Chapter 2, he set the upper bound on the labor force participation rate at its observed maximum over the sample period. He then re-estimated the model of Chapter 5. The current section is based upon Flinn's estimates, rather than the estimates of Chapter 5.

Flinn adopted our final blockwise strongly separable specification from section 5.7. One of those blocks contained semidurables, durables, and leisure. Flinn's maximum likelihood estimates of the normalized price coefficient matrix of those goods (normalized within the three-good group) is

$$\begin{bmatrix} 0.501 & 0.042 & -0.342 \\ 0.042 & 0.560 & -0.419 \\ -0.342 & -0.419 & 1.378 \end{bmatrix} \begin{array}{l} \text{(semidurables)} \\ \text{(durables)} \\ \text{(leisure)} \end{array} \quad (8.24)$$

Since Θ has been normalized within the group, all other concepts must be interpreted accordingly: the diagonal elements of W in (8.21) become conditional budget shares (the shares of the goods in the expenditure on the group), the λ_i values become the conditional income elasticities of the transformed goods (the income elasticities of these goods divided by the income elasticity of the group), and so on. Also, note that even with a constant Θ matrix, the results of the preference independence transformation change over time, because the budget shares in W are subject to change.

The variation of the transformation over time will now be illustrated. Table 8.3 gives bordered composition matrices and λ_i values at ten-year intervals. The last row of the matrix contains the column sums, and the last column contains the row sums. One transformed good accounts for more than 99 percent of the expenditure on the three-good group. The three observed goods all contribute positively to this transformed good, and its λ_i is far smaller than the two other λ_i values.

Table 8.3
Bordered composition matrices and conditional income elasticities for selected years, 1890–1955.

Semi-durables	Durables	Leisure		λ_1	λ_2	λ_3
		1890–1891				
0.186	0.091	0.720	0.997	0.99		
0.004	0.015	−0.017	0.003		6.0	
−0.003	0.001	0.002	0.000			2.9
0.188	0.107	0.705	1			
		1900–1901				
0.183	0.093	0.721	0.997	0.99		
0.004	0.015	−0.017	0.003		5.9	
−0.002	0.001	0.001	0.000			2.9
0.186	0.109	0.705	1			
		1910–1911				
0.202	0.113	0.683	0.998	0.99		
0.004	0.012	−0.015	0.002		5.2	
−0.008	0.003	0.005	0.000			2.7
0.198	0.128	0.674	1			
		1920–1921				
0.190	0.109	0.699	0.998	0.99		
0.005	0.013	−0.016	0.002		5.3	
−0.004	0.001	0.003	0.000			2.8
0.190	0.124	0.686	1			
		1930–1931				
0.142	0.105	0.750	0.997	0.99		
0.006	0.016	−0.019	0.003		5.5	
0.008	−0.003	−0.004	0.000			3.3
0.156	0.118	0.726	1			
		1940–1941				
0.127	0.126	0.743	0.996	0.99		
0.009	0.015	−0.021	0.003		5.1	
0.009	−0.006	−0.003	0.001			3.4
0.145	0.135	0.720	1			
		1950–1951				
0.082	0.117	0.795	0.994	0.97		
0.018	0.016	−0.028	0.006		5.8	
0.004	−0.005	0.002	0.000			4.2
0.104	0.127	0.769	1			

Interpretation of results

Since many durables and semidurables are time-saving goods, we believe that the first transformed good corresponds to the household's basic want for free time or "true" leisure (as opposed to "measured" leisure or nonmarket time). Time-saving devices reduce the amount of time spent by household members on menial (non "leisurely") nonmarket uses of time. The use of such devices increases the household's effective leisure. It is not surprising to note that demand for this basic want is inelastic, when we recognize that the largest contributor to it is leisure, the complement of labor supply, which is commonly believed to be highly inelastic in the long run. The main conclusion from table 8.3 therefore is that more than 99 percent of the expenditure on semidurables, durables, and leisure is accounted for by one transformed good: the acquisition of free time.

The transformed goods which we have not yet discussed are all *contrasts* between observed goods. Note that λ_2 and λ_3 take large values. The transformed good corresponding to λ_2 is a contrast between mainly durables and leisure, although semidurables play an increasing role toward the end of the sample period. A tentative interpretation is that this good corresponds to what we typically refer to as "prestige" or "status". One's durable material goods and one's work contribute positively to prestige. The high full-income elasticities for λ_2 reflects the fact that prestige is very much a luxury. The transformed good corresponding to λ_3 is also a contrast, but its share in the expenditure on the three-good group is virtually zero throughout the period.

To understand the large λ_i values, of we must recognize that the λ_i values of fig. 8.1 are conditional full-income elasticities. The unconditional

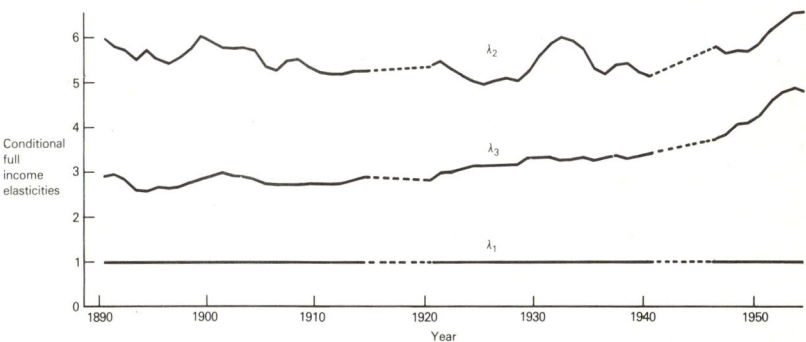

Figure 8.1. Conditional full-income elasticities of the three transformed goods, 1890–1955.

full income elasticities are only about one-half of these λ_i's, since the full-income elasticity of the three-good group is just over 0.5. Also, income differs substantially from full income. For the data used in this study, money income accounts for about two-thirds of full income.

Figure 8.1 shows the behavior of the three λ_i's. Since the curves are well separated, there are no problems in identifying the transformed goods. The current results could be pursued further by the display of other properties of the transformed goods. Such properties could include the behavior of the price and quantity indices of these goods over time and the contributions of the individual observed goods and leisure to the (full) income elasticity of each transformed goods. Further research could include a more disaggregated set of observed goods as well as disaggregation of leisure over household members.

CHAPTER 9

IMPLICIT UTILITY MODELS

9.1. Introduction

In Chapter 6 we explored and applied a highly flexible globally integrable inverse demand model, called g-hypo. The flexibility was acquired at the expense of requiring a rich parameterization. In Chapter 9 we shall explore the implicit function approach to acquiring maximum flexibility per free parameter in an attempt to decrease the number of parameters without sacrificing flexibility excessively. Although models based upon implicit utility functions contain fewer parameters than g-hypo, the estimation of implicit utility models is far *more* difficult than the estimation of g-hypo, as a result of the complexity of the structures defined by implicit utility models. Although implicit function models have advantages and are important in theory, no one yet has estimated such a model in a truly satisfactory manner. In this chapter we discuss potential methods of accomplishing that desirable, if troublesome, objective.

9.1.1. Background

Recently interest in implicit utility models has increased substantially as a result of the finding that implicit utility structures of certain types (distance or transformation functions) play a central role in the rapidly expanding literature on dual functional structures, cost of living indices, standard of living indices, and aggregation over such indices. Excellent presentations and extensions of much of that literature are available in Blackorby and Russell (1975, 1979) and in Boyce and Primont (1976). See also Gorman (1970), McFadden (1978), Diewert (1974a), Hanoch (1970), Blackorby and Russell (1976), and Emerson and Russell (1975). Implicit separability in such cases has been interpreted as referring to separability along a level surface (such as an indifference curve) of a function. When it is natural to move along a surface, implicit separability structures commonly are generated by theory.

More rigorously, implicit separability, in terms of distance functions, is equivalent to separability of each of the homothetic orderings generated by radial projections of a base indifference curve corresponding to the given utility level. Implicit weak separability is both necessary and sufficient for the equality of a pair of Allen partial elasticities of substitution with respect to some third variable. Similarly, Blackorby and Russell (1979) argue that implicit separability provides the appropriate structure for constructing theoretical cost of living indices which can be aggregated consistently into a total cost of living index. It also has been postulated analogously by Blackorby and Russell (1975) that implicit separability is relevant to problems involving motion along production possibility frontiers and utility possibility envelopes.

The central issue that has remained unexplored in this promising and elegant literature is the empirical usability of implicit utility structures (whether or not they are distance or transformation functions). The issue is clearly summarized in the concluding paragraph to Blackorby and Russell's (1979) extensive theoretical study:

> It is clear that the procedure which we have outlined raises enormous econometric problems which have not been considered in this paper at all. Implicit separability provides what seems to us to be a minimal set of maintained hypotheses which rationalize the construction of an aggregate cost of living index with a theoretically consistent set of subindices. It is our hope, therefore, that the econometric problems which this procedure generates are not insurmountable.

As we shall see in this chapter, unusual and troublesome econometric and theoretical problems arise in constructing a unique and estimable structure from such an implicit utility function. The only way that these problems can be avoided is through the use of a specialized iterative algorithm to solve for the estimates. We propose such an iterative algorithm.

9.1.2. The class of models

To see the general outline of implicit utility models, consider the equation $f(u, x) = 1$, where x is a vector of consumption quantities and u is the utility level. Rather than an implicit function definition, the function f

alternatively could be defined directly in terms of distance (transformation) or cost functions. See, for example, Blackorby and Russell (1975, 1979). Under appropriate conditions on the function f, a unique solution $u = v(x)$ to the above equation exists for u as a function of x such that the resulting function v is monotonically increasing and strictly quasiconcave. But those conditions (although sufficient for the existence of a regular neoclassical utility function, v) are not themselves sufficient for the existence of a closed form *explicit representation* of v. Hence, a neoclassical demand model can be derived from the utility function, v, without implying the existence of a closed form representation of v. A closed form representation of $v(x)$ exists only as a special case and hence only under more restrictive conditions than are necessary to derive a regular neoclassical demand model from the implicit function equation, $f(u, x) = 1$.

Hanoch (1975) has shown that strong separability of $f(u, x)$ is generally a less restrictive assumption than strong separability of $v(x)$ (although neither is less restrictive than the other if f also is a distance function). Hence, greater theoretical flexibility *per free parameter* sometimes is possible by specifying and restricting implicit utility functions rather than explicit utility functions. In this chapter we consider a demand model (the Direct Implicit Addilog or DIA) based upon a strongly separable implicit nonhomothetic utility specification. It contains as special cases a number of widely used models such as the Cobb–Douglas, the CES, and the Houthakker Direct Addilog. Unlike models based upon second-order local utility approximations, the DIA model is specified to be always globally integrable and its number of parameters increases only linearly (rather than quadratically) with the number of goods.

To further explore the restrictiveness of separability restrictions on explicit and implicit functions, observe that Hanoch (1975, p. 401) proved the following results for strong separability: (1) direct strong separability implies implicit strong separability, and (2) direct strong separability (unlike implicit strong separability) requires an implausible dependency of substitution effects upon income effects. However, explicit weak separability does not imply, and is not implied by, implicit weak separability. See Blackorby and Russell (1975, 1979). Since we use only implicit strong separability, Hanoch's result applies. For a detailed discussion of implicit utility functions, see Sato (1976).

By contrast with the DIA model, the models based upon second-order local approximation (translog, generalized Leontief, etc.) cannot be forced, through prior parameter restrictions, to be integrable to a strictly quasiconcave, monotonically increasing utility function over any *finite* region (rather than at an infinitesimal point) without seriously compromising the model's approximation properties. The empirical effects of this conflict in capabilities have been considered through simulation methods by Wales (1977), and in theory by Barnett (1979c) and by Blackorby, Primont and Russell (1977).

Models which can be forced to be integrable are usually highly restrictive. An exception is the highly flexible globally integrable g-hypo model, presented in Chapter 6. That model is more flexible than the DIA model, but at the expense of more parameters. In addition, g-hypo is marginally homothetic; the DIA is not. For a general discussion of the relative merits of the DIA model and of some competing models, see Hanoch (1975, p. 396).

9.1.3. Structural estimation with conventional algorithms

In the DIA model the first-order conditions for utility maximization plus the budget constraint and the implicit function equation jointly define a complete demand system through a system of implicit functions in quantities, prices, utility, and a Lagrange multiplier. An explicit closed form solution for the implied (reduced-form) ordinary demand system cannot be derived. Furthermore, there exists more than one complete structural (implicit) form derivable solely in terms of quantities, income, and prices, when an additive error structure is used in the structural representations. Unlike the analogous situation with reduced form demand models, FIML estimates acquired from those different potential structures can differ. As we shall see, however, the implied reduced forms, for all of the alternative structural representations, differ only in their implied imbedded error structures.

9.2. Theoretical properties of the model

9.2.1. Derivation of the model

Since the DIA is self-dual, the issues discussed in this chapter would be identical for the direct or indirect addilog case.[1] We arbitrarily select the direct utility function in illustrating the implicit addilog specification. The equation

$$\sum_i \alpha_i x_i^{-\rho_i} u^{\delta_i} = 1 \qquad (9.1)$$

---

[1] I am indebted to Ryuzo Sato for this observation.

implicitly defines the DIA utility function

$$u = v(x), \tag{9.2}$$

where the vectors $\boldsymbol{\alpha} = (\alpha_1, \ldots, \alpha_N)'$, $\boldsymbol{\rho} = (\rho_1, \ldots, \rho_N)'$, and $\boldsymbol{\delta} = (\delta_1, \ldots, \delta_N)'$ are parameters and x is a vector of goods quantities. The implicitly defined utility function, v, (of which no closed form representation exists) is globally monotonically increasing and globally strictly quasiconcave if and only if for all i

$$\alpha_i > 0 \tag{9.3}$$

and either

$$-1 < \rho_i < 0 \quad \text{and} \quad \delta_i < 0, \tag{9.4}$$

or

$$\rho_i > 0 \quad \text{and} \quad \delta_i > 0. \tag{9.5}$$

Let m be the ("representative") consumer's total expenditure on all goods ("income"), and let $p = (p_1, \ldots, p_N)'$ be the vector of market prices of the N goods. From the usual first-order conditions for constrained utility maximization, we find that the consumer's vector of demand functions is the solution for x in terms of (m, p) to

$$\frac{\rho_i \alpha_i x_i^{-\rho_i - 1} [v(x)]^{\delta_i}}{\sum_{j=1}^{N} \alpha_j x_j^{-\rho_j} \delta_j [v(x)]^{\delta_j - 1}} - \lambda p_i = 0, \quad \text{for all } i = 1, \ldots, N \tag{9.6}$$

and

$$\sum_{i=1}^{N} p_i x_i = m, \tag{9.7}$$

where λ is a Lagrange multiplier. But observe that the system ((9.6), (9.7)) contains the implicitly defined utility function $v(x)$, for which there exists no closed form representation. Hence, we cannot eliminate $v(x)$ by substitution, but must adjoin to the system ((9.6), (9.7)) the specification of v, defined implicitly by (9.1). Thus, $x = x(m, p)$ is fully defined implicitly by the solution for x to the system ((9.1), (9.6), (9.7)). As an implicit representation of $x(m, p)$, the system ((9.1), (9.6), (9.7)) has $N+2$ equations in the $N+2$ unknowns x, λ, and u. Hence, the system is complete.

Although ((9.1, (9.6), (9.7)) defines x implicitly, it does not yet provide an estimable structural model of the consumer's demand system, since λ

and u are unobservable. Furthermore, the budget identity (9.7) must be eliminated by substitution before the likelihood function can be explicitly derived. We now manipulate the equations algebraically to remove these difficulties.

First select any two first-order conditions, say the jth and kth, from (9.6), and solve simultaneously for λ and $u = v(x)$ in terms of (p, x). Substituting the resulting expressions for (λ, u) in both (9.1) and the remaining $(i \neq j$ or $k)$ equations of (9.6), we obtain the following system of N equations in the N goods quantities, x:

$$x_i^{(1+\rho_i)} = \frac{\rho_i \alpha_i p_j x_j^{(1+\rho_j)}}{\rho_j \alpha_j p_i} \left[\frac{p_j \rho_k \alpha_k x_k^{-(\rho_k+1)}}{p_k \rho_j \alpha_j x_j^{-(\rho_j+1)}} \right]^{-(\delta_j - \delta_i)/(\delta_j - \delta_k)},$$

$$(i = 1, \ldots, N; i \neq j, k), \quad (9.8)$$

$$\sum_{i=1}^{N} p_i x_i = M, \quad (9.9)$$

$$\sum_{\substack{i=1 \\ i \neq j,k}}^{N} \alpha_i x_i^{-\rho_i} \left[\frac{p_j \rho_k \alpha_k x_k^{-(\rho_k+1)}}{p_k \rho_j \alpha_j x_j^{-(\rho_j+1)}} \right]^{\delta_i/(\delta_j - \delta_k)}$$

$$+ \alpha_j x_j^{-\rho_j} \left[\frac{p_j \rho_k \alpha_k x_k^{-(\rho_k+1)}}{p_k \rho_j \alpha_j x_j^{-(\rho_j+1)}} \right]^{\delta_j/(\delta_j - \delta_k)} \left[1 + \frac{p_k \rho_j x_k}{p_j \rho_k x_j} \right] = 1. \quad (9.10)$$

We now eliminate the budget constraint by substitution. First solve (9.9) for an arbitrary element of x, say x_L. Then substitute the resulting expression for x_L into both (9.8) and (9.10). This procedure results in the following basic structural representation of the DIA demand model:

$$x_i^{(1+\rho_i)} = \frac{\rho_i \alpha_i p_j x_j^{(1+\rho_j)}}{\rho_j \alpha_j p_i} \left[\frac{p_j \rho_k \alpha_k x_k^{-(\rho_k+1)}}{p_k \rho_j \alpha_j x_j^{-(\rho_j+1)}} \right]^{-(\delta_j - \delta_i)/(\delta_j - \delta_k)},$$

$$(i = 1, \ldots, N; i \neq j, k, L) \quad (9.11)$$

$$\left[\frac{M - \sum_{\substack{i=1 \\ i \neq L}}^{N} p_i x_i}{p_L} \right]^{1+\rho_L} = \frac{\rho_L \alpha_L p_j x_j^{(1+\rho_j)}}{\rho_j \alpha_j p_L} \left[\frac{p_j \rho_k \alpha_k x_k^{-(\rho_k+1)}}{p_k \rho_j \alpha_j x_j^{-(\rho_k+1)}} \right]^{-(\delta_j - \delta_L)/(\delta_j - \delta_k)},$$

$$(9.12)$$

$$\sum_{\substack{i=1 \\ i \neq j,k,L}}^{N} \alpha_i x_i^{-\rho_i} \left[\frac{p_j \rho_k \alpha_k x_k^{-(\rho_k+1)}}{p_k \rho_j \alpha_j x_j^{-(\rho_j+1)}} \right]^{\delta_i/(\delta_j-\delta_k)}$$

$$+ \alpha_L \left[\frac{M - \sum_{\substack{i=1 \\ i \neq L}}^{N} p_i x_i}{p_L} \right]^{-\rho_L} \left[\frac{p_j \rho_k \alpha_k x_k^{-(\rho_k+1)}}{p_k \rho_j \alpha_j x_j^{-(\rho_j+1)}} \right]^{\delta_L/(\delta_j-\delta_k)}$$

$$+ \alpha_j x_j^{-\rho_j} \left[\frac{p_j \rho_k \alpha_k x_k^{-(\rho_k+1)}}{p_k \rho_j \alpha_j x_j^{-(\rho_j+1)}} \right]^{\delta_j/(\delta_j-\delta_k)} \left[1 + \frac{p_k \rho_j x_k}{p_j \rho_k x_j} \right] = 1. \quad (9.13)$$

9.2.2. Identification and normalization

The vectors δ and α require normalization for identification. The need for normalization of δ results from the homogeneity of degree zero of ((9.11), (9.12), (9.13)) in δ (so that the model is invariant to a rescaling of δ). Hence, we set an arbitrary element of δ equal to unity. Hanoch (1975) incorrectly concluded that only $N-2$ elements of δ are identified. His argument ignores the identifying information contained in (9.13) (acquired from the implicit utility function itself), which must be adjoined to the first-order conditions to complete the system. Recall that to be able to view the first-order conditions (plus the budget constraint) as themselves comprising a complete representation of demand, we require knowledge of $v(x)$ to substitute into (9.6). But we do not have a closed form representation of $v(x)$, and even if we did, it would depend upon δ in a manner providing identifying information ignored by Hanoch.

We now show that an analogous normalization is required for α, although the need for such a normalization is not immediately apparent from ((9.11), (9.12), (9.13)). The most general (limiting) special case of ((9.11), (9.12), (9.13)) is the Direct Explicit Addilog case acquired when all of the elements of δ are equal. For global identification, a model must be identified *everywhere* in its parameter space, including the subspaces of the parameter space to which we are restricted by special cases. Identification everywhere in the parameter space is assumed in all available statistical theory, including hypothesis testing theory (which does not consider the imposition of additional nonmaintained normalization restrictions under a null hypothesis). Hence, we now consider identifying restrictions in the Direct Explicit Addilog case.

All of the (ordinal) properties of demand are determined from the marginal rate of substitution function. In the general case, the DIA model's marginal rate of substitution between goods r and s is $(\rho_r \alpha_r x_r^{-\rho_r - 1} / \rho_s \alpha_s x_s^{-\rho_s - 1})[v(x)]^{\delta_r - \delta_s}$. Since a closed form representation of $v(x)$ does not exist in the general case, no explicit representation exists of the form of the dependency of $v(x)$ upon its parameters. However, in the Direct Explicit Addilog special case, $v(x)$ drops out of the marginal rate of substitution function, which then becomes homogeneous of degree zero in α. Since preferences now are seen to be invariant to rescalings of α, the demand functions also must be invariant to rescalings of α. Thus, in that region of the parameter space (the Direct Explicit Addilog special case) in which all elements of δ are equal, we find that the likelihood function is invariant to rescalings of α. Since, by the Likelihood Principle, the likelihood function is known to contain all the information in the model and data, it follows that α must be normalized. We could set an arbitrary element of α equal to unity.

In our discussion we have overlooked a subtlety. Recall that our estimation model ((9.11), (9.12), (9.13)) can approach the Explicit Addilog case arbitrarily closely, but never actually can attain it. Strictly speaking, the normalization therefore should be viewed as preventing an "almost nonidentification" problem existing near the boundary of the parameter space, rather than an exact identification problem existing on the boundary.

Our argument demonstrates zero degree homogeneity in α within some region of the parameter space, which is sufficient for nonidentification. But it may be interesting to consider the stronger property of nonidentification everywhere. In the two-good case it can be shown that an implicit reduced form exists in which the demand for each good is implicitly defined by a single equation (i.e. x_i appears for only one i in each equation). In that case, nonidentification can be proved everywhere. Since such an equation-by-equation implied reduced form does not exist in the general N-good case, that statement cannot currently be made for the N-good case (although it may be true). Hanoch (1975) maintains that an identification problem does exist everywhere in the N-good case; but (as in his treatment of δ) he reached his conclusion by overlooking the dependency of v itself upon the parameters in the first-order conditions. Unfortunately, necessary and sufficient conditions for global identification are not known for the total class of arbitrary general nonlinear models.

9.2.3. Elasticities

We now present formulae for all income, (Allen–Uzawa) substitution, and Cournot price elasticities for the DIA model. Defining s_k as the share of the kth good in total consumption expenditure, the income (or total expenditure) elasticity of demand for the ith good is

$$\eta_i = \frac{1}{(1+\rho_i)\sum_k (\delta_k s_k/\rho_k)} \left[\delta_i + \frac{\sum_k \delta_k s_k/(\rho_k+\rho_k^2)}{\sum_k s_k/(1+\rho_k)} \right]$$

for $i=1,\ldots,4$. The cross substitution elasticity between goods i and j for $i,j=1,\ldots,4$ and $i\neq j$ is

$$\sigma_{ij} = \frac{1}{(1+\rho_i)(1+\rho_j)\sum_k s_k/(1+\rho_k)},$$

while the own substitution elasticity is

$$\sigma_{ii} = \frac{1}{(1+\rho_i)^2 \sum_k s_k/(1+\rho_k)} - \frac{1}{s_i(1+\rho_i)}.$$

The Cournot price elasticitiy of good i with respect to price j for $i,j=1,\ldots,4$ is

$$\zeta_{ij} = s_j(\sigma_{ij} - \eta_i).$$

Since s_k varies over observations, all of the above elasticities also vary over observations; however, the elasticities can be evaluated at the average values of s_k ($k=1,\ldots,4$) over all observations. Since those elasticities depend upon sample size, they are not parameters, and hence meaningful standard errors do not exist.

9.3. Additive structural errors

In this section we explore the possibility of the use of additive errors in the implicit (structural) representation ((9.11), (9.12), (9.13)) of the Implicit Addilog model. In applied research with demand models, existing nonlinear FIML programs generally are used, since specialized coding of nonlinear iterative estimation algorithms is usually best left to specialists in numerical analysis. Existing coded nonlinear FIML algorithms all use additive error structures and do not permit the estimation of implicitly defined composite functions. Hence, such standard estimators can be used only with ((9.11), (9.12), (9.13)), in which the implicit utility function has been eliminated by substitution.

9.3.1. Uniqueness

The structure has $N-1$ equations in the $N-1$ dependent variables, $x_1, \ldots, x_{L-1}, x_{L+1}, \ldots, x_N$. The solution for these $N-1$ dependent variables along with the budget constraint determines the full demand vector, x. Since the underlying implicitly defined utility function, v, is strictly quasiconcave and monotonically increasing, the solution for x to ((9.11), (9.12), (9.13)) must be *unique* and cannot depend upon the selection of goods j, k, L. However, if we adjoin a conventional additive stochastic disturbance vector, ε, to ((9.11), (9.12), (9.13)), a nonuniqueness problem arises; the form of randomness induced into the behavior of x by the additive structural errors will depend upon the choice of (j, k, L). We shall consider this problem in detail. Observe that we cannot add the disturbances directly onto the reduced form, since no explicit representation of the reduced form exists.

It should, however, be observed that an additive error structure in these structural models bears no relationship to any model of rational random behavior. The additive error structure would be chosen for convenience solely to permit use of available nonlinear FIML programs. In the last section of this chapter we observe that, if convenience is neglected, we can introduce an additive error structure into the implied reduced form by defining the likelihood function as a composite function.

The nature of the nonuniqueness problem can be seen by considering the special case in which a closed form solution for $x(m, p)$ does in fact exist. Then the structural errors added onto ((9.11), (9.12), (9.13)) will be imbedded in the system's solution, $x(m, p)$, differently for different selections of (j, k, L). Although such a closed form solution does not exist in our case, the nature of the problem remains unchanged with our implicitly defined demand equations. Since the likelihood function is equal to the joint distribution of the random vector x, the dependency of that joint distribution upon our selection of (j, k, L) would induce a dependency of the parameter's FIML estimates upon (j, k, L).

To investigate the scope of this potential nonuniqueness problem, we now consider the number of different joint distributions of x that can be defined by varying (j, k, L) while maintaining additive structural errors. The following theorem demonstrates that the dependency of the FIML estimates of ((9.11), (9.12), (9.13)) upon (j, k, L) is caused solely by dependency upon (j, k). The likelihood function does not depend upon the subscript L.

Theorem 9.1. Select positive integer values for j and k such that $j, k \leq N$. Add stochastic errors onto each equation in ((9.11), (9.12), (9.13)). Then the joint distribution of x defined by ((9.9), (9.11), (9.12), (9.13)) is independent of the subscript L. Thus, the number of different FIML estimates of (δ, α, ρ) that can be generated by varying (j, k, L) in ((9.11), (9.12), (9.13)) is equal to the number of possible selections of the unordered pair (j, k). The number of such possible choices is

$$\binom{N}{2} = N(N-1)/2.$$

Proof. For a given selection of (j, k) and for any $(m, p) > 0$, the system ((9.8), (9.9), (9.10)) defines a unique transformation between the joint distribution of the additive errors and the induced singular joint distribution of the endogenous random variables x. The singularity of the distribution results from the dependency among the elements of x arising from (9.9). Hence, for fixed (j, k, m, p), the system ((9.8), (9.9), (9.10)) defines a unique (singular) joint distribution of x. Now replace (9.9) by the trivially rearranged identity

$$x_L = \frac{1}{p_L} \left[M - \sum_{\substack{i=1 \\ i \neq L}}^{N} p_i x_i \right].$$

Clearly the above statement on the transformation between the errors and x remains unchanged. But by construction, this transformation is identical to that defined by ((9.9), (9.11), (9.12), (9.13)). Hence, (with arbitrary fixed (m, p, j, k)) the (singular) joint distribution of x defined by ((9.9), (9.11), (9.12), (9.13)) is invariant to L. Q.E.D.

Barten (1969) has prove an analogous result for explicit reduced form demand models, but the nature of the problem is quite different. In the reduced form case an arbitrary stochastic equation is deleted from the specification, while in the structural case we merely delete an identity by substitution. Also, note that in our theorem we have adjoined the budget constraint (9.9) to the system ((9.11), (9.12), (9.13)). This is required to define the full joint distribution of x, since ((9.11), (9.12), (9.13)) defines only the distribution of $(x_1,\ldots,x_{L-1},x_{L+1},\ldots,x_N)$. But (9.9) contains no parameters and already has been eliminated by substitution in deriving ((9.11), (9.12), (9.13)). Hence, we could drop (9.9) when estimating ((9.11), (9.12), (9.13)).

9.3.2. Special cases

As Hanoch (1975) has pointed out, the DIA utility function contains a number of interesting special cases. However, formal hypothesis tests of those special cases are not possible within the structure defined above. For example, if $\delta_1 = \delta_2 = \cdots = \delta_N$, then an explicit closed form representation of v exists. But observe that under those restrictions, some of the exponents in ((9.11), (9.12), (9.13)) are not defined. Hence, the direct explicit addilog case is not formally nested within the estimating system ((9.11), (9.12), (9.13)). The explicit case is a limiting case, which ((9.11), (9.12), (9.13)) can approach but never attain as each of the elements of δ approach any common value. In Hanoch's formulation the same problem arises, since his ε parameter becomes undefined when all of the equality restrictions on δ are substituted into Hanoch's (1975) estimating equation (9.19).

Nevertheless, in statistics we test for exact equalities for evidence of "almost equality" rather than literally for exact equality (which we know never obtains). In fact all tests of exact equalities are known to be rejected asymptotically with any consistent hypothesis testing method. With the DIA structural model, ((9.11), (9.12), (9.13)), formal tests for "almost equality" of the elements of δ are possible, and we can define such a test in a manner such that our null hypothesis approximates exact equality (and thereby the explicit addilog case) arbitrarily well.

If the explicit addilog special case were accepted (a priori or otherwise), further special cases would become nested (within the closed form representation of the explicit case) in the conventional manner. For example, the nonhomothetic CES utility function would be acquired by equating all of the elements of ρ to a common unknown parameter ρ_0 within the explicit addilog model's structure.

In section 9.5 we shall discuss a specialized approach avoiding this problem completely. Although we shall show that the nesting problem can be avoided, the current approach, with an additive error structure, fully illustrates the problems associated with the use of conventional estimation methods with implicit utility function models.

9.4. Alternative approaches

In section 9.3 we found that the use of an additive error structure with ((9.11), (9.12), (9.13)) results in serious problems. An invariance problem exists, and a nesting problem arises relative to the interesting special cases. These issues were pursued empirically by Barnett, Kopecky, and Sato (1980) who found the problems to be very serious.

The invariance problem is particularly serious and reflects the fact that no economic justification appears to exist for the use of an additive error structure in the implicit function system ((9.11), (9.12), (9.13)). In this section we seek alternative approaches to estimation which are justifiable in principle, even if specialized computer coding is necessary to implement them.

9.4.1. Inverse demand system

One simplification would be to take logarithms of each side of eqs. (9.11) and (9.12) and then first difference each side of those equations. While this log change transformation results in a substantial simplification of the form of those equations, eq. (9.13) cannot be simplified by that means. Hence, all of the basic problems of the prior section remain.

A more fundamentally different approach is based upon the use of inverse demand systems. When direct rather than indirect utility functions are used, the form of the derived inverse demand system commonly is simpler than the form of the direct demand system. It therefore is natural to consider the form of the inverse demand system in our case.

Multiply eqs. (9.6) by x_i and divide each of the resulting equations by their sum over i. The result is

$$w_i = \frac{\rho_i \alpha_i x_i^{-\rho_i} u^{\delta_i}}{\sum_{k=1}^{N} \rho_k \alpha_k x_k^{-\rho_k} u^{\delta_k}} \qquad (i=1,\ldots,N), \qquad (9.14)$$

where $w_i = p_i x_i / m$ is the expenditure share of ith good. Eqs. (9.14) and (9.1) jointly define the inverse demand system (in share form) as composite functions. In the next subsection we explore the possibility of acquiring a representation of the inverse demand system without the need for composite functions, i.e. without the need to solve (9.1) iteratively for u, which then is used in (9.14).

9.4.2. Implicit form of inverse demand system

Multiply (9.14) through by its denominator and divide by ρ_i. Then sum over i and use (9.1) to acquire

$$\sum_{k=1}^{N} \rho_k \alpha_k x_k^{-\rho_k} u^{\delta_k} = \left(\sum_{k=1}^{N} w_k / \rho_k \right)^{-1}. \tag{9.15}$$

Substitute (9.15) into (9.14) to obtain

$$w_i = \frac{\rho_i \alpha_i}{K(w)} x_i^{-\rho_i} u^{\delta_i} \quad (i=1,\ldots,N), \tag{9.16}$$

where $K(w) = (\sum_{k=1}^{N} w_k / \rho_k)^{-1}$.

Normalize δ such that $\sum_{i=1}^{N} \delta_i = 1$. Solve (9.16) for u^{δ_i}, and compute the product $\prod_{i=1}^{N} u^{\delta_i}$, and then substitute the result into (9.16) to obtain

$$w_i \left(\sum_{j=1}^{N} \frac{w_j}{\rho_j} \right)^{N\delta_i - 1} \left(\prod_{j=1}^{N} w_j \right)^{-\delta_i} = \frac{\rho_i \alpha_i x_i^{-\rho_i}}{\left(\prod_{j=1}^{N} \rho_j \alpha_j x_j^{-\rho_j} \right)^{\delta_i}} \quad (i=1,\ldots,N).$$

Taking the logarithm of each side and letting $\theta_i = \log \alpha_i$, we get

$$\delta_i \sum_{j=1}^{N} \rho_j \log x_j - \rho_i \log x_i = \delta_i \sum_{j=1}^{N} \theta_j - \theta_i - \log \rho_i + \delta_i \left(\sum_{j=1}^{N} \log \rho_j \right)$$

$$+ \log w_i + (N\delta_i - 1)\log \left(\sum_{j=1}^{N} \frac{w_j}{\rho_j} \right)$$

$$- \delta_i \sum_{j=1}^{N} \log w_j \quad (i=1,\ldots,N). \tag{9.17}$$

Eq. (9.17), with additive errors, with w endogenous, and with x exogenous, is a considerably less deeply nonlinear structure than that derived in section 9.2. Furthermore, the interesting special cases all are nested in (9.17), although they were not nested in the structure in section 9.2, and all required normalizations can be determined globally for (9.17). Hence, as we suspected, the inverse demand system is considerably more manageable than the direct demand system.

Unfortunately, things are not as simple as they appear. Since $\sum_{i=1}^{N} w_i = 1$, the joint distribution of the endogenous variables in (9.17), with additive errors, is singular. Since the Jacobian of the transformation between the disturbances and the endogenous variables depends upon the equation deleted, we cannot simply delete an arbitrary equation as we could if we had added the disturbances onto the reduced form (9.14). An invariance problem again arises. It furthermore can be shown that (9.17) contains a redundant equation which must be replaced by the budget constraint. This replacement requires another arbitrary selection and creates a further invariance problem which is independent of the singularity problem. Hence, two potentially arbitrary selections exist.

Although we have a less deeply nonlinear structure than in section 9.2, and although we have fewer arbitrary selections, we nevertheless still have a nonlinear structural model with unresolvable invariance problems. Invariance problems inherently are very serious, and we are back with a very troublesome situation. Therefore we return to (9.14) and (9.1) directly, without attempts at simplifying substitutions.

9.4.3. The reduced form implicit demand system

The source of the problem now is clear. The additive error structures we have used with our structural models may permit the use of standard FIML estimators, but they create unavoidably fundamental methodological problems. These problems can be eliminated completely by using an additive error structure with the reduced form inverse demand system, (9.14). Since (9.14) depends upon u, which must be acquired by iterative solution of (9.1), we cannot use standard FIML estimators.

We could derive the likelihood function from (9.14) (with endogenous w and additive errors) in terms of the parameters, the exogenous variables, and u. We then could maximize the likelihood function using a gradient method with numerical differentiation and with numerical solution for u from (9.1) at each step.

The algorithm described above would resolve all of the problems encountered in this chapter. Invariance problems would disappear, hypotheses would be nested, the model would be in reduced form (in terms of composite functions), normalizations would be known and global, and the error structure could be rationalized in terms of theory. We consider these observations more than sufficient to adopt the procedure or its more easily used variant described in the next section.[2]

---

[2] The need for FIML estimation can be eliminated by use of instrumental variables estimation (see Pudney, 1980) of an implicit representation of direct demand, but iterative solution of (9.1) for u remains necessary.

9.5. Control theoretic approach

The approach proposed in the previous subsection is straightforward, provides unique maximum likelihood estimates, and possesses no problems in principle. However, computer programs for FIML estimation with such a composite likelihood function are not currently available. Nevertheless, as we shall show in this section, a variant of that estimation procedure is a special case of a class of existing constrained optimal control problems.[3] In the optimal control literature, algorithm and computer programs exist that are directly applicable to that class of problems. The use of those programs appears to provide the most promising approach to the estimation of implicit utility models.

9.5.1. The problem

The optimal control analog to estimation with a composite likelihood function is a single period problem of constrained static optimal control. The following change of notation will be needed to permit us to establish that analogy.

Let $y=(w_1,\ldots,w_N)'$, and let γ be the vector of all parameters in the implicit utility function, (9.1). We take y as endogenous and x as exogenous. In addition, let $u_t = v(x_t; \gamma)$ be the value of utility during period $t=1,\ldots,T$, where v was defined in section 9.1.

Then eq. (9.14) defines a vector valued function, g, such that (9.14) can be written as

$$y_t = g(x_t, u_t; \gamma) + \varepsilon_t, \tag{9.18}$$

for all $t=1,\ldots,T$, where the disturbances, ε_t, have been added onto the right-hand side. Similarly, eq. (9.1) defines a function, f, such that

$$f(x_t, u_t; \gamma) = 1 \tag{9.19}$$

for all $t=1,\ldots,T$. Our model then is (9.18) with u_t determined at each t by (9.19).

To simplify the notation, define the function g_t such that $g_t(\gamma, u_t) = g(x_t, u_t; \gamma)$ for all $t=1,\ldots,T$, and define the function f_t such that $f_t(\gamma, u_t) = f(x_t, u_t; \gamma)$ for all $t=1,\ldots,T$. Let **1** be the T-dimensional unit vector,

---

[3] I am indebted to Alfred Norman for pointing this fact out to me. Norman's observation forms the basis for the rest of this chapter.

and let $f = (f_1, \ldots, f_T)' - 1$. Then (9.18) and (9.19) become

$$y_t = g_t(\gamma, u_t) + \varepsilon_t \tag{9.20}$$

and

$$f(\gamma, u) = 0, \tag{9.21}$$

respectively, where $u = (u_1, \ldots, u_T)'$ and where $\mathbf{0}$ is the T-dimensional zero vector.

Despite the fact that u_t is not measurable, it is exogenous. Hence, (9.20) is a closed form explicit (reduced form) system of nonlinear equations, and the errors are in conventional additive form. Thus, the system (9.20) is in the form investigated in Chapter 4. We therefore can use eq. (4.1) and lemma 4.9 from Chapter 4 to find that maximizing the likelihood function is equivalent to minimizing the generalized variance of the fit, $|N(\gamma, u, y)|$, where

$$N(\gamma; u, y) = (1/T) \sum_{t=1}^{T} [y_t - g_t(\gamma, u_t)][y_t - g_t(\gamma, u_t)]', \tag{9.22}$$

and $y = (y'_1, \ldots, y'_T)'$. A more detailed and rigorous explanation of that result follows.

9.5.2. The optimal control analog

Let Γ be the set within which γ must lie in order for the Implicit Addilog utility function to be monotonically increasing and strictly quasiconcave. The parameter constraints defining the set Γ are (9.3), (9.4), and (9.5). Then (9.21) possesses a unique solution for u at every $\gamma \in \Gamma$. Let $D(\gamma; y)$ be the value of $|N(\gamma; u, y)|$ acquired when u is the solution to the implicit function system (9.21). Then $D(\gamma; y)$ is the generalized variance of the fit that we seek to minimize with respect to $\gamma \in \Gamma$.

The above conclusion conforms with that acquired in subsection 9.4.3. As observed in that subsection, $D(\gamma, y)$ is a composite function depending upon $|N(\gamma; u, y)|$ and upon the implicit function system (9.21). However, selecting $\gamma \in \Gamma$ to minimize $D(\gamma, y)$ is mathematically equivalent to selecting *both* $\gamma \in \Gamma$ *and* u to minimize $|N(\gamma; u, y)|$ subject to (9.21), treated as T nonlinear *constraints*. Hence, we need not treat the estimation problem as one of maximizing a composite likelihood function (or minimizing a composite generalized variance); rather, we can view the problem as one of optimizing an elementary function subject to T nonlinear constraints.

Observe that in minimizing $|N(\gamma, u, y)|$ with respect to (γ, u), we are selecting a vector of time varying unobserved variables, u, along with a vector of fixed parameters, γ. Existing FIML estimation programs generally select only fixed parameters, which do not vary over time, and usually do not permit nonlinear implicit function side constraints. However, the form of our problem is common in control theory. The control analog would be a single period problem of constrained static optimal control, in which the vector u defines the state and γ is the vector of controls, which are to be selected to minimize loss. We now derive the first-order conditions for solution to that control problem, when loss equals $|N(\gamma; u, y)|$ and when the constraints are (9.21).

9.5.3. The control algorithm

We proceed to define an algorithm permitting minimization of (9.22) subject to (9.21). Form the augmented Lagrangian as follows:

$$H(\gamma, u; y) = |N(\gamma; u, y)| + \lambda' f(\gamma, u),$$

where λ is a vector of Lagrange multipliers.

If we assume that the solution for γ is within the interior of Γ, then the necessary conditions for minimization of the augmented Lagrangian with respect to (γ, u, λ) are[4]

$$\frac{\partial H}{\partial \gamma} = 0 \quad \text{or} \quad \frac{\partial |N|}{\partial \gamma} + \left[\frac{\partial f}{\partial \gamma'}\right]' \lambda = 0, \tag{9.23}$$

$$\frac{\partial H}{\partial u} = 0 \quad \text{or} \quad \frac{\partial |N|}{\partial u} + \left[\frac{\partial f}{\partial u'}\right]' \lambda = 0, \tag{9.24}$$

$$\frac{\partial H}{\partial \lambda} = 0 \quad \text{or} \quad f(\gamma, u) = 0. \tag{9.25}$$

An algorithm, based upon first derivatives, to solve the first-order conditions ((9.23), (9.24), (9.25)) is constructed as follows.

Step 1: Guess γ.
Step 2: With that γ solve (9.25) for u by a modified Newton method.
Step 3: With that γ and u solve (9.24) for λ.

---

[4] The notation for differentiation of a vector with respect to a vector is as in eq. (8.4) of Theil (1971, p. 43).

Step 4: With that γ, *u*, and λ evaluate the left-hand side of (9.23), which is the generalized reduced gradient (analog to the gradient of the generalized variance in the unconstrained case). The result will be nonzero unless an extreme point of H has been reached. If the algorithm has not yet converged to an extreme point, then the generalized reduced gradient can be input into a conjugate gradient or variable metric algorithm to obtain the direction in which the parameters are to be changed.

Step 5: Using the algorithm selected, perform a linear search to obtain the step size (distance to be moved along direction determined in step 4).

Step 6: Check for convergence.

Step 7: If converged, stop. If not, go back to step 2.

9.5.4. Available computer programs

Computer codes to perform the above procedure exist and are described in the optimal control literature. See, for example, Nepomiastchy and Ravelli (1977/1978), Drud (1977/1978), and Mantell and Lasdon (1977/1978).

More powerful computer codes using second derivatives could also be used in implementing the algorithm described in the previous subsection. One such possibility would be adaptation of codes developed for aerospace optimization, as described in Bryson and Ho (1969).

9.6. Conclusion

In estimating models based upon implicit utility functions, the approach described in section 9.5 appears to be the most promising. The same approach is applicable to models derived from implicit function representations of indirect utility. In that case we would be estimating direct rather than inverse demand in sections 9.4 and 9.5, but all else would be analogous.

Furthermore, in the Implicit Addilog case, considered as an example in this chapter, all of the results in this chapter would be identical for an Implicit Addilog indirect (rather than direct) utility function. The reason is that the Implicit Addilog is self-dual, so that the direct utility function is Implicit Addilog if and only if the indirect utility function is Implicit Addilog.

APPENDICES

APPENDIX A

APPENDIX TO CHAPTER 2

A1. Section 2.2 proofs

In section 2.2 we asserted that if $(x, \ell_1, \ldots, \ell_{N_0})$ is the solution to problem (2.1), then

$$(x, \ell) = \left(x, \sum_{i=1}^{N_0} \ell_i + (N_h - N_0) k_0 \right)$$

is the unique solution to problem (2.2). In this section we prove that assertion.

Let

$$L_D = \sum_{i=1}^{N_0} L_D^i,$$

and define the separate problem of finding (x, ℓ_0) to

maximize $\quad u(x, \ell_0 + (N_h - N_0) k_0, N_h)$

subject to $\quad x'p + w\ell_0 = I + k_0 N_0 w,$ \hfill (A1)

$\quad\quad\quad\quad\quad N_0 k_0 \geqslant \ell_0 \geqslant N_0 k_0 - L_D; \quad x \geqslant 0.$

We shall establish a relationship between the solutions of problems (2.1) and (A1). The following lemma will be needed.

Lemma A1. Let $N_0 k_0 \geqslant \ell_0 \geqslant N_0 k_0 - L_D$. Then there exists $(\ell_1, \ldots, \ell_{N_0})$ such that $\sum_{i=1}^{N} \ell_i = \ell_0$ and $k_0 \geqslant \ell_i \geqslant k_0 - L_D^i$ for $i = 1, \ldots, N_0$.

Proof. Define a function f such that

$$f(\ell_1, \ldots, \ell_N) = \sum_{i=1}^{N_0} \ell_i.$$

Then $f(k - L_D^1, \ldots, k_0 - L_D^{N_0}) = N_0 k_0 - L_D$ and $f(k_0, \ldots, k_0) = N_0 k_0$.

Now define $A = \{(\ell_1, \ldots, \ell_{N_0}) : k_0 \geq \ell_i \geq k_0 - L_D^i\}$. Since A is a rectangle, it is a connected set. In addition, it follows that $(k_0, \ldots, k_0) \in A$ and $(k_0 - L_D^1, \ldots, k_0 - L_D^{N_0}) \in A$. But f is a continuous function, and $\ell_0 \in [N_0 k_0 - L_D, N_0 k_0]$. Hence, by the generalized Intermediate Value Theorem, we conclude that there exists $q \in A$ such that $f(q) = \ell_0$. Q.E.D.

We now prove the relationship between problems (2.1) and (A1).

Theorem A1. Let $(x^*, \ell_1^*, \ldots, \ell_{N_0}^*)$ be a solution to problem (2.1). Then $(x^*, \sum_{i=1}^{N_0} \ell_i^*)$ is a solution to problem (A1).

Proof. Let $(x^*, \ell_1^*, \ldots, \ell_{N_0}^*)$ be a solution to problem (2.1). Then by summing the inequality constraints on each ℓ_i^*, observe that $N_0 k_0 \geq \sum_{i=1}^{N_0} \ell_i^* \geq N_0 k_0 - L_D$. Also, observe that

$$x^{*\prime} p + w \sum_{i=1}^{N_0} \ell_i^* = I + k_0 N_0 w$$

and that $x^* \geq 0$. Hence $(x^*, \sum_{i=1}^{N_0} \ell_i^*)$ is feasible for problem (A1).

But suppose that $(x^*, \sum_{i=1}^{N_0} \ell_i^*)$ is not a solution to problem (A1), and let $(\tilde{x}, \tilde{\ell}_0)$ be a solution to (A1). Then since $(x^*, \sum_{i=1}^{N_0} \ell_i^*)$ is feasible for problem (A1), we see that

$$u\left(\tilde{x}, \tilde{\ell}_0 + (N_h - N_0)k_0, N_h\right) > u\left(x^*, \sum_{i=1}^{N_0} \ell_i^* + (N_h - N_0)k_0, N_h\right). \quad (A2)$$

Now since $(\tilde{x}, \tilde{\ell}_0)$ is a solution to (A1), it follows that $N_0 k_0 \geq \tilde{\ell}_0 \geq N_0 k_0 - L_D$. So by lemma A1 there exists $(\tilde{\ell}_1, \ldots, \tilde{\ell}_{N_0})$ such that $\sum_{i=1}^{N_0} \tilde{\ell}_i = \tilde{\ell}_0$ and $k_0 \geq \tilde{\ell}_i \geq k_0 - L_D^i$ for $i = 1, \ldots, N_0$. Furthermore, since $(\tilde{x}, \tilde{\ell}_0)$ is a solution to problem (A1), we know that

$$\tilde{x}' p + w \sum_{i=1}^{N_0} \tilde{\ell}_i = I + k_0 N_0 w$$

and $\tilde{x} \geq 0$. Thus $(\tilde{x}, \tilde{\ell}_1, \ldots, \tilde{\ell}_{N_0})$ is feasible for problem (2.1). But in addition it follows from (A2) that

$$u\left(\tilde{x}, \sum_{i=1}^{N_0} \tilde{\ell}_i + (N_h - N_0)k_0, N_h\right) > u\left(x^*, \sum_{i=1}^{N_0} \ell_i^* + (N_h - N_0)k_0, N_h\right).$$

So the assumed optimality of $(x^*, \ell_1^*, \ldots, \ell_{N_0}^*)$ in problem (2.1) is contradicted. Q.E.D.

Now by the strict quasiconcavity of u it can be shown that the solution to problem (A1) is unique. Then the following corollary follows easily, and provides a strong relationship between problems (2.1) and (A1).

Corollary A1. Let (x^*, ℓ_0^*) be the solution to problem (A1), and let $(\tilde{x}, \tilde{\ell}_1, \ldots, \tilde{\ell}_{N_0})$ be a solution to problem (2.1). Then

$$(x^*, \ell_0^*) = \left(\tilde{x}, \sum_{i=1}^{N_0} \tilde{\ell}_i\right).$$

Proof. Let (x^*, ℓ_0^*) be the solution to problem (A1), and suppose there exists a solution $(\tilde{x}, \tilde{\ell}_1, \ldots, \tilde{\ell}_{N_0})$ to problem (2.1) such that

$$(x^*, \ell_0^*) \neq \left(\tilde{x}, \sum_{i=1}^{N_0} \tilde{\ell}_i\right).$$

By theorem A1, it follows that $(\tilde{x}, \sum_{i=1}^{N_0} \tilde{\ell}_i)$ is a solution to problem (A1). But the solution to problem (A1) is unique. Hence, we find that

$$(x^*, \ell_0^*) = \left(\tilde{x}, \sum_{i=1}^{N_0} \tilde{\ell}_i\right),$$

which is a contradiction. Q.E.D.

In this research we shall be interested in explaining only aggregate data. So if $(x^*, \ell_1^*, \ldots, \ell_{N_0}^*)$ is the solution to problem (2.1), we need consider only the household aggregate values $(x^*, \sum_{i=1}^{N_0} \ell_i^*)$, which, by the corollary, is the solution to problem (A1). Hence, we can restrict attention to consideration of problem (A1), the solution to which contains all the information desired.

In problem (A1) add $(N_h - N_0)k_0 w$ to each side of the budget constraint and $(N_h - N_0)k_0$ to each side of the inequality constraints on ℓ_0. Then define $\ell = \ell_0 + (N_h - N_0)k_0$ and $\bar{\ell} = N_h k_0 - L_D$, and define household full income, m, by $m = I + N_h k w$. We now see that problem (A1) becomes problem (2.2).

A2. Relationship between problems (2.2) and (2.3)

In section 2.3 we apply our extended Prais–Houthakker homogeneity postulate to the solution of problem (2.2). We assert that the solution becomes the same as the solution to problem (2.3). We also assert that $\ell^* = k_0 - r_0 \bar{L}/N_h$. We prove those assertions in this section.

Letting $\lambda = 1/N_h$, we now apply the extended Prais–Houthakker postulate to the solution to problem (2.2). The result is

$$\frac{q_i}{N_h} = D_i\left(\frac{m}{N_h}, p, w, \frac{\bar{\ell}}{N_h}, 1\right), \quad i = 1, \ldots, n+1,$$

where $q = (x', \ell)'$ is the solution to problem (2.2). Now let $m^* = m/N_h$, $q^* = q/N_h$, and $\ell^* = \bar{\ell}/N_h$, and define the functions Q_i, $i = 1, \ldots, n+1$, such that $Q_i(m^*, p, w, \ell^*) = D_i(m^*, p, w, \ell^*, 1)$. Then $q_i^* = Q_i(m^*, p, w, \ell^*)$ for all $i = 1, \ldots, n+1$.

Define a function v such that $v(x^*, \ell^*, N_h) = u(x^*N_h, \ell^*N_h, N_h)$, where $\ell^* = \bar{\ell}/N_h$ and $x^* = x/N_h$. Then $v(x^*, \ell^*, N_h) = u(x, \ell, N_h)$. It can be shown that v is strictly quasiconcave and increasing in x^* and ℓ^* and that $\partial v/\partial N_h$ is negative. Dividing the budget constraint by N_h, the household decision problem becomes to choose $x^* \geq 0$ and $\ell^* \in [\bar{\ell}^*, k_0]$ to

maximize $\quad v(x^*, \ell^*, N_h)$

subject to $\quad x^{*\prime} p + \ell^* w = m^*$. (A3)

Functions f_i can be defined such that the solution to that problem can be written as $q_i^* = f_i(m^*, p, w, \ell^*, N_h)$, $i = 1, \ldots, n+1$. Then $f_i(m^*, p, w, \ell^*, N_h) = Q_i(m^*, p, w, \ell^*)$ for all i. Thus $\partial f_i/\partial N_h = 0$ for all i; and $q_i^* = Q_i(m^*, p, w, \ell^*)$, $i = 1, \ldots, n+1$, is the solution to problem (A3). Since it is the solution for arbitrary N_h, it must be the solution when $N_h = 1$. So defining u^* such that $u^*(x^*, \ell^*) = v(x^*, \ell^*, 1)$, it follows that $q_i^* = Q_i(m^*, p, w, \ell^*)$ is the solution to problem (2.3), as asserted in section 2.3. Clearly, u^* is monotonically increasing in all of its arguments and is strictly quasiconcave.

Also, observe that by corollary A1 in section A1, it was shown that at the optimum, the variable ℓ_0 of problem (2.2) is equal to the value of $\sum_{i=1}^{N_0} \ell_i$ at its optimum in problem (2.1). So with all values at their respective optima, we can write that

$$\bar{\ell} = \ell_0 + (N_h - N_0)k_0 = \sum_{i=1}^{N_0} \ell_i + (N_h - N_0)k_0.$$

It follows that

$$\ell^* = \frac{\bar{\ell}}{N_h} = \frac{1}{N_h}\left[\sum_{i=1}^{N_0} \ell_i + (N_h - N_0)k_0\right].$$

Hence, ℓ^* is household per capita leisure.

Further manipulation of ℓ^* is required to acquire a computationally operational formula. First observe that

$$\ell^* = \frac{1}{N_h}\left[\sum_{i=1}^{N_0}(k_0 - L_i) + (N_h - N_0)k_0\right],$$

and let household members $r_0 + 1, \ldots, N_0$ be unemployed, either by choice or otherwise. Then $\ell_i = k_0$ for $i = r_0 + 1, \ldots, N_0$. We now can determine that

$$\ell^* = \frac{1}{N_h}\left[\sum_{i=1}^{r_0}(k_0 - L_i) + (N_0 - r_0)k_0 + (N_h - N_0)k_0\right]$$

$$= \frac{1}{N_h}\left[\sum_{i=1}^{r_0}(k_0 - L_i) + (N_h - r_0)k_0\right].$$

So we find that

$$\ell^* = k_0 - \frac{r_0 \bar{L}}{N_h},$$

where

$$\bar{L} = \frac{1}{r_0}\sum_{i=1}^{r_0} L_i.$$

A3. Relationship between problems (2.3) and (2.5)

In section 2.3 we asserted that problem (2.3) can be restated as problem (2.5). We prove that assertion in this section.

Let Γ be any constant. Its level is arbitrary, but its constancy is required. Then define the function u_Γ such that $u_\Gamma(x^*, y) = u^*(x^*, y + k_0(1 - \Gamma))$. It can be shown that u_Γ is strictly quasiconcave and increasing in all arguments. Letting $\tilde{\ell} = \Gamma k_0 - (r_0/N_h)\bar{L}$, it follows that

$$u_\Gamma(x^*, \tilde{\ell}) = u^*\left(x^*, \tilde{\ell} + k_0(1 - \Gamma)\right) = u^*\left(x^*, k_0 - (r_0/N_h)\bar{L}\right) = u^*(x^*, \ell^*).$$

Now solving problem (2.3) for $\tilde{\ell}$ is equivalent to solving for ℓ^*, since

$$\ell^* = k_0 - \frac{r_0}{N_h}\bar{L} = \Gamma k_0 - \frac{r_0}{N_h}\bar{L} + k_0(1 - \Gamma) = \tilde{\ell} + k_0(1 - \Gamma),$$

where k_0 and Γ are fixed. Hence, problem (2.3) can be restated as to choose $x^* \geqslant 0$, $\tilde{\ell} \in [\bar{\ell}^* - k_0(1-\Gamma), \Gamma k_0]$ to

   maximize $u_\Gamma(x^*, \tilde{\ell})$

   subject to $x^{*\prime} p + \bar{\ell}^* w = m^*$ and $\bar{\ell}^* = \tilde{\ell} + k_0(1-\Gamma)$. (A4)

We now proceed to simplify the statement of problem (A4). First subtract $k_0(1-\Gamma)$ from each side of the budget constraint and define $A(\bar{\ell}^*) = [\bar{\ell}^* - k_0(1-\Gamma), \Gamma k_0]$. Define $\tilde{m}$ by $\tilde{m} = I^* + \Gamma k_0 w$, so that $\tilde{m} = m^* - k_0(1-\Gamma)w$, and let $\tilde{q} = (x^{*\prime}, \tilde{\ell})'$. Then problem (A4) can be restated as problem (2.5).

A4. Properties of the shadow price of leisure

In this section we derive the properties of the shadow price of leisure. Those properties were described in section 2.4. We begin by proving existence and uniqueness. We then prove that the shadow price of leisure declines monotonically below the wage rate as the unemployment rate increases. We provide an interpretation of the shadow price of leisure in terms of Lagrange multipliers. We also prove our characterization theorem establishing the existence of the functions f and g.

Let $(\hat{m}, p, \hat{w}) \in S_1$. Then the necessary and sufficient conditions for a solution to problem (2.10) are

$$\left.\frac{\partial u/\partial x_i}{\partial u/\partial x_j}\right|_{(\hat{x},\hat{\ell})} = \frac{p_i}{p_j}, \quad i,j = 1, \ldots, n, \tag{A5}$$

$$\left.\frac{\partial u/\partial x_k}{\partial u/\partial \ell}\right|_{(\hat{x},\hat{\ell})} = \frac{p_k}{\hat{w}}, \quad k = 1, \ldots, n, \tag{A6}$$

$$\hat{x}'p + \hat{\ell}\hat{w} = \hat{m}. \tag{A7}$$

Similarly, in problem (2.4) let $(m, p, w, \bar{\ell}) \in S$. Then since constraint (2.9) is binding, it can be eliminated by substitution. So (x^*, ℓ^*) is the solution to problem (2.4) if and only if $\ell^* = \bar{\ell}$ and x^* is the solution to

   maximize $u(x, \bar{\ell})$

   subject to $x'p = m - \bar{\ell}w$, $x \geqslant 0$.

Since $x^* > 0$ is assured by the definition of S, corner solutions for x^* can be excluded. Hence, the necessary and sufficient conditions for a solution to problem (2.4) are

$$\left.\frac{\partial u/\partial x_i}{\partial u/\partial x_j}\right|_{(x^*, \bar{\ell})} = \frac{p_i}{p_j}, \quad i, j = 1, \ldots, n, \tag{A8}$$

$$x^{*\prime} p = m - \bar{\ell} w, \quad x^* > 0. \tag{A9}$$

These conditions also follow as a special case of lemma A4 proved below. Observe that conditions (A8) depend upon $\bar{\ell}$, even though $\bar{\ell}$ is not chosen voluntarily.

The following conditions, (A10), are additional necessary conditions. They are not required for sufficiency, since the solution to (A8) and (A9) is unique.

$$\frac{\partial u/\partial x_k}{\partial u/\partial \ell} \geq \frac{p_k}{w}, \quad k = 1, \ldots, n. \tag{A10}$$

Alternatively, in problem (2.4) let $(m, p, w, \bar{\ell}) \in S^c \cap S_0$. Then constraint (2.9) is not binding. So the problem is identical to problem (2.10) with $(\hat{m}, \hat{w}) = (m, w)$ and $(m, p, w) \in S_1$. Thus, the necessary and sufficient conditions in that case are the same as those for problem (2.10).

The proofs of the results below will not necessarily be the simplest possible proofs. Readers seeking simpler proofs can aggregate over goods using Hicksian aggregation to acquire a two-dimensional problem involving leisure and aggregated goods. Geometrical proofs then can be constructed in the plane. But mathematically, the Hicksian aggregation only replaces a vector notation with a scalar notation. We present very formal proofs and analysis in this section to avoid the confusion that appears to exist in some of the literature on this subject.

The following elementary lemma is geometrically clear, but will be presented for completeness.

Lemma A2. For every $(\tilde{x}, \tilde{\ell}) > 0$, $\tilde{\ell} < k_0$, there exists $(\hat{m}, p, \hat{w}) > 0$ such that $\tilde{x} = \hat{x}(\hat{m}, p, \hat{w})$ and $\tilde{\ell} = \hat{\ell}(\hat{m}, p, \hat{w})$, and $(\hat{m}, p, \hat{w})$ is unique up to a scalar multiplicative factor.

Proof. Let $(\tilde{x}, \tilde{\ell}) > 0$ and $\tilde{\ell} < k_0$. Let

$$p_\alpha = \left.\frac{\partial u}{\partial x_\alpha}\right|_{(\tilde{x}, \tilde{\ell})} \quad \text{for } \alpha = 1, \ldots, n, \tag{A11}$$

and

$$\hat{w} = \left.\frac{\partial u}{\partial \ell}\right|_{(\tilde{x}, \tilde{\ell})}. \tag{A12}$$

Then let

$$\hat{m} = p'\tilde{x} + \hat{w}\tilde{\ell}. \tag{A13}$$

By the monotonicity of u, $(p, \hat{w}) > 0$. So $\hat{m} > 0$. Now consider whether $(\tilde{x}, \tilde{\ell})$ satisfies the conditions for a solution to problem (2.10) with $(\hat{m}, p, \hat{w})$ as first defined.

Divide (A11) with $\alpha = i$ by (A11) with $\alpha = j$ and observe that condition (A5) is satisfied. Divide (A11) with $\alpha = k$ by (A12), and observe that condition (A6) is satisfied. Also, condition (A7) is clearly satisfied by (A13). Hence $(\tilde{x}, \tilde{\ell})$ is a solution to problem (2.10) for $(\hat{m}, p, \hat{w})$ as defined in (A11), (A12), and (A13). So $\tilde{x} = \hat{x}(\hat{m}, p, \hat{w})$, and $\tilde{\ell} = \hat{\ell}(\hat{m}, p, \hat{w})$.

To prove uniqueness up to a multiplicative factor, suppose there exists $(\mathring{m}, \mathring{p}, \mathring{w}) > 0$ such that $\tilde{x} = \hat{x}(\mathring{m}, \mathring{p}, \mathring{w})$ and $\tilde{\ell} = \hat{\ell}(\mathring{m}, \mathring{p}, \mathring{w})$, but suppose there does not exist any $\lambda > 0$ such that $(\mathring{m}, \mathring{p}, \mathring{w}) = \lambda(\hat{m}, p, \hat{w})$.

Then it follows that

$$\left.\frac{\partial u/\partial x_i}{\partial u/\partial x_j}\right|_{(\tilde{x}, \tilde{\ell})} = \frac{\mathring{p}_i}{\mathring{p}_j}, \qquad i, j = 1, \ldots, n, \tag{A14}$$

and

$$\left.\frac{\partial u/\partial x_k}{\partial u/\partial \ell}\right|_{(\tilde{x}, \tilde{\ell})} = \frac{\mathring{p}_k}{\mathring{w}}, \qquad k = 1, \ldots, n, \tag{A15}$$

and

$$\mathring{p}'\tilde{x} + \mathring{w}\tilde{\ell} = \mathring{m}. \tag{A16}$$

Again divide (A11) with $\alpha = i$ by (A11) with $\alpha = j$, but now substitute the result into (A14) to get that

$$\frac{\mathring{p}_i}{\mathring{p}_j} = \frac{p_i}{p_j}, \qquad i, j = 1, \ldots, n.$$

Similarly, again divide (A11) with $\alpha = k$ by (A12), but now substitute the result into (A15) to get that

$$\frac{\mathring{p}_k}{\mathring{w}} = \frac{p_k}{w}, \qquad k = 1, \ldots, n.$$

Hence, there exists λ such that $(\mathring{p}, \mathring{w}) = \lambda(p, \hat{w})$. So by (A16), $\mathring{m} = \lambda(p'\tilde{x} + \hat{w}\tilde{\ell}) = \lambda\hat{m}$. So $(\mathring{m}, \mathring{p}, \mathring{w}) = \lambda(\hat{m}, p, \hat{w})$, which is a contradiction. Q.E.D.

The theorems below relate directly to the above lemma, except that the freedom to choose p will be removed. Theorem A1 is our existence theorem on $(\hat{m}, \hat{w})$.

Theorem A2. For any $(m, p, w, \bar{\ell}) \in S_0$, there exists a unique $(\hat{m}, \hat{w})$ such that $\hat{x}(\hat{m}, p, \hat{w}) = x^*(m, p, w, \bar{\ell})$ and $\hat{\ell}(\hat{m}, p, \hat{w}) = \ell^*(m, p, w, \bar{\ell})$. Furthermore, $(\hat{m}, \hat{w}) > 0$.

Proof. Let $(m, p, w, \bar{\ell}) \in S_0$. Suppose $\hat{\ell}(m, p, w) \geq \bar{\ell}$, so that (2.9) is not binding. Then since problem (2.4) reduces to problem (2.10), it follows that $\hat{x}(m, p, w) = x^*(m, p, w, \bar{\ell})$ and that $\hat{\ell}(m, p, w) = \ell^*(m, p, w, \bar{\ell})$. So, existence follows with $\hat{m} = m > 0$ and $\hat{w} = w > 0$. To prove uniqueness, suppose there exists $(\tilde{m}, \tilde{w}) \neq (m, w)$ such that $\hat{x}(\tilde{m}, p, \tilde{w}) = x^*$ and $\hat{\ell}(\tilde{m}, p, \tilde{w}) = \ell^*$. Then by lemma A2 there exists λ such that $(\tilde{m}, p, \tilde{w}) = \lambda(m, p, w)$. But with $p = \lambda p$, it follows that $\lambda = 1$. Hence, $(\tilde{m}, \tilde{w}) = (m, w)$, which is a contradiction.

Alternatively, suppose $\hat{\ell}(m, p, w) < \bar{\ell}$ so that constraint (2.9) is binding in problem (2.4). Then $\ell^* = \bar{\ell}$, and x^* is the solution to conditions (A8) and (A9). Now by lemma A2 there exists $(\tilde{m}, p, \tilde{w}) > 0$ such that $x^* = \hat{x}(\tilde{m}, p, \tilde{w})$ and $\bar{\ell} = \hat{\ell}(\tilde{m}, \tilde{p}, \tilde{w})$. Then by (A5)

$$\left.\frac{\partial u/\partial x_i}{\partial u/\partial x_j}\right|_{(x^*, \bar{\ell})} = \frac{\tilde{p}_i}{\tilde{p}_j}, \quad i, j = 1, \ldots, n. \tag{A17}$$

Substituting (A17) into (A8), observe that

$$\frac{p_i}{p_j} = \frac{\tilde{p}_i}{\tilde{p}_j}, \quad i, j = 1, \ldots, n.$$

Hence, there exists $\lambda > 0$ such that $\tilde{p} = \lambda p$. Let $\hat{m} = \tilde{m}/\lambda$ and $\hat{w} = \tilde{w}/\lambda$. Then $(\hat{m}, \hat{w}) > 0$. Since $\hat{x}$ and $\hat{\ell}$ are homogeneous of degree 0, it follows that

$$\hat{x}(\hat{m}, p, \hat{w}) = \hat{x}\left(\frac{\tilde{m}}{\lambda}, \frac{\tilde{p}}{\lambda}, \frac{\tilde{w}}{\lambda}\right) = \hat{x}(\tilde{m}, \tilde{p}, \tilde{w}) = x^*.$$

Similarly $\hat{\ell}(\hat{m}, p, \hat{w}) = \bar{\ell}$. Uniqueness of $(\hat{m}, \hat{w})$ again follows from lemma A2 and the fact that p is fixed. Q.E.D.

In what follows the values of $\hat{w}$ and $\hat{m}$ shown to exist in theorem A1 will be called the equivalent price of leisure (or occasionally the shadow price of leisure or just the prices of leisure) and the equivalent full-income level, respectively, corresponding to a given $(m, p, w, \bar{\ell}) \in S_0$. More formally, we state the following definitions.

Before providing a characterization of $\hat{w}$ in the next theorem, two simple lemmas will be proved. They are related to the following problems.

Problem A1. Let $(\hat{m}, p, \hat{w}) > 0$. Find $x \geq 0$ to

maximize $u(x, \hat{\ell})$

subject to $x'p = \hat{m} - \hat{\ell}\hat{w}$,

where $\hat{\ell} = \hat{\ell}(\hat{m}, p, \hat{w})$, as is defined in problem (2.10).

Problem A2. Let $(m, p, w, \bar{\ell}) > 0$. Find $x \geq 0$ to

maximize $u(x, \ell^*)$

subject to $x'p = m - \ell^* w$,

where $\ell^* = \ell^*(m, p, w, \bar{\ell})$, as defined in problem (2.4).

Lemma A3. Let $(\hat{m}, p, \hat{w}) > 0$ and let $\hat{\ell} = \hat{\ell}(\hat{m}, p, \hat{w})$, as defined in problem (2.10). Then $(\hat{x}, \hat{\ell})$ is the solution to problem (2.10) if and only if $\hat{x}$ is the solution to problem A1.

Proof. Let $(\hat{m}, p, \hat{w}) > 0$, and let $\hat{\ell} = \hat{\ell}(\hat{m}, p, \hat{w})$. Let $\hat{x}$ be the solution to problem A1, but assume that $(\hat{x}, \hat{\ell})$ is not the solution to problem (2.10). Since $\hat{x}$ is the solution to problem A1, $\hat{x}'p + \hat{\ell}\hat{w} = \hat{m}$ and $\hat{x} \geq 0$. Also, $\hat{\ell} \in [0, k_0]$ by definition of $\hat{\ell}$. Hence $(\hat{x}, \hat{\ell})$ is feasible for problem (2.10). So there must exist $\tilde{x}$ such that $(\tilde{x}, \hat{\ell})$ is feasible for problem (2.10), but such that $u(\tilde{x}, \hat{\ell}) > u(\hat{x}, \hat{\ell})$. Since $(\tilde{x}, \hat{\ell})$ is feasible for problem (2.10), $\tilde{x}'p + \hat{w}\hat{\ell} = \hat{m}$ and $\tilde{x} \geq 0$. Hence, $\tilde{x}$ is feasible for problem (2.10). Then $u(\tilde{x}, \hat{\ell}) > u(\hat{x}, \hat{\ell})$ contradicts the assumption that $\hat{x}$ is a solution to problem A1.

The converse is obvious.   Q.E.D.

Lemma A4. Let $(m, p, w, \bar{\ell}) > 0$, and let $\ell^* = \ell^*(m, p, w, \bar{\ell})$, as defined in problem (2.3). Then (x^*, ℓ^*) is the solution to problem (2.4) if and only if x^* is the solution to problem A2.

Proof. The proof is analogous to that of lemma A3.   Q.E.D.

Observe that conditions (A8) and (A9) are related to lemma A4 in a special case.

Let $\hat{S} = \{(\hat{w}, m, p, w, \bar{\ell}) > 0 : (m, p, w, \bar{\ell}) \in S\}$, and define the function, f, on $\hat{S}$ such that $f(\hat{w}, m, p, w, \bar{\ell}) = \hat{\ell}(m - \bar{\ell}(w - \hat{w}), p, \hat{w})$. We now prove the following characterization of $(\hat{m}, \hat{w})$. We shall use this characterization to solve for $(\hat{m}, \hat{w})$ in applications.

Theorem A3. Let $(m, p, w, \bar{\ell}) \in S$. If $\hat{w}$ is the equivalent price of leisure, then $\hat{m}$ is the equivalent full-income level if and only if $\hat{m} = m - \bar{\ell}(w - \hat{w})$. Furthermore, $\hat{w} > 0$ is the equivalent price of leisure if and only if it is the solution to $f(\hat{w}, m, p, w, \bar{\ell}) = \bar{\ell}$.

Proof. Let $(m, p, w, \bar{\ell}) \in S$, and let $x^* = x^*(m, p, w, \bar{\ell})$. Let $\hat{w}$ be the equivalent price of leisure. Then by (A7) if $\hat{m}$ is the equivalent full-income level, $\hat{m} = \bar{\ell}\hat{w} + x^{*\prime}p$, since $\ell^*(m, p, w, \bar{\ell}) = \bar{\ell}$ on S. But by (A9), $x^{*\prime}p = m - \bar{\ell}w$ on S. So $\hat{m} = m - \bar{\ell}(w - \hat{w})$.

Conversely, let $\hat{w}$ be the equivalent price of leisure, and let $\hat{m} = m - \bar{\ell}(w - \hat{w})$; but suppose $\hat{m}$ is not the equivalent full-income level. Now let $\tilde{m} \neq \hat{m}$ be the actual equivalent full-income level. Then by the necessary condition first proved, $\tilde{m} = m - \bar{\ell}(w - \hat{w})$. Hence, $\hat{m} \neq m - \bar{\ell}(w - \hat{w})$, which is a contradiction.

Now let $\hat{m}$ be the equivalent full-income level and $\hat{w}$ be the equivalent price of leisure. Then $\hat{\ell}(\hat{m}, p, \hat{w}) = \ell^*(m, p, w, \bar{\ell})$ by the definition of $(\hat{m}, \hat{w})$. But on S, $\ell^*(m, p, w, \bar{\ell}) = \bar{\ell}$. Using the results proved above, we get $\hat{m} = m - \bar{\ell}(w - \hat{w})$. Hence, $\hat{\ell}(m - \bar{\ell}(w - \hat{w}), p, \hat{w}) = \bar{\ell}$. So we see that $f(\hat{w}, m, p, w, \bar{\ell}) = \bar{\ell}$.

Conversely, suppose that $\hat{w} > 0$ and $f(\hat{w}, m, p, w, \bar{\ell}) = \bar{\ell}$. Let $\hat{m} = m - \bar{\ell}(w - \hat{w})$. Then $\hat{\ell}(\hat{m}, p, \hat{w}) = \bar{\ell}$. Now by (A9), $x^{*\prime}p = m - \bar{\ell}w$. So by the definition of $\hat{m}$,

$$\hat{m} = x^{*\prime}p + \bar{\ell}\hat{w}. \tag{A18}$$

Since $\hat{w} > 0$, it follows that $\hat{m} > 0$. With $(\hat{m}, \hat{w})$ as just defined and with $\hat{\ell}(\hat{m}, p, \hat{w}) = \bar{\ell}$ known, it follows from lemma A3 that the $\hat{x}(\hat{m}, p, \hat{w})$ defined in problem (2.10) is the solution to problem A1 with $\hat{\ell} = \bar{\ell}$. But by (A18), $\hat{m} - \bar{\ell}\hat{w} = x^{*\prime}p$. So problem A1 with $\hat{\ell} = \bar{\ell}$ is to find $x \geq 0$ to

maximize $\quad u(x, \bar{\ell})$

subject to $\quad x'p = x^{*\prime}p$.

Now similarly with $(m, p, w, \bar{\ell}) \in S$, it is known that $\ell^*(m, p, w, \bar{\ell}) = \bar{\ell}$. So, by lemma A4 the $x^*(m, p, w, \bar{\ell})$ defined in problem (2.4) is the solution to problem A2 with $\ell^* = \bar{\ell}$. Now by (A9), $m - \bar{\ell}w = x^{*\prime}p$. So with $\ell^* = \bar{\ell}$, problem A2 is identical to the problem immediately above. Hence, $\hat{\ell}(\hat{m}, p, \hat{w}) = \bar{\ell} = \ell^*(m, p, w, \bar{\ell})$, while both $\hat{x}(\hat{m}, p, \hat{w})$ and $x^*(m, p, w, \bar{\ell})$ are the solutions to the same problem immediately above. So $\hat{\ell}(\hat{m}, p, \hat{w}) = \ell^*(m, p, w, \bar{\ell})$, and $\hat{x}(\hat{m}, p, \hat{w}) = x^*(m, p, w, \bar{\ell})$. Thus, $\hat{w}$ is the equivalent price of leisure. Q.E.D.

The following corollary will be important below.

Corollary A2. Let $(m, \mathbf{p}, w, \bar{\ell}) \in S_0$. Then the equivalent price of leisure, $\hat{w}$, satisfies $0 < \hat{w} \leq w$. If $(m, \mathbf{p}, w, \bar{\ell}) \in S$, then $0 < \hat{w} < w$.

Proof. Let $(m, \mathbf{p}, w, \bar{\ell}) \in S_0 \cap S^c$, so that (2.9) is not binding in problem (2.4). Then $\hat{w} = w$.

Alternatively, suppose $(m, \mathbf{p}, w, \bar{\ell}) \in S$, so that (2.9) is binding. Then by theorem A2, the equivalent price of leisure, $\hat{w}$, is the solution to $f(\hat{w}, m, \mathbf{p}, w, \bar{\ell}) = \bar{\ell}$. It is desired to examine f in the vicinity of $\hat{w} = 0$. Since f is defined on $\hat{S}$, f is not defined at $\hat{w} = 0$. So we must take the limit (which easily can be shown to exist) as $\hat{w} \to 0$ to find that

$$\lim_{\hat{w} \to 0} f(\hat{w}, m, \mathbf{p}, w, \bar{\ell}) = \lim_{\hat{w} \to 0} \hat{\ell}(m - \bar{\ell}w, \mathbf{p}, \hat{w}) = \lim_{\hat{w} \to 0} \hat{\ell}(x^{*\prime}\mathbf{p}, \mathbf{p}, \hat{w}) \text{ by (A3)}.$$

So with leisure approaching a free good as $\hat{w} \to 0$, it follows that

$$\lim_{\hat{w} \to 0} f(\hat{w}, m, \mathbf{p}, w, \bar{\ell}) = k_0$$

by nonsaturation. Hence,

$$\lim_{\hat{w} \to 0} f(\hat{w}, m, \mathbf{p}, w, \bar{\ell}) > \bar{\ell}, \quad \text{since } \bar{\ell} < k_0.$$

But f is continuous in $\hat{w}$ since $\hat{\ell}$ and $m - \bar{\ell}(w - \hat{w})$ are. So there exists $\delta > 0$ such that if $0 < \hat{w} < \delta$, then $f(\hat{w}, m, \mathbf{p}, w, \bar{\ell}) > \bar{\ell}$. Furthermore, $f(w, m, \mathbf{p}, w, \bar{\ell}) = \hat{\ell}(m, \mathbf{p}, w) < \bar{\ell}$ by the definition of S. In summary, observe that

$$f(\hat{w}, m, \mathbf{p}, w, \bar{\ell}) \begin{cases} < \bar{\ell}, & \text{if } \hat{w} = w, \\ > \bar{\ell}, & \text{for } \hat{w} \in (0, \delta). \end{cases}$$

So, by the continuity of f in $\hat{w}$ there exists $\hat{w} \in (0, w)$ such that $f(\hat{w}, m, \mathbf{p}, w, \bar{\ell}) = \bar{\ell}$. By theorems A1 and A2 the solution to that equation is unique. Q.E.D.

Hence, we see that the shadow price of leisure never can exceed the wage rate, and will be strictly less than the wage rate when unemployment exists. We now prove that the shadow price of leisure equals the wage rate *only* at full employment.

Corollary A3. Let $(m, \mathbf{p}, w, \bar{\ell}) \in S_0$. Then $\hat{w} = w$ if and only if $\hat{\ell}(m, \mathbf{p}, w) \geq \bar{\ell}$.

Proof. Suppose $\hat{\ell}(m, \mathbf{p}, w) \geq \bar{\ell}$. Then condition (2.9) is not binding in problem (2.4), so $\hat{w} = w$. Conversely, suppose $\hat{w} = w$ but $\hat{\ell}(m, \mathbf{p}, w) < \bar{\ell}$. Then $(m, \mathbf{p}, w, \bar{\ell}) \in S$. So by corollary A2, $\hat{w} < w$, which is a contradiction. Q.E.D.

Now by theorem A2 and the uniqueness result of theorem A1 the solution for $\hat{w}$ to

$$f(\hat{w}, m, p, w, \bar{\ell}) = \bar{\ell} \tag{A19}$$

is unique for each $(m, p, w, \bar{\ell}) \in S$. Hence, there exists a function, now to be defined as g, on S such that $\hat{w} = g(m, p, w, \bar{\ell})$ is the solution for $\hat{w}$ to (A19).

It has been argued that for fixed (m, p, w) the price of leisure declines monotonically as unemployment increases. See, for example, Owen (1970), Christensen (1968), and Grossman (1973). The following lemmas must be proved before that result can be verified.

Lemma A5. Let $\bar{\ell} < k_0$ be as given in problem (2.4), and let $(\hat{m}, p, \hat{w}) \in S_1$. Then it follows that

$$\bar{\ell} \frac{\partial \hat{\ell}}{\partial \hat{m}} + \frac{\partial \hat{\ell}}{\partial \hat{w}} < 0.$$

Proof. Let $(\hat{m}, p, \hat{w}) \in S_1$. Then by assumption 2.2, $(\partial \hat{\ell}/\partial \hat{m})(k_0 - \bar{\ell}) > \partial h/\partial \hat{w}$. But

$$\frac{\partial h}{\partial \hat{w}} = \frac{\partial \hat{\ell}(\hat{I} + k_0 \hat{w}, p, \hat{w})}{\partial \hat{w}} = \frac{\partial \hat{\ell}}{\partial \hat{m}} k_0 + \frac{\partial \hat{\ell}}{\partial \hat{w}}.$$

So $(\partial \hat{\ell}/\partial \hat{m})(k_0 - \bar{\ell}) > (\partial \hat{\ell}/\partial \hat{m}) k_0 + \partial \hat{\ell}/\partial \hat{w}$, or

$$-\bar{\ell} \frac{\partial \hat{\ell}}{\partial \hat{m}} - \frac{\partial \hat{\ell}}{\partial \hat{w}} > -k_0 \frac{\partial \hat{\ell}}{\partial \hat{m}} + k_0 \frac{\partial \hat{\ell}}{\partial \hat{m}} = 0.$$

Hence, we see that $\bar{\ell}(\partial \hat{\ell}/\partial \hat{m}) + \partial \hat{\ell}/\partial \hat{w} < 0$. Q.E.D.

Lemma A6. Let $(m, p, w, \bar{\ell}) \in S_0$, let $\hat{w}$ be the equivalent price of leisure, and let $\hat{m}$ be the equivalent full-income level. Then $(\hat{m}, p, \hat{w}) \in S_1$.

Proof. Let $(m, p, w, \bar{\ell}) \in S_0$, let $\hat{w}$ be the equivalent price of leisure, and let $\hat{m}$ be the equivalent full-income level. From $(m, p, w, \bar{\ell}) \in S_0$ it follows that $\bar{\ell} \leq \ell^*(m, p, w, \bar{\ell}) < k_0$, $x^*(m, p, w, \bar{\ell}) > 0$, and $(m, p, w, \bar{\ell}) > 0$. But by the definition of $(\hat{m}, \hat{w})$, it follows that $(\hat{m}, \hat{w}) > 0$, $\ell^*(m, p, w, \bar{\ell}) = \hat{\ell}(\hat{m}, p, \hat{w})$, and $x^*(m, p, w, \bar{\ell}) = \hat{x}(\hat{m}, p, \hat{w})$. Then since $\bar{\ell} > 0$, we conclude that $(\hat{m}, p, \hat{w}) > 0$, $\hat{x}(\hat{m}, p, \hat{w}) > 0$, and $0 < \hat{\ell}(\hat{m}, p, \hat{w}) < k_0$. Hence $(\hat{m}, p, \hat{w}) \in S_1$. Q.E.D.

Theorem A4. Let $(m, p, w, \bar{\ell}) \in S$. Then $\partial g/\partial \bar{\ell} < 0$.

Proof. Let $(m, \boldsymbol{p}, w, \bar{\ell}) \in S$, and let $\hat{w}$ be the equivalent price of leisure. Then
$$\hat{w} = g(m, \boldsymbol{p}, w, \bar{\ell}), \tag{A20}$$
and $f(\hat{w}, m, \boldsymbol{p}, w, \bar{\ell}) = \bar{\ell}$, or
$$\hat{\ell}(\hat{m}, \boldsymbol{p}, \hat{w}) = \bar{\ell}, \tag{A21}$$
where
$$\hat{m} = m - \bar{\ell}(w - \hat{w}) \tag{A22}$$
is the equivalent full-income level. Substitute (A22) and then (A20) into (A21) to get:
$$\hat{\ell}\left(m + \bar{\ell}\left(g(m, \boldsymbol{p}, w, \bar{\ell}) - w\right), \boldsymbol{p}, g(m, \boldsymbol{p}, w, \bar{\ell})\right) = \bar{\ell}.$$
Differentiate with respect to $\bar{\ell}$ to get
$$\frac{\partial \hat{\ell}}{\partial \hat{m}} \left\{ \left[g(m, \boldsymbol{p}, w, \bar{\ell}) - w \right] + \bar{\ell} \frac{\partial g}{\partial \bar{\ell}} \right\} + \frac{\partial \hat{\ell}}{\partial \hat{w}} \frac{\partial g}{\partial \bar{\ell}} = 1,$$
or
$$\frac{\partial \hat{\ell}}{\partial \hat{m}} g(m, \boldsymbol{p}, w, \bar{\ell}) - \frac{\partial \hat{\ell}}{\partial \hat{m}} w + \bar{\ell} \frac{\partial g}{\partial \bar{\ell}} \frac{\partial \hat{\ell}}{\partial \hat{m}} + \frac{\partial \hat{\ell}}{\partial \hat{w}} \frac{\partial g}{\partial \bar{\ell}} = 1,$$
or
$$\left(\bar{\ell} \frac{\partial \hat{\ell}}{\partial \hat{m}} + \frac{\partial \hat{\ell}}{\partial \hat{w}} \right) \frac{\partial g}{\partial \bar{\ell}} = 1 - \frac{\partial \hat{\ell}}{\partial \hat{m}} g(m, \boldsymbol{p}, w, \bar{\ell}) + \frac{\partial \hat{\ell}}{\partial \hat{m}} w,$$
or
$$\frac{\partial g}{\partial \bar{\ell}} = \frac{1 - \frac{\partial \hat{\ell}}{\partial \hat{m}} g(m, \boldsymbol{p}, w, \bar{\ell}) + \frac{\partial \hat{\ell}}{\partial \hat{m}} w}{\bar{\ell} \frac{\partial \hat{\ell}}{\partial \hat{m}} + \frac{\partial \hat{\ell}}{\partial \hat{w}}}.$$

But $g(m, \boldsymbol{p}, w, \bar{\ell}) = \hat{w}$. So it follows that
$$\frac{\partial g}{\partial \bar{\ell}} = \frac{1 + \frac{\partial \hat{\ell}}{\partial \hat{m}} (w - \hat{w})}{\bar{\ell} \frac{\partial \hat{\ell}}{\partial \hat{m}} + \frac{\partial \hat{\ell}}{\partial \hat{w}}}.$$

Now by lemma A6, $(\hat{m}, \boldsymbol{p}, \hat{w}) \in S_1$, since $(m, \boldsymbol{p}, w, \bar{\ell}) \in S \subset S_0$. So lemma A5 can be applied to conclude that $\bar{\ell}(\partial \hat{\ell}/\partial \hat{m}) + \partial \hat{\ell}/\partial \hat{w} < 0$, and assumption

2.1 can be invoked to conclude that $\partial \hat{\ell}/\partial \hat{m} > 0$. Furthermore, $w - \hat{w} > 0$ follows from corollary A2. Hence, $\partial g/\partial \bar{\ell} < 0$.   Q.E.D.

Kuhn–Tucker conditions

Let $(m, p, w, \bar{\ell}) \in S_0$, and consider problem (2.4). First we change the budget constraint of problem A1 to be $x'p + \ell w \leq m$. This is a trivial change, since the monotonicity of the utility function ensures that the budget constraint will be binding. The feasible set for problem A1 is then $A = \{(x, \ell) \geq 0;\ \bar{\ell} \leq \ell \leq k_0,\ x'p + \ell w \leq m\}$. Since the interior of A is non-empty, it is easy to verify that the regularity conditions for the Kuhn–Tucker necessary conditions are satisfied. The usual Kuhn–Tucker assumption of the concavity of u is not needed, since the sufficient conditions for an optimum will not be required. See Hadley (1974, ch. 6) or Kuhn and Tucker (1951, theorem 1). We are now in a position to provide simplified proofs of theorem A2 and of half of corollary A2 in a manner utilizing a directly formulated and revealing expression for the equivalent price of leisure. The nature of the insight provided by the Kuhn–Tucker approach differs from that provided by the previous approach.

The Lagrangian for the revised problem (2.4) is

$$\mathcal{L} = u(x, \ell) + \lambda_1(\ell - \bar{\ell}) + \lambda_2(k_0 - \ell) + \lambda_3(m - x'p - \ell w).$$

Let (x^*, ℓ^*) be the solution to problem (2.4). Then by the Kuhn–Tucker conditions it is necessary that

$$\frac{\partial \mathcal{L}}{\partial x_\alpha} = \frac{\partial u}{\partial x_\alpha}\bigg|_{(x^*, \ell^*)} - \lambda_3^* p_\alpha \leq 0, \quad \text{for } \alpha = 1, \ldots, n, \tag{A23}$$

with equality if $x_\alpha^* > 0$;

$$\frac{\partial \mathcal{L}}{\partial \ell} = \frac{\partial u}{\partial \ell}\bigg|_{(x^*, \ell^*)} + \lambda_1^* - \lambda_2^* - \lambda_3^* w \leq 0, \tag{A24}$$

with equality if $\ell^* > 0$;

$$\frac{\partial \mathcal{L}}{\partial \lambda_1} = \ell^* - \bar{\ell} \geq 0, \qquad \text{with equality if } \lambda_1^* > 0; \tag{A25}$$

$$\frac{\partial \mathcal{L}}{\partial \lambda_2} = k_0 - \ell^* \geq 0, \qquad \text{with equality if } \lambda_2^* > 0;$$

$$\frac{\partial \mathcal{L}}{\partial \lambda_3} = m - x^{*\prime} p - \ell^* w \geq 0, \quad \text{with equality if } \lambda_3^* > 0; \tag{A26}$$

$$(x^*, \ell^*) \geq 0 \quad (\lambda_1^*, \lambda_2^*, \lambda_3^*) \geq 0.$$

Now $(x^*, \ell^*) > 0$ on S_0, so conditions (A23) and (A24) hold with equality. Now by condition (A25), if $\lambda_2^* > 0$, then $k_0 - \ell^* = 0$. But on S_0, $\ell^* < k_0$. Hence $\lambda_2^* = 0$. So the necessary conditions reduce to

$$\left.\frac{\partial u}{\partial x_\alpha}\right|_{(x^*, \ell^*)} = \lambda_3^* p_\alpha, \quad \text{for } \alpha = 1, \ldots, n, \tag{A27}$$

$$\left.\frac{\partial u}{\partial \ell}\right|_{(x^*, \ell^*)} + \lambda_1^* - \lambda_3^* w = 0, \tag{A28}$$

$$\ell^* - \bar{\ell} \geqslant 0, \quad \text{with equality if } \lambda_1^* > 0, \tag{A29}$$

$$(x^*, \ell^*) \geqslant \mathbf{0}; \quad \ell^* \leqslant k_0; \quad x^{*\prime} p + \ell^* w = m;$$

$$(\lambda_1^*, \lambda_3^*) \geqslant \mathbf{0}. \tag{A30}$$

Now divide (A27) with $\alpha = i$ by (A28) with $\alpha = j$ to get that

$$\left.\frac{\partial u/\partial x_i}{\partial u/\partial x_j}\right|_{(x^*, \ell^*)} = \frac{p_i}{p_j}, \quad \text{for } i, j = 1, \ldots, n. \tag{A31}$$

Similarly, divide (A27) with $\alpha = k$ by (A28) to get that

$$\left.\frac{\partial u/\partial x_k}{\partial u/\partial \ell}\right|_{(x^*, \ell^*)} = \frac{\lambda_3^* p_k}{\lambda_3^* w - \lambda_1^*}, \quad \text{for } k = 1, \ldots, n. \tag{A32}$$

We next seek $(\hat{w}, \hat{m})$ such that (x^*, ℓ^*) will be a solution to problem (2.10); that is to say, such that (A5), (A6), and (A7) will be satisfied at (x^*, ℓ^*).
Let $\hat{w} = w - \lambda_1^*/\lambda_3^*$, and let $\hat{m} = x^{*\prime} p + \ell^* \hat{w}$. Then clearly condition (A7) is satisfied at (x^*, ℓ^*). Next observe that

$$\frac{\lambda_3^* p_k}{\lambda_3^* w - \lambda_1^*} = \frac{\lambda_3^* p_k}{\lambda_3^* \hat{w}} = \frac{p_k}{\hat{w}}, \quad \text{for } k = 1, \ldots, n.$$

So by (A32),

$$\left.\frac{\partial u/\partial x_k}{\partial u/\partial \ell}\right|_{(x^*, \ell^*)} = \frac{p_k}{\hat{w}}, \quad \text{for } k = 1, \ldots, n,$$

demonstrating that condition (A6) is satisfied at (x^*, ℓ^*). Finally, observe that by (A31), condition (A5) is satisfied. Thus, existence of $(\hat{w}, \hat{m})$ has been proved.

To prove uniqueness, observe that for given $\hat{w}$ the choice of $\hat{m}$ is clearly unique. So it remains only to prove the uniqueness of $\hat{w}$. Suppose there exists another equivalent price of leisure, $\tilde{w} \neq w - \lambda_1^*/\lambda_3^*$. Then at (x^*, ℓ^*) it follows from (A6) that

$$\left.\frac{\partial u/\partial x_k}{\partial u/\partial \ell}\right|_{(x^*, \ell^*)} = \frac{p_k}{\tilde{w}}, \quad \text{for } k = 1, \ldots, n.$$

Hence by (A32),

$$\frac{p_k}{\tilde{w}} = \frac{\lambda_3^* p_k}{\lambda_3^* w - \lambda_1^*} = \frac{p_k}{\hat{w}}, \quad k = 1, \ldots, n.$$

So $\tilde{w} = \hat{w}$, which is a contradiction. Furthermore, we know that

$$\hat{w} = p_k \left.\frac{\partial u/\partial \ell}{\partial u/\partial x_k}\right|_{(x^*, \ell^*)} > 0, \quad k = 1, \ldots, n,$$

by the monotonicity of u, and then $\hat{m} = x^{*\prime} p + \hat{w} \ell^* > 0$, since $\ell^* \geq \bar{\ell} > 0$. So $(\hat{w}, \hat{m}) > 0$. Hence, theorem A2 has been verified.

The explanatory power of the Kuhn–Tucker necessary conditions is particularly evident in illustrating the results of part of corollary A2 to theorem A3. Recall that

$$\hat{w} = w - \frac{\lambda_1^*}{\lambda_3^*}. \tag{A33}$$

Now by (A27) and the monotonicity of u, observe that

$$\lambda_3^* = \frac{\partial u/\partial x_\alpha |(x^*, \ell^*)}{p_\alpha} > 0,$$

while by (A30) we know that $\lambda_1^* \geq 0$. Hence, $\hat{w} \geq w$, as is the conclusion of half of corollary A2.

More important than verifying a few of our previous results, the above Kuhn–Tucker theory provides the new and revealing direct characterization of the equivalent price of leisure exhibited in (A32) above. That result will now be interpreted. Recall that in general a Lagrange multiplier λ_i is the marginal value of relaxing the ith constraint. In this case it then follows that λ_3^* is the marginal utility of increasing income m, while λ_1 is the marginal utility of increasing labor demand, ℓ, with all consumption quantities adjusted optimally. So we can write $\lambda_3^* = \partial u/\partial m$ and $\lambda_1^* = \partial u/\partial \ell$. But $\partial u/\partial m$ is the shadow price of income in utility units, while $\partial u/\partial \ell$ is the shadow price of labor demand in utility units. Adopting the notation $p_m = \partial u/\partial m$ and $p_{\bar{\ell}} = \partial u/\partial \ell$, we can write that $\lambda_3^* = p_m$ and $\lambda_1^* = p_{\bar{\ell}}$.

Returning to (A33), we now observe that $p_{\bar{\ell}} = p_m(w - \hat{w})$. Multiplying through by $\bar{\ell}$, it then follows that

$$p_{\bar{\ell}} d\bar{\ell} = p_m \left[(w - \hat{w}) d\bar{\ell} \right]. \tag{A34}$$

To interpret this result, view $\hat{L}(\hat{m}, p, \cdot) = k - \hat{\ell}(\hat{m}_0, p, \cdot)$ for constant $(\hat{m}, p)$ as a labor supply curve, and let $L_D(w)$ be the labor demand function. Recalling that $\hat{m} = m - \ell(w - \hat{w})$, observe that $\hat{m}$ varies with changes in $\hat{w}$, $\bar{\ell}$, w, and m. So when we vary $\hat{w}$ and $\bar{\ell}$ below, compensating changes in m could be viewed as implicit, to keep $\hat{m}$ constant. The level at which $\hat{m}$ will be held constant is the level corresponding to the actual current value of $(m, p, w, \bar{\ell})$.

Let constraint (2.9) of problem (2.4) be binding at the current value of $(m, p, w, \bar{\ell})$. Then when $(\hat{m}, \hat{w})$ are the equivalent values corresponding to the actual (m, w), we have that $\hat{\ell}(\hat{m}, p, \hat{w}) = \bar{\ell}$. Letting $\bar{L} = k - \bar{\ell}$, we can now draw fig. A1. Observe that $\hat{L}$ is not the usual labor supply function. Now from fig. A1 we can view w as the demand price of labor and $\hat{w}$ as its supply price. So $w - \hat{w}$ is the excess demand price and $\bar{L}(w - \hat{w})$ is "excess" expenditure on labor input by firms.

Let $\bar{L}$ change to $\bar{L} - d\bar{L}$, and refer to fig. A2. Observe that $-d\bar{L}(w - \hat{w})$ is the infinitesimal change in "excess" expenditure on labor input resulting from $d\bar{L}$. But since $d\bar{\ell} = -d\bar{L}$, we see that $d\bar{\ell}(w - \hat{w})$ is the marginal (incremental) decrease in "excess" expenditure on labor input resulting from $d\bar{\ell}$. Thus, $p_m[(w - \hat{w})d\bar{\ell}]$ is the utility value (in a cardinal sense) of that change, or equivalently the incremental utility of $d\bar{\ell}$. Note that it is negative. So those who remain employed after the decrease in employment lose some of their "excess" income. But recall that in some sense $p_{\bar{\ell}}$ is itself a shadow price of $\bar{\ell}$. In terms of the concepts just introduced, eq. (A34) explains the sense in which $p_{\bar{\ell}}$ is a shadow price.

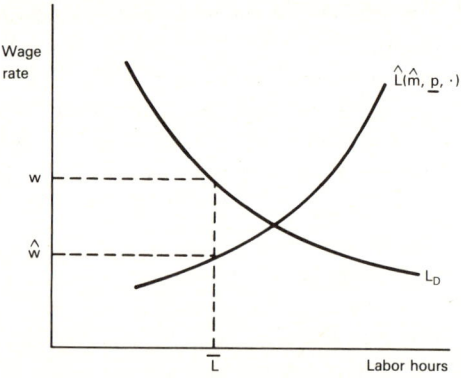

Figure A1. Excess demand price of leisure.

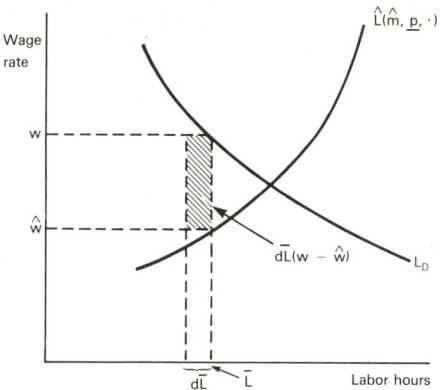

Figure A2. A shadow price interpretation of the equivalent price of leisure.

Finally, dividing $d\bar{l}$ back out of (A34), it becomes clear that $\hat{w}$ is chosen such that $p_m(w-\hat{w})$ is the shadow price, $p_{\bar{l}}$. Observe that in $p_m(w-\hat{w})$ the marginal utility of income, p_m, merely converts the units of the excess demand price $w-\hat{w}$ to utility units. Hence, we find that when $k_0 - \hat{l}(\hat{m}, p, \cdot)$ is viewed as a supply curve, $\hat{w}$ is chosen such that the shadow price of labor demand, $p_{\bar{l}}$, is equal to the excess demand price for labor, $w-\hat{w}$, in utility units.

A5. Extension to the full-employment boundary

In section 2.5 we defined the function g on S. In this section we extend the function g to a function g^* defined on S^* such that S^* contains the full-employment boundary of S as well as S itself. We also prove the existence of the function ξ^*, and we prove that $\partial \xi^*/\partial \hat{w} > 0$.

Let $A = \{(\hat{w}, m, p, w) > 0: \hat{w} = g(m, p, w, \bar{l}), (m, p, w, \bar{l}) \in S, 0 < \bar{l} < k_0\}$. Now by theorem A4 in section A4, g is monotone in $\bar{l}$. Hence, its inverse in $\bar{l}$ exists and has domain A. So define ψ on A to be that inverse. Then $\bar{l} = \psi(\hat{w}, m, p, w)$ for $(\hat{w}, m, p, w) \in A$, and by theorem A4, $\partial \psi/\partial \hat{w} < 0$. Observe that equivalently ψ is the solution for $\bar{l}$ to $f(\hat{w}, m, p, w, \bar{l}) = \bar{l}$. Thus, we have shown that for each $(\hat{w}, m, p, w) \in A$, f has a unique fixed point in $\bar{l}$.

Now define ξ on A such that $\xi(\hat{w}, m, p, w) = k_0 - \psi(\hat{w}, m, p, w)$, and let $\bar{L} = k_0 - \bar{l} =$ per capita man-hours employed. Then $\bar{L} = \xi(\hat{w}, m, p, w)$ for all $(\hat{w}, m, p, w) \in A$. So ξ determines per capita man-hours employed if $\hat{w}$ is the equivalent price of leisure when $(m, \boldsymbol{p}, w)$ is the market data. Observe that for given values of $(\hat{w}, m, \boldsymbol{p}, w) \in A$, $\xi(\hat{w}, m, \boldsymbol{p}, w)$ lies *on* the labor supply function of problem (2.10). When applied to a model derived from a community utility function, the function g, determining the equivalent price of leisure, is the result of primary interest. But in specifying the equivalent price of leisure for the Rotterdam model, the inverse function ψ and the related function ξ will be seen to be in a more convenient form. Our version of the Rotterdam model will not be dependent upon the existence of a community utility function.

Now by the definition of S and therefore of A, the possibility $\hat{\ell}(m, \boldsymbol{p}, w) \geq \bar{\ell}$ (i.e. the possibility of full employment) is excluded on A and on S. Equivalently, the possibility $w = \hat{w}$ is excluded, since by theorem A3 in section A4, $w = \hat{w}$ if and only if full employment exists. But g is defined on S, and ψ and ξ on A. Since empirical applications of this theory rest on the specification of g or ξ, this is an undesirable situation. While the primary objective of these functions is to correct w down to $\hat{w}$, a unified approach capable of dealing also with full employment would be desirable. So we now extend the domains of g and ξ to include the full-employment case.

First observe that in this analysis the case of a strictly positive excess demand for labor does not differ from the case of exact labor market clearing. In either case, condition (2.9) of problem (2.4) is not binding, and problem (2.4) reduces to problem (2.10). Hence, if $\hat{\ell}(m, \boldsymbol{p}, w) > \bar{\ell}$, we can increase $\bar{\ell}$ to equal $\hat{\ell}$ without affecting the analysis. So the case of $\hat{\ell} > \bar{\ell}$ will be excluded from consideration. This does not mean that an excess demand for labor cannot exist. It means that $\bar{\ell}$ can be redefined without affecting this analysis. In brief, $\bar{L} = k_0 - \bar{\ell}$ has been defined such that it is no longer always the per capita demand for labor. It now is only the demand for labor when an excess supply of labor exists. Otherwise $\bar{L}$ is set equal to the per capita supply of labor. In terms of the data, $\bar{L}$ is equal to per capita man-hours employed in either case.

In symbols, if L_D = per capita labor demand, then $\bar{\ell}$ is defined by

$$\bar{\ell} = \begin{cases} k_0 - L_D, & \text{if } \hat{\ell}(m, \boldsymbol{p}, w) < k_0 - L_D, \\ \hat{\ell}(m, \boldsymbol{p}, w), & \text{if } \hat{\ell}(m, \boldsymbol{p}, w) \geq k_0 - L_D. \end{cases} \quad (A35)$$

So g and ξ need only be extended to their domains' boundary region on which $\hat{\ell}(m, \boldsymbol{p}, w) = \bar{\ell}$. Hence, we wish to extend g to a function g^* defined on

$$S^* = \{(m, \boldsymbol{p}, w, \bar{\ell}) \in S_0 : \hat{\ell}(m, \boldsymbol{p}, w) \leq \bar{\ell}\},$$

which is all of S_0, when $\bar{\ell}$ is determined as in (A35) above. Similarly, we wish to extend ψ and ξ to functions ψ^* and ξ^* defined on

$$A^* = \{(\hat{w}, m, \boldsymbol{p}, w) > \boldsymbol{0} : \hat{w} = g^*(m, \boldsymbol{p}, w, \bar{\ell}),$$

$$(m, \boldsymbol{p}, w, \bar{\ell}) \in S^*, 0 < \bar{\ell} < k_0\}.$$

Observe that $S^* - S$ is the desired full employment boundary region on which $\hat{\ell}(m, \boldsymbol{p}, w) = \bar{\ell}$.

Now on S, define g^* such that $g^*|_S = g$. Similarly, on A define ψ^* such that $\psi^*|_A = \psi$. Then it remains only to define ξ^*, ψ^*, and g^* on the boundary regions $A^* - A$ and $S^* - S$, where $\hat{\ell}(m, \boldsymbol{p}, w) = \bar{\ell}$. Recall that g explains the equivalent price of leisure in terms of $(m, \boldsymbol{p}, w, \ell)$. But on the full-employment boundary regions we know that $\hat{w} = w$. Hence, define g^* on $S^* - S$ such that $g^*|_{S^* - S} = w$. In applications we get the same result by using the formula derived for g on all of S^*. As seen in the Cobb–Douglas example of subsection 2.5.3, $g(m, \boldsymbol{p}, w, \bar{\ell})$ reduces to w at full employment.

Similarly, recall that the objective of ψ was to relate the per capita man-hour employment level, ℓ, to the equivalent price of leisure, $\hat{w}$, at given $(m, \boldsymbol{p}, w) > \boldsymbol{0}$. Since $\hat{\ell}(m, \boldsymbol{p}, w) = \bar{\ell}$ and $\hat{w} = w$ on $A^* - A$, $k_0 - \bar{\ell}$ does that itself on $A^* - A$. So define ψ^* such that $\psi^*(\hat{w}, m, \boldsymbol{p}, w) = \hat{\ell}(m, \boldsymbol{p}, w)$ for all $(\hat{w}, m, \boldsymbol{p}, w) \in A^* - A$. Observe that on $A^* - A$, $\hat{w}$ is a redundant explanatory variable, since $\hat{w} = w$ on $A^* = A$. Again, in applications the formula derived for ψ can be used on all of A^*, since it will reduce to $\hat{\ell}(m, \boldsymbol{p}, w)$ on $A^* - A$.

Finally, by analogy to the definition of ξ, define ξ^* on all of A^* in the obvious manner as $\xi^* = k_0 - \psi^*$. Now as shown previously, $\partial \xi / \partial \hat{w} > 0$. Similarly, we expect that on $A^* - A$,

$$\frac{\partial \xi^*}{\partial \hat{w}} = \frac{\partial \xi^*}{\partial w} = \frac{\partial}{\partial w}\left[k_0 - \hat{\ell}(m, \boldsymbol{p}, w)\right] = -\frac{\partial \hat{\ell}(m, \boldsymbol{p}, w)}{\partial w} > 0$$

by the discussion following assumption 2.2, with the variable $\hat{w}$ changed to w merely as a matter of notation. So we shall expect that $\partial \xi^* / \partial \hat{w} > 0$ everywhere on A^*.

APPENDIX B

APPENDIX TO CHAPTER 3

B1. Integrability and aggregation theory

B1.1. Integrability theory

As we have seen, the theoretical properties of eqs. (3.18) provided by theorem 3.2 do not depend for their validity upon integrability of the aggregate system (3.18). Nevertheless, we shall find it useful to explore the integrability properties of (3.18).

The following definitions will be required.

Definition B1. We shall say that (3.18) "corresponds with" an aggregate demand system $a(m, p)$, if $a(m, p) = (1/N)\sum_{c=1}^{N} q_c(m_c(t), p(t))$ for some collection of neoclassical demand systems $q_c(m_c, p)$, $c = 1, \ldots, N$, and if the system of differential equations (3.18) can be solved for $\bar{q} = (Q_1, \ldots, Q_n)'$ such that $\bar{q} = a(m(t), p(t))$ for $t \in T$.

Definition B2. We shall say that (3.18) "corresponds with" the aggregate demand system of a "representative consumer", if (3.18) corresponds with an aggregate demand system $a(m, p)$ and if there exists a function b such that $b(M(t), p(t)) = a(m(t), p(t))$ for every $t \in T$.

Definition B3. We shall say that (3.18) is integrable if (3.18) corresponds with the aggregate demand system of a representative consumer, and if there exists a strictly quasiconcave, monotonically increasing (community) utility function U, such that at every $t \in T$, $\bar{q} = b(m(t), p(t))$ maximizes $U(\bar{q})$ subject to $\bar{q}'p \leq M$.

We have *no* prior reason to believe that (3.18) necessarily must *or should* "correspond with" any aggregate demand system. It is well known that limits of sequences of functions can have fundamentally different properties from those of any of the functions in the sequence and commonly will not be bijectively related to any element or finite collection of elements of the function sequence. In fact (3.18) is a fundamentally different sort of construct from an aggregate demand function system, and in general *none* of the relationships in definitions 3.1, 3.2, or 3.3 need obtain. Furthermore, it was our intent to *ensure* that no such correspondences could exist, since little is known about the properties of aggregate demand systems (except under extremely strong assumptions) and hence of *any* system of equations directly derivable from an aggregate demand system.

Observe the nature of (3.18) itself. It has hybrid properties, in the sense that some of its factors were introduced into the equation only in the limit as N goes to infinity, while others are defined for finite N. For example, $\overline{M}$ and W_i depend upon N, while the macrocoefficients appeared in the limit as N goes to infinity. But functions depending upon N tend to depend upon income through the finite sample of incomes m, while the functionals that appeared in the limit depend upon income through the distribution functions F_t and H_t. With (3.18) depending upon income through an income distribution function *as well as* upon m or M, it is clear that (3.18) is a fundamentally different sort of construct from an aggregate demand function system. None of the relationships in definitions 3.1, 3.2, or 3.3 can be expected to obtain; this is immediately evident from the dependence of (3.18) upon t through F_t and H_t as well as through $(m(t), p(t))$. This form of time dependence is not permitted in definitions 3.1, 3.2, and 3.3.

To escape from the unacceptably restrictive implications of available theorems on aggregate demand systems, we must break the links that exist when the properties in definitions 3.1, 3.2, and 3.3 obtain, and we must pass to a fundamentally different function space. We have done *precisely* that. The strong results in theorems 3.1 and 3.2 were rendered logically possible by the lack of any need for "correspondence" (in the sense of definitions 3.1, 3.2, or 3.3) between (3.18) and an aggregate demand system, whether or not integrable.

Although we have no reason to impose upon (3.18) restrictions sufficient for *aggregate* integrability, we now consider what would happen if we did. First we presume that we have imposed some set of restrictions sufficient for (3.18) to correspond with an aggregate demand system. That would require, at the least, that the dependency of (3.18) upon F_t and H_t be eliminated. We now seek *further* conditions sufficient for (3.18) to be integrable. Gorman (1953) has proved that the aggregate demand system defined in definition 3.1 is integrable in the sense of definition 3.3 if and only if each consumer has parallel linear Engel curves. Such a severe restriction on consumer preferences cannot be accepted, and we have induced randomness into the taste determining factors s_c specifically to account for more general preference variability. As observed by Phlips (1974, p. 19), Gorman's result obtains "under totally unrealistic conditions". Nevertheless, we now follow Yoshihara (1969) in introducing even greater restrictiveness.

We shall refer to a function property as being origin-closed if it would obtain even if each consumer's consumption set, S_c, contained the origin (so that the consumer can survive with consumption even at the origin). McFadden synonymously used the term "global" to refer to the widely used origin-closed case. But we elsewhere use global to mean "everywhere on the *given* consumption set". Although the origin-closed case is restrictive, the sole generalization that has found widespread empirical use is the translation of the origin of R^n to a subsistence consumption bundle; the translated non-negative orthant then is used as the consumption set. The generalization of origin-closed properties to the resulting affine space is obvious. A further, but less common, generalization is provided by Gorman's polar form. A simple proof of the following well-known result follows.

Theorem B.1. If (3.18) is origin-closed integrable, then all consumers' demand functions for all goods are identical and have unitary income elasticities.

Proof. As we have seen, all consumers must have parallel linear Engel curves if (3.18) is to be integrable. But it is well known that demand systems with parallel linear Engel curves are origin-closed integrable if and only if they have unitary income elasticities. This is easily seen as follows. The demand function $q_{ic}(m_c, \boldsymbol{p})$ has linear Engel curves if and only if $q_{ic}(m_c, \boldsymbol{p})$ is of the form $a_{ic}(\boldsymbol{p}) + b_i(\boldsymbol{p})m_c$. That function is origin-closed integrable if and only if $a_{ic}(\boldsymbol{p}) = 0$. Hence, we find that $q_{ic}(m_c, \boldsymbol{p})$ has linear Engel curves and also is origin-closed integrable if and only if $q_{ic}(m_c, \boldsymbol{p})$ is of the form $b_i(\boldsymbol{p})m_c$, which has unitary income elasticities.
Q.E.D.

Detailed consideration of the origin-closed case in aggregation can be found in Chipman (1974), Eisenberg (1961), Katzner (1970, p. 139), and Green (1964, pp. 44–50). As we shall see below, an analogous result, derived under the *same origin-closed assumption*, is precisely that for which Yoshihara (1969) criticized the Rotterdam model's particular parameterization of (3.18). In fact we see that under this assumption *no* aggregate demand system and *no* theoretical system (3.18) will be integrable unless each consumer's demand function has unitary income elasticity. The proper conclusion (now widely accepted by theorists) is that integrability of any aggregate demand system (whether or not its domain includes the origin) is extremely unlikely and should not be assumed exclusively on theoretical grounds. However, we do believe, for *empirical* reasons, that aggregate integrability can be a useful and entirely justifiable *functional regularity* condition, and we ourselves have maintained aggregate integrability for that purpose in Chapters 6 and 7. But in the current theoretical chapter we shall not and *need not* impose restrictions sufficient for aggregate integrability.

Much recent literature has appeared on the theoretical implications of aggregation over consumers. Since Gorman's conditions are both necessary and sufficient for aggregate integrability, the recent literature can say nothing further on the issues we have defined above, which are the relevant issues in considering the critique of the Rotterdam model. However, the recent literature explores results weaker than aggregate integrability, and such results may be useful in motivating the construction of future models. Hence, we discuss that literature in the next subsection.

B1.2. Recent aggregation literature

In the general equilibrium literature, McFadden, Mas-Colell, Mantel, and Richter (1974), Debreu (1974), Sonnenschein (1973), and Mantel (1974, 1976) have demonstrated that very little is known about aggregate demand functions and aggregate excess demand functions. We have seen that such functions generally are not integrable. In considering potentially weaker results, Sonnenschein (1973, p. 404) observes that his proofs provide "a striking indication that the budget and homogeneity restrictions largely exhaust the empirical implications of the utility hypothesis for market demand functions, even under the strong hypothesis that community income is shared equally". He concludes (1973, p. 406) that at the aggregate level "there is little left of demand theory beyond homogeneity and balance...it remains an empty (empirical) box".

Muellbauer (1975) has considered the possibility of acquiring weaker results than Gorman's (1953), but under stronger conditions than those accepted in the above general equilibrium literature. Simmons (1979) has extended Muellbauer's results to include leisure demand. This possibility also has been considered by Diewert (1976a), but only under the empirically impracticable assumption that the number of consumers is less than the number of goods. Muellbauer (1975) seeks the existence of a shadow income level such that aggregate demand would be integrable if the representative consumer were allocated the shadow level of income. When the shadow level of income equals aggregate per capita income, Muellbauer's (1975) results reduce to Gorman's results. Since the existing empirical literature allocates measured aggregate per capita income to the representative consumer, Muellbauer's promising results cannot be used to rationalize existing models postulating integrable aggregate demand. That approach, called the stratification approach by Wold and Juréen (1953), was originated in 1895 by Pareto. It has more recently been considered by Green (1964, p. 67) and by Diewert (1976).

As we have observed earlier, the random sampling approach to modeling income and taste differences could be used directly with aggregate demand functions rather than with our transformation of demand theory. If preferences are viewed to be the same for all consumers, as assumed in Diewert's (1976) version, then the stratification approach reduces to a model of a representative consumer faced with random income. But it is the existence of that representative consumer which is at issue. In fact, Sonnenschein (1973) and Mantel (1976) have shown that the problem exists even when all incomes vary proportionately, so that income distribution remains constant. The source of the problem is differences in tastes over consumers rather than variations in income distribution over time. But to capture variations in tastes and income distribution, it would require knowledge of the joint distribution of income and all of the taste determining stratifying variables, s_c, which generally cannot themselves reasonably be specified, although there has been some progress in the direct modeling of some elements of s_c (see, for example, Muellbauer, 1977).

B2. The remainder terms

Let us consider the goods and estimates in the tables on pp. 188–189 of Theil (1975). As has been pointed out to me by Theil, we can expect, for his data, that both θ_i and $(\text{var } w_{jc})^{1/2}$ will be well below 0.1. Hence, the aggregation bias of the (i, j)th Slutsky coefficient will be well below $|\rho_{ij}/100|$ in absolute value. Now we may view ρ_{ij} as the correlation coefficient of $m_c\mu_{ic} = \partial(p_i q_{ic})/\partial \log m_c$ and w_{jc} in the consumer population. There appears to be no reason whatsoever to believe that this quantity should differ appreciably from zero, and it cannot exceed 1. Hence for $i \neq j$, it follows that $|\gamma_{ij}(t)|$ is likely to fall well below 0.001 uniformly in $t \in T$. Hence, for those goods, the aggregation bias of the off-diagonal Slutsky coefficient will be less than 0.001 in absolute value for all $t \in T$. This is very modest by comparison with the Slutsky coefficient estimates presented by Theil in those tables. His unconstrained off-diagonal estimates average 0.032 in absolute value. Nevertheless, the potential complications that could result from this previously unrecognized (although perhaps commonly small) off-diagonal aggregation bias may merit further theoretical and empirical exploration.

Under our assumptions, the matrix $[\gamma_{ij}(t)]$ need not be symmetric. Whenever our speculations about its magnitude are not applicable, the powerful Slutsky symmetry result of theorem 3.2 could be swamped by nonsymmetric aggregation bias, but the desired symmetry condition is $\gamma_{ij}(t) - \gamma_{ji}(t) = 0$ for all $i \neq j$. By the triangle inequality, $|\gamma_{ij}(t) - \gamma_{ji}(t)| \leq |\gamma_{ij}(t)| + |\gamma_{ji}(t)|$. Hence, smallness of $|\gamma_{ij}(T)|$ for all $i \neq j$ is sufficient, but not necessary, for $[\gamma_{ij}(t)]$ to be almost symmetric. Direct speculations on the magnitude of $|\gamma_{ij}(t) - \gamma_{ji}(t)|$ would provide a much lower upper bound. But we shall not consider such a direct bound, since the stronger conditions of smallness of each individual $|\gamma_{ij}(t)|$ for all $i \neq j$ permits more informative interpretation of the macroparameters.

Similar consideration of the diagonal elements of $[\gamma_{ij}(t)]$ suggests that $\gamma_{ii}(t)$ typically will be less than 0.01 in absolute value for all $t \in T$ and probably will be positive. That upper bound on $|\gamma_{ii}(t)|$ follows from the same considerations presented in the previous discussion of $\gamma_{ij}(t)$ for $i \neq j$. Positivity results from the properties of ρ_{ii}, which relates $m_c\mu_{ic}$ and w_{ic} for the same good i. It appears plausible, on the average, that consumers whose tastes yield a relatively large w_{ic} also have a large μ_{ic}. If this speculation were true, then ρ_{ii} and hence $\gamma_{ii}(t)$ would be positive. Hence the coefficients of $d \log p_i/dt$ in (3.28) may be slightly smaller than $\bar{\pi}_i$.

Although our a priori upper bound on the diagonal elements of $[\gamma_{ij}(t)]$ is larger than that on the off-diagonal elements, the off-diagonal bound is of more concern through its relationship with the empirically powerful Slutsky symmetry condition. Also, observe that Theil's unconstrained estimates of the diagonal elements of the Slutsky matrix average 0.067, as opposed to only 0.032 for the off-diagonal elements. Hence, greater diagonal aggregation bias is empirically tolerable.

The magnitude of the $a_i(t)$ term

Observe that

$$\alpha_i(t) = \text{cov}\left[\frac{d\log m_c}{dt}, \frac{m_c}{Em_c}(\mu_{ic} - \bar{\mu}_i)\right] = \theta_i \rho_i \left(\text{var}\frac{d\log m_c}{dt}\right)^{1/2},$$

where ρ_i is the correlation coefficient between $m_c(\mu_{ic} - \bar{\mu}_i)/Em_c$ and $d\log m_c/dt$ in the consumer population and where θ_i is the positive square root of

$$\theta_i^2 = \frac{1}{(Em_c)^2} E\left[m_c^2(\mu_{ic} - \bar{\mu}_i)^2\right].$$

Hence, $\alpha_i(t)$ is a nonrandom function of time, which can be expressed as a multiple, $\theta_i \rho_i$, of the standard deviation of the logarithmic income rates of change across consumers. It could be observed at this point that the sums over i of $\alpha_i(t)$, $\beta_i(t)$, $\gamma_{ij}(t)$, $\rho_{ij}\theta_i$, and $\rho_i\theta_i$ are all zero, while the sum of $\gamma_{ij}(t)$ over j also is zero. The coefficient θ_i is a dispersion measure of the ith marginal budget share across consumers, in the sense that it is a non-negative number which vanishes if the μ_{ic} values for this i are equal to $\bar{\mu}_i$ with unit probability. The dispersion measure is weighted towards the rich through the squared income weighting of the squared discrepancies between μ_{ic} and $\bar{\mu}_i$.

The nature of the connection between $\alpha_i(t)$ and income distribution is clear from the fact that $\text{var}(d\log m_c/dt)$ and therefore $\alpha_i(t)$ vanish when all incomes change proportionately. As Sonnenschein (1973) has shown, proportional income distribution is a weaker assumption than aggregate demand integrability. An alternative manner in which $\alpha_i(t)$ could be zero is if either θ_i or ρ_i were zero. In the rest of this subsection we shall consider assumptions under which ρ_i is zero. Hence, those assumptions (which are unrelated to income proportionality) can be used in cases in which income proportionality is an inappropriate assumption. The intent of this subsection's discussion of potential assumption structures is to suggest that the term $\alpha_i(t)$ typically will be small. In fact, we suspect that even if none of the assumptions discussed in this section was applicable, the *complete* global remainder term (3.24) still commonly would be small. By Schwartz's inequality we know that $\text{cov}(v_c, k_{ic})$ is bounded by $[\text{var}(v_c)\,\text{var}(k_{ic})]^{1/2}$. We would expect this bound to be small relative to Em_c in a developed economy in which the variability that induces randomness into (v_c, k_{ic}) is small relative to Em_c. Hence $\text{cov}(v_c, k_{ic})/Em_c$ typically will be small.

Theil has aggregated the relative price version of the Rotterdam model over consumers. His derivation could be restructured and reinterpreted to prove that the entire term (3.24) is of stochastic order $o_p(1)$. That desirable result would be considerably stronger than ours below. However, Theil's assumptions are far too strong for our purposes and inherently accept a particular parameterization of (3.18). We shall, however, implicitly use Theil's stronger assumptions with the model's alternative relative price version.

Although assumption 3.1 will be accepted throughout our analysis, a further more restrictive assumption will be used solely in the remainder of this subsection. That assumption can be viewed as consistent with the two-stage sampling procedure (discussed previously) in which income paths are sampled independently of tastes.

Assumption B1. For each $t \in T$ and each $c = 1, \ldots, N$, the random vector s_c is stochastically independent of $m_c(t)$.

Assumption B1 is a stochastic analog to the conventional assumption that income does not appear in the consumer's utility function. This stochastic assumption is used also by Green (1964, pp. 66–77). Nevertheless, one would expect that some of the factors affecting the consumer's intertemporal income prospects may also affect his tastes. Consider, for example, hereditary and environmental factors. Hence, assumption B1 (which we shall not maintain) is not weak.

We now consider an additional assumption.

Assumption B2. At any $t \in T$, the logarithmic rate of change of the cth randomly drawn consumer's income, $d \log m_c / dt$, is stochastically independent of his logarithmic level of income $\log m_c(t)$. We also assume that $\log m_c(t)$ is a differentiable second-order stochastic process. That is to say, we assume that $E(\log m_c(t))^2$ is finite for all $t \in T$. The value of this assumption can be seen from the following theorem.

Theorem B2. If assumptions B1 and B2 obtain, then $\alpha_i(t)$ is uniformly zero for all $t \in T$.

Proof. Recall that $k_{ic} = m_c(\mu_i(m_c, p, s_c) - \bar{\mu}_i)$. But under assumptions B1 and B2 (s_c, m_c) is stochastically independent of $d \log m_c / dt$. Thus, k_{ic} is stochastically independent of $d \log m_c / dt$, and our theorem follows from (3.25). Q.E.D.

The interpretation of assumption B1 is transparent and has been discussed above. Assumption B2 is a regularity condition on the stochastic process $\log m_c(t)$. We now investigate the class of stochastic processes consistent with that regularity condition, and we argue that the class of admissible processes is large and plausible.

Define the cth consumer's income share by $r_c(t) = m_c(t)/NM$, and let the income share allocation be $r(t) = (r_1(t), \ldots, r_n(t))'$. We shall show that under assumption B2 income shares are generated by a stochastic process having a property resembling a weak local version of the "absolutely fair game" property of martingales.

Property B1. Let $c \in \{1, \ldots, N\}$. Then if assumptions 3.1 and B2 obtain, it follows at any $t \in T$ that[1]

$$E[\,dr_c(t)/dt\,|\,r(t)\,] = 0. \tag{B1}$$

Proof. For the cth drawn consumer, we have that $\log r_c(t) = \log m_c - \log NM$. So

$$\frac{dr_c(t)}{dt} = r_c(t) \frac{d\log m_c}{dt} - \frac{m_c}{(NM)^2} \sum_{k=1}^{N} \frac{dm_k}{dt}$$

$$= r_c(t) \frac{d\log m_c}{dt} - r_c(t) \sum_{k=1}^{N} r_k(t) \frac{d\log m_k}{dt}. \tag{B2}$$

Now let $A(t) = E[d\log m_c/dt\,|\,r(t)]$, which we shall show not to depend upon c. By assumptions 3.1 and B2, $d\log m_c(t)/dt$ is distributed independently of $r_c(t)$, $c = 1, \ldots, N$. Thus, we see that $A(t) = E[d\log m_c(t)/dt]$, which is the same for all $c = 1, \ldots, N$. So from (B2), we find that

$$E[\,dr_c(t)/dt\,|\,r(t)\,] = r_c(t) A(t) \left[1 - \sum_{k=1}^{N} r_k(t)\right] = 0,$$

since $\sum_{k=1}^{N} r_k(t) = 1$.   Q.E.D.

By property B1 the cth consumer's expected rate of change in income share conditional upon the current income share allocation $r(t)$ is zero, regardless of the current income distribution. This condition appears to be reasonable in a stable capitalistic economy. We now demonstrate that the

---

[1] Strictly speaking, all results on conditional expectations should be followed by the qualifications [a.s.].

above property of the stochastic income distribution would be satisfied if $r(t)$ were *any* vector valued continuous time martingale.

Following Breiman (1968, p. 300), we shall say that $r(t)$ is a vector valued martingale, if $E[r(t)|r(\tau), \tau \leq t_0] = r(t_0)$ for all t_0, $t \geq 0$ such that $t_0 \leq t$. We shall prove that this condition is stronger than condition (B1). This result is stated below as property B2 of assumption B2.

Property B2. Let $c \in \{1, \ldots, N\}$ and assume that there exists an integrable random variable Y such that

$$|[r_c(t+\Delta t) - r_c(t)]/\Delta t| \leq Y \quad [\text{a.s.}] \tag{B3}$$

for all $(t, \Delta t)$ such that $\Delta t > 0$ and $t, t + \Delta t \in T$. If $r(t)$ is a continuous time vector valued martingale, then condition (B1) obtains.

Proof. Since $r(t)$ is a martingale, we know that for each $c = 1, \ldots, N$ $E[r_c(t+\Delta t)|r(t)] = r_c(t)$ for all $(t, \Delta t)$ such that $\Delta t > 0$ and $t, t + \Delta t \in T$. Hence, we can determine that $E[r_c(t+\Delta t) - r_c(t)|r(t)] = r_c(t) - r_c(t) = 0$. Thus, we have that

$$E\big[(r_c(t+\Delta t) - r_c(t))/\Delta t \,|\, r(t)\big] = 0. \tag{B4}$$

Now $[r_c(t+\Delta t) - r_c(t)]/\Delta t \xrightarrow{\text{a.s.}} dr_c(t)/dt$ as $\Delta t \to 0$, since $r_c(t)$ is differentiable. Taking the limit of (B4) as $\Delta t \to 0$, we acquire (B1) from (B3) and the Conditional Form of the Lebesgue Dominated Convergence Theorem (see, for example, Tucker, 1967, p. 216). Q.E.D.

It should be observed that the converse of property B2 is not true. Neither property B1 nor assumption B2 implies that $r(t)$ is a martingale. So conditions (B1) is *weaker* than the widely used martingale property. In fact, our property (B1) is much weaker than the familiar martingale property. Heuristically, our condition (B1) tells us that the cth consumer's expected (although not necessarily actual) differential income share change is independent of his current share. The martingale property would establish independence between his expected future differential share changes and *all* of his past income share experience.

The above derivation and discussion of properties B1 and B2 is intended to suggest that assumption B2 is not unreasonable. In fact, the class of admissible processes $m_c(t)$ defined by assumption B2 is large and includes many of the most widely used stochastic processes. Consider, for example, property B3 of assumption B2.

Property B3. Let assumption 3.1 obtain, and let $\log m_c(t) = f(t) + x_c(t)$, where $f(t)$ is *any* nonstochastic function of time and $x_c(t)$ is *any* differentiable stationary Gaussian process. Then $\log m_c(t)$ satisfies assumption B2.

Proof. By example 1 on p. 138 of Hoel, Port, and Stone (1972), it follows immediately that $d \log m_c(t)/dt$ is uncorrelated with $\log m_c(t)$ for all $t \in T$, since any Gaussian process is a second-order process. But by Hoel, Port, and Stone (1972, p. 139), the derivative of a Gaussian process is also Gaussian. Our property follows immediately. Q.E.D.

Our Gaussian assumption is used only to acquire a "strict sense" property. If we were satisfied with a "wide sense" property, we would acquire the same result with the Gaussian assumption replaced by the very weak assumption that $(x(t))^2$ has finite expectation for all $t \in T$. For the difference between strict sense and wide sense properties of stochastic processes, see Doob (1953, p. 77).

Of course, the converse of property B3 is not true. We see again that assumption B2 imposes reasonable conditions on $m_c(t)$. It is interesting to observe that in nonlinear models with fixed coefficients, similar restrictions on the sequences of explanatory variables is required, but then only to assure consistency of one's estimates. See Malinvaud's (1970a) condition (v) on p. 331. Although Malinvaud's results are for nonlinear generalized least squares, we shall show that similar regularity conditions are needed with the nonlinear MLE. We now have considered two alternative assumption structures which are sufficient for $\alpha_i(t)$ to be zero. Necessary conditions would be much weaker. We believe that $\alpha_i(t)$ typically will be small.

B3. The Rotterdam model specification

B3.1. Derivation of eq. (3.29).

Integrating (3.28) (under our assumptions) with respect to time from t to $\bar{t}$, we get that for $i = 1, \ldots, n$

$$\int_t^{\bar{t}} W_i \frac{d \log Q_i}{dt} dt = \int_t^{\bar{t}} \bar{\mu}_i \frac{d \log \overline{M}}{dt} dt + \sum_{j=1}^{n} \int_t^{\bar{t}} \bar{\pi}_{ij} \frac{d \log p_j}{dt} dt. \quad \text{(B5)}$$

We now shall define $\overline{W}_i, i = 1, \ldots, n$, such that

$$\int_t^{\bar{t}} W_i (d \log Q_i / dt) dt = \overline{W}_i \int_t^{\bar{t}} (d \log Q_i / dt) dt,$$

so that

$$\int_t^{\bar{t}} W_i(\mathrm{d}\log Q_i/\mathrm{d}t)\,\mathrm{d}t = \overline{W}_i\mathrm{D}Q_{it}. \tag{B6}$$

If $\mathrm{d}\log Q_i/\mathrm{d}t$ is positive over $(t,\bar{t})$, as is most common for normal goods, the Mean Value Theorem for Integrals (Buck, 1965, p. 106) assures us that there exists $t^*\in(t,\bar{t})$ such that $\overline{W}_i = W_i(t^*)$. In general, we can expect $\overline{W}_i$ to lie in a local neighborhood of $W_i(t)$ and $W_i(\bar{t})$, regardless of the size of $\mathrm{d}\log Q_i/\mathrm{d}t$. Hence, for small Δt we can approximate $\overline{W}_i$ by W_{it}^*. Applying similar reasoning to the right-hand side of (B5), the right-hand side becomes

$$\bar{\mu}_i \int_t^{\bar{t}} \frac{\mathrm{d}\log \overline{M}}{\mathrm{d}t}\,\mathrm{d}t + \sum_{j=1}^n \bar{\pi}_{ij}\mathrm{D}p_{jt},$$

where $\bar{\mu}_i$ and $\bar{\pi}_{ij}$ are evaluated at t. Also, by similar reasoning and by the results on p. 332 of Theil (1971), we find that $\mathrm{D}\overline{M}_t$ provides a finite change approximation to $\int_t^{\bar{t}}(\mathrm{d}\log \overline{M}/\mathrm{d}t)\,\mathrm{d}t$. Then (3.29) follows from this result and results (B5) and (B6). Q.E.D.

B3.2. Properties of assumption 3.3

Assumption 3.3 does not exclude sample paths of (3.30) and (3.31) exhibiting either increasing or decreasing trends or even exhibiting cycles in response to variations in $m_c(t)$ and $p(t)$ over time. Consider, for example, the processes $z(t)=Zt+c$ and $x(t)=X\cos\lambda_1 t + Y\sin\lambda_2 t + k$, $t\in T$, where $(c,k,\lambda_1,\lambda_2)>0$ are constants, and (X,Y,Z) are random variables with zero means. Furthermore, *all* stationary stochastic processes (including the widely used stationary Gaussian process) and many widely used nonstationary processes have constant mean functions (including the Wiener process or Brownian motion, martingales, and symmetric random walks).

In fact *any* arbitrary function of time is a sample path of any of an infinite number of stochastic processes having constant mean function. Suppose, for example, we seek some arbitrary path $f(t)$. Then consider the process $x(t)$ having path $f(t)$ with probability $\frac{1}{2}$ and path $-f(t)$ with probability $\frac{1}{2}$, so that $Ex(t)=0$ for all $t\in T$. Use of assumption 3.3 would be somewhat analogous to the use of uniform priors in Bayesian statistics, since it would impose no prior tendency in any predetermined direction. However, it should be recognized that if we were to accept assumption 3.3, we would pass from the purely theoretical result (3.18) to a parameterized special case.

Although we shall not maintain assumption 3.3, we shall consider the implications of its exact satisfaction. Since our approach is designed for use in the usual case in which a community utility function need not exist, we would hope that assumption 3.3 need not imply Gorman's (necessary and sufficient) conditions for the existence of a community utility function. This possibility can be dispelled by the counterexample of a population of Cobb–Douglas consumers having different Cobb–Douglas utility functions (different parameters). Engel curves then will not be parallel, violating Gorman's conditions. But if all consumers had constant income shares in community income, the income weighted average of the microcoefficients of any subset of the consumers would be constant over time. Taking the probability limit as the number of consumers in the subset go to infinity, we would find that the macrocoefficients would be constant, and assumption 3.3 would be satisfied.

We also wonder whether assumption 3.3 implies homotheticity of preferences or any other such implausible restrictions on preferences. Again we provide a counterexample. Let all consumers have identical tastes with nonlinear Engel curves. We immediately have contradicted homotheticity. We place no further restrictions on preferences. Let relative prices remain constant over time, but let price levels vary (nonstochastically and proportionately) over time such that $m_c(t)$ divided by a numeraire price is generated by any arbitrary strong-sense stationary stochastic process. The macroparameters again can be shown to be constants. Recall that each consumer's marginal budget shares and Slutsky coefficients depend solely upon relative prices and numeraire-price-deflated income. Hence, our macroparameters are the mean functions of stochastic processes having identical marginal distributions at all t. Constancy of the macroparameters follows immediately. The purpose of this counterexample is to illustrate that constancy of the macroparameters does not depend exclusively upon preferences. The macroparameters are the mean functions of the stochastic processes (3.30) and (3.31), which depend *jointly* upon the price paths and the income stochastic process as well as upon the tastes of infinite consumers and upon the random vector s_c. Also, observe that assumption 3.3 depends upon these *actual* joint distributions and paths, not upon every possible such joint distribution and path.

B3.3. The Rotterdam model's integrability properties

As we have seen in section B1, we have no reason to believe that (3.18) is or should be integrable. Hence, we have no reason to believe that any empirical specification of our approximation to (3.18) is or should be integrable. Yet the integrability properties of the Rotterdam model have been the subject of the existing theoretical work on the model. Therefore we shall explore those properties in this section. We shall see that (3.29) will be integrable only under extraordinary conditions; but in theorem B1 we already have seen that *even the general theoretical construct (3.18)* will be integrable only under similar extraordinary conditions.

The lack of a correspondence between the model and an integrable aggregate demand system could severely limit the model's usefulness if it prevented the model from forecasting Q_{t+1}. But no such problem exists. The model is designed to forecast value share transitions; see Theil (1975, p. 39). Hence, if we know the value shares for period t, we can forecast next period's value shares and thereby Q_{t+1} for given M_{t+1} and p_{t+1}.

The existing results on the model generally were deduced from its limit as the finite changes "approach" differentials. We delete ε_{it} from (3.29) and replace the finite changes with differentials to get that

$$W_i \mathrm{d}\log Q_i = \bar{\mu}_i \left[\mathrm{d}\log M - \sum_{k=1}^{n} W_k \mathrm{d}\log p_k \right]$$
$$+ \sum_{j=1}^{n} \bar{\pi}_{ij} \mathrm{d}\log p_j, \qquad i = 1, \ldots, n.$$

Yoshihara (1969) proved the following theorem, which is central (in one form or another) to the existing theoretical results on the Rotterdam model. Although we shall consider the implications of this theorem in detail, perhaps it should be evident immediately that the widely discredited possibility of existence of a community utility function must provide a conspicuously poor criterion for judging a demand model. This fact is now widely recognized by theoreticians. See, for example, footnote 1 of Willig (1976).

Theorem B3. The system of equations (B7) is origin-closed integrable to a community utility function only at those parameter values for which (B7) is origin-closed integrable to a Cobb–Douglas *community* utility function.

Yoshihara's proof (applied to his aggregate data) was derived in terms of the model's relative price version. But the proof is equally as applicable to the absolute price version. Although Yoshihara's was the first published proof, other proofs now exist. McFadden (1964) has shown that the result can be weakened slightly if the origin-closed condition is dropped.

We shall define the "feasible parameter set" to be the set of admissible parameter values satisfying the theoretical macrocoefficient restrictions of theorem 3.2. The Cobb–Douglas demand system satisfies (B7) only on a proper subset of that feasible parameter set, although our theoretical foundations obtain *everywhere* on the feasible parameter set. In fact it is easily shown that (B7) is integrable (to a Cobb–Douglas demand system) only on a negligible *Lebesgue measure zero* subset of the feasible parameter set. We see from inspection of the feasible parameter set that the number of free parameters in that set far exceeds the number of free parameters of a Cobb–Douglas system. Hence, it follows immediately that the Cobb–Douglas result can obtain only on a parameter subspace having lower dimension than that of the admissible parameter set itself. Thus, by theorem B1 the model is integrable only on that lower dimensional (and thereby Lebesgue product measure zero) section of the feasible parameter set. Although theorem B1 is correct, it informs us of the model's properties (such as unitary income elasticities) almost nowhere (in the language of measure theory).

To impute the result of theorem B1 to the model *in general* is analogous to basing a conclusion on an event which has probability measure zero. Furthermore, any model can be reduced to an absurdity by imposing additional severe restrictions on the parameters. For the Cobb–Douglas properties to apply to the model's applications, users of the Rotterdam model would have had to impose parameter constraints sufficient to restrict the model to the Cobb–Douglas subset of the feasible parameter set. This has never been done.

It is far more instructive to consider the complement of the previously (and correctly) analyzed, but negligible, Lebesgue measure zero Cobb–Douglas parameter subset. The model is not integrable on that complement, and hence the model is not integrable "almost everywhere". This fact appears to have been recognized by Deaton (1974a, 1974b). But our theoretical macroparameter restrictions, provided by theorem 3.2, are implied under assumptions 3.1 and 3.2 by *micro* integrability. Those restrictions do not result from or imply aggregate integrability, and they were acquired under assumptions which are vastly weaker than those necessary and sufficient for aggregate integrability.

From our previous results and discussions we see now that the properties of the Rotterdam model are closely related to implications of highly general economic theory. In general, neither the *theoretical* construct (3.18) nor *any* aggregate demand system will be origin-closed integrable except in a pathological case. As seen in theorem B1, the exceptional case obtains when all consumers' income elasticities for each good are unity. Analogously, the Rotterdam model's aggregate "differential form" (B7) will not be origin-closed integrable except on a Lebesgue measure zero subset of the model's feasible parameter set. As seen in theorem B1, the exceptional case obtains when a Cobb–Douglas community utility function exists (in which case the aggregate income elasticity for each good is unity). Furthermore, we have seen that aggregate integrability of general theoretical demand systems (as well as of the Rotterdam model) remains implausible when the origin-closed assumption is removed. But our theoretical system (3.18), *unlike* an aggregate demand system, has the known global properties provided by theorem 3.2 whenever our weak assumptions 3.1 and 3.2 are maintained; and the Rotterdam model locally approximates (3.18) at *any* point in the model's feasible parameter set (not just within the Lebesgue measure zero Cobb–Douglas subset). We do not "approximate" aggregate integrability: we do not use it, need it, or accept it at all.

Although macro integrability now has been shown to be irrelevant to our results, one still might ask whether micro integrability could imply implausible restrictions on the Rotterdam model; at the micro level, integrability *is* a reasonable admissibility conditions. To apply theorem B1 or any of its variants to the micro system (3.14), its microcoefficients must have constant sample paths (independent of variations in $p(t)$ and $m_c(t)$ over time). But the microcoefficient sample paths are not constant. They can vary with variations in both $p(t)$ and $m_c(t)$ over time. As we have observed in tautology 3.1, the macrocoefficients would be exactly constant (which we do not assume anyway) if and only if the stochastic processes (3.30) and (3.31) had constant mean functions. But as we have seen earlier, constancy of the mean function of those processes does not imply constancy of the processes themselves, and it certainly does not imply constancy of the microcoefficients (either over consumers or over time). Hence, the critique does not apply at the micro level.

Alternatively, one might attempt to apply the Rotterdam model directly to the behavior of a single consumer simply by setting $N = 1$ and viewing the single consumer as the total population. But the model was derived by taking stochastic limits as N goes to infinity. If one were to set $N = 1$, none of our stochastic convergence results would obtain. Hence, we would be left with our original stochastically varying nonstationary microcoefficients, and we therefore would not be able to apply the argument of the model's critics.

B4. Locally integrable models

B4.1. Flexibility of locally integrable models

Recently a number of models have appeared having sufficient parameters to provide a second-order local approximation to an arbitrary community utility function. They include the translog, generalized Cobb–Douglas, and generalized Leontief models along with a number of other models based upon such quadratic transformations. In terms of the aggregate demand system (rather than an unobservable cardinal utility function), these models provide a first-order local approximation. But we have seen that the Rotterdam model also has sufficient parameters for a local first-order approximation (although to a different theoretical construct). Hence, claims of the superior "flexibility" of these models are not readily assessed in terms of the flexibility of the functional forms themselves. We shall have to consider the models' integrability properties.

The flexibility of these models is severely restricted, and in some cases totally destroyed (as with the translog), if global integrability is imposed. Hence, users of these models generally seek only local integrability. As a result, we shall refer to these models as the class of "locally integrable" models. The approximation properties of these models are known only if integrability is imposed a priori at no more than *a single infinitesimal point* of approximation. If we insist *in advance* (either through an understood agreement, to be enforced as an admissibility condition after the estimates become available, or through prior parameter restrictions) that such a model must be integrable over some predetermined *finite* region, then the model's abilities as an arbitrary first-order approximator are lost. Yet in fact users of these models frequently (implicitly or explicitly) do seek integrability over the finite region (preferably the convex closure) of the observed data, since the model's behavior otherwise is suspect.

Blackorby, Primont, and Russell (1977) have shown that if integrability is required a priori over any finite region, the models become subject to serious theoretical limitations in their ability to model the preferences even of the representative consumer. These limitations become especially troublesome if separability conditions are imposed, as is commonly desirable when the number of free parameters otherwise would be large. Alternatively, our g-hypo model in Chapter 6 is both flexible and *globally* integrable. But g-hypo, like the locally integrable models, does assume the existence of a representative consumer, and hence is better suited to maintaining and using theory (for its functional regularity conditions) than to testing it. Alternatively, if integrability over a finite region is not required in advance, the functional behavior of the "locally integrable" models can be troublesome. See Wales (1977).

Furthermore, we know that the representative consumer and his community utility function exist over any finite region only under entirely implausible conditions. Those who claim superior properties for the class of locally integrable functional forms do so on the grounds that such models permit aggregate integrability to a larger class of community utility functions over the region of the data. It is a strange convention which leads to selection of a model on the basis of its flexibility under entirely implausible conditions. The fact that the Rotterdam model is restrictive on a Lebesgue measure zero subset of its parameter space (on which even theory dictates restrictiveness) is hardly a serious limitation. But in the usual and truly important case in which the representative consumer does *not* exist, the class of locally integrable models, unlike the Rotterdam model, has only a distant and barely understood link with economic theory.

B4.2. Tests of theory

It has widely been asserted that empirical tests of the theoretical results of theorem 3.2 with the Rotterdam model implicitly test for the existence of a double log community utility function. See, for example, Christensen, Jorgenson, and Lau (1975) and Phlips (1974, pp. 56, 58, 89, and 94). As we have seen, those assertions are not correct. However, tests of theory with the locally integrable models *do* test for aggregate integrability which we have seen is a theoretically pathological case. Hence, the locally integrable models are well designed to test for inherently implausible theoretical restrictions, which obtain only under far stronger conditions than our assumptions 3.1 and 3.2. Furthermore, the *prior* imposition of integrability of the popular translog functional form over the local but finite region of the data is no easy task, if even possible, without maintaining Cobb–Douglas preferences, and integrability cannot be expected to obtain if not imposed.

It is important to understand that tests for macro integrability of locally integrable models are tests for fundamentally different conditions from the necessary *micro* integrability conditions provided by our theorem 3.2. We test for the results of theorem 3.2 with the Rotterdam model. In testing integrability with the locally integrable models, the maintained hypothesis is the existence of the models themselves. But here the necessary and sufficient conditions are Gorman's extremely strong conditions of linear Engel curves which are parallel for all consumers. The null hypothesis merely adds micro theory to Gorman's Engel curve restrictions. Before we even consider the mild transition from the maintained to the null hypothesis, we should consider the approximating properties of the patently unacceptable *maintained* hypothesis, on which the existence of the locally integrable models themselves depend. The alternative to the maintained hypothesis is rejection of the model itself.

Theoreticians accept micro integrability and (strongly) question parallel linear Engel curves. Hence, the interesting hypothesis test, relative to the necessary and sufficient conditions for macro integrability, would be to maintain the weak assumption of micro integrability and test the null hypothesis of parallel linear Engel curves. But that which is approximated by the locally integrable models exists if and only if parallel linear Engel curves obtain. Hence users of those models must *maintain* the interesting null hypothesis. In that case the above procedure would lead to equality of the null and maintained hypothesis, rendering rejection logically impossible. The locally integrable models *cannot test for macro integrability* at all. The most that can be done in testing theory with such models is to maintain the strong assumption of parallel linear Engel curves and test the weak assumption of micro integrability. This, of course, is precisely the reverse of the interesting economic test and is methodologically convoluted. Under these circumstances it is not surprising that tests of "theory" with these models have rejected the restrictions (such as symmetry) required to permit adequate precision of the models' parameter estimators. See, for example, Christensen, Jorgenson, and Lau (1975) and Berndt, Diewert, and Darrough (1977). By contrast the Rotterdam model's symmetry restrictions have been accepted empirically by Theil (1971, 1975) and Deaton (1974a).

APPENDIX C

APPENDIX TO CHAPTER 4

C1. Eisenpress nonlinear FIML program

C1.1. Introduction

In Part II we compute full information maximum likelihood estimates of some deeply nonlinear systems of equations. To provide the ability to complete that research, we invested considerable time and resources, with the assistance of Kenneth Kopecky, John Davison, Harry Eisenpress, and John Greenstadt, in the construction of a sophisticated nonlinear FIML program. In this appendix we provide general user information for that program. We have found the program to be particularly powerful and reliable in the estimation of a large number of unusually complicated nonlinear systems.

Our objective in this programming effort was to provide a very powerful, reliable, and user-oriented program. It was our objective to provide a program that would converge as certainly as possible with as large a class of models as possible and with as littler user effort as possible. We were willing to sacrifice execution time for user convenience and reliability. Although newer algorithms are capable of achieving more rapid convergence in some cases, we found that our objectives were best served by extending the capabilities of the highly sophisticated coding and nested numerical analysis techniques contained within the existing Eisenpress nonlinear FIML program.

The Eisenpress program requires and analytically computes third-order partial derivatives (although only second-order partials are needed when the model is in reduced form). Newer algorithms do not require such high-order derivatives, and hence can converge in less computing time, when they do converge. However, the use of the analytic derivatives in the

Eisenpress program along with the use of unusually sophisticated programming and contingent numerical analysis techniques provides high reliability and user convenience. We have extended those capabilities substantially.

C1.2. General information

The Eisenpress–Greenstadt package is an IBM user-contributed program which estimates the parameters of a nonlinear equation or of a system of such equations. The equation or system may be nonlinear in the parameters and/or in the independent or dependent variables. In a system of equations, the system is estimated simultaneously by full information maximum likelihood (FIML). A nonlinear single equation least squares (NLSQ) estimation stage is available to provide initial conditions for the nonlinear FIML estimation stage. The NLSQ stage should be bypassed for models in structural form, since this stage provides a consistent estimator only for models in reduced form. If the user does not wish to use the NLSQ stage, he may supply his own estimates for the initial conditions of the nonlinear FIML stage.

The system consists of two programs, one preparatory in nature, the other for the actual solutions; the PL-1 Optimizing Compiler and Linkage Editor are used as well. The preparatory program, DIRIV, accepts the analytic statement of the problem and generates PL-1 code for the equations and their derivatives as a subroutine called CHAIN; FORMAC symbolic mathematical subroutines are used by DIRIV to perform formal analytic differentiation and simplification. CHAIN is then compiled and link-edited to the second program, NLFI, which contains the algorithm for the numerical solution of the estimation problem. NLFI is then executed.

General documentation for the original unrevised program is provided in a publication of the SHARE Program Library Agency. This appendix contains the program description with:
    (a) an outline of the relevant mathematical and statistical information,
    (b) restrictions,
    (c) range and precision information,
    (d) structure of input decks (Decks A and B) for control, equations, and data,
    (e) interpretation of output, and
    (f) listings of job control language and cataloged procedures.

The Eisenpress–Greenstadt program is very powerful, but any nonlinear FIML estimator inherently can be very expensive to use. Nonlinear FIML is the most sophisticated nonlinear structural estimator known, and it is the only available estimator providing asymptotically efficient estimates for nonlinear structural models (see, for example, Jorgenson and Laffont, 1974). Furthermore, our extended Eisenpress–Greenstadt program is the most powerful of the currently existing nonlinear FIML programs. However, the price for this sophistication can be formidable execution time, especially for models in structural rather than reduced form. Timing can range from a minute or two, including compilation and link-edit, to an hour or more, depending upon initial conditions and analytic complexity. Large systems may require regions in excess of one million bytes. The program's use should be limited to problems that are intractable to lesser means; in those cases, analytic techniques should be used as far as possible to simplify the problem prior to submission to the program's treatment. With models of moderate complexity, Wymer's (1977) RESIMUL program is well worth trying.

We have made many substantial changes to the Eisenpress program's processing of equations, differentiation of equations, and to the search algorithm itself. However, the program is based upon the same fundamental mathematical algorithm. For a discussion of that algorithm, see Eisenpress and Greenstadt (1966). The supporting statistical theory is contained in Chapter 4.

Since we have revised and extended the program substantially, the original documentation on the output is only suggestive of the general features of the current output. The current job control language (JCL) is totally different from the originally documented JCL. However, to facilitate use, the current JCL has been incorporated into cataloged procedures. The numerical (Deck B) input is the same as that used in the original program except for the insertion of the desired convergence criterion (commonly 10^{-7}) between the fourth and fifth entries on the first card of Deck B.

C1.3. Limitations

Our version of the program will treat a system of 20 equations in 50 variables with 80 observations per variable. The analytic expression for each equation can be up to 2000 characters in length, including imbedded blanks. As many as 20 parameters per equation are permitted. The revised program provides comprehensive messages indicating the local behavior of the system over the region searched. The algorithm is strictly uphill and possesses only two failure modes. It will fail if the model is locally unidentified or if the implied reduced form (and therefore the model itself) does not exist uniquely in the neighborhood being searched. An appropriate message will be printed in either case, and new initial conditions should be tried. It should be noted, however, that repeated failure of such jobs may occur, since both failure modes tend to indicate extremely poor model behavior locally and sometimes globally. In such cases the model should be respecified or other data used or both.

C1.4. Error codes and failure modes

In addition to the two internal failure modes, execution can be terminated through external system (ONCODE) intervention. This occurs in two cases. The system terminates execution if the logarithm of a nonpositive number is encountered at the initial conditions or if division by zero is encountered anywhere (ONCODE = 320). The most likely cause of an oncode termination is a parameter which has become too small (an underflow) and can no longer be distinguished from zero. To avoid such terminations at the beginning of NLFI's execution, do not use exact zeros as initial conditions for parameters. If the termination should occur after the first iteration, restart the program with the initial conditions determined as follows: increase any parameters that have become very small while simultaneously using the latest estimates as initial conditions for the remaining parameters. When the source of the problem is not immediately evident from the latest parameter estimates, the precise parameters requiring a change in value can be determined by locating the statement where execution was terminated. The statement number will be printed out with the error message. If the error occurred within NLFI, the listing of NLFI can be useful. Otherwise (and most likely), the error occurred within CHAIN, which is printed out prior to every execution. Sometimes these terminations indicate that a binding inequality constraint exists on the parameters, and should be imposed by substitution. For example, some models become undefined if a parameter, θ, becomes negative. In that case, eliminate θ by substituting $\theta = \phi^2$ and estimate ϕ.

The cataloged procedures used with this program do not use PL-1 compiler optimization, since the optimizer contains unresolved bugs. But optimization commonly decreases execution time by about 30 percent.

With complicated jobs, the NOPT compiler parameter should be overridden with OPT(TIME) to permit optimization. If optimization fails, either the "Protection Exception" or the "Privileged Operation Exception" oncode message will be printed during execution. In that case, the user *must* return to the cataloged procedure's default use of the more expensive NOPT (no optimization) option.

C1.5. Input design

When coding equations for Deck A (analytic input), the subscripts for the parameter vector should be assigned so that the parameters with the highest degree of nonlinearity in the model receive the lowest parameter subscript. This assignment is essential for the successful compilation of complicated models and also can substantially reduce execution time. If the same equations are to be estimated more than once (e.g. with different data), the analytic output from DIRIV should be stored during the first run. If the model possesses equality or inequality side restrictions on the parameters, the restrictions should be eliminated by substitution. For example, if a parameter, θ, must satisfy $-2 \leq \theta \leq 2$, then eliminate θ by substituting $\theta = 2 \sin \phi$ into the model, and estimate ϕ.

C1.6. Job control language

The following JCL should be used to execute the cataloged procedures EISENSET, EISENADD, and EISENCLG to perform differentiation in multiple steps, followed by compilation, link editing, and execution of NLFI.

```
//jobname     JOB     job accounting information
//stepname    EXEC    EISENSET
//SYSIN       DD      *
/*
//stepname    EXEC    EISENADD            (repeat this step for
                                           each equation)
//SYSIN       DD      *
             Deck A control card          (repeat identical card
                                           for each
                                           EISENADD step)
```

Card containing only the   (increment at each
   equation number   step)
Equation statement as described
  for Deck A in SHARE document
/*
//stepname   EXEC   EISENCLG
//LKED.SYSIN   DD *
     INCLUDE A (EISEN2)
/*
//GO.SYSIN DD *
     Deck B as described in SHARE document, with
     convergence criterion added.
/*

The code for CHAIN may be cataloged and saved by including the following DD override cards within the above deck setup.

After // EXEC EISENSET card, add:

//INPUT2 DD DSN = user supplied dsname,
//   DISP = (NEW,PASS),
//   SPACE = (CYL,(1, 1),RLSE), UNIT = TS03330,
//   DCB = (RECFM = FB,LRECL = 80,BLKSIZE = 3120)

After each // EXEC EISENADD card, add:

//INPUT2 DD DSN = dsname supplied above,
//   DISP = (MOD,PASS)

After // EXEC EISENCLG card, add:

//PL1L.SYSIN DD DSN = dsname of INPUT2,
//   DISP = (OLD,CATLG,DELETE)

To reuse derivatives stored by the preceding, create a single step job executing only the EISENCLG step. Use the same deck setup as for the EISENCLG step without stored derivatives, but follow the "//stepname

EXEC EISENCLG" card by the following card:

//PL1L.SYSIN   DD   DSN=dsname above, DISP=OLD

Other possibilities also may be tried for more specialized purposes, such as to add one or more equations to a previously stored model (use EISENADD as above, followed by EISENCLG), or to store a load module of the completed model (rather than just its uncompiled derivatives) for repeated use (override LKED.SYSLMOD in EISENCLG to create a member of a PDS, then on later execution use a JOBLIB card to identify the PDS and execute PGM=member name, in order to execute the load module). But the general procedures described above satisfy the objectives of nearly all conventional applications of this program.

C1.7. Cataloged procedures

We now provide listings for the three cataloged procedures used in the above JCL. Parts of these procedures relate explicitly to the Federal Reserve Board's computer systems. The user should adapt these procedures to his own computer system.

The EISENSET procedure

The listing for the EISENSET procedure follows.

```
XXEISENSET PROC
 *** THIS PROCEDURE IS THE FIRST PREPARATORY STEP
 *** FOR THE EISENPRESS FIML PROGRAM. IT CREATES A
 *** DATA SET, INPUT2, TO RECEIVE THE EQUATIONS
 *** OF THE SUBROUTINE CHAIN, TO BE CREATED BY
 *** THE DIFFERENTIATION PROGRAM DIRIV AND COM-
 *** PILED AND LINKED TO THE FIML PROGRAM NLFI
 *** ITSELF.
XX    EXEC PGM=DIRIV
XXSTEPLIB  DD   DSN=FRB.LIBPD,DISP=SHR
XXSYSUT1   DD   DSN=&UT1,UNIT=DKLO,
XX              SPACE=(CYL,(1,1),RLSE),
XX              DCB=(RECFM=F,BLKSIZE=829)
```

```
XXSYSPRINT DD SYSOUT=A
XXINPUT2   DD   DSN=&&INPUT2,DISP=(NEW,PASS),
XX              UNIT=DKLO,
XX   SPACE=(CYL,(1,1),RLSE),
XX   DCB=(RECFM=FB,LRECL=80,BLKSIZE=3120)
```

The EISENADD procedure

The listing for the EISENADD procedure follows.

```
XXEISENADD PROC
*** THIS PROCEDURE CONTINUES THE PREPARATORY STEP
*** FOR THE EISENPRESS FIML PROGRAM, IT CALLS
*** THE DIFFERENTIATION ROUTINE DIRIV TO CREATE
*** EQUATIONS FOR THE DATASET INPUT2. THE CATA-
*** LOGUED PROCEDURE EISENSET MUST BE CALLED TO
*** CREATE INPUT2; THE PRESENT PROCEDURE MUST
*** BE USED TO PROCESS EACH EQUATION.
XX   EXEC PGM=DIRIV
XXSTEPLIB DD DSN=FRB.LIBPD,DISP=SHR
XXSYSUT1   DD DSN=&UT1,UNIT=DKLO,
XX              SPACE=(CYL,(1,1),RLSE),
XX              DCB=(RECFM=F,BLKSIZE=829)
XXSYSPRINT DD SYSOUT=A
XXINPUT2   DD   DSN=&&INPUT2,DISP=(MOD,PASS)
```

The EISENCLG procedure

The listing for the EISENCLG procedure follows.

```
XXEISENCLG PROC
*** THIS PROCEDURE IS THE OPERATIONAL STEP OF THE
*** EISENPRESS FIML PROGRAM. IT COMPILES THE
*** SUBROUTINE CHAIN WHICH HAS BEEN PREPARED BY
*** THE PROCEDURES EISENSET AND EISENADD, AND
*** LINKS THEM INTO THE LOAD MODULE WHICH IS
*** EXECUTED.
```

Appendix C   331

```
XXPL1L EXEC   PGM = IELOAA,
XX            PARM = 'F(I),NSEQ,NOPT,MAR(2,80),OF,GS'
XXSYSIN DD    DSN = &&INPUT2,DISP = (OLD,DELETE)
XXSYSPRINT    DD SYSOUT = A
XXSYSLIN DD   DSNAME = &LOADSET,
XX            DISP = (MOD,PASS),UNIT = DSKLO,
XX            SPACE = (CYL,(5, 1)),
XX            DCB = (RECFM = FB,LRECL = 80,BLKSIZE = 3120)
XXSYSUT1 DD   UNIT = DSKLO,SPACE = (1024,(300,60),,CONTIG),
XX            SEP = (SYSPRINT, SYSLIN),
XX            DCB = BLKSIZE = 1024
```

Program source code

The program consists of two PL-1 procedures. A listing of the latest version of the program is available upon request from Kenneth Kopecky, John Davison, or the author at the Federal Reserve Board. The user is advised to begin with the publically unrevised version of the Eisenpress program and modify the coding to agree with the latest available.

C2. Chapter 4 proofs

Proof of lemma 4.3. By the triangle inequality, it follows that $|X_t - c| \leq |X_t - X_{mt}| + |X_{mt} - c|$. So $[|X_t - c| > \varepsilon] \subset [|X_t - X_{mt}| + |X_{mt} - c| > \varepsilon]$. Then for all $m = 1, 2, \ldots$, we know that

$$P[|X_t - c| > \varepsilon] \leq P[|X_{mt} - c| > \varepsilon - |X_t - X_{mt}|]. \tag{C1}$$

Now since $X_{mt} \xrightarrow{a.s.} X_t$ as $m \to \infty$ uniformly in t, we can choose m_0 such that if $m \geq m_0$, then $|X_{mt} - X_t| < \delta$ [a.s.] uniformly in t for arbitrary $\delta > 0$. Then for any $m \geq m_0$, it follows that $\varepsilon - |X_{mt} - X_t| > \varepsilon - \delta$ [a.s.] uniformly in t, and hence $[|X_{mt} - c| > \varepsilon - |X_t - X_{mt}|] \subset [|X_{mt} - c| > \varepsilon - \delta]$ [a.s.] uniformly in t. So $P[|X_{m_0 t} - c| > \varepsilon - |X_t - X_{m_0 t}|] \leq P[|X_{m_0 t} - c| > \varepsilon - \delta] \to 0$ as $t \to \infty$, and by (C1) it follows that $P[|X_t - c| > \varepsilon] \to 0$ as $t \to \infty$. Q.E.D.

Proof of lemma 4.6. By property 4.1 and assumption 4.1 it follows that $(1/T)\mathcal{G}_T(\boldsymbol{\theta}) \to M(\Omega^{-1})$ as $T \to \infty$. To prove the analogous result for $(1/T)\mathcal{G}_T(\boldsymbol{\theta})$, we observe that by property 4.2 there exists a nonsingular

matrix valued transformation Q such that $(1/T)\mathcal{J}_T(\theta) = \frac{1}{2}Q(\Omega)$. Since $Q(\Omega)$ does not depend upon T, we see immediately $(1/T)\mathcal{J}_T(\theta) \to \frac{1}{2}Q(\Omega)$ as $T \to \infty$.
Q.E.D.

Proof of lemma 4.7. Let $\delta > 0$. Then we see that $[|X_t| > \delta] \subset [|Y_t| > \delta]$. So it follows that $0 \leq P[|X_t| > \delta] \leq P[|Y_t| > \delta] \to 0$ as $t \to \infty$. Hence $P[|X_t| > \delta] \to 0$ as $t \to \infty$.
Q.E.D.

Proof of lemma 4.8. For notational convenience we suppress the T subscript from $\tilde{\gamma}_T$. Now let

$$r_T = \frac{1}{T} \sum_{t=1}^{T} \sum_{r,s=1}^{n} h_{trk}(\tilde{\gamma}) \sigma_{rs} h_{tsj}(\tilde{\gamma}),$$

where $\sigma_{rs} = [S_T]_{rs}$. Then by the multivariate Mean Value Theorem,

$$r_T = \frac{1}{T} \sum_{t=1}^{T} \sum_{r,s=1}^{n} h_{trk}(\gamma_0) \sigma_{rs} h_{tsj}(\gamma_0)$$

$$+ \frac{1}{T} \sum_{t=1}^{T} \sum_{r,s=1}^{n} \frac{\partial}{\partial \gamma'} \left[h_{trk}(\gamma) \sigma_{rs} h_{tsj}(\gamma) \right]_{\gamma = \gamma^*} (\tilde{\gamma} - \gamma_0), \qquad (C2)$$

where γ^* is on the line between γ_0 and $\tilde{\gamma}$. Now

$$\frac{1}{T} \sum_{t=1}^{T} \sum_{r,s=1}^{n} h_{trk}(\gamma_0) \sigma_{rs} h_{tsj}(\gamma_0)$$

$$= \frac{1}{T} \sum_{t=1}^{T} \left. \frac{\partial g_t'}{\partial \gamma_k} \right|_{\gamma = \gamma_0} S_T \left. \frac{\partial g_t}{\partial \gamma_j} \right|_{\gamma = \gamma_0} = [M_T(S_T)]_{kj}$$

$$= [M(\Omega_0^{-1})]_{kj} + o_p(1) \text{ by lemma 4.4} \qquad (C3)$$

Let

$$P_T = \frac{1}{T} \sum_{t=1}^{T} \sum_{r,s=1}^{n} \frac{\partial}{\partial \gamma'} \left[h_{trk}(\gamma) \sigma_{rs} h_{tsj}(\gamma) \right]_{\gamma = \gamma^*} (\tilde{\gamma} - \gamma_0).$$

Then

$$P_T = \frac{1}{T} \sum_{t=1}^{T} \sum_{r,s=1}^{n} \sigma_{rs} h_{trk}(\gamma^*) \left. \frac{\partial h_{tsj}(\gamma)}{\partial \gamma'} \right|_{\gamma = \gamma^*} (\tilde{\gamma} - \gamma_0)$$

$$+ \frac{1}{T} \sum_{t=1}^{T} \sum_{r,s=1}^{n} \sigma_{rs} h_{tsj}(\gamma^*) \left. \frac{\partial h_{trk}(\gamma)}{\partial \gamma'} \right|_{\gamma = \gamma^*} (\tilde{\gamma} - \gamma_0).$$

So

$$0 \leq |P_T| \leq \frac{1}{T} \sum_{t=1}^{T} \sum_{r,s=1}^{n} |\sigma_{rs}| \left| h_{trk}(\gamma^*) \frac{\partial h_{tsj}}{\partial \gamma'} \right|_{\gamma=\gamma^*} |\tilde{\gamma} - \gamma_0|$$

$$+ \frac{1}{T} \sum_{t=1}^{T} \sum_{r,s=1}^{n} |\sigma_{rs}| \left| h_{tsj}(\gamma^*) \frac{\partial h_{trk}}{\partial \gamma'} \right|_{\gamma=\gamma^*} |\tilde{\gamma} - \gamma_0|.$$

But by assumption 4.2, there exists a vector of constants $c \geq 0$ such that

$$\left| h_{trk}(\gamma^*) \frac{\partial h_{tsj}}{\partial \gamma'} \right|_{\gamma=\gamma^*} < c'$$

and

$$\left| h_{tsj}(\gamma^*) \frac{\partial h_{trk}}{\partial \gamma'} \right|_{\gamma=\gamma^*} < c'.$$

So

$$0 \leq |P_T| \leq \frac{2}{T} c' |\tilde{\gamma} - \gamma_0| \sum_{t=1}^{T} \sum_{r,s=1}^{n} |\sigma_{rs}|.$$

Now σ_{rs} does not depend upon t (although it does depend upon T). So $0 \leq |P_T| \leq 2c' |\tilde{\gamma} - \gamma_0| |\Sigma_{r,s=1}^n \sigma_{rs}|$. But $S_T = \Omega_0^{-1} + o_p(1)$. So since $|\cdot|$ is a continuous function, $|\sigma_{rs}| = |[\Omega_0^{-1}]_{rs}| + o_p(1)$. Furthermore, $|\tilde{\gamma} - \gamma_0| = o_p(1)$. So by Slutsky's theorem, it follows that $2c' |\tilde{\gamma} - \gamma_0| |\Sigma_{r,s=1}^n \sigma_{rs}| = o_p(1)$. Hence, by lemma 4.7, $P_T = o_p(1)$. So by (C2) and (C3), we see that $r_T = [M(\Omega_0^{-1})]_{kj} + o_p(1)$.   Q.E.D.

Proof of lemma 4.9. For notational convenience we suppress the T subscript from $\tilde{\theta}_T$ and $\tilde{\gamma}_T$. Then by property 4.3 we can conclude that

$$-\frac{1}{T} d^2 \log L(\theta | y, x)|_{\theta=\tilde{\theta}} = \frac{1}{2} \text{tr}\left[(S_T^{-1} d\Omega)^2 (2 S_T^{-1} N - I) \right]$$

$$- \text{tr}\left[S_T^{-1} d\Omega S_T^{-1} d\tilde{N} \right] + \frac{1}{2} \text{tr}(S_T^{-1} d^2 \tilde{N}), \quad \text{(C4)}$$

where $\tilde{N} = N(\tilde{\gamma})$, and where $d^i \tilde{N} = [d^i N]_{\gamma=\tilde{\gamma}}$ for $i = 1, 2$. Now by lemma 4.1, $\tilde{N} = \Omega_0 + o_p(1)$, while $S_T^{-1} = \Omega_0^{-1} + o_p(1)$. So since the first term on the right of (C4) is a continuous function of $(\tilde{N}, S_T^{-1})$, we see that the first term on the right of (C4) satisfies

$$\frac{1}{2} \text{tr}\left[(S_T^{-1} d\Omega)^2 (2 S_T^{-1} \tilde{N} - I) \right] = \frac{1}{2} \text{tr}(\Omega_0^{-1} d\Omega)^2 + o_p(1). \quad \text{(C5)}$$

Furthermore, by property 4.4, we find that

$$d\tilde{N} = -\frac{1}{T} \sum_{k=1}^{q} \sum_{t=1}^{T} \left[\tilde{\varepsilon}_t \frac{\partial g_t'(\gamma)}{\partial \gamma_k} \bigg|_{\gamma=\tilde{\gamma}} + \frac{\partial g_t(\gamma)}{\partial \gamma_k} \bigg|_{\gamma=\tilde{\gamma}} \tilde{\varepsilon}_t' \right] d\gamma_k, \tag{C6}$$

where $\tilde{\varepsilon}_t = y_t - g_t(\tilde{\gamma})$. But $\tilde{\varepsilon}_t = \varepsilon_t + [g_t(\gamma_0) - g_t(\tilde{\gamma})]$. So

$$\frac{1}{T} \sum_{t=1}^{T} \tilde{\varepsilon}_t \frac{\partial g_t'(\gamma)}{\partial \gamma_k} \bigg|_{\gamma=\tilde{\gamma}}$$

$$= \frac{1}{T} \sum_{t=1}^{T} \varepsilon_t \frac{\partial g_t'}{\partial \gamma_k} \bigg|_{\gamma=\tilde{\gamma}} + \frac{1}{T} \sum_{t=1}^{T} [g_t(\gamma_0) - g_t(\tilde{\gamma})] \frac{\partial g_t'}{\partial \gamma_k} \bigg|_{\gamma=\tilde{\gamma}}. \tag{C7}$$

Now by assumption 4.2 there exists a scalar constant K such that $h_{tik}(\tilde{\gamma}) < K$ uniformly in $t = 1, \ldots, T$. So

$$0 \leq \left| \frac{1}{T} \sum_{t=1}^{T} [g_{tj}(\gamma_0) - g_{tj}(\tilde{\gamma})] h_{tik}(\tilde{\gamma}) \right| \leq \frac{K}{T} \sum_{t=1}^{T} |g_{tj}(\gamma_0) - g_{tj}(\tilde{\gamma})|$$

$$\leq K \max_{t \leq T} |g_{tj}(\gamma_0) - g_{tj}(\tilde{\gamma})|, \quad \text{for } j, k = 1, \ldots, n.$$

By lemmas 4.5 and 4.7 it follows that

$$\frac{1}{T} \sum_{t=1}^{T} [g_t(\gamma_0) - g_t(\tilde{\gamma})] \frac{\partial g_t'}{\partial \gamma_k} \bigg|_{\gamma=\tilde{\gamma}} = o_p(1). \tag{C8}$$

Furthermore, by the multivariate Mean Value Theorem, we know that

$$\frac{1}{T} \sum_{t=1}^{T} \varepsilon_{ti} h_{tjk}(\tilde{\gamma}) = \frac{1}{T} \sum_{t=1}^{T} \varepsilon_{ti} h_{tjk}(\gamma_0)$$

$$+ \left[\frac{1}{T} \sum_{t=1}^{T} \varepsilon_{ti} \frac{\partial h_{tjk}}{\partial \gamma'} \right]_{\gamma=\gamma^*} (\tilde{\gamma} - \gamma_0), \quad \text{for } i, j = 1, \ldots, n, \tag{C9}$$

where γ^* is on the line between γ_0 and $\tilde{\gamma}$. Now by assumption 4.2 $h_{tjk}(\gamma_0)$ is bounded uniformly in t. Hence, by property 4.12, it follows that

$$\frac{1}{T} \sum_{t=1}^{T} \varepsilon_{ti} h_{tjk}(\gamma_0) = o_p(1). \tag{C10}$$

Now by assumption 4.2, $\partial h_{tjk}/\partial \gamma_r$ is bounded uniformly in t ($r = 1, \ldots, n$). So there exists a constant K_1 such that $|\partial h_{tjk}/\partial \gamma_r| < K_1$ for all $t = 1, \ldots, T$. So

$$0 \leq \left| \frac{1}{T} \sum_{t=1}^{T} \varepsilon_{ti} \frac{\partial h_{tjk}}{\partial \gamma_r} \right|_{\gamma=\gamma^*} \leq K_1 \left[\frac{1}{T} \sum_{t=1}^{T} |\varepsilon_{ti}| \right] = K_1 c + o_p(1).$$

by Khintchine's theorem, where $c = E|\varepsilon_{ti}|$. The expectation is taken with respect to the law of ε_t with $\Omega = \Omega_0$. So

$$0 \leq \left\| \left[\frac{1}{T}\sum_{t=1}^{T} \varepsilon_{ti}\frac{\partial h_{tjk}}{\partial \gamma'}\right]_{\gamma=\gamma^*} (\tilde{\gamma}-\gamma_0) \right\| \leq o_p(1).$$

By lemma 4.7,

$$\left[\frac{1}{T}\sum_{t=1}^{T} \varepsilon_{ti}\frac{\partial h_{tjk}}{\partial \gamma'}\right]_{\gamma=\gamma^*} (\tilde{\gamma}-\gamma_0) = o_p(1). \tag{C11}$$

Hence, by (C9), (C10), and (C11), we see that

$$\frac{1}{T}\sum_{t=1}^{T} \varepsilon_{ti}h_{tjk}(\tilde{\gamma}) = o_p(1), \quad \text{for } i,j = 1,\ldots,n.$$

So

$$\frac{1}{T}\sum_{t=1}^{T} \varepsilon_t \frac{\partial g'_t}{\partial \gamma_k}\bigg|_{\gamma=\tilde{\gamma}} = o_p(1). \tag{C12}$$

Then by (C7), (C8), and (C12), it follows that

$$\frac{1}{T}\sum_{t=1}^{T} \tilde{\varepsilon}_t \frac{\partial g'_t(\gamma)}{\partial \gamma_k}\bigg|_{\gamma=\tilde{\gamma}} = o_p(1), \quad k = 1,\ldots,q. \tag{C13}$$

Then obviously it also follows that

$$\frac{1}{T}\sum_{t=1}^{T} \frac{\partial g_t(\gamma)}{\partial \gamma_k}\bigg|_{\gamma=\tilde{\gamma}} \tilde{\varepsilon}'_t = o_p(1), \quad k = 1,\ldots,q. \tag{C14}$$

So, by (C6), (C13), and (C14) we see that $d\tilde{N} = o_p(1)$. But recall that $S_T^{-1} = \Omega_0^{-1} + o_p(1)$. So

$$\text{tr}\left[S_T^{-1} d\Omega S_T^{-1} d\tilde{N}\right] = o_p(1). \tag{C15}$$

We can substitute into property 4.5 to get that

$$d^2\tilde{N} = \frac{1}{T}\sum_{t=1}^{T}\sum_{j,k=1}^{q}\left[2\frac{\partial g_t(\gamma)}{\partial \gamma_j}\bigg|_{\gamma=\tilde{\gamma}}\frac{\partial g'_t(\gamma)}{\partial \gamma_k}\bigg|_{\gamma=\tilde{\gamma}}\right.$$

$$\left.- \tilde{\varepsilon}_t \frac{\partial^2 g'_t}{\partial \gamma_k \partial \gamma_j}\bigg|_{\gamma=\tilde{\gamma}} - \frac{\partial^2 g_t}{\partial \gamma_k \partial \gamma_j}\bigg|_{\gamma=\tilde{\gamma}}\tilde{\varepsilon}'_t\right]d\gamma_j d\gamma_k. \tag{C16}$$

We can show that

$$\frac{1}{T}\sum_{t=1}^{T} \tilde{\varepsilon}_t \frac{\partial^2 g'_t}{\partial \gamma_k \partial \gamma_j}\bigg|_{\gamma=\tilde{\gamma}} = o_p(1) \tag{C17}$$

by the same method in proving (C13), and again it follows immediately that

$$\frac{1}{T}\sum_{t=1}^{T}\frac{\partial^{2}g_{t}}{\partial\gamma_{k}\partial\gamma_{j}}\bigg|_{\gamma=\tilde{\gamma}}\tilde{\varepsilon}'_{t}=o_{p}(1). \tag{C18}$$

So, by (C16), (C17), and (C18) it follows that

$$\operatorname{tr}(S_{T}^{-1}d^{2}\tilde{N})$$

$$=\operatorname{tr}\left\{S_{T}^{-1}\left[\frac{1}{T}\sum_{t=1}^{T}\sum_{j,k=1}^{q}2\frac{\partial g_{t}(\gamma)}{\partial\gamma_{j}}\bigg|_{\gamma=\tilde{\gamma}}\cdot\frac{\partial g'_{t}(\gamma)}{\partial\gamma_{k}}\bigg|_{\gamma=\tilde{\gamma}}\right]d\gamma_{j}d\gamma_{k}\right\}+o_{p}(1)$$

$$=2\sum_{t=1}^{T}\sum_{k,j=1}^{q}\frac{1}{T}\operatorname{tr}\left[S_{T}^{-1}\frac{\partial g_{t}(\gamma)}{\partial\gamma_{j}}\bigg|_{\gamma=\tilde{\gamma}}\frac{\partial g'_{t}(\gamma)}{\partial\gamma_{k}}\bigg|_{\gamma=\tilde{\gamma}}\right]d\gamma_{j}d\gamma_{k}+o_{p}(1)$$

$$=2\sum_{t=1}^{T}\sum_{j,k=1}^{q}\frac{1}{T}\operatorname{tr}\left[\frac{\partial g'_{t}(\gamma)}{\partial\gamma_{k}}\bigg|_{\gamma=\tilde{\gamma}}\cdot S_{T}^{-1}\frac{\partial g_{t}(\gamma)}{\partial\gamma_{j}}\bigg|_{\gamma=\tilde{\gamma}}\right]d\gamma_{j}d\gamma_{k}+o_{p}(1)$$

$$=2\sum_{j,k=1}^{q}\left[\frac{1}{T}\sum_{t=1}^{T}\frac{\partial g'_{t}(\gamma)}{\partial\gamma_{k}}\bigg|_{\gamma=\tilde{\gamma}}S_{T}^{-1}\frac{\partial g_{t}(\gamma)}{\partial\gamma_{j}}\bigg|_{\gamma=\tilde{\gamma}}\right]d\gamma_{j}d\gamma_{k}+o_{p}(1).$$

So by lemma 4.8 we see that

$$\operatorname{tr}(S_{T}^{-1}d^{2}\tilde{N})=2\sum_{k=1}^{q}\sum_{j=1}^{q}\left[M(\Omega^{-1})\right]_{kj}d\gamma_{j}d\gamma_{k}+o_{p}(1)$$

$$=2d\gamma'M(\Omega_{0}^{-1})d\gamma+o_{p}(1).$$

Hence,

$$\operatorname{tr}(S_{T}^{-1}d^{2}\tilde{N})=2d\gamma'M(\Omega_{0}^{-1})d\gamma+o_{p}(1). \tag{C19}$$

So, by (C4), (C5), (C15), and (C19) we see that

$$-\frac{1}{T}d^{2}\log L(\theta|y,x)|_{\theta=\tilde{\theta}}=\tfrac{1}{2}\operatorname{tr}(\Omega_{0}^{-1}d\Omega)^{2}+d\gamma'M(\Omega_{0}^{-1})d\gamma+o_{p}(1).$$

Q.E.D.

Proof of theorem 4.1. We know by property 4.6 that

$$-\frac{1}{T}E_{\theta_{0}}d^{2}\log L(\theta_{0}|y,x)=\tfrac{1}{2}\operatorname{tr}(\Omega_{0}^{-1}d\Omega)^{2}+d\gamma'M_{T}(\Omega_{0}^{-1})d\gamma.$$

But by the definition of $M(\cdot)$, $M_{T}(\Omega_{0}^{-1})\to M(\Omega_{0}^{-1})$ as $T\to\infty$. So it follows that

$$-\frac{1}{T}E_{\theta_0}d^2\log L(\theta_0|\,y,x) \underset{T\to\infty}{\to} \tfrac{1}{2}\mathrm{tr}(\Omega_0^{-1}d\Omega)^2 + d\gamma' M(\Omega_0^{-1})d\gamma.$$

Hence, by lemma 4.9, we find that

$$-\frac{1}{T}d^2\log L(\theta|\,y,x)|_{\theta=\tilde{\theta}} = \lim_{T\to\infty}\left[-\frac{1}{T}E_{\theta_0}d^2\log L(\theta_0|\,y,x)\right] + o_p(1),$$

where we have suppressed the subscript T in $\tilde{\theta}_T$.

Now recalling that

$$I_T(\theta_0) = -E_{\theta_0}\left[\frac{\partial^2 \log L(\theta_0|\,y,x)}{\partial\theta\partial\theta'}\right],$$

it follows that

$$-\frac{1}{T}\frac{\partial^2 \log L(\theta|\,y,x)}{\partial\theta\partial\theta'}\bigg|_{\theta=\tilde{\theta}} = \lim_{T\to\infty}\frac{1}{T}I_T(\theta_0) + o_p(1)$$
$$= I(\theta_0) + o_p(1),$$

or that $(1/T)B_T(\tilde{\theta}) = I(\theta_0) + o_p(1)$. Hence, $TB_T^{-1}(\tilde{\theta}) = I^{-1}(\theta_0) + o_p(1)$, since the inverse of a matrix is a continuous function of all of the elements of the original matrix. Q.E.D.

Proof of corollary 4.1. This result follows immediately from theorem 4.1 and the fact that $\theta_0 \overset{p}{\to} \theta_0$ trivially. Q.E.D.

Proof of lemma 4.10. If we assume or verify conditions sufficient to permit the interchange of differentiation and integration, this lemma follows immediately. To avoid the need for dealing with such conditions, we evaluate the expectation directly.

By property 4.7, we know that

$$d\log L(\theta|\,y,x) = -\frac{T}{2}\{\mathrm{tr}[\Omega^{-1}d\Omega(I-\Omega^{-1}N(\gamma))] + \mathrm{tr}(\Omega^{-1}dN)\}.$$

So it follows that

$$E_\theta d\log L(\theta|\,y,x)$$
$$= -\frac{T}{2}\mathrm{tr}[\Omega^{-1}d\Omega(I-\Omega^{-1}E_\theta(N(\gamma)))] - \frac{T}{2}\mathrm{tr}[\Omega^{-1}E_\theta(dN)].$$

(C20)

Now $E_\theta(N(\gamma)) = (1/T)[T\Omega] = \Omega$. So the first term on the right of (C20) is zero. Also, by property 4.8, we know that $E_\theta(dN) = 0$. Hence $E_\theta d\log L(\theta|y, x) = 0$.

So we can easily see that

$$E_{\theta_0}\left[\frac{\partial \log L(\theta|y, x)}{\partial \theta}\right]_{\theta=\theta_0} = 0. \qquad \text{Q.E.D.}$$

Proof of lemma 4.11. The result follows from lemma 4.10 by setting $T=1$, and observing that the origin in time is arbitrary. Q.E.D.

Proof of lemma 4.12. By setting $T=1$ in property 4.7, we can determine that

$$d\log f_t(y_t|\theta) = -\tfrac{1}{2}\text{tr}\big[(I-\Omega^{-1}N_t)\Omega^{-1}d\Omega\big] - \tfrac{1}{2}\text{tr}(\Omega^{-1}dN_t), \qquad (C21)$$

where $N_t = \varepsilon_t\varepsilon_t' = [y_t - g_t(\gamma)][y_t - g_t(\gamma)]'$.

We now determine the gradient of $\log f_t(y_t|\theta)$ with respect to θ by evaluating the two terms on the right-hand side of (C21).

Consider the second term on the right-hand side of (C21). If we define $s_{tkj} = [N_t]_{kj}$ and $\omega^{ik} = [\Omega^{-1}]_{ik}$, then we know that $[\Omega^{-1}dN_t]_{ij} = \sum_{k=1}^n \omega^{ik}ds_{tkj}$. Then it follows that $\text{tr}(\Omega^{-1}dN_t) = \sum_{i,k=1}^n \omega^{ik}ds_{tki}$. Setting $T=1$ in property 4.4, we can conclude that

$$\text{tr}(\Omega^{-1}dN_t) = -\sum_{i,k=1}^n\sum_{r=1}^q \omega^{ik}\big(\varepsilon_{tk}h_{tir}(\gamma) + h_{tkr}(\gamma)\varepsilon_{ti}\big)d\gamma_r, \quad \text{for all } t.$$

So referring back to (C21), we find that

$$\begin{aligned}
\frac{\partial \log f_t(y_t|\theta)}{\partial \gamma_r}\bigg|_{\theta=\theta_0} &= \frac{1}{2}\sum_{i,k=1}^n \omega_0^{ik}\big[\varepsilon_{tk}h_{tir}(\gamma_0) + h_{tkr}(\gamma_0)\varepsilon_{ti}\big] \\
&= \sum_{i,k=1}^n \varepsilon_{tk}\omega_0^{ik}h_{tir}(\gamma_0) \\
&= \frac{\partial g_t'}{\partial \gamma_r}\bigg|_{\gamma=\gamma_0}\Omega_0^{-1}\varepsilon_t.
\end{aligned} \qquad (C22)$$

Similarly, to evaluate the first term on the right of (C21), we define the random matrix A_t such that $A_t = -\tfrac{1}{2}(I-\Omega^{-1}N_t)\Omega^{-1}$. Then the first term on the right-hand side of (C21) is $\text{tr}(A_t d\Omega)$. Letting $a_{tik} = [A_t]_{ik}$ and $\omega_{kj} = [\Omega]_{kj}$, we have that $[A_t d\Omega]_{ij} = \sum_{k=1}^n a_{tik}d\omega_{kj}$. Hence, it follows that

$\mathrm{tr}(A_t \mathrm{d}\Omega) = \sum_{i,k=1}^n a_{tik} \mathrm{d}\omega_{ki}$. Thus,

$$\frac{\partial \log f_t(\mathbf{y}_t|\boldsymbol{\theta})}{\partial \omega_{ki}} = a_{tik} = a_{tki}$$

or

$$\left.\frac{\partial \log f_t(\mathbf{y}_t|\boldsymbol{\theta})}{\partial \Omega}\right|_{\boldsymbol{\theta}=\boldsymbol{\theta}_0} = -\tfrac{1}{2}\Omega_0^{-1} - \Omega_0^{-1}(\boldsymbol{\varepsilon}_t\boldsymbol{\varepsilon}_t')\Omega_0^{-1}.$$

So we see that any element of $\partial \log f_t(\mathbf{y}_t|\boldsymbol{\theta})/\partial \Omega|_{\boldsymbol{\theta}=\boldsymbol{\theta}_0}$ is linear in the elements of $\boldsymbol{\varepsilon}_t\boldsymbol{\varepsilon}_t'$ and generates a collection of identically and independently distributed random variables as t varies over $t=1,\ldots,T$. Hence, there exist identically and independently distributed random vectors $\mathbf{h}_t$, $t=1,\ldots,T$, and a matrix of constants G_{ij} for any $i,j=1,\ldots,n$ such that

$$\left.\frac{\partial \log f_t(\mathbf{y}_t|\boldsymbol{\theta})}{\partial \omega_{ij}}\right|_{\boldsymbol{\theta}=\boldsymbol{\theta}_0} = G_{ij}\mathbf{h}_t, \qquad t=1,\ldots,T. \tag{C23}$$

Now define the identically and independently distributed random vectors $\mathbf{u}_t$, $t=1,\ldots,T$, such that $\mathbf{u}_t = (\boldsymbol{\varepsilon}_t', \mathbf{h}_t')'$. Then from (C22) and (C23) we can construct matrices of constants K_t such that

$$\left.\frac{\partial \log f_t(\mathbf{y}_t|\boldsymbol{\theta})}{\partial \boldsymbol{\theta}}\right|_{\boldsymbol{\theta}=\boldsymbol{\theta}_0} = K_t \mathbf{u}_t \tag{C24}$$

where, by assumption 4.2, every element of K_t is bounded uniformly in $t=1,2,\ldots$. Now let

$$r_{t,T} = \int_{[\|z\|>\delta\sqrt{T}]} \|z\|^2 \mathrm{d}F_{\boldsymbol{\theta}_0,t}(z)$$

$$= \int \|z\|^2 I_{[\|z\|>\delta\sqrt{T}]} \mathrm{d}F_{\boldsymbol{\theta}_0,t}(z), \tag{C25}$$

where $I_{[\cdot]}$ is the indicator function, and let G_{Ω_0} be the distribution function of $\mathbf{u}_t$. Observe that G_{Ω_0} is the same for all $t=1,2,\ldots$. We now proceed to investigate the properties of $r_{t,T}$.

Define the random vector $\mathbf{s}$ by $\mathbf{s} = \partial \log f_t(\mathbf{y}_t|\boldsymbol{\theta})/\partial \boldsymbol{\theta}|_{\boldsymbol{\theta}=\boldsymbol{\theta}_0}$, and let H be the distribution function of $\|\mathbf{s}\|^2 I_{[\|\mathbf{s}\|>\delta\sqrt{T}]}$. Then since $\|\mathbf{s}\|^2 I_{[\|\mathbf{s}\|>\delta\sqrt{T}]}$ is a Borel function of $\mathbf{s}$ and $\|K_t\mathbf{u}\|^2 I_{[\mathbf{u}:\|K_t\mathbf{u}\|>\delta\sqrt{T}]}$ is a Borel function of $\mathbf{u}$, we find from section 2.6.1 of Rao (1973) that

$$\int \|z\|^2 I_{[\|z\|>\delta\sqrt{T}]} \mathrm{d}F_{\boldsymbol{\theta}_0,t}(z) = \int x \mathrm{d}H(x)$$

$$= \int \|K_t\mathbf{u}\|^2 I_{\{\mathbf{u}:\|K_t\mathbf{u}\|>\delta\sqrt{T}\}} \mathrm{d}G_{\Omega_0}(\mathbf{u}).$$

So we have that

$$r_{t,T} = \int \|K_t u\|^2 I_{\{u: \|K_t u\| > \delta\sqrt{T}\}} dG_{\Omega_0}(u). \tag{C26}$$

Letting K_{ti} be the ith row of K_t, we see that

$$\|K_t u\|^2 = \sum_{i=1}^{p} (K_{ti} u)^2 = \left| \sum_{i=1}^{p} K_{ti} u K_{ti} u \right| \leq \sum_{i=1}^{p} |K_{ti}| \|u\| \|K_{ti}\| \|u\|$$

$$= \sum_{i=1}^{p} [|K_{ti}| \|u\|]^2.$$

But recall that every element of K_t is bounded uniformly in t. So there exists a vector of constants $c \geq 0$ such that

$$\|K_t u\|^2 \leq \sum_{i=1}^{p} [c'|u|]^2 = p[c'|u|]^2. \tag{C27}$$

Thus, it follows by (C26) that

$$|r_{t,T}| \leq \int_{[\|K_t u\| > \delta\sqrt{T}]} p[c'|u|]^2 dG_{\Omega_0}(u).$$

Now by (C27) we know that $\|K_t u\| \leq p^{1/2} c'|u|$. So it follows that $[\|K_t u\| > \delta\sqrt{T}] \subset [p^{1/2} c'|u| > \delta\sqrt{T}]$. Then independently of t, we see that

$$\int_{[\|K_t u\| > \delta\sqrt{T}]} p[c'|u|]^2 dG_{\Omega_0}(u) \leq \int_{[p^{1/2} c'|u| > \delta\sqrt{T}]} p[c'|u|]^2 dG_{\Omega_0}(u).$$

Hence,

$$|r_{t,T}| \leq \int_{[p^{1/2} c'|u| > \delta\sqrt{T}]} p[c'|u|]^2 dG_{\Omega_0}(u)$$

independently of t.

Then since $[p^{1/2} c'|u| > \delta\sqrt{T}] \to \phi$ as $T \to \infty$, we can conclude from the absolute continuity of the indefinite integral, that

$$\left| \frac{1}{T} \sum_{t=1}^{T} r_{t,T} \right| \leq \frac{1}{T} \sum_{t=1}^{T} |r_{t,T}| \leq \int_{[pc'|u| > \delta\sqrt{T}]} pc'|u| dG_{\Omega_0}(u) \underset{T \to \infty}{\to} 0.$$

So we have shown that $(1/T) \sum_{t=1}^{T} r_{t,T} \to 0$ as $T \to \infty$. Q.E.D.

Proof of lemma 4.13. By the definition of a_T we know that

$$\frac{1}{\sqrt{T}} a_T(\theta_0) = \frac{1}{\sqrt{T}} \sum_{t=1}^{T} \frac{\partial \log f_t(y_t|\theta)}{\partial \theta} \bigg|_{\theta=\theta_0}.$$

Furthermore, by lemma 4.11 we know that

$$E_{\theta_0}\left[\frac{\partial \log f_t(y_t|\theta)}{\partial \theta}\right]_{\theta=\theta_0} = 0.$$

So if we let

$$\Omega_t = \text{var}_{\theta_0}\left[\frac{\partial \log f_t(y_t|\theta)}{\partial \theta}\right]_{\theta=\theta_0},$$

we see that

$$\Omega_t = E_{\theta_0}\left[\frac{\partial \log f_t(y_t|\theta)}{\partial \theta}\frac{\partial \log f_t(y_t|\theta)}{\partial \theta'}\right]_{\theta=\theta_0}$$

$$= -E_{\theta_0}\left[\frac{\partial^2 \log f_t(y_t|\theta)}{\partial \theta \partial \theta'}\right]_{\theta=\theta_0}.$$

So it follows that

$$\frac{1}{T}\sum_{t=1}^{T}\Omega_t = -\frac{1}{T}E_{\theta_0}\left[\frac{\partial^2 \log L(\theta|y,x)}{\partial \theta \partial \theta'}\right]_{\theta=\theta_0}$$

$$= \frac{1}{T}I_T(\theta_0) \to I(\theta_0) \text{ as } T \to \infty.$$

We can now appeal to lemma 4.12 and the multivariate Central Limit Theorem (see, for example, Dhrymes, 1970, p. 108, or Rao, 1973, ch. 2, problem 4.7) to conclude that

$$\frac{1}{\sqrt{T}}\sum_{t=1}^{T}\frac{\partial \log f_t(y_t|\theta)}{\partial \theta}\bigg|_{\theta=\theta_0} \xrightarrow{\mathcal{L}} N(0, I(\theta_0)) \text{ as } T \to \infty. \qquad \text{Q.E.D.}$$

Finally we can prove our theorem, asserting that $\hat{\theta}$ is asymptotically normally distributed.

Proof of theorem 4.2. By the multivariate Mean Value Theorem, it follows that

$$\frac{1}{T}\frac{\partial \log L(\theta|y,x)}{\partial \theta_i}\bigg|_{\theta=\hat{\theta}} = \frac{1}{T}\frac{\partial \log L(\theta|y,x)}{\partial \theta_i}\bigg|_{\theta=\theta_0}$$

$$+ \frac{1}{T}\frac{\partial}{\partial \theta'}\frac{\partial \log L(\theta|y,x)}{\partial \theta_i}\bigg|_{\theta=\theta^*}(\hat{\theta}-\theta_0)$$

$$= \frac{1}{T}a_{Ti}(\theta_0) - \frac{1}{T}b'_{Ti}(\theta^*)(\hat{\theta}-\theta_0), \qquad (C28)$$

where b'_{Ti} is the ith row of $B_T(\theta)$, and θ^* is on the line between $\hat{\theta}$ and θ_0.

But the left-hand side of (C28) equals zero, by the definition of the ML estimator. So we see that

$$0 = \frac{1}{T}a_{Ti}(\theta_0) - \frac{1}{T}b'_{Ti}(\theta^*)(\hat{\theta} - \theta_0),$$

or that

$$0 = \frac{1}{T}a_T(\theta_0) - \frac{1}{T}B_T(\theta^*)(\hat{\theta} - \theta_0).$$

Hence, we find that

$$\hat{\theta} - \theta_0 = \left[\frac{1}{T}B_T(\theta^*)\right]^{-1}\left[\frac{1}{T}a_T(\theta_0)\right] = TB_T^{-1}(\theta^*)\left[\frac{1}{T}a_T(\theta_0)\right],$$

or

$$\sqrt{T}(\hat{\theta} - \theta_0) = TB_T^{-1}(\theta^*)\left[\frac{1}{\sqrt{T}}a_T(\theta_0)\right]. \tag{C29}$$

Since θ^* is between $\hat{\theta}$ and θ_0, it is clear that $0 \leq |\theta^* - \theta_0| \leq |\hat{\theta} - \theta_0|$. But $|\hat{\theta} - \theta_0| = o_p(1)$. So, by Lemma 4.7, we conclude that $\theta^* = \theta_0 + o_p(1)$. Hence, it follows from theorem 4.1 that $TB_T^{-1}(\theta^*) = I^{-1}(\theta_0) + o_p(1)$. So by (C29) we find that

$$\sqrt{T}(\hat{\theta} - \theta_0) = \left[I^{-1}(\theta_0) + o_p(1)\right]\left[\frac{1}{\sqrt{T}}a_T(\theta_0)\right],$$

or that

$$\sqrt{T}(\hat{\theta} - \theta_0) = I^{-1}(\theta_0)\left[\frac{1}{\sqrt{T}}a_T(\theta_0)\right] + o_p(1)\left[\frac{1}{\sqrt{T}}a_T(\theta_0)\right].$$

By lemma 4.13 and Slutsky's theorem, it follows that

$$o_p(1)\left[\frac{1}{\sqrt{T}}a_T(\theta_0)\right] = o_p(1).$$

So

$$\sqrt{T}(\hat{\theta} - \theta_0) = I^{-1}(\theta_0)\left[\frac{1}{\sqrt{T}}a_T(\theta_0)\right] + o_p(1).$$

The first term on the right-hand side of that equation is a continuous function of $(1/\sqrt{T})a_T(\theta_0)$. So by lemma 4.13 it follows that

$$I^{-1}(\theta_0)\left[\frac{1}{\sqrt{T}}a_T(\theta_0)\right] \xrightarrow[T \to \infty]{\mathcal{L}} N(0, I^{-1}(\theta_0)).$$

Hence, by Slutsky's theorem, we conclude that

$$\sqrt{(T)}(\hat{\boldsymbol{\theta}}-\boldsymbol{\theta}_0) \xrightarrow{\mathcal{L}} N(\mathbf{0}, \boldsymbol{I}^{-1}(\boldsymbol{\theta}_0)).$$ Q.E.D.

Proof of corollary 4.2. Since α is the first elements of $\boldsymbol{\theta}$, this corollary follows immediately from theorem 4.2. Q.E.D.

Proof of corollary 4.3. By the block diagonality of $\boldsymbol{I}_T(\boldsymbol{\theta})$, theorem 4.2, and the definition of $\boldsymbol{I}(\boldsymbol{\theta})$, we see that

$$\sqrt{(T)}(\hat{\gamma}-\gamma_0) \xrightarrow[T\to\infty]{\mathcal{L}} N\left(0,\left[\lim_{T\to\infty}\frac{1}{T}\mathcal{I}_T(\boldsymbol{\theta}_0)\right]^{-1}\right).$$

But $(1/T)\mathcal{I}_T(\boldsymbol{\theta}_0) \xrightarrow[T\to\infty]{} \mathcal{I}(\boldsymbol{\theta}_0)$ by the definition of $\mathcal{I}(\cdot)$. So the corollary follows from the fact that matrix inversion is a continuous function of the elements of the original matrix. Q.E.D.

Proof of lemma 4.14. Observe that $\boldsymbol{I}(\boldsymbol{\theta}_0)[\sqrt{(T)}(\hat{\boldsymbol{\theta}}-\boldsymbol{\theta}_0)]$ is a continuous function of $\sqrt{(T)}(\hat{\boldsymbol{\theta}}-\boldsymbol{\theta}_0)$. So, by theorem 4.2 it follows that $\boldsymbol{I}(\boldsymbol{\theta}_0)[\sqrt{(T)}(\hat{\boldsymbol{\theta}}-\boldsymbol{\theta}_0)] \xrightarrow[T\to\infty]{\mathcal{L}} \boldsymbol{I}(\boldsymbol{\theta}_0)N(\mathbf{0},\boldsymbol{I}^{-1}(\boldsymbol{\theta}_0))$. But since $\boldsymbol{I}(\boldsymbol{\theta}_0)N(\mathbf{0},\boldsymbol{I}^{-1}(\boldsymbol{\theta}_0))=N(\mathbf{0},\boldsymbol{I}(\boldsymbol{\theta}_0))$, we see that $\boldsymbol{I}(\boldsymbol{\theta}_0)[\sqrt{(T)}(\hat{\boldsymbol{\theta}}-\boldsymbol{\theta}_0)] \xrightarrow[T\to\infty]{\mathcal{L}} N(\mathbf{0},\boldsymbol{I}(\boldsymbol{\theta}_0))$. Hence, by lemma 4.13 our result follows immediately. Q.E.D.

Proof of lemma 4.15. $\boldsymbol{I}^{-1}(\boldsymbol{\theta}_0)[(1/\sqrt{T})\boldsymbol{a}_T(\boldsymbol{\theta}_0)]$ is a continuous function of $(1/\sqrt{T})\boldsymbol{a}_T(\boldsymbol{\theta}_0)$. So by lemma 4.13 it follows that $\boldsymbol{I}^{-1}(\boldsymbol{\theta}_0)[(1/\sqrt{T})\boldsymbol{a}_T(\boldsymbol{\theta}_0)] \xrightarrow{\mathcal{L}} N(\mathbf{0},\boldsymbol{I}^{-1}(\boldsymbol{\theta}_0))$ as $T\to\infty$. Our result now follows immediately from theorem 4.2 Q.E.D.

Proof of theorem 4.3. Rao (1973, sect. 6e.3) has proved this result for the case of identically and independently distributed observations. Although he wrote the likelihood ratio in the form of λ^*, his proof does not establish that the maximum likelihood estimator is a consistent root of the likelihood function. So in fact it is λ_T, which is based upon a consistent root, to which his proof applies.

At the end of that section he observed that the result can be extended to nonidentically distributed observations, if our results in theorem 4.2, lemma 4.6, and lemma 4.15 obtain. Q.E.D.

Proof of theorem 4.4. Partition $B_T(\theta)$ such that

$$B_T(\theta) = \begin{bmatrix} c_T \theta & a_T'(\theta) \\ a_T(\theta) & D_T(\theta) \end{bmatrix},$$

where

$$c_T(\theta) = -\frac{\partial^2 \log L(\theta| y, x)}{\partial \alpha^2}.$$

Then it follows that

$$\left[B_T^{-1}(\theta) \right]_{11} = \frac{1}{c_T(\theta) - a_T'(\theta) D_T^{-1}(\theta) a_T(\theta)}. \tag{C30}$$

By (4.3) we know that $e(\alpha, k(\alpha| y, x)| y, x) = 0$ for all $\alpha \in R$. Differentiating with respect to α, we find that

$$\frac{\partial}{\partial \alpha} e(\alpha, k(\alpha| y, x)| y, x) = 0,$$

or

$$\frac{\partial}{\partial \alpha} e(\alpha, \phi| y, x) \bigg|_{\phi = k(\alpha| y, x)} + \frac{\partial}{\partial \phi'} e(\alpha, \phi| y, x) \bigg|_{\phi = k(\alpha| y, x)} \frac{\partial k(\alpha| y, x)}{\partial \alpha} = 0,$$

or

$$\frac{\partial \log L(\theta| y, x)}{\partial \alpha \partial \phi} \bigg|_{\phi = k(\alpha| y, x)} + \frac{\partial \log L(\theta| y, x)}{\partial \phi' \partial \phi} \bigg|_{\phi = k(\alpha| y, x)} \frac{\partial k(\alpha| y, x)}{\partial \alpha} = 0,$$

for all $\alpha \in R$. Rearranging, we find that

$$\frac{\partial k(\alpha| y, x)}{\partial \alpha} = - \left[\frac{\partial \log L(\theta| y, x)}{\partial \phi' \partial \phi} \right]^{-1}_{\phi = k(\alpha| y, x)} \frac{\partial \log L(\theta| y, x)}{\partial \alpha \partial \phi} \bigg|_{\phi = k(\alpha| y, x)}$$

$$= -D_T^{-1}(\alpha, k(\alpha| y, x)) a_T(\alpha, k(\alpha| y, x)). \tag{C31}$$

Now $L^*(\alpha| y, x) = L(\alpha, k(\alpha| y, x)| y, x)$. So by (4.1) it follows that

$$\frac{\partial \log L^*(\alpha| y, x)}{\partial \alpha} = \frac{\partial \log L(\alpha, \phi| y, x)}{\partial \alpha} \bigg|_{\phi = k(\alpha| y, x)}$$

$$+ \frac{\partial \log L(\alpha, \phi| y, x)}{\partial \phi'} \bigg|_{\phi = k(\alpha| y, x)} \frac{\partial k(\alpha| y, x)}{\partial \alpha}$$

$$= \frac{\partial \log L(\theta| y, x)}{\partial \alpha} \bigg|_{\phi = k(\alpha| y, x)}.$$

Letting
$$H(\theta | y, x) = \frac{\partial \log L(\theta | y, x)}{\partial \alpha},$$
we see that
$$\frac{\partial \log L^*(\alpha | y, x)}{\partial \alpha} = H(\alpha, k(\alpha | y, x) | y, x).$$
Differentiating with respect to α, we find that
$$\frac{\partial^2 \log L^*(\alpha | y, x)}{\partial \alpha^2} = \frac{\partial H(\alpha, \phi | y, x)}{\partial \alpha}\bigg|_{\phi = k(\alpha | y, x)}$$
$$+ \frac{\partial H(\alpha, \phi | y, x)}{\partial \phi'}\bigg|_{\phi = k(\alpha | y, x)} \frac{\partial k(\alpha | y, x)}{\partial \alpha},$$
or
$$\frac{\partial^2 \log L^*(\alpha | y, x)}{\partial \alpha^2} = \frac{\partial \log L(\theta | y, x)}{\partial \alpha^2}\bigg|_{\phi = k(\alpha | y, x)}$$
$$+ \frac{\partial \log L(\theta | y, x)}{\partial \phi' \partial \alpha}\bigg|_{\phi = k(\alpha | y, x)} \frac{\partial k(\alpha | y, x)}{\partial \alpha}.$$
So we see that
$$-\frac{\partial^2 \log L^*(\alpha | y, x)}{\partial \alpha^2} = c_T(\alpha, k(\alpha | y, x))$$
$$+ a'_T(\alpha, k(\alpha | y, x)) \frac{\partial k(\alpha | y, x)}{\partial \alpha}$$
$$= c_T(\alpha, k(\alpha | y, x))$$
$$- a'_T(\alpha, k(\alpha | y, x)) D_T^{-1}(\alpha, k(\alpha | y, x))$$
$$\times a_T(\alpha, k(\alpha | y, x))$$

by (C31). Hence it follows that
$$\left[-\frac{\partial^2 \log L^*(\alpha | y, x)}{\partial \alpha^2} \right]^{-1}$$
$$= \frac{1}{c_T(\alpha, k(\alpha | y, x)) - a'_T(\alpha, k(\alpha | y, x)) D_T^{-1}(\alpha, k(\alpha | y, x)) a_T(\alpha, k(\alpha | y, x))}.$$
$$= \left[B_T^{-1}(\alpha, k(\alpha | y, x)) \right]_{11}$$

by (C30). So we see that
$$\left[-\frac{\partial^2 \log L^*(\alpha| y, x)}{\partial \alpha^2}\right]^{-1}_{\alpha=\hat{\alpha}} = \left[B_T^{-1}(\hat{\alpha}, k(\hat{\alpha}| y, x))\right]_{11}.$$

It is clear that
$$\left[\begin{array}{c}\hat{\alpha}\\k(\hat{\alpha}| y, x)\end{array}\right] = \hat{\boldsymbol{\theta}},$$

where $\hat{\boldsymbol{\theta}}$ is our maximum likelihood estimate of $\boldsymbol{\theta}$. So
$$\left[-\frac{\partial^2 \log L^*(\alpha| y, x)}{\partial \alpha^2}\right]^{-1}_{\alpha=\hat{\alpha}} = \left[B_T^{-1}(\hat{\boldsymbol{\theta}})\right]_{11}. \qquad \text{Q.E.D.}$$

APPENDIX D

APPENDIX TO CHAPTER 5

D1. Data sources

We acquired consumption data from Kuznets (1961). From Kuznets' tables R-9 and R-10 we can find consumption expenditure in each of the four categories for the years 1919–1955 both in current prices and in 1929 prices. The index year for all deflators will be 1929. The data is tabulated at the end of this appendix. Table D1 lists expenditure in each category in index year prices as "quantity". The columns called "prices" are implicit price deflators computed by dividing expenditure in current prices by expenditure in 1929 prices. The category called "leisure" will be described below.

Observe that the data in our table D1 extends backwards to 1890, while Kuznets' tables R-9 and R-10 begin in 1919. To extend Kuznets' tables R-9 and R-10 back to 1890, we use his tables R-27 and R-28 which provide five-year moving averages for the four categories extending back into the nineteenth century. Since those tables overlap the years covered by tables R-9 and R-10, it was possible to decompose the moving averages to find the underlying unpublished annual data. In all instances we used variant III of Kuznets' data, since variant III is based upon conventions most closely in agreement with those now in use by the Department of Commerce. Observe that our data covers the years 1890–1955.

To acquire per capita consumption, we need population data. That data was acquired from the *Historical Statistics of the United States from Colonial Times* (1960, p. 7). Series A1 was used back to 1930 where the series begins. For the years prior to 1930 the series was extended using series A2 and the instructions in the footnote to the table. That choice was made to permit maximum agreement with Commerce Department consumption conventions.

Wage rate data was acquired as follows. First it was necessary to acquire earnings per full-time equivalent employee. This was acquired for the years

Table D1

Prices and quantities of perishables (P), semidurables (SD), durables (D), services (S), and leisure (L), 1890–1955.

Year	Population (thousands)	Quantities[a]					Prices[b]				Leisure consumption[c]		Wage rate[d]	Unemployment rate (%)
		P	SD	D	S	L	P	SD	D	S	Γ=1.0	Γ=.48		
1890	63056	6.80	3.05	1.95	6.20	101.26	0.603	0.541	0.426	0.532	193.48	60.48	0.147	4.0
1891	64361	8.55	3.12	2.09	6.25	103.18	0.497	0.516	0.493	0.536	197.15	61.41	0.149	5.4
1892	65666	7.85	3.27	2.32	5.70	104.85	0.561	0.511	0.414	0.605	200.34	61.84	0.149	3.0
1893	66970	9.10	3.14	1.97	6.40	107.98	0.538	0.478	0.462	0.453	206.32	65.07	0.141	11.7
1894	68275	8.90	2.87	1.82	6.20	111.91	0.449	0.460	0.368	0.492	213.83	69.83	0.130	18.4
1895	69850	9.10	3.45	2.20	7.50	112.68	0.516	0.435	0.355	0.507	215.30	68.54	0.135	13.7
1896	70885	10.00	3.32	2.24	7.20	115.45	0.420	0.425	0.393	0.514	220.59	71.09	0.136	14.4
1897	72189	9.70	3.62	2.52	7.00	117.13	0.500	0.434	0.341	0.564	223.81	71.55	0.137	14.5
1898	73494	10.60	3.69	2.37	7.85	119.52	0.476	0.420	0.384	0.452	228.37	73.37	0.137	12.4
1899	74799	11.60	4.02	2.77	8.70	119.76	0.461	0.453	0.368	0.494	228.83	71.07	0.146	6.5
1900	76094	11.60	4.05	2.60	9.50	122.02	0.526	0.494	0.415	0.516	233.15	72.66	0.151	5.0
1901	77585	13.50	4.42	2.84	10.30	123.47	0.493	0.455	0.451	0.534	235.92	72.29	0.158	4.0
1902	79160	12.70	4.67	3.07	9.80	125.06	0.563	0.465	0.427	0.582	238.96	72.01	0.170	3.7
1903	80632	13.60	4.94	3.02	11.20	126.92	0.540	0.466	0.467	0.509	242.52	72.46	0.172	3.9
1904	82165	14.10	4.87	3.02	11.70	130.79	0.521	0.487	0.454	0.530	249.91	76.61	0.176	5.4
1905	83820	14.10	5.15	3.35	12.50	132.16	0.567	0.505	0.472	0.572	252.52	75.73	0.178	4.3
1906	85437	16.00	5.47	3.89	13.80	133.78	0.534	0.550	0.496	0.572	255.63	75.43	0.183	1.7
1907	87000	16.70	5.47	3.72	13.80	136.01	0.575	0.561	0.513	0.601	259.89	76.40	0.193	2.8
1908	88709	14.60	5.49	3.07	13.70	141.63	0.603	0.528	0.541	0.558	270.62	83.52	0.193	8.0
1909	90492	16.60	5.92	3.92	15.20	142.86	0.596	0.561	0.503	0.582	272.98	82.12	0.202	5.1
1910	92407	16.60	5.75	4.00	15.50	145.60	0.657	0.565	0.533	0.619	278.20	83.30	0.213	5.9
1911	93868	18.00	6.32	3.99	16.30	147.71	0.600	0.547	0.546	0.620	282.83	84.25	0.216	6.7
1912	95331	18.20	6.67	4.27	15.80	149.17	0.665	0.550	0.564	0.665	285.02	83.95	0.221	4.6
1913	97227	18.60	6.94	4.22	16.70	152.76	0.661	0.569	0.618	0.629	291.89	86.82	0.234	4.3
1914	99118	19.10	6.57	3.97	16.70	157.67	0.623	0.559	0.622	0.677	301.28	92.23	0.238	7.9
1915	100549	17.60	6.40	4.05	17.00	161.11	0.676	0.555	0.625	0.712	307.85	95.78	0.239	8.5
1916	101966	19.00	7.02	5.14	18.80	160.41	0.753	0.685	0.696	0.750	306.50	91.44	0.264	5.1
1917	103414	18.70	6.57	5.12	18.80	161.59	1.048	0.977	0.803	0.798	308.76	90.65	0.303	4.6
1918	104550	19.60	6.34	4.17	19.20	161.81	1.189	1.293	0.962	0.859	309.18	88.67	0.381	1.4
1919	105063	19.60	6.62	5.37	20.70	166.54	1.219	1.317	1.065	0.787	318.21	96.62	0.448	1.4

Appendix D

Table D1 (*continued*).

Year	Population (thousands)	Quantities[a]				Prices[b]					Leisure consumption[c]		Wage rate[d]	Unemployment rate (%)
		P	SD	D	S	L	P	SD	D	S	L	Γ=1.0	Γ=.48		
1920	106466	20.60	5.75	5.30	22.50	169.88	1.282	1.757	1.242	0.916	0.877	324.60	100.05	0.519	5.2
1921	108541	21.50	6.92	4.29	24.30	179.70	0.991	1.186	1.242	0.992	0.716	343.37	114.44	0.499	11.7
1922	110055	22.20	7.82	5.47	23.80	179.31	0.928	1.083	1.062	0.987	0.774	342.61	110.49	0.475	6.7
1923	111950	23.10	8.61	7.15	25.40	179.13	0.961	1.114	1.032	1.004	0.907	342.28	106.16	0.502	2.4
1924	114113	24.90	7.97	7.45	28.70	184.94	0.924	1.136	0.995	1.017	0.869	353.37	112.69	0.512	5.0
1925	115832	24.70	8.78	8.38	25.20	186.51	0.992	1.083	1.005	1.028	0.917	356.37	112.07	0.517	3.2
1926	117399	25.80	8.83	9.30	28.60	187.79	1.012	1.126	0.943	1.024	0.962	358.82	111.21	0.525	1.8
1927	119038	26.30	9.91	8.83	29.20	191.50	0.977	1.019	0.948	1.017	0.959	365.91	114.85	0.542	3.3
1928	120501	26.20	9.89	9.04	31.20	194.02	1.004	1.031	0.951	1.006	0.942	370.72	116.57	0.544	4.2
1929	121770	27.20	10.40	9.21	33.40	195.50	1.000	1.000	1.000	1.000	1.000	373.56	116.73	0.564	3.2
1930	123188	26.50	9.36	7.45	32.60	202.55	0.947	0.952	0.961	0.957	0.864	387.02	127.20	0.560	8.9
1931	124129	26.50	9.27	6.40	31.00	209.22	0.800	0.831	0.856	0.894	0.676	399.78	137.93	0.533	16.3
1932	124949	24.80	8.22	4.86	28.50	216.88	0.690	0.686	0.751	0.825	0.491	414.41	150.88	0.485	24.1
1933	125690	24.70	7.44	4.72	28.20	218.37	0.688	0.700	0.735	0.759	0.438	417.25	152.15	0.447	25.2
1934	126485	26.50	7.81	5.38	28.90	220.02	0.766	0.809	0.783	0.754	0.531	420.40	153.63	0.492	22.0
1935	127362	27.70	8.44	6.63	30.30	219.19	0.816	0.797	0.771	0.759	0.573	418.82	159.20	0.505	20.3
1936	128181	31.00	9.29	8.18	32.20	216.18	0.819	0.797	0.770	0.773	0.629	413.07	142.72	0.505	17.0
1937	128961	32.50	9.27	8.60	34.00	215.42	0.843	0.837	0.805	0.800	0.730	411.62	139.63	0.545	14.3
1938	129969	33.20	9.37	7.05	33.40	221.57	0.795	0.812	0.807	0.808	0.641	423.37	149.25	0.546	19.1
1939	131028	34.50	10.30	8.35	33.90	221.34	0.783	0.787	0.799	0.808	0.689	422.92	146.56	0.557	17.2
1940	132122	36.10	10.70	9.57	35.30	221.33	0.795	0.796	0.812	0.813	0.767	422.91	144.25	0.577	14.6
1941	133402	38.40	11.50	11.00	36.90	218.17	0.862	0.878	0.878	0.843	0.977	416.88	135.51	0.650	9.9
1946	141389	49.10	13.40	12.20	47.60	231.32	1.287	1.590	1.303	1.048	1.932	442.00	143.79	1.108	3.9
1947	144126	48.40	12.70	14.60	49.30	237.74	1.467	1.740	1.411	1.130	2.063	454.26	150.28	1.183	3.9
1948	146631	48.70	12.50	15.10	51.30	242.69	1.554	1.848	1.470	1.195	2.232	463.72	154.45	1.277	3.8
1949	149188	49.60	12.60	15.90	52.60	250.53	1.512	1.738	1.484	1.230	2.225	478.71	164.05	1.339	5.9
1950	151683	51.10	12.70	19.20	55.60	254.51	1.532	1.740	1.490	1.257	2.342	486.31	166.40	1.389	5.3
1951	154360	52.60	12.60	17.10	57.50	256.55	1.662	1.881	1.585	1.311	2.637	490.21	164.40	1.491	3.3
1952	157028	54.20	13.20	16.90	59.70	261.14	1.696	1.833	1.574	1.355	2.783	498.98	167.79	1.566	3.1
1953	159636	56.20	13.20	18.90	61.70	265.69	1.689	1.833	1.577	1.412	2.955	507.67	170.97	1.655	2.9
1954	162417	57.10	13.10	19.00	63.30	274.37	1.697	1.832	1.547	1.449	2.867	524.25	181.70	1.713	5.6
1955	165270	60.00	13.80	22.90	66.40	278.07	1.682	1.826	1.559	1.471	3.048	531.33	182.75	1.769	4.4

[a] Billions of dollars in 1929 prices.
[b] Price indices equal 1 in 1929 base year.
[c] Billions of man-hours per year.
[d] Dollars per hour.

1900–1946 from column 2, table A-16, of Lebergott (1964). To find the data for the years prior to 1900, it was necessary to utilize Lebergott's table A-19, which extended back into the nineteenth century. However, table A-19 contains annual earnings for nonfarm employees, while we seek earnings for all employees. Now Lebergott's table A-17 contains nonfarm earnings for the same years as those covered by table A-16. So the third column of table A-17 was regressed on the third column of table A-16 to acquire a relationship between nonfarm earnings and the earnings of all full-time equivalent employees. A linear regression was forced through the data point for 1900 to ensure a perfect splice. The fit was very good, and linearity was clearly acceptable. The resulting regression was then used to adjust the nonfarm data in table A-19, column 3, to total labor force data. By this process we acquired annual earnings per full-time equivalent employee for the years 1890–1946.

To acquire wage rate data for the years 1890–1946, we divided our annual earnings data by the population data in our table D1. Wage rate data for the years 1946–1955 was acquired by extrapolating the 1946 wage rate using percentage changes computed from the BLS hourly earnings index in table C-12 of the Bureau of Labor Statistics (1973) *Employment and Earnings*. For a discussion of the merits of that index, which became available in April of 1973, see the Bureau of Labor Statistics (1971, 1972). It is insensitive to interindustry employment shifts and is purported to be the best available index of percentage changes in the wage rate. The resulting wage rate series can be found in table D1.

Data on E is found by computing $1-U$, where U is the unemployment rate. The unemployment rate was found in Lebergott (1964, table A-3), and it is tabulated in our table D1. Man-hours were found in Kendrick (1961, table A-X, column 1) for the years 1890–1953. For the years 1954–1955, table 5.1 of Knowles (1960) was used. Since Knowles data source was unpublished data gathered by Kendrick, the splice between Knowles' and Kendrick's data was direct.

Leisure consumption was computed in accordance with section 5.1.

APPENDIX E

APPENDIX TO CHAPTER 7

E1. Other monetary assets

In this appendix we use the model (7.12) to acquire tentative estimates of elasticities of substitution between various monetary assets not considered in Chapter 7. Although the models used in Chapter 7 were selected for their applicability to the purposes of sections 7.8 and 7.9, we do not design different models for each of the cases in this appendix. Although (7.12) was conveniently available to us, other more flexible models would have been preferable in a more systematic treatment of some of the cases we consider only briefly in this appendix.

Table E1 contains our estimates of θ and the implied elasticities of substitution. In some of the three asset cases a model permitting different elasticities of substitution between pairs of assets could be preferable, although we frequently re-estimated various two-good combinations. By using model (7.12) in each case, we have not attempted to nest all of the cases within one model (utility tree).

In addition we have not adjusted the yields on small time deposits for early redemption penalties. In short, in this appendix we applied a readily available model (from our work in Chapter 7) to additional readily available data. The quality of the match between the data and model in this appendix is not always high, and the results therefore are considerably more tentative than those in Chapter 7 itself.

Table E1
Substitution elasticities between other monetary substitutes.

Goods	Quarters	θ	Elasticity of substitution (σ)
1. Transaction balances 2. Passbook savings (3 institutions)	1970(1)–1978(1)	0.597[a] (0.22)	0.283[a]
1. Passbook savings (3 institutions) 2. Small time at CBs 3. Large nonnegotiable CDs at CBs	1968(1)–1974(4)	0.0[b] (0.18)	0.0[c]
Same as above	1970(1)–1978(1)	0.42 (0.133)	0.19
1. Passbook savings (3 institutions) 2. Small time (3 institutions) 3. Negotiable and nonneg. CDs at CBs	1968(1)–1975(4)	0.63[b] (0.201)	0.306
Same as above	1970(1)–1978(1)	0.716[b] (0.099)	0.365
1. Passbooks savings (3 institutions) 2. Large non-negotiable CDs at CBs	1968(1)–1974(4)	0.0 (0.499)	0.0[c]
Same as above	1970(1)–1978(1)	0.60 (0.16)	0.29
1. Passbook savings (3 institutions) 2. Small time at CBs	1968(1)–1974(4)	0.0 (0.21)	0.0[c]
Same as above	1970(1)–1978(1)	0.0 (0.21)	0.0[c]
1. Small time at CBs 2. Large nonnegotiable CDs at CBs	1968(1)–1974(4)	0.0 (0.93)	0.0[c]
Same as above	1970(1)–1978(1)	0.55 (0.21)	0.26
1. Small time (3 institutions) 2. Large non-negotiable CDs at CBs	1968(1)–1975(4)	0.0 (0.92)	0.0[c]
Same as above	1970(1)–1978(1)	0.60 (0.13)	0.287
1. Small time (3 institutions) 2. Large negotiable CDs at CBs	1968(1)–1975(4)	0.0 (1.99)	0.0[c]
Same as above	1970(1)–1978(1)	0.76 (0.11)	0.4
1. Small time at CBs 2. Small time at S&Ls 3. Small time at MSBs	1967(1)–1975(4)	0.0[b] (0.73)	0.0[c]

Table E1 (*continued*).

Same as above	1970(1)–1978(1)	0.60 (0.13)	0.287
1. Small time at CBs 2. Small time at S&Ls	1970(1)–1978(1)	0.0 (0.49)	0.0[c]
1. Small time at MSBs 2. Small time at CBs	1970(1)–1978(1)	0.0 (1.09)	0.0[c]
1. Small time at S&Ls 2. Small time at MSBs	1970(1)–1978(1)	3.35 (0.36)	12.82
1. Passbook savings at CBs 2. Passbook savings at S&Ls 3. Passbook savings at MSBs	1966(1)–1975(4)	1.08 (0.059)	0.75
Same as above	1970(1)–1978(1)	1.94 (0.239)	2.66

Note: Asymptotic standard errors are in parentheses.

[a] From section 7.9.

[b] Joint parameter, under assumption that σ is the same for all pairs of the three goods.

[c] Small positive number, since $\sigma > 0$ was imposed during estimation.

BIBLIOGRAPHY

Abbott, M. and O. Ashenfelter (1976), "Labor Supply, Commodity Demand, and the Allocation of Time", *Review of Economic Studies*, 43, 389–412.
Amemiya, Takeshi (1974), "The Nonlinear Two-Stage Estimator", *Journal of Econometrics*, 2, 105–110.
Amemiya, Takeshi (1975), "The Nonlinear Limited Information Maximum Likelihood Estimator and the Modified Nonlinear Two Stage Least Squares Estimator", *Journal of Econometrics*, 3, 375–386.
Amemiya, Takeshi (1977), "The Maximum Likelihood and the Nonlinear Three-Stage Least Squares Estimator in the General Nonlinear Simultaneous Equation Model", *Econometrica*, 45, 955–968.
Anderson, Ronald (1979), "Perfect Price Aggregation and Empirical Demand Analysis", *Econometrica*, 47, 1209–1230.
Arrow, K. and F. Hahn (1971), *General Equilibrium Analysis* (Holden Day, San Francisco).
Ashenfelter, Orley and James Heckman (1974), "The Estimation of Income and Substitution Effects in a Model of Family Labor Supply", *Econometrica*, 42, 73–85.
Bahadur, R. R. (1964), "On Fisher's Bound for Asymptotic Variances", *Annals of Mathematical Statistics*, 35, pp. 1545–1552.
Bard, Yonathan (1973), *Nonlinear Parameter Estimation* (Academic Press, New York).
Barnett, William A. (1973), "The Effects of Bliss on Welfare Economics", *Journal of Economic Issues*, 7, 29–45.
Barnett, William A. (1976), "Maximum Likelihood and Iterated Aitken Estimation of Nonlinear Systems of Equations", *Journal of the American Statistical Association*, 71, 354–360.
Barnett, William A. (1977a), "Pollak and Wachter on the Household Production Function Approach", *Journal of Political Economy*, 85, 1073–1082.
Barnett, William A. (1977b), "Recursive Subaggregation and a Generalized Hypocycloidal Demand Model", *Econometrica*, 45, 1117–1136.
Barnett, William A. (1979a), "Random Sets and Confidence Procedures", *Rocky Mountain Journal of Mathematics*, 9, no. 3, 453–461.
Barnett, William A. (1979b), "The Joint Allocation of Leisure and Goods Expenditure", *Econometrica*, 45, 1117–1136.
Barnett, William A. (1979c), "Theoretical Foundations for the Rotterdam Model", *Review of Economic Studies*, 46, 109–130.
Barnett, William A. (1979d), "The User Cost of Money", *Economics Letters*, 1, 145–149.
Barnett, William A. (1980a), "Economic Monetary Aggregation: An Application of Aggregation and Index Number Theory", *Annals of Applied Econometrics* (supplement to the *Journal of Econometrics*), 14, 11–48.
Barnett, William A. (1980b), "Economic Monetary Aggregates: Reply", *Annals of Applied Econometrics* (supplement to the *Journal of Econometrics*), 14, 57–59.
Barnett, William A. (1980c), "Divisia Indices", in: Norman Johnson and Samuel Kotz, eds., *Encyclopedia of Statistical Sciences*, vol. 1 (Wiley, New York), forthcoming.
Barnett, William A. and Paul A. Spindt (1979), "The Velocity Behavior and Information Content of Divisia Monetary Aggregates", *Economics Letters*, 4, 51–57.
Barnett, William A., D. Beck, E. Ettin, J. Kalchbrenner, D. Lindsey, R. Porter, T. Simpson,

and P. Tinsley (1979), "A Proposal for Redefining the Monetary Aggregates", *Federal Reserve Bulletin*, 65, 13–42.

Barnett, William A., Kenneth Kopecky, and Ryuzo Sato (1980), "Estimation of Implicit Utility Demand Models", *European Economic Review*, forthcoming.

Barnett, W., E. Offenbacher, and P. Spindt (1981), "New Concepts of Aggregated Money", *Journal of Finance* (Papers and Proceedings of the Thirty-ninth Annual Meeting of the American Finance Association), forthcoming.

Barten, A. P. (1964), "Consumer Demand Functions under Conditions of Almost Additive Preferences", *Econometrica*, 32, 1–38.

Barten, A. P. (1969), "Maximum Likelihood Estimation of a Complete System of Demand Equations", *European Economic Review*, 1, 7–73.

Barten, A. P. (1970), "Réflexions sur la construction d'un système empirique des fonctions de demande", *Cahiers du Seminarie d'Econometrie*, 12, 67–80.

Barten, A. P. (1974), "Complete Systems of Demand Equations: Some Thoughts about Aggregation and Functional Form", *Recherches Economiques de Louvain*, 40, 1–18.

Becker, G. S. (1965), "A Theory of the Allocation of Time", *The Economic Journal*, 75, 493–517.

Berndt, E. R. and N. E. Savin (1975), "Estimation and Hypothesis Testing in Singular Equation Systems with Autoregressive Disturbances", *Econometrica*, 43, 937–957.

Berndt, E. R., W. E. Diewert, and M. N. Darrough (1977), "Flexible Functional Forms and Expenditure Distributions: An Application to Canadian Consumer Demand Functions", *International Economic Review*, 18, 651–676.

Berndt, E. R., B. H. Hall, R. E. Hall, and J. A. Hausman (1974), "Estimation and Inference in Nonlinear Structural Models", *Annals of Economic and Social Measurement*, 3, 653–666.

Betancourt, R. R. (1971a), "Intertemporal Allocation under Additive Preferences: Implications for Cross-Section Data", *Southern Economic Journal*, 37, 458–468.

Betancourt, R. R. (1971b), "The Estimation of Price Elasticities from Cross Section Data under Additive Preferences", *International Economic Review*, 12, 283–292.

Bickel, Peter J. (1967), "Some Contributions to the Theory of Order Statistics", in: Lucien M. LeCam and Jerzy Neyman, eds., *Proceedings of the Fifth Berkeley Symposium on Mathematical Statistics and Probability* (University of California Press, Berkeley), pp. 575–591.

Bisignano, J. (1974), "Real Money Substitutes", *International Economic Review*, forthcoming.

Blackorby, C. and R. Russell (1975), "Implicit Separability and Duality Theory", Discussion Paper No. 75–12 (University of California, Department of Economics, San Diego).

Blackorby, C. and R. Russell (1976), "Functional Structure and the Allen Partial Elasticities of Substitution: An Application of Duality Theory", *Review of Economic Studies*, 43, 285–291.

Blackorby, C. and R. Russell (1979), "Indices and Subindices of the Cost of Living and the Standard of Living", *International Economic Review*, forthcoming.

Blackorby, C., R. Boyce, and R. Russell (1978), "Estimation of Demand Systems Generated by the Gorman Polar Form; A Generalization of the S-Branch Utility Tree", *Econometrica*, 46, 345–364.

Blackorby, C., D. Primont, and R. R. Russell (1977), "On Testing Separability Restrictions with Flexible Functional Forms", *Journal of Econometrics*, 5, 195–209.

Blackorby, C., D. Primont, and R. R. Russell (1978), *Duality, Separability, and Functional Structure* (Elsevier North-Holland, New York).

Boyce, R. and D. Primont (1976), "An Econometric Test for Cost of Living Subindexes", mimeographed (Data Resources, Inc., Cambridge and University of British Columbia, British Columbia).

Breiman, L. (1968), *Probability* (Addison-Wesley, Reading, Massachusetts).

Brooks, R. B. (1970), "Diagonalizing the Hessian Matrix of the Consumer's Utility Function", Doctoral dissertation (University of Chicago).

Brown, Murray and Dale H. Heien (1972), "The S-Branch Utility Tree: A Generalization of the Linear Expenditure System", *Econometrica*, 40, 737–747.
Bryson, A. E. and Y. C. Ho (1969), *Applied Optimal Control* (Blaisdell, Waltham).
Buck, R. C. (1965), *Advanced Calculus* (McGraw-Hill, New York).
Bureau of Labor Statistics, Department of Labor (1971), *Monthly Labor Review*, December.
Bureau of Labor Statistics, Department of Labor (1972), *Monthly Labor Review*, February.
Bureau of Labor Statistics, Department of Labor (1973), *Employment and Earnings*, 19, no. 7, January.
Byron, R. P. (1970a), "The Restricted Aitken Estimation of Sets of Demand Relations", *Econometrica*, 38, 816–830.
Byron, R. P. (1970b), "A Simple Method for Estimating Demand Systems under Separable Utility Assumptions", *Review of Economic Studies*, 37, 261–274.
Chetty, V. K. (1969), "On Measuring the Nearness of Near-Moneys", *American Economic Review*, 59, 270–281.
Chipman, J. S. (1974), "Homothetic Preferences and Aggregation", *Journal of Economic Theory*, 8, 26–38.
Christensen, L. R. (1968), "Savings and the Rate of Return", Doctoral dissertation (University of California, Berkeley).
Christensen, L. R. and D. W. Jorgenson (1968), "Intertemporal Optimization and the Explanation of Consumer Behavior", presented at Meetings of the Econometric Society, December.
Christensen, L. R. and M. E. Manser (1977), "Estimating U.S. Consumer Preferences for Meats with a Flexible Utility Function," *Journal of Econometrics*, 5, 37–53.
Christensen, L. R., D. W. Jorgenson, and L. J. Lau (1975), "Transcendental Logarithmic Utility Functions", *American Economic Review*, 65, 367–383.
Clements, K. W. (1976), "A Linear Allocation of Spending-Power System: A Consumer Demand and Portfolio Model", *Economic Record*, 52, 182–198.
Clements, K. W. and Phuong Nguyen (1979), "Money Demand, Consumer Demand, and Relative Prices in Australia", *Economic Record*, forthcoming.
Clements, K. W. and H. Theil (1979), "A Cross-Country Analysis of Consumption Patterns", Center for Mathematical Studies in Business and Economics Report 7924 (University of Chicago, Chicago).
Conkwright, N. B. (1957), *Introduction to the Theory of Equations* (Ginn, Boston).
Darrough, M. N. (1975), "Intertemporal Allocation of Consumption, Savings, and Leisure: An Application Using Japanese Data", Doctoral dissertation (University of British Columbia, British Columbia).
Darrough, M. N. (1977), "A Model of Consumption and Leisure in an Intertemporal Framework", *International Economic Review*, 18, 677–696.
Deaton, A. (1974a), "The Analysis of Consumer Demand in the United Kingdom, 1900-1970", *Econometrica*, 42, 341–368.
Deaton, A. (1974b), "A Reconsideration of the Empirical Implications of Additive Preferences", *Economic Journal*, 81, 338–347.
Deaton, A. (1978), "Specification and Testing in Applied Demand Analysis", *Economic Journal*, 88, 524–536.
Debreu, G. (1959), *Theory of Value* (John Wiley & Sons, New York).
Debreu, G. (1974), "Excess Demand Functions", *Journal of Mathematical Economics*, 1, 15–21.
Denny, M. (1974), "The Relationship between Functional Forms for Production Systems", *Canadian Journal of Economics*, 7, 21–31.
Dewhurst and Associates (1955), *America's Needs and Resources* (Twentieth Century Fund, New York).
Dhrymes, P. J. (1970), *Econometrics* (Harper and Row, New York).
Diewert, W. E. (1974a), "Applications of Duality Theory", in: M. Intriligator and K.

Kendrick, eds., *Frontiers of Quantitative Economics*, vol. 2 (North-Holland, Amsterdam), pp. 106–171.
Diewert, W. E. (1974b), "Intertemporal Consumer Theory and the Demand for Durables", *Econometrica*, 42, 497–516.
Diewert, W. E. (1976a), "Generalized Slutzky Conditions for Aggregate Consumer Demand Functions", Discussion paper 76-05 (University of British Columbia, British Columbia).
Diewert, W. E. (1976b), "Exact and Superlative Index Numbers", *Journal of Econometrics*, 4, 115–146.
Dixon, P. B. (1975), *The Theory of Joint Maximization* (Elsevier North-Holland, New York).
Dolby, G. R. (1972), "Generalized Least Squares and Maximum Likelihood Estimation of Non-Linear Functional Relationships", *Journal of Royal Statistical Society*, Series B, 34, 393–400.
Donovan, Donal J. (1978), "Modelling the Demand for Liquid Assets: An Application to Canada", *International Monetary Fund Staff Papers*, 25, 676–704.
Doob, J. L. (1953), *Stochastic Processes* (Wiley, New York).
Drud, Arne (1977/1978), "An Optimization Code for Nonlinear Econometric Models Based on Sparse Matrix Techniques and Reduced Gradients", *Annals of Economic and Social Measurement*, 6, 563–580.
Economic Report of the President (1973), (Government Printing Office, Washington, D.C.).
Eisenberg, E. (1961), "Aggregation of Utility Functions", *Management Science*, 7, 337–350.
Eisenpress, H. and J. Greenstadt (1966), "The Estimation of Nonlinear Econometric Systems", *Econometrica*, 34, 851–861.
Emerson, R. and R. R. Russell (1975), "The Structure of Consumer and Produced Duality Theory", Discussion Paper 74-6 (University of California Department of Economics, San Diego).
Fair, R. C. (1972), "A Full-Information Maximum Likelihood Program", *Econometrica*, 40, 773.
Fisher, F. M. (1966), *The Identification Problem in Econometrics* (McGraw-Hill, New York).
Fisher, I. (1922), *The Making of Index Numbers* (Houghton Mifflin, Boston).
Flinn, Christopher, J. (1978), "A Preference Independence Transformation Involving Leisure", Center for Mathematical Studies in Business and Economics Report 7847 (University of Chicago, Chicago).
Friedman, A. (1970), *Foundations of Modern Analysis* (Holt, New York).
Friedman, M. and A. Schwartz (1970), *Monetary Statistics of the United States: Estimates, Sources, Methods* (Columbia University Press, New York).
Frisch, R. (1930), "Necessary and Sufficient Conditions Regarding the Form of an Index Number Which Shall Meet Certain of Fisher's Tests", *Journal of American Statistical Association*, 25, 297–406.
Fuss, Melvyn A. (1977), "The Demand for Energy in Canadian Manufacturing", *Journal of Econometrics*, 5, 89–116.
Gallant, R. A. (1975a), "The Power of the Likelihood Ratio Test of Location in Nonlinear Regression Models", *Journal of the American Statistical Association*, 70, 198–203.
Gallant, R. A. (1975b), "Seemingly Unrelated Nonlinear Regression", *Journal of Econometrics*, 3, 35–50.
Gallant, R. A. (1977), "Three-Stage Least-Squares Estimation for a System of Simultaneous, Nonlinear, Implicit Equations", *Journal of Econometrics*, 5, 71–88.
Goldberger, A. S. (1967), "Functional Form and Utility: A Review of Consumer Demand Theory", Systems Formulation, Methodology, and Policy Workshop Paper no. 6703 (Social Systems Research Institute, University of Wisconsin).
Goldfeld, S. M. (1976), "The Case of the Missing Money", *Brookings Papers on Economic Activity*, 3, 683–730.
Goldfeld, S. M. and R. E. Quandt (1972), *Nonlinear Methods in Econometrics* (North-Holland, Amsterdam).

Goldman, S. M. and H. Uzawa (1964), "A Note on Separability in Demand Analysis", *Econometrica*, 32, 387–398.
Gorman, W. M. (1953), "Community Preference Fields", *Econometrica*, 21, 63–80.
Gorman, W. M. (1970), "Quasi-Separable Preferences, Costs and Technologies", mimeographed (London School of Economics, London).
Green, H. A. J. (1964), *Aggregation in Economic Analysis* (Princeton University Press, Princeton).
Green, H. A. J. (1971), *Consumer Theory* (Penguin, Baltimore).
Grossman, M. (1973), "Unemployment and Consumption: Note", *American Economic Review*, 63, 208–213.
Hadley, G. (1974), *Nonlinear and Dynamic Programming* (Addison-Wesley, Reading, Massachusetts).
Hall, R. E. (1973), "The Specification of Technology with Several Kinds of Outputs", *Journal of Political Economy*, 3, 878–892.
Hanoch, G. (1970), "Generation of New Production Functions through Duality" (Harvard Institute of Economic Research, Cambridge).
Hanoch, G. (1975), "Production and Demand Models with Direct and Indirect Implicit Additivity", *Econometrica*, 43, 395–419.
Hartley, H. O. (1964), "Exact Confidence Regions for the Parameters in Non-Linear Regression Laws", *Biometrika*, 51, 347–353.
Hasenkamp, G. (1975), "Index Numbers and Sub-Systems of Demand Equations", presented at the Third World Congress of the Econometric Society, Toronto.
Hatanaka, Michio (1979), "On the Efficient Estimation Methods for the Macro-Economic Models Nonlinear in Variables", *Journal of Econometrics*, forthcoming.
Hausman, Jerry A. (1975), "An Instrumental Variable Approach to Full-Information Estimators for Linear and Certain Nonlinear Econometric Models", *Econometrica*, 43, 727–738.
Heckman, J. (1974), "Shadow Prices, Market Wages, and Labor Supply", *Econometrica*, 42, 676–694.
Hoel, P., S. Port, and C. Stone (1972), *Introduction to Stochastic Processes* (Houghton Mifflin, Boston).
Hood, W. C. and T. C. Koopmans (1953), *Studies in Econometric Methods* (John Wiley and Sons, New York).
Houthakker, H. S. (1962), "Additive Preferences", *Econometrica*, 28, 244-257; errata, 30 (1962) 633.
Hulten, C. R. (1973), "Divisia Index Numbers", *Econometrica*, 63, 1017–1026.
Huzurbazar, V. S. (1948), "The Likelihood Equation, Consistency, and Maxima of the Likelihood Function", *Annals of Eugenics (London)*, 14, 185–200.
Jennrich, R. I. (1969), "Asymptotic Properties of Non-Linear Least Squares Estimators", *Annals of Mathematical Statistics*, 40, 633–643.
Jorgenson, D. W. and Jean-Jacques Laffont (1974), "Efficient Estimation of Nonlinear Simultaneous Equations with Additive Disturbances", *Annals of Economic and Social Measurement*, 3, 615–640.
Jorgenson, D. W. and L. Lau (1975), "The Structure of Consumer Preferences", *Annals of Economic and Social Measurement*, 4, 49–101.
Jorgenson, D. W. and L. Lau (1977), "Statistical Tests of the Theory of Consumer Behavior", in: H. Albach, E. Helmstädter and R. Henn, eds., *Quantitative Wirtschaftsforschung* (J. C. B. Mohr, Tübingen), pp. 383–394.
Journal of Political Economy (1973), 81, no. 2, part II, March/April, supplement.
Journal of Political Economy (1974), 82, no. 2, part II, March/April, supplement.
Kadiyala, K. R. (1972), "Production Functions and Elasticity of Substitution", *Southern Economic Journal*, 38, 281–284.
Katzner, D. W. (1970), *Static Demand Theory* (Macmillan, London).
Keller, W. J. (1976), "A Nested CES-Type Utility Function and its Demand and Price-Index

Functions", *European Economic Review*, 7, 175–186.
Kendall, M. G. and A. S. Stuart (1961), *The Advanced Theory of Statistics*, vol. 2 (Hafner, New York).
Kendrick, J. W. (1961), *Productivity Trends in the United States* (Princeton University Press, Princeton).
Kiefer, N. M. (1975), "Quadratic Utility, Labor Supply, and Commodity Demand", in: S. M. Goldfeld and R. E. Quandt, eds., *Studies in Nonlinear Estimation* (Ballinger, Cambridge), pp. 167–179.
Kiefer, N. M. (1977), "A Bayesian Analysis of Commodity Demand and Labor Supply", *International Economic Review*, 18, 209–218.
Kiefer, N. M. and J. MacKinnon (1976), "Small Sample Properties of Demand System Estimates", in: S. M. Goldfeld and R. E. Quandt, eds., *Studies in Nonlinear Estimation* (Ballinger, Cambridge), pp. 181–210.
Klein, Benjamin (1974), "Competitive Interest Payments on Bank Deposits and the Long-Run Demand for Money", *American Economic Review*, 64, 931–949.
Knowles, J. W. (1960), "The Potential Economic Growth in the United States", Study Paper no. 20, Joint Economic Committee, 86th Congress of the United States (Government Printing Office, Washington, D. C.), January.
Koopmans, T. C. (1957), *Three Essays on the State of Economic Science* (McGraw-Hill, New York).
Koopmans, T. C., H. Rubin, and R. B. Leipnik (1950), "Measuring the Equation Systems of Dynamic Economics", in: T. C. Koopmans, ed., *Statistical Inference in Dynamic Economic Models*, Cowles Commission Monograph 10 (John Wiley and Sons, New York), pp. 53–237.
Kuhn, H. and A. Tucker (1951), "Nonlinear Programming", in: J. Neyman, ed., *Proceedings of the Second Berkeley Symposium on Mathematical Statistics and Probability* (University of California Press, Berkeley), pp. 481–492.
Kuznets, S. (1952), ed., *Income and Wealth of the United States, Trends and Structures*, Income and Wealth Series II, International Association for Research in Income and Wealth (Bowes and Bowes, Cambridge, England).
Kuznets, S. (1961), *Capital in the American Economy* (National Bureau of Economic Research, New York).
Laitinen, K. (1978), "Why is Demand Homogeneity So Often Rejected?", *Economics Letters*, 1, 187–192.
Laitinen, K. and H. Theil (1979), "Supply and Demand of the Multiproduct Firm", *European Economic Review*, forthcoming.
Lancaster, K. J. (1966), "A New Approach to Consumer Theory", *Journal of Political Economy*, 74, 132–157.
Lange, O. (1942), "Theoretical Derivation of Elasticities of Demand and Supply: The Direct Method", *Econometrica*, 10, 193–214.
Lazarsfeld, P. and J. Rosenberg (1971), *The Language of Social Research* (Free Press, New York).
Lebergott, S. (1964), *Manpower in Economic Growth* (McGraw-Hill, New York).
Leser, C. E. V. (1963), "Forms of Engel Functions", *Econometrica*, 31, 694–703.
Lluch, C. (1973), "The Extended Linear Expenditure System", *European Economic Review*, 4, 21–32.
Maks, J. A. H. (1978), "Consistency and Consumer Behavior in the Netherlands, 1921-1962", *European Economic Review*, 11, 343–362.
Malinvaud, E. (1966), *Statistical Methods of Econometrics* (North-Holland, Amsterdam).
Malinvaud, E. (1970a), "The Consistency of Nonlinear Regression", *Annals of Mathematical Statistics*, 41, 956–969.
Malinvaud, E. (1970b), *Statistical Methods of Econometrics* (North-Holland, Amsterdam).
Mantel, R. R. (1974), "On the Characterization of Aggregate Excess Demand", *Journal of Economic Theory*, 7, 348–353.

Mantel, R. R. (1976), "Homothetic Preferences and Community Excess Demand Functions", *Journal of Economic Theory*, 12, 197–201.
Mantell, J. B. and L. S. Lasdon (1977/1978), "A GRG Algorithm for Econometric Control Problems", *Annals of Economic and Social Measurement*, 6, 581–598.
McFadden, Daniel (1964), "Notes on Professor Theil's Demand System", mimeographed (University of California, Berkeley).
McFadden, D. (1978), "Cost, Revenue, and Profit Functions", in: M. Fuss and D. McFadden, eds., *Production Economics: A Dual Approach to Theory and Applications* (North-Holland, Amsterdam).
McFadden, D., A. Mas-Colell, Rolf Mantel, and Marcel K. Richter (1974), "A Characterization of Community Excess Demand Functions", *Journal of Economic Theory*, 9, 361–374.
Meisner, J. F. (1979a), "The Sad Fate of the Asymptotic Slutsky Symmetry Test for Large Systems", *Economics Letters*, 2, 231–234.
Meisner, J. F. (1979b), "Alternative Demand Models for Close Substitutes", *Economics Letters*, 3, 77–80.
Meisner, J. F. and K. W. Clements (1979), "Specific Complements and the Demand for Money in Australia", *Economics Letters*, forthcoming.
Mossin, A. (1968), "Time Horizons and Terminal Capital", *Swedish Journal of Economics*, 70, 200–220.
Muellbauer, J. (1975), "Aggregation, Income Distribution and Consumer Demand", *Review of Economic Studies*, 62, 524–544.
Muellbauer, J. (1976), "Community Preferences and the Representative Consumer", *Econometrica*, 44, 979–999.
Muellbauer, J. (1977), "Testing the Barten Model of Household Composition Effects and the Cost of Children", *The Economic Journal*, 87, 460–487.
Mundlak, Y. and A. Razin (1969), "Aggregation, Index Numbers and the Measurement of Technical Change", *The Review of Economics and Statistics*, 51, 166–175.
Nasse, P. (1970), "Analyse des effets de substitution dans un système complet de fonctions de demande", *Annales de l'Inséé* (Institut National de la Statistique et des Etudes Economiques), 5, 81–110.
Nepomiastchy, Pierre and Alain Ravelli (1977/1978), "Adapted Methods for Solving and Optimizing Quasi-Triangular Econometric Models", *Annals of Economic and Social Measurement*, 6, 555–562.
Nerlove, Marc, (1974), "Household and Economy: Toward a New Theory of Population and Economic Growth", *Journal of Political Economy*, 82, March/April supplement, 200–218.
Offenbacher, Edward K. (1979), "The Substitutability of Monetary Assets", mimeographed (Board of Governors of the Federal Reserve System, Washington, D. C.).
Owen, J. D. (1964), "The Demand for Recreation in the United States, 1900–1961", Doctoral dissertation (Columbia University, New York).
Owen, J. D. (1970), *The Price of Leisure* (McGill-Queen's University Press, Montreal).
Owen, J. D. (1971), "The Demand for Leisure", *Journal of Political Economy*, 79, 56–76.
Parkin, J. M., R. J. Cooper, J. R. Henderson, and M. K. Danes (1975), "An Integrated Model of Consumption, Investment, and Portfolio Decisions", in: *Papers in Monetary Economics*, vol. 2 (Reserve Bank of Australia, Sydney), pp. 1–59.
Parks, R. W. (1969), "Systems of Demand Equations: An Empirical Comparison of Alternative Functional Forms", *Econometrica*, 37, 629–650.
Paulus, J. D. (1972), "The Estimation of Large Systems of Consumer Demand Equations Using Stochastic Prior Information", Doctoral dissertation (University of Chicago, Chicago).
Paulus, J. D. (1975), "Mixed Estimation of Complete Demand Equations", *Annals of Economic and Social Measurements*, 4, 117–132.
Pearce, I. F. (1964), *A Contribution to Demand Analysis* (Oxford University Press, London).
Phillips, P. C. B. (1976), "On the Iterated Minimum Distance Estimator and the Quasi-Maximum Likelihood Estimator", *Econometrica*, 44, 449–460.

Phlips, L. (1974), *Applied Consumption Analysis* (North-Holland, Amsterdam).
Phlips, L. (1978), "The Demand for Leisure and Money", *Econometrica*, 46, 1025–1044.
Pollak, R. A. (1976), "Habit Formation and the Long-Run Utility Functions", *Journal of Economic Theory*, 13, 272–297.
Pollak, R. A. and M. L. Wachter (1975), "The Relevance of the Household Production Function and its Implications for the Allocation of Time", *Journal of Political Economy*, 83, 255–277.
Pollak, R. A. and M. L. Wachter (1977), "Reply: Pollak and Wachter on the Household Production Approach", *Journal of Political Economy*, 85, 1083–1086.
Pollak, R. and T. Wales (1969), "Estimation of the Linear Expenditure System", *Econometrica*, 37, 611–628.
Powell, A. (1966), "A Complete System of Consumer Demand Equations for the Australian Economy Fitted by a Model of Additive Preferences", *Econometrica*, 34, 661–675.
Powell, A., T. V. Hoa, and R. H. Wilson (1968), "A Multi-Sectoral Analysis of Consumer Demand in the Post-War Period", *Southern Economic Journal*, 35, 109–120.
Prais, S. J. and H. S. Houthakker (1971), *Analysis of Family Budgets* (Cambridge University Press, Cambridge).
Pudney, S. E. (1980), "Disaggregated Demand Analysis: The Estimation of a Class of Large Nonlinear Demand Equations", *Review of Economic Studies*, 47, 875–892.
Quirk, James and Rubin Saposnik (1968), *Introduction to General Equilibrium Theory and Welfare Economics* (McGraw-Hill, New York).
Radner, R. (1968), "Competitive Equilibrium under Uncertainty", *Econometrica*, 36, 31–58.
Rao, C. R. (1973), *Linear Statistical Inference and its Applications* (John Wiley and Sons, New York).
Rothenberg, T. J. (1973), *Efficient Estimation with a Priori Information*, Cowles Foundation Monograph 23 (York University Press, New Haven).
Samuelson, P. A. (1947), *Foundations of Economic Analysis* (Atheneum, New York).
Samuelson, P. A. (1950), "The Problem of Integrability in Utility Theory", *Economica*, 17, 355–385.
Samuelson, P. A. and S. Swamy (1974), "Invariant Economic Index Numbers and Canonical Duality: Survey and Synthesis", *American Economic Review*, 64, 566–593.
Sato, Ryuzo (1976), "The Implicit Formulation and Non-Homothetic Structure of Utility Functions", in: H. Albach, E. Helmstädter, and R. Henn, eds., *Quantitative Wirtschaftsforschung* (J. C. B. Mohr, Tübingen), pp. 580–595.
Shiller, Robert J. (1979), "The Volatility of Long-Term Interest Rates and Expectations Models of the Term Structure", *Journal of Political Economy*, 37, 1190–1219.
Silvey, S. D. (1959), "The Lagrange Multiplier Test", *Annals of Mathematical Statistics*, 30, 389–407.
Simmons, P. (1979), "A Theorem on Aggregation across Consumers in Neoclassical Labour Supply", *Review of Economic Studies*, 46, 737–740.
Solari, Luigi (1971), *Théorie des Choix et Fonctions de Consommation Semi-Agrégées* (Librarie PROZ, Geneva).
Sonnenschein, H. (1973), "The Utility Hypothesis and Market Demand Theory", *Western Economic Journal*, 11, 404–410.
Stone, J. R. N. (1953), *The Measurement of Consumers' Expenditure and Behavior in the United Kingdom, 1920–1938*, vol. 1 (Cambridge University Press, Cambridge, England).
Swamy, P. A. V. B. (1971), *Statistical Inference in Random Coefficients Regression Models* (Springer-Verlag, New York).
Theil, H. (1967), *Economics and Information Theory* (North-Holland, Amsterdam).
Theil, H. (1971), *Principles of Econometrics* (Wiley, New York).
Theil, H. (1972), *Statistical Decomposition Analysis* (North-Holland, Amsterdam).
Theil, H. (1975), *Theory and Measurement of Consumer Demand*, vol. 1 (North-Holland, Amsterdam).

Theil, H. (1976), *Theory and Measurement of Consumer Demand*, vol. 2 (North-Holland, Amsterdam).
Theil, H. (1977), "The Independent Inputs of Production", *Econometrica*, 45, 1303–1327.
Theil, H. (1979), "Equicorrelated Substitutes and Nasse's Extension of the Linear Extension System", *Economics Letters*, 3, 81–84.
Theil, H. (1980), *The Systemwide Approach to Microeconomics* (University of Chicago Press, Chicago).
Theil, H. and R. B. Brooks (1970), "How Does the Marginal Utility of Income Change when Real Income Changes?", *European Economic Review*, 2, 218–239.
Theil, H. and K. Laitinen (1979), "Maximum Likelihood Estimation of the Rotterdam Model under Two Different Conditions", *Economics Letters*, 2, 239–244.
Tinsley, P., P. Spindt, and M. Friar (1980), "Indicator and Filter Attributes of Monetary Aggregates: A Nit-Picking Case for Disaggregation", *Journal of Econometrics*, 14, 61–69.
Törnquist, L. (1936), "The Bank of Finland's Consumption Price Index", *Bank of Finland Bulletin*, 10, 1–8.
Triplett, Jack E. (1976), "The Measurement of Inflation: a Survey of Research on the Accuracy of Price Indices", in: Paul H. Earl, ed., *Analysis of Inflation* (D.C. Heath, Lexington, Massachusetts), pp. 19–82.
Tucker, H. G. (1967), *A Graduate Course in Probability* (Academic Press, New York).
United States Bureau of the Census (1960), *Historical Statistics of the United States, Colonial Times to 1957* (Government Printing Office, Washington, D.C.).
United States Department of Agriculture (1968a), *Food: Consumption, Prices, Expenditures* (United States Government Printing Office, Washington, D.C.).
United States Department of Agriculture (1968b), *Supplement to Food: Consumption, Prices, Expenditures* (United States Government Printing Office, Washington, D.C.).
Wald, A. (1949), "Note on the Consistency of the Maximum Likelihood Estimate", *Annals of Mathematical Statistics*, 20, 595–602.
Wales, T. J. (1977), "On the Flexibility of Flexible Functional Forms: An Empirical Approach", *Journal of Econometrics*, 5, 183–193.
Wegge, Leon L. (1965), "Identifiability Criteria for a System of Equations as a Whole", *The Australian Journal of Statistics*, 7, 67–77.
Weiss, L. (1971), "Asymptotic Properties of Maximum Likelihood Estimators in Some Nonstandard Cases", *Journal of American Statistical Association*, 66, 345–350.
Weiss, L. (1973), "Asymptotic Properties of Maximum Likelihood Estimators in Some Nonstandard Cases, II", *Journal of American Statistical Association*, 68, 428–430.
Weiss, L. (1975), "The Asymptotic Distribution of the Likelihood Ratio in Some Nonstandard Models", *Journal of the American Statistical Association*, 70, 204–208.
Willig, R. D. (1976), "Integrability Implications for Locally Constant Demand Elasticities", *Journal of Economic Theory*, 12, 391–401.
Willis, Robert J. (1973), "A New Approach to the Economic Theory of Fertility Behavior", *Journal of Political Economy*, 81, March/April supplement, 14–64.
Wold, H. and L. Juréen (1953), *Demand Analysis* (Wiley, New York).
Wolfowitz, J. (1965), "Asymptotic Efficiency of the Maximum Likelihood Estimator", *Theory of Probability and its Applications*, 10, 247–254.
Working, H. (1943), "Statistical Laws of Family Expenditure", *Journal of the American Statistical Association*, 38, 43–56.
Wymer, C. R. (1977), "Computer Programs: RESIMUL Manual", International Monetary Fund, manuscript.
Yoshihara, K. (1969), "Demand Functions: An Application to the Japanese Expenditure Pattern," *Econometrica*, 37, 257–274.

AUTHOR INDEX

Abbott, M., 4, 9, 10, 29, 30, 100, 113, 123, 127, 133
Afriat, S.N., 187
Amemiya, T., 75, 236
Anderson, R., 203
Arrow, K., 191
Ashenfelter, O., 4, 9, 10, 29, 30, 100, 113, 123, 127, 133

Bahadur, R.R., 91
Bard, Y., 77
Barnett, W.A., 10, 55, 59, 75, 95, 96, 116, 171, 185, 203, 219, 222, 227, 229, 231, 233, 236, 262, 271
Barten, A.P., 43, 52, 69, 115, 269
Beck, D., 219, 229
Becker, G.S., 21, 190, 250, 254
Berndt, E.R., 77, 92, 214, 321
Betancourt, R.R., 4, 10
Bickel, P.J., 81
Bisignano, J., 191
Blackorby, C., 92, 161, 189, 259, 260, 261, 262, 319
Boyce, R., 92, 259
Breiman, L., 312
Brooks, R.B., 69, 233, 249
Brown, M., 159
Bryson, A.E., 277
Buck, R.C., 181, 314
Byron, R.P., 48

Chapman, D., 103, 121, 139, 140
Chetty, V.K., 191
Chipman, J.S., 305
Christensen, L.R., 4, 5, 9, 10, 14, 39, 50, 56, 109, 110, 293, 320, 321
Clements, K.W., 73, 191
Conkwright, N.B., 247
Cooper, M.J., 191

Danes, M.K., 191
Darrough, M.N., 10, 126, 321
Davison, J., 323, 331
Deaton, A., 69, 317, 321
Debreu, G., 306
Denny, M., 161
Dewhurst, J.F., 101
Dhrymes, P.J., 89, 341
Diewert, W.E., 10, 191, 204, 220, 221, 222, 224, 226, 231, 239, 243, 247, 259, 307, 321
Dixon, P.B., 26, 192
Donovan, D.J., 191, 192
Doob, J.L., 313
Drud, A., 277

Eisenberg, E., 305
Eisenpress, H., 77, 160, 166, 236, 323, 324, 329, 330, 331
Emerson, R., 259
Ettin, E., 219, 229

Fair, R.C., 103, 121, 139, 140
Fisher, F.M., 238, 240, 242, 251
Fisher, I., 188, 189, 193, 203, 204, 217, 220, 221, 222, 231
Flinn, C.J., 233, 249, 255
Friar, M., 228
Friedman, A., 191
Friedman, M., 185, 191
Frisch, R., 188, 189, 251, 254
Fuss, M.A., 203, 214

Gallant, R.A., 76, 77, 95, 236
Goldberger, A.S., 45, 46, 47, 129
Goldfeld, S.M., 76, 89
Goldman, S.M., 10, 12
Gorman, W.M., 72, 159, 259, 304, 305, 307, 315, 321

Green, H.A.J., 10, 162, 163, 199, 200, 201, 305, 307, 310
Greenstadt, J., 160, 323, 324, 325
Grossman, M., 5, 39, 50, 109, 293

Hadley, G., 295
Hahn, F., 191
Hall, R.E., 77, 236, 239
Hall, B.H., 77
Hanoch, G., 259, 261, 262, 265, 266, 270
Hartley, H.O., 89
Hasenkamp, G., 165
Hatanaka, M., 76
Hausman, J.A., 76, 77
Heckman, J., 6, 30, 32
Heien, D.H., 159
Henderson, J.R., 191
Ho, Y.C., 277
Hoa, T.V., 5
Hoel, P., 313
Houthakker, H.S., 5, 23, 24, 25, 55, 152, 261, 283, 284
Hulten, C.R., 221, 231
Huzurbazar, V.S., 89

Jennrich, R.I., 76, 77, 80, 83
Jorgensen, D.W., 4, 9, 14, 56, 77, 193, 194, 320, 321, 325
Juréen, L., 307

Kadiyala, K.R., 161
Kalchbrenner, J., 219, 229
Katzner, D.W., 12, 178, 179, 180, 305
Keller, W.J., 165
Kendall, M.G., 89
Kendrick, J.W., 350
Kiefer, N.M., 10, 127, 166
Klein, B., 199, 205
Knowles, J.W., 350
Koopmans, T.C., 76, 96, 103, 121, 238
Kopecky, K., 271, 323, 331
Kuhn, H., 35, 295, 297
Kuznets, S., 27, 29, 99, 100, 128, 347

Laffont, J., 77, 325
Laitinen, K., 94, 133, 138
Lancaster, K.J., 190, 250, 254
Lange, O., 179

Lasdon, L.S., 277
Lau, L., 56, 320, 321
Lazarsfeld, P., 248
Lebergott, S., 350
Leipnik, R.B., 76, 96, 103, 121
Leontief, W., 187
Leser, C.E.V., 73
Lindsey, D., 219, 229
Lluch, C., 58

MacKinnon, J., 166
Maks, J.A.H., 192
Malinvaud, E., 7, 75, 76, 77, 78, 79, 80, 81, 82, 83, 84, 85, 86, 88, 91, 313
Manser, M.E., 56
Mantell, R.P., 277, 306, 307
Mas-Colell, A., 306
McFadden, D., 259, 305, 306, 316
Meisner, J.F., 73, 94
Mincer, J., 4
Mossin, A., 65
Muellbauer, J., 20, 306, 307
Mundlak, Y., 166

Nasse, P., 73
Nepomiastchy, P., 277
Nerlove, M., 19
Nguyen, P., 191
Norman, A., 274

Offenbacher, E.K., 191, 199, 205, 213, 231
Owen, J.D., 4, 5, 6, 10, 12, 39, 50, 111, 293

Parkin, J.M., 191
Parks, R.W., 152
Patinkin, D., 191
Paulus, J.D., 67, 69
Pearce, I.F., 26, 178, 179, 180
Phillips, P.C.B., 80, 91
Phlips, L., 56, 58, 191, 305, 320
Pollak, R.A., 165, 198, 211, 233, 234, 236, 242, 243, 244, 245, 246, 247, 248
Port, S., 313
Porter, R., 219
Powell, A., 5
Prais, S.J., 5, 23, 24, 25, 55, 283, 284
Primont, D., 161, 189, 259, 262, 319
Pudney, S.E., 273

Quandt, R.E., 76, 89
Quirk, J., 191

Rao, C.R., 65, 91, 339, 341, 343
Ravelli, A., 277
Razin, A., 169
Richter, M.K., 306
Rosenberg, J., 248
Rothenberg, T.J., 91
Rubin, H., 76, 96, 103, 121
Russell, R., 92, 161, 189, 259, 260, 261, 262, 319

Samuelson, P.A., 19, 179, 187, 188, 198
Saposnik, R., 191
Sato, R., 261, 262, 271
Savin, N.E., 214
Schwartz, A., 185
Shiller, R.J., 205
Silvey, S.D., 79
Simmons, P., 306
Simpson, T., 219, 229
Solari, L., 161, 162, 165
Sonnenschein, H., 306, 307, 309
Spindt, P., 227, 228, 231
Stone, C., 313
Stone, J.R.N., 42, 45, 152
Strotz, R.H., 58
Stuart, A.S., 89
Swamy, P.A.V.B., 69
Swamy, S., 187, 188, 198

Theil, H., 9, 11, 39, 43, 52, 54, 55, 59, 60, 61, 62, 63, 67, 68, 69, 73, 100, 112, 115, 117, 121, 123, 136, 137, 138, 144, 147, 148, 149, 150, 163, 201, 220, 221, 222, 223, 226, 227, 228, 230, 231, 233, 249, 250, 251, 252, 276, 307, 308, 310, 314, 316, 321
Tinsley, P., 219, 228, 229
Törnquist, L., 221, 222, 223, 226, 227, 228, 230, 231
Triplett, J.E., 204
Tucker, A., 35, 295, 297
Tucker, H.G., 312

Uzawa, H., 10, 11

Wachter, M.L., 233, 234, 236, 242, 243, 244, 245, 246, 247, 248
Wald, A., 83
Wales, T., 165, 262, 320
Wegge, L.L., 238
Weiss, L., 91
Willig, R.D., 316
Willis, R.J., 19
Wilson, R.H., 5
Wold, H., 307
Wolfowitz, J., 91
Working, H., 73
Wymer, C.R., 77, 236, 325

Yoshihara, K., 56, 305, 316

Zellner, A., 121

SUBJECT INDEX

Accounting practices, monetary aggregation, 188, 216
Additive preferences. *See* Strong separability of preferences
Affine origin, transformation to, 164–165, 305
Aggregation over consumers:
  with existence of representative consumer, 26, 31–32, 136, 159–160, 187, 204, 251, 263, 303–307
  with existence of representative household, 5, 26–27, 55, 250
  general case, 65, 303–304
  with leisure, 306
  limiting stochastic transformation, 57, 63, 65, 135
    aggregated system, 63
    asymptotic aggregation bias of Slutsky macrocoefficients, 68, 73, 307–308
    components of remainder term, 66, 114, 131–133; magnitudes, 307–313
    empirical income distribution function, 61
    macrocoefficients, 61
    random microcoefficients, 60–61
    remainder term (definition), 64
    theoretical income distribution function, 61, 309–313
    theoretical restrictions, 65
  methods:
    mean demand function, 65
    recent aggregation literature, 306–307
    stochastic convergence approach, 39, 61
    stratification approach, 307
    Also see Integrability, aggregate
Aggregation over goods:
  conditions for consistent linear aggregation, 219
  conditions for consistent three-stage decision, 11, 162–163
  conditions for consistent two-stage decision, 4–5, 8–13, 40, 42, 133, 160–162, 185, 199–201, 208, 213, 217, 259
  aggregate commodity consumption, 10
  differential consistency, 201
  conditions for selection of components of aggregate, 218
  conditions for separation of labor supply from consumer demand, 3, 9, 133–135, 154
  Hicksian aggregation, 287
  Also see Index numbers; Recursive structures; Monetary aggregation
Aggregation, recursive. *See* Recursive structures: recursive aggregation
Antonelli matrix, 179, 183

BAN estimators, 91
Basic wants, 250, 258
Bayesian estimation, 127, 169
Benchmark asset (definition), 194, 199, 205
Bergson demand system, 239
Best CUAN estimators, 91
Beverages, demand for. *See* WS-branch utility function: estimates
Bonds. *See* Benchmark asset (definition)

Cardinal utility, 135–136, 178, 250–251, 319
Category utility function, 201
Causality. *See* Household production function approach: causality
Cereals, demand for. *See* WS-branch utility function: estimates
Certificates of deposit. *See* Large certificates of deposit; Time deposits
CES (Constant Elasticity of Substitution) utility function:
  homothetic, 207, 209, 212–213, 261
  nonhomothetic, 270

Subject index

Cobb–Douglas utility, 39–42, 56, 160, 239–240, 247, 261, 301, 315, 317–320
Commodities (definition of) in household production function approach. *See* Household production function approach: definitions: commodities
Composite likelihood function, 271, 274
Computer programs:
  FIML estimation:
    Chapman–Fair, 103n, 121, 139–140
    Eisenpress–Barnett, 77, 160, 236, 323–331; job control language and cataloged procedures, 327–331; user instructions, 323–327
    Harvard's TSP, 77, 236
    NBER programs, 77
    Wymer's RESIMUL, 77, 236, 325
  GLS estimation, finite step:
    Zellner Three Stage Least Squares, 121
  iterated Aitken estimation:
    Harvard's TSP, 83
  optimal control, 277
Community utility function, 44
  Also see Integrability, aggregate; Locally integrable demand systems
Conditional income elasticities, 255
Constant-commodity-consumption goods demand functions (in household production function approach), definition, 235
Consumption characteristics, 190–192, 233
Consumption function:
  full, 9, 14
  Modigliani–Brumberg–Ando, 14
Consumption set, 58
Contrasts, transformed goods as, 257
Convexity of preferences, 160, 171, 178
Corner solutions:
  Kuhn–Tucker conditions, 6, 35, 295–299
  labor market, 17, 20, 23, 30–42
  Also see Inequality constraints on parameters; Price of leisure (shadow)
Correspondence with an aggregate demand system, 303
Cost function, 236, 261
  Also see Hybrid Diewert joint cost function
Cost of living index, true, 195, 204, 259–260
Cournot aggregation (definition), 46

Covariance matrix, error. *See* Error covariance matrix
Cramer–Rao variances, 89
Cross effects (definition), 171
CSE (Constant Slutsky Elasticity) model, 44–49, 101–113
  differential form, 45–46
  empirical specification, 48, 52
  estimation, 50, 101–113
    precision of price of leisure specification's parameter estimator, 108–109
    ridge lines of likelihood function, 109–110
    robustness to rescaling of leisure consumption, 105
  simplification of form, 46–47
Currency, 185, 187
  Also see Transactions balances; Monetary aggregation

Dairy products, demand for. *See* WS-branch utility function: estimates
Data and data sources:
  durables consumption and prices, 99–100, 347–349
  food quantities and prices, 169–170
  hours available per able-bodied person, 100
  interest rates, 205–206
  labor force participation, 101
  leisure consumption, 100, 347–350
  marginal tax rate, 206
  monetary asset balances, 205
  perishables consumption and prices, 99, 347–349
  population, 204, 347–349
  price of leisure, 100
  semidurables consumption and prices, 99, 347–349
  services consumption and prices, 99, 347–349
  Swedish, 152
  unemployment rate, 348–350
  upper bound on labor force participation rate, 100–101
  wage rate, 347–350
Demand deposits, 187
  Also see Transactions balances; Monetary aggregation

Subject index

Demand homogeneity, 46–47, 51
Demand systems. *See* CSE (Constant Slutsky Elasticity) model; Cobb–Douglas utility; CES (Constant Elasticity of Substitution) utility function; Rotterdam Model, absolute price version; Rotterdam Model, relative price version; WS-branch utility function; G-hypo (generalized hypocycloidal) utility function; Translog model; Generalized Leontief model; Generalized Cobb–Douglas utility; Gorman's polar form; S-branch demand system; Differential approach; Direct (Explicit) Addilog utility function; DIA (Direct Implicit Addilog) model; IIA (Indirect Implicit Addilog) model; Indirect Addilog Model; Locally integrable demand systems; Linear expenditure system; Double log demand model; Bergson demand system
Depressions and recessions, 8, 107
Development, economic, 5
DIA (Direct Implicit Addilog) model:
  control theoretic approach to estimation: the algorithm, 276–277; available computer programs, 277
  the optimal control analog, 274–276
  derivation of the model, 262–265
  elasticities, 267
  identification and normalization, 265–266
  inverse demand system:
    implicit form, 272–273
    reduced form, 273
  special cases, 270
  structural estimation with conventional algorithms, 262, 265–270
    additive structural errors, 267–270
    nonuniqueness of estimator, 268–270
  Also see Implicit utility models
Differential approach, 11, 55n, 251
Direct (Explicit) Addilog utility function, 261, 265–266, 270
Distance function, 259–261
Divisia index. *See* Index numbers: statistical: Divisia
Double log demand model, 49
Duality:
  between direct and inverse demand, 160, 178–184
  dual functional structures (general), 259
  duality between price and quantity aggregates, 159, 188–189, 192, 195n, 200, 202–203, 216
  in household production function approach, 246
Durables demand:
  estimation of function, 103–154
  forecasting, 8
  interaction with demand for leisure. *See* Leisure demand: interaction with demand for durables
  preference independence transformation, 254–258
Durable goods:
  stability of historical income share, 7, 108
  time-saving, 7, 113, 136, 257
  user cost of, 197

Econometric models, large, 4
Eggs, demand for. *See* WS-branch utility function: estimates
Elasticity of substitution, 210, 215, 218, 351–354
Engle aggregation (definition), 46
Engle's law, 11
Entropy, 227
Environmental factors, 310
Error covariance matrix:
  block diagonal, 175
  singularity, 45, 49, 52–53, 77, 115, 170, 269
Errors-in-the-variables, 166
Error structure:
  autoregressive, 144, 147–148, 166, 214–215
  nonlinearly imbedded, 262, 268
  tests. *See* Rotterdam model (general): residual analysis and error structure tests
Euclidean distance normalization. *See* WS-branch utility function: normalization of parameters
Expectations. *See* Intertemporal allocation: expectations

Factor demand function, 236
  Also see Hybrid Diewert joint cost function

Fats and oils, demand for. *See* WS-branch utility function: estimates
Feasible parameter set, 317
Filters, 228n
Firms, 200, 220
Flexible functional forms. *See* Locally integrable demand systems
Food:
  demand modeling, 159–184
  price forecasting. *See* Forecasting, price
Forecasting, price, 159, 179
Free time, 257
Frisch price index. *See* Index numbers: statistical: Frisch
Fruits and vegetables, fresh, demand for. *See* WS-branch utility function: estimates
Fruits and vegetables, processed, demand for. *See* WS-branch utility function: estimates
Full-employment-equivalent income level. *See* Shadow income level, definition
Full-employment-equivalent price of leisure. *See* Price of leisure (shadow)
Full income, 7–8, 10, 13, 21–22, 107–108, 123, 255, 258
Full wealth, 13, 22
Functional structure, theory of, 189

Galois theory, 247
Generalized Cobb-Douglas model. *See* Locally integrable demand systems
General equilibrium theory, 56, 305
Generalized least squares, nonlinear:
  finite step, 6–7, 75, 79, 121–122, 137–142
  iterated (to convergence), 77, 82
Generalized Leontief model. *See* Locally integrable demand systems
Generalized variance of fit, 77, 102, 104, 275
G-hypo (generalized hypocycloidal) utility function. *See* WS-branch utility function: g-hypo (generalized hypocycloidal) special case
Goods (definition of) in household production function approach. *See* Household production function approach: definitions: goods
Gorman's polar form, 305
Growth models, 34

Habit formation, 176, 184, 198, 212–213
Hereditary factors, 310
Homogeneity of demand, 6, 199
Homogeneous separability. *See* Homothetic separability
Homothetic preferences, 10–11, 41, 133–134, 142, 161, 163–164, 187, 189, 192, 194, 197–198, 200–203, 209n, 213, 217, 260, 306, 315
Homothetic separability, 14, 42, 161, 199, 217
Household model (theory):
  able-bodied household members, 22–31
  adult equivalent scale, 20
  age-sex composition of household, 20, 25
  change in notation, 29
  household capital (nonlabor) income, 19–31, 34, 123
  household savings, 19–31
  household size, 19–31
  labor force participation rate, 17–18, 25, 30, 113
    Also see Household model (theory): rescaling of available hours
  non-able-bodied household members, 21–31
  per capita leisure, 25–26, 113
  Prais-Houthakker homogeneity postulate, 24
    extended, 5, 23–26, 55, 283–285
  proofs (appendix), 281–286
  representative household. *See* Aggregation over consumers: with existence of representative household
  rescaling of available hours, 27–29
    upper bound on labor force participation rate, 28, 255
  supernumerary leisure, 29
  unemployment, 18, 20–42, 113
    Also see Price of leisure (shadow)
Household production function approach, 233–249
  causality, 248
  definitions:
    commodities, 234
    goods, 234
    shadow prices, 234
  estimation methods, 236
  household reduced form, 237

household structural form, 235–236
  equivalence class, 246
household technology, 18, 190, 233, 235–236, 250
  structural change, 190–192, 233, 245
  Also see Joint production
identification of structural form, 238–242
  example, 239–242
measurement problem, 248
nonsingularity of structural disturbance covariance matrix, 237–238
Pollak and Wachter critique, 242–249
  example of resolution, 247–248
  the issue, 244–248
  shadow price approach, 246–247
Housing, demand for, 126
Human capital, 39
Hybrid Diewert joint cost function, 239–240, 247

Identification:
  almost nonidentification, 266
  of labor supply, 17, 124–125
  with nonlinearity in variables:
    order conditions, 242
    rank conditions, 242
  of relative price version of Rotterdam model, 53
IIA (Indirect Implicit Addilog) model, 262, 277
  Also see Implicit utility models
Implicit strong separability, 261
Implicit utility models, 259–277
  definition of class of models, 260–262
  Direct Implicit Addilog model. *See* DIA (Direct Implicit Addilog) model
  Indirect Implicit Addilog model. *See* IIA (Indirect Implicit Addilog) model
  potential uses, 259–260
  Also see Implicit strong separability; Implicit weak separability
Implicit weak separability, 260–261
Income effects, 12, 261
Income flexibility, 54, 138–143, 251, 254
Index numbers:
  functional (true, exact, or economic), 185–187
  weights, monetary asset components, 186
  Also see Aggregation over goods

statistical, 185–186, 204, 219–222
  arithmetic average, 231
  bias and freakishness, 231
  circularity test, Fisher's 231
  Diewert-superlative, 221
  Divisia: price index, 11, 252, 254; quantity index, 186, 189, 221, 251–252, 254; real income: *See* Real income, log change
  exact, 220
  factor reversal test, Fisher's, 203, 220, 231, 251
  Fisher ideal, 204, 221–223, 231
  Frisch, 11, 254
  Leontief price index, 210, 216
  Törnquist–Theil discrete time approximation to the Divisia, 221–231
  weights, 222
  Also see Monetary aggregation
Indirect Addilog Model, 152
Indirect utility function, 152, 195n, 201, 262, 277
Inequality constraints on parameters, 160, 164–165, 208, 210
Inflation rate, 197, 229
Information matrix, 85, 87, 96
Information theory:
  average information inaccuracy measure of fit, 7, 149–154
    Rotterdam model with leisure, 150–153
    Rotterdam model without leisure, 153–154
  theory, 149–150
  information content of monetary aggregates, 186, 220, 227–230
    sample estimates, 228–229
    time series estimates, 230
Insatiability assumption, 59n
Instrumental variables estimation, 203–204, 273n
Integrability, aggregate:
  definition, 303
  as functional regularity condition, 306
  general-theory, 303–306
  global, 43–44, 56, 66, 114, 159, 171, 207, 261–262, 300, 303–307, 309, 315–319, 321
  local. *See* Locally integrable demand systems

origin closed, 305
Intertemporal allocation, 13–15, 58, 193–194, 228
  expectations, 14, 58, 193–194, 197, 205
  rational, 205
  intertemporal preference separability, 58, 123
  intertemporal utility function, 13, 58, 194–195, 211
  rate of time preference, 58, 196
  replanning, 14, 58, 195
  wealth constraint, 13–14, 58, 196
Invariance problem, 271, 273
  Also see DIA (Direct Implicit Addilog) model: structural estimation with conventional algorithms: nonuniqueness of estimator
Inverse demand systems, 159, 180
  Also see WS-branch utility function: Duality: between direct and inverse demand
Iterated Aitken estimation, nonlinear. *See* Generalized least squares, nonlinear

Joint production, 239, 242
  Also see Hybrid Diewert joint cost function

Kuhn–Tucker conditions. *See* Corner solutions: Kuhn–Tucker conditions

Labor force participation rates. *See* Household model (theory): labor force participation rate
Labor supply. *See* Leisure demand
Large certificates of deposit, 186, 351–353
  Also see Monetary aggregation
Leisure, true. *See* Free time
Leisure demand:
  as derived demand, 3, 5, 25
  estimation of function, 6, 101–154
  inelasticity, 34, 103, 124
  interaction with demand for durables, 7–8, 12, 103–105, 107–108, 110, 113, 122–123, 125, 127, 129–130, 132, 134–135, 138, 140–142, 152, 154
  interaction with demand for recreational goods, 4, 12

  joint modeling with goods demand, 4, 6–8, 10, 101–154
  preference independence transformation, 254–258
  separability from goods demand, 133–135, 193
  stability of historical income share, 7, 107, 152, 154
  Also see CSE (Constant Slutsky Elasticity) model; Price of leisure (shadow); Identification: of labor supply; Rotterdam model (general); Rotterdam model, absolute price version; Rotterdam model, relative price version
Likelihood function:
  concentrated, 94, 97
  properties (in theory), 85–86
Linear expenditure system, 11, 42, 142, 152
Linear homogeneity of preferences. *See* Homothetic preferences
Liquidity, 185, 211
Locally integrable demand systems:
  aggregate integrability, 57, 72–73, 319–320
  flexibility of, 319
  functional behavior, 178, 319–320
  generalized Cobb–Douglas, 43, 71, 319
  generalized Leontief, 43, 68, 71, 127, 261, 319
  translog:
    direct, 160, 261
    indirect, 43, 68, 70–71, 126–127, 261, 319–320
  tests of theory, 320–321
  Also see Taylor series local approximation
Luxury goods, 12

Marginal budget shares, 59
Marginal homotheticity, 163, 197, 207, 262
Marginal propensity to consume. *See* Marginal budget shares
Maximum likelihood estimation, linear in parameters (nonlinear in variables), 76
Maximum likelihood estimation, linear in variables (nonlinear in parameters), 76
Maximum likelihood estimation, nonlinear:
  asymptotic covariance matrix, 88–89
  nuisance parameters, 6, 96–98
  asymptotic efficiency, 6, 91–92

asymptotic likelihood ratio test statistic, 6, 92–95
  simplification of the statistic, 94–95
asymptotic normality, 6, 90–91, 341–343
asymptotic standard error of only one parameter estimator, 98
consistency (strong), 82
consistency (weak), 6, 80–83
  proofs (appendix), 331–346
  uniqueness of estimator, 83
Mean of order $\rho_r/2$. See WS-branch utility function: normalization of parameters
Means of payment, money as, 185
Measure theory, 61n, 95, 311n, 317
Meats, demand for. See WS-branch utility function: estimates
Mixed estimation, 169
ML estimator, 83
Monetary aggregation:
  consistent with rational economic behavior:
    conditional current period allocation, 199–202
    intertemporal allocation, 193–196
  empirical selection of components, 217–219, 351–354
  functional (exact) aggregates, 187–219
    estimation for passbook accounts over institution types, 207–212, 216–217
    estimation recursively over transaction balances and passbook subaggregate, 212–215
    theoretical index number properties, 209–210, 215–216
  government interest rate setting, 212
  statistical index numbers, 219–231
    Divisia index (Törnquist–Theil), definition, 221
    velocity of aggregate and example, 222–227
    information content of aggregate. See Information theory: information content of monetary aggregates
  Also see Index numbers; Aggregation over goods; Recursive structures; User cost of monetary assets
Monetary assets, substitutability between, 218n, 351–354

Monetary services, 211
Money, demand for:
  utility approach, 191
  Also see Monetary aggregation
Moneyness, 185–186, 211
Monopsony, 244

Naive forecast, 152
New home economics, 18, 239, 243–244
  Also see Household production function approach
Numeraire good, 179

On-the-job training, 39
Optimal control, constrained. See DIA (Direct Implicit Addilog) model: control theoretic approach to estimation
Own effects (definition), 171

Partial adjustment, 209, 211–213
Passbook accounts, aggregation over institution types, 185, 187, 201, 207–212
  Also see Monetary aggregation
Perishables demand, estimation of function, 103–154, 254
Portfolio allocation, 189
  Also see Monetary aggregation: consistent with rational economic behavior
Poultry, demand for. See WS-branch utility function: estimates
Prais–Houthakker homogeneity postulate, extended. See Household model (theory): Prais–Houthakker homogeneity postulate, extended
Predictors, MARL, 228n
Preference independence, 250, 252
  Also see Strong separability of preferences: complete
Preference independence transformation, 249–258
  application to durables, semidurables, and leisure, 254–258
    interpretation of results, 257–258
    the transformation, 254–256
  basic constructs and definitions, 250–252
  composition matrix of transformation, 253, 256

income elasticities of transformed goods, 253, 256
  conditional, 255
normalization of preferences, 251
normalized price coefficients, 252
the transformation, 252–254
Prestige, 257
Price of leisure (shadow):
  with approximate demand systems, 36–39, 48–50
    specification, 38, 48; special cases, 50
  assumptions, 33–34
    Also see Household model (theory)
  Cobb–Douglas example, 39–42
  consistency of estimated specification with theory, 110
  definitions, 35, 289
  equivalent price of leisure ratio, 40
  existence, 35, 286–288
  extension of function to full employment boundary, 299–301
  extraneous estimation, 50, 111–113
    Also see CSE (Constant Slutsky Elasticity) model; leisure demand
  graphic representation, 299
  historical comparison with market wage rate, 106–107
  proofs (appendix), 286–301
  properties of function, 35, 292–295
  solution for, 36, 290–291
    as fixed point, 36
  with unemployment, 5–6, 8, 13, 17, 31–42, 113, 286–299
  uniqueness, 35, 289
  without weak separability in leisure, 113
Price of money, 185, 188
  Also see User cost of monetary assets
Principal component transformation, constrained, 253
Production possibility frontiers, 260

Quasiconcavity of utility function. *See* Convexity of preferences

Rational random behavior, 268
Real income, log change, 46, 48, 52, 53, 60, 101, 115
Recessions. *See* Depressions and recessions

Recursive structures:
  estimation, 165–167, 202–204, 214
  intertemporally, 58, 165
  recursive aggregation, 159, 161, 166, 187, 189
  utility tree, 165–166, 174, 200, 351
  Also see Aggregation over goods: conditions for consistent two-stage decision
Rental price of monetary assets. *See* User cost of monetary assets
Replanning. *See* Intertemporal allocation: replanning
Representative consumer, 303. *Also see* Aggregation over consumers: with existence of representative consumer
Representative household. *See* Aggregation over consumers: with existence of representative household
Residual analysis. *See* Rotterdam model (general): residual analysis and error structure tests
Rotterdam model, absolute price version:
  asymptotic Slutsky aggregation bias. *See* Slutsky symmetry: asymptotic aggregation bias
  elasticity aggregates, 118–120, 122–124
  estimation, 120–135, 144–155
    robustness to rescaling of leisure data, 128–131
    robustness to variations in parameter of price of leisure specification, 124–131
  finite changes, 68–69, 313–314
  Slutsky matrix, 52, 115
    negative semidefiniteness, 51, 65, 115, 122
  specification, 51–52, 68–72, 115–120
  test for intercept, 131–133
  test for weak separability in leisure, 133
  theoretical foundations, 6, 43–44, 48, 55–73, 114–120, 307–318
    global remainder term. *See* Aggregation over consumers, limiting stochastic transformation: components of remainder term
    local remainder term, 71
  weak separability test, 116–117, 133–135
Rotterdam model, relative price version:
  aggregation over consumers, 310

estimation, 135–155
  block additive, 136–142
  completely additive, 142–143
  generalization, 73
  income flexibility. *See* Income flexibility
  negative definiteness of price coefficient matrix, 53, 140
  specification, 53–55
Rotterdam model (general):
  asymptotic covariance matrix of omitted parameter estimators, 54, 137–139, 141–142
  constancy of coefficients, 56–57, 69–72, 314–315
  critique, 56–57, 317–318, 320–321
  information theoretic measure of fit. *See* Information theory: average information inaccuracy measure of fit
  integrability properties, 72, 315–318
  marginal budget shares, 52–53, 115, 122
  residual analysis and error structure tests, 144–149
  with leisure, 7, 37, 50, 114–155
  Also see Rotterdam model, relative price version; Rotterdam model, absolute price version

Samuelsonian finesse, 19
Savings deposits. *See* Passbook accounts, aggregation over institution types
S-branch demand system, 29, 159, 184
Schwartz inequality, 309
Self-dual preferences, 262
Semidurables demand:
  estimation of function, 103–154
  preference independence transformation, 254–258
  stability of income share over time, 7
Separability. *See* Strong separability of preferences; Weakly separable preferences; Homothetic separability; Recursive structures; Implicit strong separability; Implicit weak separability; Intertemporal allocation: intertemporal preference separability
Separating hyperplane, 234
Services demand, estimation of function 103–154, 254

Shadow income level, definition, 35
  Also see Price of leisure (shadow)
Shadow price approach to household production function approach. *See* Household production function approach: shadow price approach
Shadow prices (definition of) in household production function approach. *See* Household production function approach: definitions: shadow prices
Shephard's lemma, 235
Simultaneous bias, 184
Slutsky coefficients (definition), 59
Slutsky symmetry:
  asymptotic aggregation bias, 73, 131–133
  magnitude, 307–308
  definition, 46, 52
Social sciences, "soft", 248
Specific interactions (specific complementarity or specific substitutability), 7, 49, 53, 113, 138, 142
Standard of living index, 259
Status, 257
Strong separability of preferences:
  blockwise, 49, 53, 135–142, 151–153, 159, 174–178, 255
  complete, 49, 142–143, 151–153, 174–176, 233, 250, 261
Strotz consistent planning, 58
Substitution effects, 12, 225, 231, 261
Sugar and sweeteners, demand for. *See* WS-branch utility function: estimates
Superior goods, 161
Supernumerary values, 29, 42, 142, 161–164, 197–199, 201, 207, 213
  augmented, 162

Tail area of test (definition), 95
Taste-determining factors (definition), 59, 310
Tastes, shifts in. *See* Time trends and shifts in tastes, unexplained
Taxes:
  effect on user cost of monetary assets, 197
  wage and commodity, 4, 113
Taylor series local approximation, 56, 68, 71–72, 178, 204, 261, 319
Term structure theory, 205

Tie-in-sales, 244
Time deposits:
  aggregation over, 187
  elasticities of substitution with other monetary assets, 185–186, 351–354
  Also see Monetary aggregation
Time series model, ARIMA, 230
Time trends and shifts in tastes, unexplained, 5, 7, 67, 113, 131–133, 152, 190
Transactions balances:
  elasticities of substitution with other monetary assets, 215, 351–354
  nested aggregation over passbook accounts, 185, 212–217
  Also see Monetary aggregation
Transactions technology, 191
Transformation function, 259–261
Translog model. *See* Locally integrable demand systems
Two stage decision. *See* Aggregation over goods: conditions for consistent two-stage decision

Unemployment. *See* Household model (theory): unemployment; Price of leisure (shadow); Depressions and recessions; Identification: of labor supply
User cost of monetary assets, 188, 196–197
Utility functions. *See* Demand systems
Utility possibility envelopes, 260
Utility tree. *See* Recursive structures: utility tree

Value share transitions, 316
Velocity of money, 185–186, 188, 192

Wars:
  First World War:
    private rationing, 100, 145, 255
    structural change after, 148–149, 152
  Second World War:
    rationing, 100, 145, 170, 255
    structural change after, 7, 154
Weakly separable preferences:
  empirical tests, 49, 126, 133–135, 137
  in theory, 10, 12–13, 41, 67, 116–117, 142, 159, 161, 187, 189, 193–194, 200–201, 217
Working–Leser demand model, 73
WS-branch utility function, 161–184
  estimation procedure. *See* Recursive structures: estimation
  estimates:
    blockwise estimation of disaggregated branches, 170–174
    elasticities, 181–184
    joint estimation of disaggregated branches, 174–176
    recursive estimation of aggregate stage, 176–178
  g-hypo (generalized hypocycloidal) special case, 169, 172–184, 259, 262, 319
  hypocycloid of four cusps (or astroid), 169
  inverse demand system, derivation, 163–164
  normalization of parameters, 167–168